NZ Business
(signed)

The Rich List

18 April 2004

ALSO BY GRAEME HUNT

Introduction to Sharemarket Investment, 1985, 1986, 1987.

Scandal at Cave Creek: A Shocking Failure in Public Accountability, 1996.

Why MMP Must Go: The Case for Ditching the Electoral Disaster of the Century, 1998.

Hustlers, Rogues & Bubble Boys: White-collar Mischief in New Zealand, 2001.

The Rich List

Wealth and Enterprise
in New Zealand
1820-2003

Graeme Hunt

REED

To my children, Robert (14) and Ellen (12), who, with any luck, will grow up with a healthy respect for hard work and wealth-creation.

Published by Reed Books, a division of Reed Publishing (NZ) Ltd,
39 Rawene Rd, Birkenhead, Auckland (www.reed.co.nz),
in association with Waddington Press Ltd, Auckland.
Reed has associated companies, branches and
representatives throughout the world.

This book is copyright. Except for the purpose of fair reviewing, no part of this publication may be reproduced or transmitted in any form or by any means, electronic or mechanical, including photocopying, recording, or any information storage and retrieval system, without permission in writing from the publisher. Infringers of copyright render themselves liable to prosecution.

ISBN 0 7900 0917 X

© Graeme John Hunt 2003

The author asserts his moral rights in the work.

First published 2000
This edition 2003

Printed in New Zealand

Contents

Foreword *by Nevil Gibson*	vii
Acknowledgments	ix
Author's note	x
Prologue	xi
1. The pre-treatyites	1
2. Merchant might, runholder wealth	29
3. Crony capitalism	80
4. Brave new world	123
5. Wealth and welfare	171
6. 1987's long hangover	224
Epilogue	277
Appendices	
A. *NBR Rich List 2003*	282
B. *NBR* Business Hall of Fame 1994–2003	288
C. *NBR* Sporting Rich 2003	293
Bibliography	295
Indices	
A. Individuals and families	309
B. Businesses and organisations	319
C. Properties, ships, boats and horses	330

Foreword

Many New Zealanders find it hard to celebrate or accept success of the financial kind. It's known as the 'Kiwi curse' or the tall-poppy syndrome. Yet there is a continuing fascination with wealth — who has it, how they made and how to do it.

The *National Business Review Rich List* was born in the heady days of the sharemarket and property booms of the mid-1980s. It is now an accepted term in the New Zealand lexicon. Attitudes to wealth have not changed much since then, even though there is more of it. New Zealand remains an egalitarian society, ready to embrace many differing races and cultures regardless of material circumstance.

An important element in this is a commitment to equality of opportunity. Governments have found it relatively easy to take away a New Zealander's earnings through tax. Yet they would not dare to destroy the individual's right to make the most of their lives. So while attitudes to wealth may send out mixed messages, the entrepreneurial spirit remains strong.

New Zealand ranks high among nations where businesses can easily be launched, although it does not fare so well when it comes to making them successful. Some of this may be due to the pioneering can-do spirit — one that continues today as people from both free and repressed societies settle here to seek a better way of life for them and their families. For many it may mean starting at the bottom, the way a lot of businesses do, and fighting the odds — since along with New Zealand's freedom to do business in an honest manner goes a heavy burden of compliance and regulation.

The bulk of New Zealanders in business remain small scale and are likely to be satisfied to stay that way. But the real advances in society come from those prepared to risk much more. *NBR*'s *Rich List* is a compendium of those relatively few who have been able to beat the odds, often by overcoming early failure. It combines the household names of people who have made fortunes from providing goods and services people want with the more private businesses that work away from the public eye.

Graeme Hunt has edited the *Rich List* for *NBR* since 1994. He has spent much more time preparing this book, now in its extensively revised second edition. It contains more examples of how a wide range of individuals and their families made commercial history and then went on to reinvest their success back into the community.

It is a pleasing feature of an egalitarian and trusting society that these community-minded and philanthropic gestures are so prevalent. Life in our large and small cities would not be so attractive without the generous support for civic facilities, educational institutes, leisure activities and charities that comes from a prosperous business sector.

The Rich List (the book) celebrates the best of how the free-enterprise system, based on the right of people to own property and create wealth, has contributed to New Zealand's history. Mr Hunt is to be congratulated for providing a long-overdue balance to this nation's story by focusing on people who in their vision, passion and achievement have spread riches that can be shared by everyone.

Nevil Gibson
Editor-in-chief
National Business Review
August 2003

Acknowledgments

This book would not have been possible without the support of many people and the patience of many more. I am especially grateful to the following who read parts of the manuscript, spotted mistakes and offered helpful advice (in alphabetical order): historian Dr Michael Bassett, public relations manager Owen Cook, *National Business Review* editor-in-chief Nevil Gibson, historian Dr Jim McAloon, Emeritus Professor Russell Stone, *NBR* subeditor and author Paul Verdon and Auckland Research Centre history librarian David Verran. Special thanks are also due to Susan Brierley, who did a superb job editing a complicated text; Reed Publishing senior editor Peter Dowling, who directed the project patiently and professionally and at all times offered wise counsel; former *NBR* reporter Aimee McClinchy; and researcher Kirsten Trainor Smith, who assisted with illustrations and copyright clearance. Numerous other people, including family members of some of those included in the book and some of the subjects themselves, also assisted with information or offered help. They include: Chris Adams, Cedric Allan, Brian Allison, Barbara Barker, Anna Bidwill, Euan Bidwill, Reg Birchfield, Joe Bolton, Graham Bush, Mick Calder, Angela Caughey, Constance Clark, Grant Common, Brian Corban, Morton Coutts, Hugh de Lacy, Rob Fenwick, Anthony Flude, John Hambling, David Hay, Deborah Hill Cone, Michael Horton, Dick Hubbard, Pauline Hughes, the late Beverley Hunt, Ian Hunter, Chris Hutching, David Irving, Anne Irwin, Vaughan Jeffs, Robin Judkins, Bob Kerridge, John Kerridge, Rolly Kerridge, Deborah LaHatte, Lincoln Laidlaw, Ken Leeming, Peter Levin, Kerry McCarthy, Gordon McLauchlan, John Ormond, Warren Paine, Renée Patterson, Hugh Perrett, David Picot, Bill Preston, Diana Robinson, Doug Ross, Peter Russell, John Sax, David Smythe, John Stacpoole, Peter Shirtcliffe, Fleur Snedden, Ian Stuart, Jan van der Heyden, Doug Walker, Ray Wattie, Sue Westbury, Richard Wigley, Gail Williamson and Dave Youngson.

Author's note

Sources

Business historiography has a weak tradition in New Zealand but *The Dictionary of New Zealand Biography*, which I have drawn on heavily for a number of the nineteenth-century and early twentieth-century profiles, was especially useful. Russell Stone's excellent *Makers of Fortune* is an unequalled source for those studying nineteenth-century Auckland business history. Michael Bassett's *Sir Joseph Ward* is one of the few biographies that provides a detailed financial snapshot of a major political figure. L.G.D. Acland's *The Early Canterbury Runs* was my Bible on pastoralism. Angela Caughey's *An Auckland Network* helped me understand the relationships among Auckland shopkeepers and traders in the late nineteenth and early twentieth centuries. Yvonne van Dongen's *Brierley* still provides the best assessment of the corporate raider a decade after it was published. David Grant's *Bulls, Bears & Elephants* has a valuable chapter explaining the aftermath of the 1987 sharemarket crash. The *National Business Review* (*NBR*), and especially its *Rich Lists*, provided much of the financial detail and colour missing from conventional accounts of leading wealth-creators. The size of the bibliography underscores the huge job of identifying and tracking wealth over 180 years or so of European settlement in New Zealand.

Names

Throughout the text I have generally referred to individuals by their commonly used first name or initials where appropriate, unless the person tends to be known by more than one first name (such as John Logan Campbell or John Robert Godley) or where it is unclear which first name is favoured. In some instances a nickname has been used in preference to the first name because the nickname is better known. Where a person is titled, the honorific has been used. It has been placed in parentheses in some instances — e.g. (Sir) — to indicate the honour had not been awarded at that time. Full names are contained in the index.

Prologue

The secrets of wealth and wealth-creation in New Zealand are only now being uncovered. Our history since the arrival of the first Europeans tells much about governors, land wars, political leaders, Maori renaissance and sporting prowess, but little about those who brought wealth to New Zealand or who created it here by endeavour or stealth.

Business historiography — the writing of history about the firms and companies that created many of New Zealand's richest people — is in its infancy 180 years after the beginnings of European settlement.

Those books that recount the history of successful enterprises only occasionally unlock the secrets of success; more often they are dry, fawning accounts of enterprises' first 50 or 100 years, written by dull former company secretaries or uninspiring retired journalists.

The absence in New Zealand of public recognition of the importance of private wealth and enterprise is reflected in the fact that the country's Business Hall of Fame (now sponsored by the *National Business Review*) was established only in 1994, many years after the Sports Hall of Fame, and 153 years after William Brown and Dr John Logan Campbell set up shop in a tent in Auckland's Commercial Bay.

Modern New Zealand's founding fathers were not just politicians and warriors; they included whalers, bankers, sawmillers, shopkeepers, speculators and squatters, people who harnessed their capital and know-how for substantial private gain and, in many cases, significant public benefit.

These rich and influential people were no more a uniform class in the early years of settlement than they are today. 'The rich' is simply a label I and others like me use to describe those who hold or create wealth. It is not their personal virtues or vices that separate them from other New Zealanders but their enterprise and achievements.

The Rich List is not an academic treatise on wealth New Zealand-style but, I trust, a readable and entertaining overview of those who made it (in wealth terms), those who tried and failed, and those who would like to have.

It provides a broad-brush look at our rich and enterprising citizens from the earliest days of European settlement to the start of the new millennium. It is written not as a history (although it contains much history) but as an inspiration to those who place individual endeavour before that of the state. As a result, some pioneer runholders, shopkeepers and industrialists whom readers might consider should have been included in the book are not.

Their exclusion is either because they do not warrant inclusion — perhaps because their wealth or enterprise was not what some people think it was — or because their occupational group or interests have been amply or better represented by others. (This is especially true of nineteenth-century runholders and a number of the post-millennium rich.) Conversely, others who were not personally rich but whose enterprise or endeavours created wealth have been included.

Identifying the true rich, especially in the nineteenth century and the first half of the twentieth, is no easy task. I have been highly selective, even more so than during my ten years as editor of the *NBR Rich List*.

I make no apology for this — it is a practice commentators on wealth adopt worldwide. *Forbes*' annual list of international billionaires does not include New Zealand's only family of (Kiwi-dollar) billionaires, the Todds of Wellington, because it considers them 'too boring'. The Todds, unlike some of New Zealand's lesser and gaudier rich, have no problem with being snubbed. Like so many of New Zealand's old-money rich they shun publicity about their wealth, presumably on the grounds that discussion of richness and wealth-creation is tacky. Many New Zealanders on the poverty line share a similar view.

This is an Anglo-Saxon characteristic, not an American one. It is easy to imagine a New York City ghetto-dweller envying the owner of an unattended Mercedes S-Class, and being more likely to steal it for personal use than anything else. The lager lout who sees a similar vehicle in Wolverhampton, England, will probably spraypaint it in the colours of his soccer team or slash the tyres. The New Zealand hoon will more than likely scratch the fine metallic paintwork down one side with a coin or do his best to tear off the emblem.

The hostility some New Zealanders feel toward public displays of wealth resembles working-class attitudes in the United Kingdom far more than the prejudices of blue-collar Americans but New Zealand society today is poles apart from Britain. This was not planned by promoters of organised settlement in New Zealand like Edward Gibbon Wakefield. They wanted New Zealand to develop a gentler form of the British class system — one where deserving settlers would slowly improve their lot, but not at the expense of established interests — rather than robust egalitarianism. That was not to be. Still, New Zealanders' emotional attitudes to wealth and the behaviour of the wealthy, especially the attitudes of those who live off the state, reflect the country's British heritage.

Listeners to evening talkback radio, for instance, can testify that many callers who attack company directors for profiteering, tax fiddles or fraud (such as the notorious wine-box transactions) see nothing wrong in claiming the dole illegally or cheating on accident compensation.

Fortunately, attitudes are changing: New Zealanders are today more willing to discuss wealth and wealth-creation than they were before the free-market economic reforms of the 1980s or even when the first New Zealand *Rich List* was published in 1986. In many households and workplaces, however, wealth remains as taboo a subject as religion.

If it has done nothing else, *NBR*'s annual *Rich List* has put the topic of wealth squarely in the ladies' knitting circle, the works canteen and the rugby club, whether the patrons like it or not.

No *Rich List* in my experience has survived a day published without protests from clergy, tut-tuts from Radio New Zealand socialists, objections from people on the list and complaints from others upset they have not been included.

The overall reaction has been one of intense (and sometimes prurient) interest from people of all walks of life, some of whom would not normally read the *National Business Review*. While many New Zealanders might consider discussion of wealth in bad taste, or even highly offensive, they want to read about it nonetheless.

It was this intense interest that prompted Reed Publishing to approach me about producing a book on New Zealand's rich. I was only too willing to oblige and *NBR*, which provides much of my income and where I have worked for many years, gave me 100 per cent support, as did the writers who contribute regularly to *NBR*'s *Rich List*.

For those who prefer to read about poverty, child molestation, indigenous land rights, industrial relations or gender equity, this is not the book for you. For the majority of New Zealanders who get on with life, have a sense of humour and retain the Kiwi can-do attitude, this book has important lessons and messages.

It will, I hope, correct some of the myths that attach to the rich — that their success is the product of good fortune, dishonesty or both. To be sure, some of New Zealand's wealthy have prospered as a result of luck, unethical behaviour or sharp practice but the idle, the greedy and the fraudsters (of whom there are comparatively few) have for the most part paid a hefty price for their behaviour — business failure, bankruptcy, family break-up, prison and, in some cases, suicide.

Throughout the book I have included top-ten wealth lists — for 1840, 1855, 1876, 1906, 1936, 1966, 1987, 1997 and 2003. These are based on available information, some of it limited, and a number of assumptions have had to be made. In the absence of any official tables of private wealth — and thank goodness we do not have a government preparing them — these provide a snapshot of the scale and nature of individual and family fortunes. They also allow readers to compare New Zealand private wealth with that overseas.

This gives us the opportunity to assess New Zealand's wealth-creating abilities and gauge whether we are doing enough to retain those who provide capital and jobs.

Graeme John Hunt
Auckland
August 2003

1

The pre-treatyites

*A person must be uncommonly hard pushed
if he cannot get a living in New Zealand.*

Lt Thomas McDonnell, trader of Horeke, 1830s

No exact date exists for New Zealand's emergence from a place of discovery to one of economic value but from the 1790s ships from North America and India (the latter belonging to the East India Company), armed with copies of maps and journals prepared by Captain James Cook nearly a generation earlier, were plying New Zealand waters. Their business was exclusively commodity based: seal skins, whale oil and timber. Such contact as there was with Maori, the tangata whenua of these temperate South Pacific islands, was hit and miss. Sometimes the inhabitants seemed friendly, at other times downright hostile, even violent. What is clear is that once contact was made, there was no turning back for European or Maori. The former, having tasted the country's riches, hankered for more; the latter, having glimpsed or sampled European technology, were unwilling or unable to return to their old ways.

That New Zealand was abundant in natural riches had been apparent to visitors since Captain Cook. At the time of first contact, indeed, many Maori tribes were rich in terms of land, forest and fisheries. Yet using the criteria of wealth applied by modern economists, it is impossible to assess the worth of Maori individuals at the time or, for that matter, for many decades following (though, in modern times, some have tried in Treaty of Waitangi claims). Part of the difficulty in assessing Maori wealth is that Maori ownership of land, waka, pounamu and other goods was (and in many cases still is) a collective undertaking. Early Maori society lacked a convenient measure of wealth, such as a minted currency, that can be related easily to the present day. Nevertheless, it was contact between Maori and European that provided the first impetus for wealth-creation in New Zealand. The contact came not just through visiting ships and shore parties but from deserters, some of them former convicts, 'going bush'. While this group, which formed the nucleus of the Pakeha-Maori — Europeans who chose to live with, and like, Maori — was relatively few in number, its influence on tribal society, especially among Nga Puhi in the north, was considerable. Pakeha-Maori were agents for change, whether as exalted additions to the tribe or as semi-slaves.

The Musket Wars that turned Maori society on its head from 1806 until the mid-1840s — a period of unprecedented intertribal 'cleansing' and slaughter — owe something to Pakeha-Maori, even if they did not participate actively in the warfare (and there are documented cases where they did). The musket allowed Maori warlords to do far more efficiently what they had already done in the pre-contact period: gain material advantage over traditional enemies and exact revenge for real or imagined wrongs or insults.

Maori willingness to accept European technology, not just muskets but ironware and other goods, paved the way for settlement and long-term trade. Entrepreneurs could look beyond commodities and deal with the locals, irrespective of the racial views they might hold about Polynesian society. There had been little such dealing in Australia. The structure of Aboriginal society was alien to settlers and administrators alike and Aborigines, despite the good intentions of one or two enlightened officials, were treated as a nuisance akin to agricultural pests. In New Zealand it was clear to the early merchant traders and timbermillers who were putting down roots in the north that their very existence depended on dealing with a dominant, armed and volatile indigenous population.

The country's outer reaches, especially the bottom of the South Island and Stewart Island, were different. There, weather and the availability of shipping and supplies played a far greater role in business success than fraternisation with the tangata whenua. Captain William Stewart (1776?–1851), a Scots-born former Royal Navy officer, was among the first to recognise the potential for organised trade in the south. In 1824 he attracted interest from T. & D. Asquith in England in a proposal to establish a timber, flax and trading settlement on Stewart Island. Stewart knew the region well, having served for several years as a captain on sealing ships around the subantarctic islands and the South Island. For years he was thought to have been the first officer on the historic 1809 voyage of the *Pegasus* who proved South Cape — the name Captain Cook had given to Stewart Island in 1770 — to be an island. In fact, that was the work of another mariner of the same name. (The Stewart outline chart of the whole island and the detailed chart of Port Pegasus, on the island's southeastern coast — the effort of this lesser-known William Stewart — completed an Admiralty chart of the region that had been unfinished since 1791, and remained in use until 1840.)

Name confusion notwithstanding, Stewart, the ex-sealer, succeeded in having the *Prince of Denmark* and *Lord Rodney* dispatched to Stewart Island in 1826 to get the Port Pegasus settlement under way. He also persuaded an English shipbuilder based in the Bay of Islands, George Cooke, and seven sawyers to move to Port Pegasus. But the venture failed and Stewart went to ground before reportedly being jailed in Sydney for debt. He later returned to Stewart Island and piloted HMS *Herald* when Lt-Col. Thomas Bunbury arrived in 1840 to proclaim British sovereignty. One of his most successful employees was Captain John Howell (1810?–74) who set up a whaling station for Jones at Jacobs River, Southland, and later founded Riverton.

Johnny Jones (1808/09?–69), a fiery Sydney entrepreneur, had none of Stewart's education and few of the hydrographic skills of Stewart's namesake, but he was able to launch a substantial business in New Zealand nonetheless. Like Stewart, he initially gave scant consideration to Maori interests because southern Maori numbers were relatively low. Jones had to adopt a different tack later on, however, when he began to move into large-scale land speculation. But in 1835, when he joined forces with Edwin Palmer to buy a whaling station at Preservation Inlet on the wild Fiordland coast and, soon after, the schooner *Sydney Packet* for whaling, making money was his prime concern. Jones was only 26 or 27 years old but he was already rich, and undoubtedly New Zealand's wealthiest pioneer at that time. Little is known of his background — his mother is believed to have been a convict — but somehow Jones had saved sufficient money from working on sealing and whaling ships, and later as a waterman ferrying people across Port Jackson (now Sydney Harbour), to acquire interests in three whaling ships by 1830. Starting with the whaling station at Preservation Inlet in 1834, he acquired a controlling interest in the South Island whaling industry, employing about 280 men in seven stations around the south and east coasts.

In 1838 Jones bought a year-old shore whaling station at Waikouaiti Bay, Otago, where the town of Karitane now stands, from two insolvent Sydney merchants, at a cost of £225. In 1838–39 he extended his interests with the purchase of huge tracts of land — about 40,500 ha (nearly 100,000 acres) — from local Maori. As the whaling station struggled Jones turned his attention to colonising, establishing settlements at the northern end of Waikouaiti Bay,

Whaler-turned-businessman Johnny Jones (1808/09?–69) craved respectability in his later years. He dressed, according to one critic, 'like a prosperous farmer in his Sunday best'. Otago Settlers Museum

about 9 km from the whaling station, Prospect Farm on flat land close to the sea (now Matanaka-by-the-Beach) and later, Cherry Farm on the ridge behind Cornish Head (Matanaka). The first settlers, about a dozen families, with 20 head of cattle and provisions, arrived at their new home in February 1840. As this venture unfolded, Jones took part in an even bigger gamble. He had

Farm building, left, dating from the 1840s, at Matanaka, Otago, which is testimony to the early colonising efforts of Johnny Jones.
OTAGO SETTLERS MUSEUM

persuaded several South Island Maori leaders not to cede their lands to the Crown, and now, nervous that his holdings were in danger if the South Island became a British possession, he joined forces with New South Wales lawyer-speculator William Wentworth (1790–1872) and three others to buy all unsold Maori land in the South Island for £200. This acquisition was said to cover about 800,000 ha (nearly two million acres) but it ran foul of New South Wales Governor Sir George Gipps' anti-landsharking proclamation. Jones was allowed the maximum 1035 ha (2560 acres) under law, and it took him 27 years of haggling to get an additional 3500 ha (8650 acres).

Jones and his family arrived at Waikouaiti in 1843 and later built a homestead at Matanaka (which survives today with a barn, granary and stables). As whaling declined Jones concentrated on developing his holdings, introducing sheep, cattle and horses, and, with the founding of Dunedin in 1848, providing food to immigrants at fair prices. Matanaka remained the headquarters of his shipping and trading enterprise until he and his family moved to Dunedin in 1854.

By the time of his death fifteen years later Jones' reputation had changed from that of a sometimes violent whaler and feudal farm owner to a mercantile elder statesman — the man who printed his own bank notes and established the Harbour Steam Navigation Co (the forerunner to the Union Steam Ship Co). He is also remembered as being fair in business dealings and generous in time and money to a number of causes. His donations of land and grants to the

Anglican, Roman Catholic, Presbyterian and Methodist communities probably earn him the dubious title of New Zealand's first business philanthropist. A distinguished-looking man, once unkindly described as dressed like a prosperous farmer in his Sunday best, Jones used his wealth to acquire a mantle of respectability even if he remained rough around the edges. His fine Dunedin property, Fern Hill, which the Jones family acquired in 1854 for £550 from Captain Edmund Bellairs, a retired soldier and founding member of New Zealand's upper house (the Legislative Council), is testimony to a battler made good. He replaced Bellairs' wooden home with a stone mansion that survives today, ironically as a gentlemen's club, the Dunedin Club.

Jones' move to Dunedin reflected his growing commercial interests and the educational needs of his children (he had eleven, of whom nine survived infancy). It was also part of a gentrification process for a man without breeding, unwilling to talk about his Sydney origins and once described as one of Sydney's 'Forty Thieves'. Jones' business prowess was finally recognised officially in 1999, 130 years after his death, by his posthumous induction into the Business Hall of Fame.

The Weller brothers, who were the first settlers of note in Otago, shared much of Jones' true grit but came from a more genteel background. Unlike Jones they were not in the country long enough to be counted among Dunedin's founding fathers. Edward Weller (1814?–93) and his brother Joseph (1804–35), who were originally from Folkestone in Kent, England, came from Sydney to Otago Harbour in 1831, establishing a shore whaling station at the water's edge below the Maori village of Otakou. Another brother, George (1805–75), stayed in Sydney to run the family business. The Otago station, with 80 cottages, tri-works, slipways, and sheds, was badly damaged by fire in 1832 — the first of several setbacks for the firm. Edward was kidnapped by Maori in 1833 and had to be ransomed, the station was under the threat of attack by Maori the following year and in 1835 Joseph died of tuberculosis and a measles epidemic swept through the local Maori population.

None of these early mishaps dented the confidence of Edward Weller although George, nine years Edward's senior, did his share of worrying. The firm was able to launch a 61-tonne schooner, *Joseph Weller*, in 1833 (built by William Stewart's former shipbuilder, George Cooke), rebuild the station and establish it as the headquarters of a seven-station whaling empire in the South Island which, over ten months in 1836/37, earned £8000 from whaling alone. The Wellers also made money from farming and selling timber, spars, flax, fish, artefacts and preserved Maori heads. They even tried exporting whale oil directly to London but were forced to pay duty as foreigners — there was no

Edward Weller (1814?–93), left, and George Weller (1805–75), two of three brothers whose whaling station in Otago Harbour laid the foundations for permanent settlement in the region. OTAGO SETTLERS MUSEUM

register or flag for New Zealand ships before 1834 — and the project had to be abandoned.

Stiff competition from Johnny Jones from the mid-1830s and a falling whale harvest after 1837 hurt the business and encouraged the Wellers to speculate on land. By 1840 they had acquired more than 1.2 million ha (three million acres), most of it for a token consideration, but, like Jones, they ran foul of Governor Gipps' restrictions on land purchases. In 1841 all thirteen of their claims were rejected. By this time Edward had handed over the Otago station to his brother-in-law, George Schultze, and returned to Australia. He remained in New South Wales, where he farmed until his death by drowning during flooding in 1893.

Jones and the Wellers had few chances in business but they took them all.

Other settlers in the north of the country — on the Hokianga Harbour and in the Bay of Islands — had the advantages of a better climate, huge stands of kauri timber (ideal for spars), relative closeness to Sydney, and Maori who were more used to the ways of European business than those in the south. But they struggled for the sort of success that came naturally to Jones and the Weller brothers.

One of the earliest northern settlers with the potential to become rich was Ranulph Dacre (1797–1884), the son of an army officer from Hampshire, England. He joined the Royal Navy in 1810, and on the *Spartan* was a shipmate of novelist-to-be Frederick Marryat. He served in the war of 1812 but resigned in 1816, aged just nineteen, to captain a schooner trading in the West Indies, Australia and the Pacific. In 1824 Dacre visited New Zealand as part-owner of the schooner *Endeavour* which called at Whangaroa, north of the Bay of Islands. From 1825–31 he traded between Australia, New Zealand and London before settling and marrying in Sydney.

In 1834 Dacre set up a mercantile and shipping agency with William Wilks to trade in whale oil, sandalwood, kauri timber, greenstone and flax, and he made frequent trips to New Zealand for spars and sawn timber for the Royal Navy. He acquired land at Mangonui in the Far North, Mercury Bay on the Coromandel Peninsula and Mahurangi, north of Auckland, for timber, shipbuilding, trading and raising stock. Dacre, who was an honest trader not intimidated by bullying or threats, obtained timber and land rights from Maori and employed skilled Maori workers, despite setbacks which included the destruction of buildings and a vessel. He was also part of a New Zealand delegation of speculators and merchants who interviewed the British consul to New Zealand, Captain William Hobson, in Sydney in January 1840 about his intentions toward the colony.

Dacre was one of the first exporters of greenstone from New Zealand. He shipped two tonnes to China, but the Opium War between Britain and China held up the cargo in Manila and he lost heavily. Despite this and other setbacks for his New Zealand operations, by 1840 he was one of Sydney's leading merchants, owning a wharf, ships, a cattle station and other property in addition to his New Zealand interests. He was appointed a magistrate, and a director of the Union Bank of Australia and the Sydney Alliance Insurance Co. Dacre became insolvent in the 1842–44 depression, losing much of his property, but he slowly recovered. In 1844 he established a business relationship with James Macky, part of the Nathan trading house in Auckland, dividing his time between Sydney and Auckland. In 1848 he bought the 1349-ha (3334-acre) Weiti block near Orewa, north of Auckland, which his sons, Henry and Life

Septimus, farmed as a cattle station (Henry's restored brick cottage, built in 1855 or 1856 at Karepiro Bay, remains today). Another of Dacre's sons, Charles, farmed nearby on the Whangaparaoa Peninsula.

In 1854 Dacre went into partnership as a merchant and shipping agent with James Macky's brother, Thomas, and bought more land, including 1618 ha (4000 acres) at Omaha, northeast of Warkworth. The Dacre family moved from Sydney to Auckland in 1859, by which time T. Macky & Co was a prominent trading enterprise. The family settled at Eden Cr, on the slopes of Official Bay. Dacre was active in the Anglican synod and a patron of the now-demolished St Paul's Church. His wealth increased during his retirement and he was able to provide well for his family. In 1882 he and his family owned 3642 ha (9000 acres) of land, worth nearly £10,000. He died in England two years later.

Thomas McDonnell (1788–1864) was another who had a background in the Royal Navy. He rose to the rank of lieutenant and served in the Napoleonic Wars before joining the East India Company as a ship's captain. By 1828 he was a merchant and shipowner, trading in various goods, including Chinese opium. In January 1831 McDonnell bought the 400-tonne barque *Sir George Murray* at auction in Sydney — the ship had been seized for sailing without a register — and the failed sawmilling and shipyard business at Deptford (now Horeke) on the Hokianga where she had been built. The deal is said to have included 2071 ha (5120 acres) of land. The business, founded in 1826 or earlier, was New Zealand's first commercial shipyard and had been owned by the Sydney firm of Raine & Ramsay (later Raine Ramsay & Browne), which was among the first to identify the commercial potential of the kauri trade. The shipyard had built three vessels, but collapsed in 1830, shortly after the *Sir George Murray* was built. The work was completed by the shipyard superintendent, Captain David Clark (1766?–1831), who delivered the vessel to Sydney but later became a casualty of the takeover.

A former partner in the failed Raine Ramsay & Browne, Scots-born merchant Gordon Browne, went on to establish a timber spar station at Mahurangi, north of Auckland, in 1832 and build New Zealand's first water-powered sawmill at Mercury Bay on the Coromandel Peninsula in 1836, while working with Ranulph Dacre. Browne was declared insane about 1841 — he died in 1844 — and Dacre is thought to have appointed American trader-speculator William Webster (1815–97), part-owner of a copper mine on Great Barrier Island, to take over. A year earlier Dacre had put up bail of £12,000 to have Webster released from Sydney debtors' prison. As for the Horeke enterprise, McDonnell was keen to do more than run a timber business-cum-shipyard. He wasted little time, sailing the *Sir George Murray* to Horeke in March 1831 with family, servants and settlers. During the next few years he established a mini-empire that included an impressive house for its time — known as the Cottage — orchards, vineyards, workers' houses and seventeen cannon (used for ceremonial purposes rather than protection). He also ran cattle.

McDonnell built up his business with help from Clark's replacement, George Russell, who had been at the Sydney sale when McDonnell bought the *Sir George Murray*, and had taken possession of the Horeke property until he arrived. Russell worked with McDonnell, either as his manager or partner, until 1839 when he bought land at the rival timber settlement of Kohukohu, 5 km downstream on the other side of the harbour from Horeke. McDonnell's business was always a battle, not least because his Ulster temper cost him friendships with other settlers and the nearby Wesleyan mission station at Mangungu, although he kept local Maori on side for a time. In 1835 he became honorary additional British resident to James Busby at Waitangi, but he was temperamentally unsuited to the job and fell out with the hapless Busby, quitting a year later. His sole achievement in office was to capture the crew of the schooner *Industry* and send them in irons to Hobart Town, Van Diemen's Land (now Hobart, Tasmania) to stand trial for the murder of their captain at sea.

McDonnell extended the boundaries of his Horeke settlement in 1836 and acquired a large area of timberland at Motukaraka, but in 1839 he sold the bulk of his holdings to the New Zealand Company. After 1840 he battled incessantly with the Crown to have the land purchases validated, creating much ill will among Hokianga Maori in the process. In 1858, by which time his empire had all but collapsed, he was granted land near Whangarei which he quickly sold. He then retired to Auckland, where he died in 1864 after falling from his horse.

McDonnell's eldest son, Thomas (1831/33?–99) — egotistical, flamboyant and hotheaded like his father — became a military leader of note in the 1860s land wars, rising to the rank of colonel. His most important command was in the battle against Titokowaru at Te Ngutu-o-te-manu, South Taranaki, in 1868, where his one-time friend, Major Gustavus von Tempsky, was killed. Thomas jnr was awarded the New Zealand Cross in 1884 for his reconnaissance with von Tempsky at Paparata, south of Auckland, 21 years earlier. His brothers, William, George and Edward, also served in the colonial forces.

Thomas snr was not alone in trying to build a Hokianga empire. In 1820 the eccentric French aristocrat-adventurer, Charles, Baron de Thierry (1793–1864), masterminded a deal at Cambridge University, England, to acquire 16,187 ha (40,000 acres) on the Hokianga to establish an independent colony. The middleman in the purchase was Anglican missionary Thomas Kendall, who was visiting Cambridge with Nga Puhi warlord Hongi Hika and his

Charles, Baron de Thierry (1793–1864), whose attempts to create a New Zealand empire based on dubious property holdings on the Hokianga failed by 1840. AUCKLAND CITY LIBRARIES, N.Z., A10827

nephew, Waikato, officially to help compile a Maori dictionary. The price paid for the land: 36 axes. The financially strapped de Thierry, whose parents had fled revolutionary France in 1793, failed to win Dutch or French support for the venture. But his talk of becoming sovereign chief of the Hokianga so alarmed the British resident, James Busby, traders and missionaries that in

1835 Busby persuaded 34 chiefs to sign a declaration of independence and seek Crown protection. Undeterred, two years later de Thierry led a group of colonists from Sydney to the Hokianga in the vain hope of establishing an independent colony. The colony failed, in no small part due to the combined opposition of McDonnell and local Maori, and de Thierry had to be content with 323 ha (800 acres), not the 16,187 ha bought on his behalf by Kendall. Nevertheless, de Thierry stayed on until the Northern War forced him to settle in Auckland.

Toward the end of his life he experimented with flax-processing and manufactured millboard, and by his death in 1864 he had achieved some financial success. While he might seem a comic figure today, de Thierry won the hearts of many, not least the Roman Catholic bishop of Western Oceania, Jean Baptiste Pompallier, whose cause he championed (all the more surprising because de Thierry was a Protestant), and Governor George Grey.

Frederick Maning (1811/12?–83), a Dublin-born Anglo-Irishman from a comfortable background, also dreamed of riches on the Hokianga. Like McDonnell, he was a wheeler-dealer — cunning and underhand — who could get on with Maori. Unlike McDonnell, he crossed the racial divide, living as a Pakeha-Maori, fathering an illegitimate half-Maori child and later taking a Maori wife, the sister of a local chief, who bore him four children. Maning arrived in the Hokianga in 1833 and with a business partner acquired land at Kohukohu. He was a trader — in timber, pork and potatoes — until selling up in 1837 and returning to Hobart Town, where his Irish parents and siblings had made their home. Two years later he was back on the Hokianga, this time buying a tract of land for £4 cash and £80 in goods from Maori at Onoke, at the mouth of the Whirinaki River. It was here that his family was born and where, for more than 40 years, he made his home. Maning did not get on with Lt-Governor Hobson, who felt Maning had persuaded chiefs not to sign the Treaty of Waitangi when it came to Mangungu on 12 February 1840 (Maning's brother-in-law, Hauraki, was one who did not sign). During the Northern War, however, Maning provisioned Maori on the government side and joined a war party against Hone Heke.

In 1850 Maning started sawmilling in the Hokianga, doing quite well, and by the early 1860s he was supplying timber for his Hobart-based brothers' ships. His brothers' business collapsed in 1864, about the time Maning's father died. As the eldest son and the main beneficiary of his father's will, he was able — and, perhaps, morally obliged — to assist the Tasmanian branch of the family. Maning was not exceptionally wealthy but he stayed in the north and prospered long after others had moved south. He is best known for his books, now classics, *Old New Zealand* and *A History of the War in the North of New Zealand Against the Chief Heke, in the Year 1845*, and his time as a judge on the Native Land Court. His final years were troublesome: widowed in 1847, he turned against things Maori in old age, became alienated from his children and developed a paranoid fear that they were plotting to kill him. His flight to Auckland in 1880, deserting a dying, paralysed daughter, gave him some respite before his death from cancer three years later. His house at Onoke, built in 1839 or 1840, survives as a reminder of one of the country's more interesting traders. Built mainly of heart kauri, it is set on kauri floor joists mounted on large boulders half set into the ground. It contains some fine hand-planed kauri panelling. The walls are also bullet-proof (at least to early nineteenth-century weapons) — a reminder that living on the Hokianga in the early days was far from safe.

Two other prominent northern traders, James Clendon and Gilbert Mair, easily qualify for entry into the pioneering rich list. Clendon (1800–72), probably the richest and most successful businessman in the north, was another with a seagoing background, being born in Deal, Kent, the son of a Cinque Ports pilot. Clendon and his brother, John, established a shipowning business in London. In 1828 he captained a ship taking female prisoners to Port Jackson (Sydney) and later went on to New Zealand for spars. He was accompanied by his pregnant wife, who gave birth to their second child off the Hokianga in early 1829. Three and a half years later Clendon was back in New Zealand, arriving on his schooner *Fortitude* with his business partner, Samuel Stephenson. It was the start of a highly successful business career that put him second only to Johnny Jones in wealth before 1840. In 1830 Clendon had acquired 89 ha (220 acres) at Okiato near Kororareka (now Russell) from the Nga Puhi chief Pomare II, and two years later he opened a trading store at Okiato. In 1837 he added another 32 ha (80 acres) to the Okiato estate and the following year 1352 ha (3342 acres) at Manawaora on the seaward coast which became a farm — reputedly the first to export wool from New Zealand. Business grew in the trade of provisions, flax and timber, surviving an early mishap in 1833 when the *Fortitude* was stranded briefly on the Hokianga and plundered by local Maori.

Clendon was a man of standing, and an outspoken critic of crime and drunkenness in the Bay of Islands. He was alarmed in 1834 when a Maori burglar shot at the British resident, James Busby, and the following year he drained his rum casks in a forlorn effort to encourage sobriety. He got on with Busby, supporting him in uniting northern tribes against de Thierry's grandiose ambitions in 1835. Clendon was also a master at mixing diplomacy and business. As US consul from 1838 to 1841 — a post more symbolic than real, since for much of that time there was no government to be accredited to — he gained considerable business from the many American ships visiting the Bay of Islands. But he also did some good. In 1839, for instance, he worked with Busby in investigating a report that an American boy from the US whaler *Hannibal* had been abducted and was being kept in a grogshop. The captain of the *Hannibal*, supported by other captains, landed and demolished the grogshop. Clendon was also appointed president of the New Zealand Banking Co, which opened the colony's first bank in Kororareka in 1840.

Clendon was prepared to lose much of his American business by supporting the plans of the British consul, William Hobson, to extend British sovereignty to New Zealand. His fortunes picked up temporarily when the new administration selected his Okiato property as the site for the capital. After much haggling, he sold 121 ha (300 acres), his comfortable ten-room house overlooking the harbour, a jetty, a store, two cottages and other buildings for £15,000 — £2000 for the land and £13,000 for the improvements. His asking price had been £23,000 but Governor Gipps of New South Wales, concerned that Clendon's title had not been established in accordance with his January 1840 land proclamation, baulked at the deal, even at the lower figure, and banned the sale of town lots. This deprived Clendon of a further £15,000 he had hoped to make and in the end he received only £2250 in cash and compensatory land elsewhere — mostly 4046 ha (10,000 acres) between Papatoetoe and Papakura, South Auckland, including what is now Manurewa and Wiri (Manukau City Centre). This was said to be worth 1s 6d an acre but was unsaleable at that price in the depressed market of the 1840s.

Clendon sold part of his South Auckland holding for 1s 3d an acre and farmed his Manawaora land in the Bay of Islands while becoming a justice of the peace, an ex officio member of New Zealand's first Legislative Council (1840–44) and after that a police magistrate, his jurisdiction eventually extending to the Hokianga. He was also collector of customs for the Hokianga from 1857. His wife died in 1855, leaving him with six children, and he remarried the following year, his new partner producing eight children. The family moved to Kerikeri briefly before settling at Herd's Pt (now Rawene) on the Hokianga in 1862, where Clendon continued dispensing the law until his retirement from the bench. The last few years before his death in 1872 were spent as a merchant, selling beer, wine and spirits. Clendon's last home, one of many he enjoyed in his busy career, survives today as Rawene's most historic building. While not large by modern standards, it was considered commodious for its day. It was also the first home in Rawene to have glass windows.

Gilbert Mair (1799?–1857), a ship's carpenter and the son of a shipowner from Peterhead, Scotland, has the distinction of helping Anglican missionary Henry Williams build the third vessel of European design in New Zealand and the first in the nineteenth century — the 60-tonne schooner *Herald*, built for Williams' Church Missionary Society. The *Herald*, which Mair commanded, was launched at Paihia in 1826 but was wrecked on the Hokianga bar in 1828. Mair then built a smaller replacement, the *Karere*, which was launched in 1830.

Mair, who was highly respected for his honesty and hospitality, acquired 159 ha (394 acres) from Maori at Te Wahapu Inlet, 4.8 km south of Kororareka, where he established a prosperous trading station, wharf and ship-repair yard complete with carpenters, sawyers, a blacksmith and a bootmaker. He took William Powditch as a partner from 1832 to 1835. With his brother William (who later drowned), Mair exploited kauri gum long before the industry began in earnest, being the first to export it to America. Timber and flax were also exported to Sydney.

In 1835 Mair completed building what is now New Zealand's oldest church, Christ Church, Kororareka. The family's six-room house at Te Wahapu burned down in 1836, and a two-storey replacement, completed that year, comprised a drawing room, dining room, kitchen, four bedrooms on the ground floor, and three upstairs. Two rooms were added later. Around 1837 Mair went into partnership with James Busby to mill timber at Ngunguru, near Whangarei, but the venture failed. Another with Clendon in 1838–39, to use their newly acquired barque *Independence* (renamed *Tokerau*) for trading, also failed. Mair was also behind a shore whaling station venture on Whale Island in the eastern Bay of Plenty.

Mair lobbied hard to have Britain declare New Zealand a colony and was involved in a vigilante movement, the Kororareka Association, formed in 1838 to clamp down on crime, drunkenness and sailors jumping ship in the Bay of Islands. Association members were required to own a musket, pistols, ammunition and a cutlass. One of its punishments including stripping, tarring and feathering offenders before drumming them out of town.

In 1840, with whaling on the wane, Mair decided to sell up, hopeful of persuading the government to buy his property as a site for the new capital. Although it was valued at £13,990 compared with the £23,000 asking price for Clendon's Okiato property nearby, surveyor-general Felton Mathew dismissed Mair's valuation as 'ludicrous', persuading Hobson to buy Clendon's land in what must rate as the most blatant example of jobbery in the Hobson administration. Even at the knocked-down price of £15,000, Okiato was still more expensive than Te Wahapu and close to 40 ha (100 acres) smaller.

Mair then leased Te Wahapu as a going concern to an American, US vice-consul Captain William Mayhew, and in 1842 he offered Mayhew a 999-year term — a virtual sale — for £7000. But Mair apparently received only £900 in cash and goods, and most of the balance, represented by promissory notes, was never paid. The lease to Mayhew included Toretore Island — valued at £2000 and part of Mair's original purchase of Te Wahapu — but the government took it without compensation because its deep-water frontage made it valuable for naval purposes. This placed Mair in financial difficulty when, in 1844, Mayhew's assignee, H.G. Smith, claimed a £2000 refund.

By this time Mair was well ensconced in Whangarei, where he and his family moved in December 1842, taking up 728 ha (1800 acres) for farming. He called his new home Deveron after the Mair home parish in Scotland. The family fled to Auckland briefly during the Northern War, fearing a Maori attack, but returned without incident. Today the Mair settlement is an inner-city suburb of Whangarei known as Mairtown. The city's bush-clad Mair Park was given to the town by the family. Gilbert Mair died prematurely in 1857, survived by twelve children, several of whom made their mark in New Zealand history:

▶ Robert Mair (1830–1920), the eldest son, was a prominent local government administrator and registrar of electors in Whangarei;

▶ William Mair (1832–1912) rose to the rank of major in the New Zealand Militia in command of the Arawa auxiliary force operating against rebel Hauhau in the Bay of Plenty. He was also a resident magistrate and a judge of the Native Land Court;

▶ Henry Mair (1836–81) was a captain in the colonial forces, raised the Opotiki Volunteer Forest Rangers, and served in a number of skirmishes against the rebels in the eastern Bay of Plenty. After the war he became a South Seas trader, and later a labour recruiter; he was murdered in the New Hebrides (now Vanuatu); and

▶ Gilbert Mair jnr (1843–1923) became a surveyor and interpreter, his intense interest in Maoridom arising from meeting Maori while helping his father in the kauri-gum business. He served with distinction in the land wars, rising to the rank of captain in the colonial forces and winning the New Zealand Cross for heading off an attack on Rotorua by Te Kooti in 1870. He is the only European to be admitted full chieftainship of the Arawa tribe. Unlike his father, he never achieved financial success.

A member of the family, well known in the 1990s for holding political views different from those of his distinguished forebears, is Maori activist Ken Mair (born 1956).

Four other entrepreneurs, all but one with links to the north, are contenders for entry in a pre-1840 rich list: Phillip Tapsell, John Harris, John Montefiore and Joel Samuel Polack.

Phillip Tapsell (1777?–1873) was the assumed name of Danish-born seaman-adventurer Hans Homman Jensen Falk, adopted so that he could serve on British ships when Britain and Denmark were at war. (The name Tapsell is a corruption of 'topsail'.) Tapsell was an early visitor to the Bay of Islands in whaling ships. In 1823, while serving on the *Asp*, he was married to a Maori woman by Anglican missionary Thomas Kendall in what was claimed to be the first European-style marriage to take place in New Zealand. His wife decamped the same day. Tapsell did not settle in New Zealand permanently until 1830, when he was married again, this time by Samuel Marsden, promoter of the Anglican mission in New Zealand, to a sister of a Nga Puhi chief.

At the invitation of the Arawa chiefs of Rotorua, Tapsell settled at Maketu in the Bay of Plenty where, as agent for a Sydney firm, he supplied muskets, gunpowder and other goods in exchange for flax. He engaged large numbers of Maori to work in the swamps to prepare flax fibre for export, and between peacemaking in tribal disputes and fighting off criticism from Anglican missionaries over his arms dealing Tapsell established a sound business.

He took a high-ranking Arawa Maori as his wife after his second wife died, eventually marrying her in a ceremony conducted by Bishop Pompallier. In 1836 Tapsell's business suffered a huge blow when Maketu pa in the Bay of Plenty was burned in an intertribal dispute. Tapsell lost more than £4000 in trade goods, buildings and about 120 tonnes of dressed flax, and it was only after missionary intervention that he and his heavily pregnant wife were released. He was forced to leave the district, and lost his contract with his Sydney principal. Although he was engaged by another Sydney merchant and went into partnership with John Middlemas at Whakatane, Tapsell never recovered from the Maketu setback and his new venture suffered a series of reverses. In 1848 he was forced to supplement his income by boatbuilding. He acquired White Island, an active volcano, and Whale Island off the Bay of Plenty coast and for a while lived with his daughter and son-in-law, who ran a store on Whale Island. In 1866 Tapsell failed to obtain a pension from the government in recognition of his reputed leadership of the party that had recaptured the brig *Wellington* from escaped convicts 40 years earlier. He died at Maketu in 1873, in his late nineties. Today the large Tapsell family is one of

Phillip Tapsell (1777?–1873), the Danish-born seaman-adventurer, born Hans Homman Jensen Falk, who settled at Maketu in the Bay of Plenty in 1830 and became one of the country's most prominent traders. Pictured here with his daughter, Kataraina.
Reed Publishing Photo Library

the more prominent in Maoridom. A former speaker of Parliament, Sir Peter Tapsell (born 1930), is the leading member.

John Harris (1808–72) was Gisborne's first trader, like Tapsell a pioneer in the flax trade. He was born in Cornwall, England, joined the Royal Navy as a boy, but quit through ill health and joined relatives in Australia as a twelve- or thirteen-year-old. He worked there until English-born trader Joseph Montefiore sent him with two colleagues to Poverty Bay in early 1831 to establish a flax business. Aged just 23, Harris set himself up initially at Awapuni Lagoon, on the lower reaches of the Waipaoa River, before moving to the west bank of the Turanganui River. In 1832 or 1833 he married a high-ranking Ngati Porou woman. Harris eventually bought the trading post off Montefiore and later acquired land at Opou, near Awapuni, where he built his house. He might also have owned land at Ruataniwha in Hawke's Bay. Harris was a pioneer pastoralist as well as the co-founder of the first whaling station in Poverty Bay — established next to his store on the west bank of the Turanganui River in 1837. By the early 1850s he was the most substantial settler in Poverty Bay, owning five of the district's twenty weatherboard houses and more livestock than his fellow Europeans. His land claims also survived government scrutiny in 1869.

Harris generally got on with missionaries William and Jane Williams, although they were not impressed by what they considered to be his licentious behaviour. He remarried in 1854 — his first wife had died — but his new wife later moved back to Auckland with their two children, leaving him depressed. He committed suicide on a visit to Auckland in 1872.

The only other Gisborne trader to compare with Harris, although not in the pre-treaty years, was Captain George Read (1814/15?–78), a former whaler who set up on the Kaiti side of the Turanganui River in 1852, not far from Harris' first store. A short, fiery man with a powerful personality, Read was also an extensive pastoralist, who by 1876 owned or leased interests in 29 separate blocks of land in an area extending upriver as far as Makauri and south to the Waipaoa rivermouth. He was also a director of the Poverty Bay Petroleum & Kerosene Co, and is remembered for building Poverty Bay's first hotel, the Albion Club, in 1866.

John Israel Montefiore (1807–98) was, as his middle name suggests, a member of the early Jewish community in New Zealand. A cousin of Joseph Montefiore, the merchant who had set Harris up in New Zealand, he arrived in Sydney in 1829 and left for Tauranga two years later in search of tradeable commodities such as flax, pork and potatoes. In 1836 he moved to the Bay of Islands, where he worked as a merchant and acquired land at Manawaora Bay near James Clendon's farm. He is said to have set up there as a ship's chandler.

John Montefiore (1807–98), a prominent Auckland Jewish merchant, was a founder of the Auckland Savings Bank in 1846. He was left to manage the merchant firm of Brown & Campbell when the partners were overseas in 1856 but was sacked in 1859 after being accused of wild property speculation and mismanagement.
COURTESY ASB BANK

An aloof but honourable man, he was considered one of the better-bred merchants in the Bay of Islands.

Montefiore returned to Sydney in late 1836 but was back in the Bay of Islands in March 1840, the month after the Treaty of Waitangi was signed. He set up shop as a food supplier and ship's chandler in Kororareka, close to other Jewish traders including Joel Samuel Polack and David Nathan (later to become a leading merchant in Auckland). Nathan's second wife, whom he married in 1878, was a daughter of Joseph Montefiore.

In 1841 John Montefiore moved to the new capital, Auckland, and at the first land auction bought on behalf of Sydney-based clients. His business grew and he acquired significant properties in what is now the central business district. He was also a founder of the Auckland Savings Bank, which opened in 1847. In about 1850 he returned to London, but was persuaded to come back five years later by Dr John Logan Campbell to run Brown & Campbell in the absence of Campbell and co-proprietor, William Brown. During this tenure in Auckland Montefiore helped set up the Auckland Chamber of Commerce in

1856, and was its chairman a year later. But Brown & Campbell struggled and Montefiore was sacked in 1859 for mismanagement and foolhardy land speculation. He sold most of his assets and returned to England where he died.

Joel Samuel Polack (1807–82), whom Montefiore had known at Kororareka, also hailed from London. He came to New Zealand in 1831 and after briefly trading on the Hokianga with Joseph Montefiore (who also had a trading station at Kawhia Harbour), and exploring the region, moved to the Bay of Islands. There Polack acquired several tracts of land and built a sizeable house, Parramatta, on a 3.6-ha (nine-acre) site at the north end of Kororareka beach. He established a significant merchant business, including the country's first brewery in 1835, but his interests extended well beyond profit. He had a keen interest in Maori welfare, not least the danger that unorganised European settlement posed to Maori society. Indeed, his brewery was aimed at encouraging Maori to drink beer instead of overproof spirits.

Polack returned to England in 1838, publishing accounts of his New Zealand experiences in two books, but he was back in New Zealand in 1842, this time as a colonist, promoting settlement by auctioning land into quarter-acre lots. Like other trader-speculators, his land dealings came under scrutiny from the Crown. But the real blow came on 11 March 1845 when Kororareka was sacked by Hone Heke and Kawiti in the first battle of the Northern War. A stockade had been built around Polack's house to provide protection for the town's women and children, and powder and ammunition for the defence had been stored there. The magazine blew up, reputedly ignited by a spark from a defender's pipe, destroying everything. Polack claimed the total loss came to £2600 but he failed to get compensation from the government. In 1845 he shifted to Auckland, where he enjoyed some success in trading and land speculation, before moving to California in 1850. He died in San Francisco in 1882.

The number of possible entrants in a rich list before 1840 is small and the level of wealth minor compared with the fortunes built up by Canterbury runholders, Dunedin industrialists and Auckland businessmen in the second half of the nineteenth century. It could have been larger had a number of pre-treaty land claims been upheld and the Bay of Islands not entered a prolonged slump following the removal of the capital to Auckland. Had Edinburgh-born James Busby (1802–71), who paved the way for British sovereignty, succeeded with his plans to establish a township called Victoria on his Waitangi claim, the north might have retained some of its economic clout. It is easy to dismiss Busby as a rampant speculator — his extensive land purchases in 1839 near Waitangi and at Waimate (now Waimate North), Ngunguru and Whangarei give that impression — but he had been farming and trading since arriving in New

Zealand in 1833 and had earlier worked 809 ha (2000 acres) in New South Wales, where he indulged his passion for viticulture. By 1838 he had also imported sheep and bullocks into New Zealand and was establishing a vineyard, extensive vegetable gardens and a forest nursery at Waitangi. The Victoria township venture failed, along with a timbermilling business established with Gilbert Mair near Whangarei. A sheep and cattle station at Whangarei, launched in 1840–41 at a cost of more than £4000, also failed and by the mid-1840s Busby had to mortgage the Waitangi holdings to pay his debts. Most of his remaining life was spent in litigation or taking petitions against various governments to have his land claims honoured. His case was finally settled in 1868, three years before his death, but much of the compensation was eaten up in legal costs.

The leading Anglican missionary in the Bay of Islands, Henry Williams (1792–1867), was one of several Church Missionary Society (CMS) members who had acquired large landholdings in the 1830s. Williams ultimately fared better than Busby despite a campaign against him and his CMS colleagues by Governor Grey. Grey questioned the validity of Williams' and others' titles to their lands, despite their legitimacy having been upheld by Grey's predecessor, Captain Robert FitzRoy. Grey suggested, without evidence, that the missionary acquisitions had contributed to Maori disaffection and to the Northern War. In 1848 landgrabbing charges were brought against Williams' CMS colleague, former chief protector of aborigines and CMS New Zealand secretary George Clarke (1798–1875), in a test case before the Supreme Court. Although the court rejected Grey's allegations, the CMS in London sacked Clarke nevertheless. Williams, the most outspoken of the missionaries, suffered the same fate, having become an embarrassment to his bishop, George Selwyn, who sided with Grey. Williams, still a priest and archdeacon of Waimate, quit Paihia and went farming with his family on the disputed lands at Pakaraka, inland from the Bay of Islands, where he built his home, appropriately named the Retreat, in 1851. With the help of his softer-natured brother, evangelical missionary William Williams (1800–78), he was reinstated to the CMS in 1854.

While Henry Williams' massive contribution to the Treaty of Waitangi, the Maori language and to peaceful relations between Europeans and Maori remain his epitaph, Grey's land-grabbing allegations continue to dog the family to this day. Some 800 direct descendants today own more land than any other family in New Zealand — large tracts on the North Island's East Coast and in the Bay of Plenty, Hawke's Bay and the Wairarapa — worth at least $30 million. The East Coast fortune was built up by Henry's second son, Samuel (1822–1907), whose achievements as a missionary and educationalist were equalled only by

Anglican missionary Henry Williams (1792–1867), who was accused by Governor George Grey of land-grabbing and sacked by the Church Missionary Society for refusing to surrender disputed holdings. There is no evidence his land titles were other than legitimate.
CHARLES BAUGNIET, ALEXANDER TURNBULL LIBRARY, C-020-005

his skills as a grazier. Samuel's impressive career included founding an Anglican mission school for Maori in Central Hawke's Bay, Te Aute College, in 1854. He died at Te Aute with an estate worth nearly £430,000. This was after providing for an extended family and donating generously over many years to missionary work and educational causes. Today, questions are asked about whether Samuel should be remembered as a father of Maori secondary education or as a major landowner and developer providing for his large family. The book *East Coast Pioneers*, published in 1998, has gone some way toward restoring Samuel's standing.

Several other Williams made significant contributions to the family's fortunes and standing, including the following:

▶ Henry Williams' fourth son, Thomas Coldham Williams (1825–1912), known as T.C. In 1858 he married Anne Beetham, a member of a pioneering sheepfarming family in the Wairarapa. T.C. went into partnership with the Beethams, expanding their Brancepeth station near Masterton and establishing a large Williams clan in the Wairarapa. Family members still farm in the region, including the 530-ha (1300-acre) Te Parae stud, carved out of the original Brancepeth estate;

Te Rau Kahikatea, home of the third Anglican bishop of Waiapu, (William) Leonard Williams (1829–1916). The house, built in 1875, is pictured in about 1885. W.F. CRAWFORD COLLECTION, GISBORNE MUSEUM & ARTS CENTRE/TE WHARE TAONGA O TE TAIRAWHITI, GISBORNE

- William Williams' grandson, Heathcote Beetham Williams (1868–1961), known as H.B.; a wealthy grazier, businessman and benefactor. In 1923 he funded (Sir) Robert Kerridge's purchase of a Gisborne picture theatre, the first step toward creating a nationwide chain that at its height owned 75 per cent of New Zealand's cinemas. H.B. became a 50:50 partner in the venture and the Williams family retained a strong interest until the ill-fated merger of Kerridge Odeon Corporation with David Phillips' investment company, Pacer Pacific Corporation, in 1987;

- H.B.'s younger brother, Arnold Beetham Williams (1870–1965), known as A.B.; a farmer, businessman and benefactor who developed the 2400-ha (5930-acre) Puketiti station near Te Puia Springs, on the East Coast, from the early 1900s. It is now run by Desmond Williams, one of his three adopted children. The large homestead, built in 1907–08 from American oregon with matai and rimu interior panelling, survives;

- Henry Williams' grandson, Kenneth Stuart Williams (1870–1935), a skilled pastoralist, who ran the large Matahiia station, southwest of Ruatoria, from 1898. With three cousins he set up the Waiapu Returned Soldiers' Trust to assist soldiers returning from World War I to obtain their own farms, and also helped struggling farmers survive the Depression. But Kenneth is best remembered as a popular and energetic politician — chairman of Waiapu County Council (1909–20), first chairman of Waiapu Hospital & Charitable Aid Board (1903), first chairman of Tokomaru Harbour Board (1910–19), Reform Party MP (1920–35) and minister of public works and minister in charge of roads and public buildings (1926–28). He introduced petrol tax in 1927. An excellent horseman, he was also a founder of the Waiapu Racing Club and owned several racehorses;

- H.B.'s younger son, Heathcote Beetham Williams (born 1922), known as Bill, who heads the Turihaua station on the coast northeast of Gisborne, where the Williams are prominent cattle breeders. He is also a businessman and benefactor. Turihaua, farmed since 1886, is now run largely by his second son, Hamish. Bill's eldest son, Marcus, an environmentalist, organic farmer and stockbreeder, was one of the first deer-farmers on the East Coast, starting at Turihaua in 1978 before acquiring a 160-ha Tolaga Bay property he named Sequoia.

The Williams have stayed loyal to farming during increasingly difficult times in the meat and wool industry. Their presence is everywhere — in Te Rau Kahikatea, the fine Victorian Gothic home Leonard Williams built in Derby St,

Gisborne, in 1875; in the family's numerous charitable bequests; their association with Te Aute College; their contribution to Maori language and education; and their involvement with stock-and-station agency Williams & Kettle, a listed Napier-based company that dates back to 1880. If they were land-grabbers — the allegation levelled by Grey at Henry Williams — they have more than done their penance.

Before 1840 it is relatively easy to categorise New Zealand's rich. There were not many of them; with the exception of Jones and Tapsell they were English or Scots; most had a seafaring background (Stewart, Jones, the Wellers, Dacre, McDonnell, Clendon, Mair, Harris and even Henry Williams). Most had learned to speak Maori and some — Maning, Polack and the Williams — had developed a specialist knowledge of Maori culture. Several took Maori wives or mistresses. (In addition to those mentioned, Edward Weller had two short relationships which produced children; the haughty John Montefiore, despite being contemptuous of Maori customs and habits, had a part-Maori daughter; Polack lived on the Hokianga for a time with a Maori 'chief girl'; and Clendon's second wife was part-Maori.) Two of the early rich, Maning and Tapsell, became true Pakeha-Maori. And many children of the early rich also took Maori wives or mistresses (Mairs and de Thierrys are good examples). This high level of fraternisation between the races is not surprising given the small number of Europeans (especially European women) living in New Zealand before 1840 and the need most traders had to do business with local Maori chiefs or warlords, sometimes directly under their tutelage. Relations were not easy — traders and missionaries complained that their houses, ships and stores were not infrequently pillaged by local Maori — but the incidences of violence against the trader-settlers before 1840 were relatively few. McDonnell, for instance, failed to get on with his European neighbours but was able to build up his business in Horeke in the 1830s because he developed respect for, and earned the respect of, local Maori.

There were few rules before 1840, and virtually no state bureaucracy. Traders could keep the proceeds of their endeavours in the absence of a customs tariff or an Inland Revenue Department. But there was only a slim chance of compensation if their ships ran aground or sank (as happened occasionally) or their houses were ransacked or burned (also not uncommon). Even in the early years after New Zealand became a British dependency, as Polack found to his cost when his house and business were destroyed in the attack on Kororareka in 1845, the government had neither the wherewithal nor the will to pay compensation.

This was the true, unadulterated free market — strong on quick-wittedness

The Rich List *
January 1840

Top ten families/individuals with their main sources of wealth

1. **Jones, John** (1808/09?–69) *Whaling, shipping*

2. **Clendon, James Reddy** (1800–72) *Trading, farming*

3. **Polack, Joel Samuel** (1807–82) *Trading, brewing*

4. **Mair, Gilbert snr** (1799?–1857) *Trading, shipping*

5. **Harris, John Williams** (1808–72) *Trading, whaling*

6. **Dacre, Ranulph** (1797–1884) *Trading, timber*

7. **McDonnell, Thomas snr** (1788–1864) *Trading, timber*

8. **Weller brothers** *Whaling*
   Edward Weller (1814?–93) and George Weller (1805–75).

9. **Williams family** *Land, farming*
   Mainly interests associated with Henry Williams' family in the Bay of Islands.

10. **Maning, Frederick Edward** (1811/12?–83) *Trading*

---

* This list relates more to the earnings potential and business activities of the people named than to their nominal landholdings. Many land claims were disallowed or scaled back severely after 1840. Hence, land alone does not qualify as wealth for this list. An exception is Henry Williams (1792–1867), whose family retained their extensive holdings after the signing of the Treaty of Waitangi. Two other possible entrants, trader John Montefiore (1807–98) and his cousin Joseph, have been excluded because they were not in the country in January 1840 and their wealth cannot be calculated. (John Montefiore, later one of Auckland's rich, left New Zealand in 1836 and did not return until March 1840.) In the case of Ranulph Dacre and the Weller brothers, Sydney-based wealth has been taken into account.

and entrepreneurship but, unlike the free market of today, operating in the absence of local capital. Before 1840 — indeed, before the 1860s — it was virtually impossible to raise money locally. There was not even a bank in New Zealand until 1840. Foreign capital, either speculative from London or the proceeds of successful trading in Sydney, formed the basis of New Zealand's pre-treaty business development.

New Zealand was hardly an El Dorado but it was not without promise. It was made for soldiers of fortune like Dacre, McDonnell, Mair and Clendon who could work without rules or bend the few that existed. Ultimately the shopkeepers and those landowners who survived the post-treaty land inquisitions were the ones to carry their fortunes through to the second half of the nineteenth century.

2

Merchant might, runholder wealth

The whole and entire object of everyone here is making money, the big fishes eating the little ones.

DR JOHN LOGAN CAMPBELL, MERCHANT OF AUCKLAND, 1840

The Auckland that greeted Dr John Logan Campbell and William Brown in 1840 was unprepossessing if not downright unattractive. There was no town and no infrastructure — just a government store, a tidal creek emptying into a swamp and a shingle beach. But for the Scots pair, who had met in 1839, gone their own ways and then reunited, Auckland was the best of a bad lot.

Brown (1809/10?–98), a Dundee lawyer in his thirties, was the older of the two by seven years and therefore the senior partner of 'the firm'. He had originally planned to buy land in Adelaide but after ten unhappy months there he and his wife, Jessie (née Smith), took the *Palmyra* to Sydney. On board they met Campbell (1817–1912), a newly qualified Edinburgh surgeon whose father had armed him with £1000 to go sheepfarming in Australia. The Browns and Campbell parted at Sydney — Brown to look at prospects in the Bay of Islands and Campbell to investigate wool-growing in New South Wales.

Campbell quickly became disillusioned with the drought-stricken colony and left for Port Nicholson (now Wellington) in March 1840 on the *Lady Lilford*. After a fortnight living in a tent and exploring the Hutt Valley he was unimpressed with the area, and left on the *Lady Lilford* for the Hauraki Gulf. The ship dropped anchor at Waiau (now Coromandel) where, by chance, he met Brown and rekindled their friendship. After three months' stay on the

Coromandel Peninsula, Brown and Campbell left with two other Scots for the Hauraki Gulf. Although they were initially unsuccessful in buying land in Auckland, in May 1840 Brown and Campbell bought the 60-ha (148-acre) island Motukorea (now Browns Island), 2 km off the southern shore of the Waitemata Harbour. Here they raised pigs. But their aim had always been to buy land and settle in the capital-to-be and in December that year, barely three months after Auckland was founded, the firm of Brown & Campbell was up and running. It was Auckland's first European trading enterprise, operating out of what Campbell described as an 'historic' tent in Commercial Bay (or Shore Bay as the locals preferred), a stone's throw from the water. This primitive start heralded a 31-year business partnership that would make Brown and Campbell Auckland's richest citizens by the mid-1850s, and create an enterprise that would form a pillar of a major late-twentieth-century public company, Lion Nathan.

Timing was everything. Brown and Campbell signalled their intention to be part of Auckland's future when, in April 1841, they bought a town lot at auction — Auckland's first Crown auction — on the south side of what was then the main thoroughfare, Shortland Cr (now Shortland St), above O'Connell St. Two months later they built a warehouse at the front of the lot, using ready-sawn timber Campbell had brought down from the north. With the leftover timber they built a cottage at the rear for the Browns; Campbell also lived in a back room for a period. A second storey was later added to the warehouse. Acacia Cottage remained on the site until 1920 when it was moved to Cornwall Park, where it remains Auckland's oldest surviving house.

In 1844 the partners made their first shipment of New Zealand produce to England, buying the barque *Bolina* to send flax, manganese, kauri timber and kauri gum. The Browns also travelled to the UK as Jessie required medical treatment. With capital from William Gibson, a sleeping partner in St Andrews, Scotland — invested through an allied firm next door, Gibson & Mitchell — Brown & Campbell expanded into auctioneering, a shipping agency, importing, land speculating and trading with Maori. The partners' knowledge of Maori custom — most of it gained from their time together on the Coromandel and in negotiating to buy Motukorea — and their willingness to put in the hard toil required in a pioneering society gave them a head start over most early Auckland traders.

Campbell remarked that Auckland in the 1840s had 'parsons without churches and magistrates without courts'. Yet this absence of infrastructure, he noted, did not stop the people of Auckland from being Christian and properly behaved. So it was with the pioneer merchants. Despite the lack of local capital, boundless opportunities in the absence of rules and ordinances made business attractive. The 'restrictions' tended to be more personal than market related — boredom and a lack of home comforts. Brown and Campbell fell prey to both and were lured back to the comfortable life in Europe — Brown for good, Campbell for many years. Had their resident managers not let them down when they were overseas, the founders of Brown & Campbell (later called Brown Campbell & Co and, after 1897, the Campbell & Ehrenfried Co) would have been but a footnote in history.

Despite romantic tales of the 'lively capital' from historian Una Platts and flowery accounts of the region's fine harbours, good soils and stands of timber from New Zealand's second attorney-general, William Swainson, Auckland in the early 1840s was an economic backwater and a dreary garrison town. Such social life as there was revolved around the governor's tiny court and occasional horseracing meetings. Entrepreneurs like Brown and Campbell, who did not hesitate to mix business and politics, could earn a good living, but in the absence of a local capital market there was little other than land on which to spend their newly created wealth and, without roads or railways, nowhere easy to travel to. Perhaps this accounts for the keenness of Brown, Campbell and others to write about their observations of Maori society and to maintain numerous other interests.

Brown was involved in politics in the 1850s (a member of the House of Representatives [MHR] in the central government and superintendent of the Auckland province); he owned Auckland's first stable newspaper, the *Southern Cross*, for many years, and he studied phrenology. Campbell also entered politics (like Brown, an MHR and provincial superintendent); he developed a passion for the visual arts, and he was an addicted international traveller. The partners' ability to trade, rather than rely on their education or well-heeled family connections, was the factor that separated them from thousands of other upper middle-class Victorians dotted around the British Empire. When they rested on their laurels in the mid-1850s and decided the firm could do without them, they nearly came unstuck. In 1856 their joint assets totalled £110,000. In 1871, Campbell was forced to take control of Brown Campbell & Co because Brown would not return from Britain to take his turn at running the business. Brown's share of the dissolved partnership was just £40,000. He could have had much more but the attractions of London — which included a fine home at Bayswater — and family commitments were too great.

Another merchant-trader who enjoyed early success in Auckland was Thomas Henderson (1810–86). With Scots brothers Henry and John Macfarlane (the latter Henderson's brother-in-law) he founded the timbermilling/shipping firm Henderson & Macfarlane, owner of the Pacific Island Traders fleet which became the Circular Saw Line. A blacksmith-engineer by trade, Henderson was about the same age as William Brown. He also hailed from Brown's home town in Scotland, Dundee. Demonstrating the business dexterity that brought Brown and Campbell success, Henderson speculated in the first government land sales, built one of the town's first hotels, the Commercial, and set about exploiting timber in the Waitakere Ranges, west of Auckland. By the late 1850s he was one of Auckland's more prosperous citizens. His credit standing was such that in 1863 he was able to raise £15,000 in Melbourne on his own account to recruit military settlers to New Zealand — this was after a bank there refused to advance more than £10,000 on New Zealand government letters of credit. Henderson's home epitomised his confidence — a brick, two-storey, twin-gable mansion in Emily Pl, Official Bay, it was built in the early 1860s at a cost of between £5000 and £8000. For a time it was the only home on Auckland's skyline to rival the second Government House (which replaced an earlier one destroyed by fire in 1848). But Henderson's success was not to last. His business suffered losses through increased competition, fires and shipwrecks, wiping away much of the family fortune (see chapter 3).

Auckland trader David Nathan (1816–86) was more fortunate. An Orthodox Jew from London who had chanced his arm briefly at Kororareka before settling in Auckland, he shared a similar rise in fortune to Brown, Campbell and Henderson, starting in 1840 with the purchase of 1011 ha (2500 acres) in Manurewa from James Clendon, at the knock-down price of 1s 3d an acre.

Nathan started business in a tent on the Auckland foreshore and in August 1841 built a wooden store on the corner of Shortland Cr and High St, a few doors down the hill from Brown & Campbell. He was briefly in partnership with Israel Joseph, a Jewish auctioneer who had been his neighbour in Kororareka, and who later set up a dry-goods store in Commercial Bay. Nathan's business followed a similar pattern to Brown & Campbell and, like them, he invested heavily in property. Nathan's marriage ceremony in 1841 was the first Jewish service in New Zealand, and the town's first regular Jewish services were held in a room in his Shortland Cr store from 1843. With John Montefiore he obtained a Crown grant for a 4046-sq m (one-acre) Jewish cemetery on the corner of Karangahape Rd and Symonds St. Nathan was widowed in 1864 and later married a daughter of Montefiore's cousin, Joseph.

Nathan played an important role in the development of Auckland business and local government. He retired in 1868 after establishing the merchant house L.D. Nathan & Co for his sons, Laurence and Alfred. He laid the foundation stone for the Auckland synagogue across the road from the

David Nathan (1816–86), an Orthodox Jew from London who created a highly successful trading business in Auckland in 1841 that today forms part of trans-Tasman brewer Lion Nathan.
COURTESY ASB BANK

Northern Club in 1884, and died at his fine home, Bella Vista, on nearby Waterloo Quadrant two years later. (Built in 1863 from imported bricks at a reputed cost of more than £5000, Bella Vista survives, with additions, as Newman Hall.) Nathan had earlier lived at St Keven's, Karangahape Rd, a stone house built for him in 1848. This provided shelter to Governor Grey after Government House burned down that year, and was lived in by other notables before returning to the Nathan family; after it had been restored following a fire, it was occupied by Laurence Nathan (1846–1905). From the 1880s Alfred Nathan (1850–1931) lived near his father's home in an elegant Italianate townhouse, Wickford, in the then merchant princes' row, Princes St. Wickford, the interiors of which were said to rival any townhouse in London, today serves as the University of Auckland registry. Alfred was president of the nearby Northern Club from 1917–19.

The Nathan business, a competitor of Brown & Campbell for many years, was destined to become part of it. In 1988, 147 years after David Nathan set

The interior of Wickford, the Italianate Auckland townhouse of Jewish merchant Alfred Nathan (1850–1931). It was said to rival any townhouse in London. Much altered since Nathan's time, it serves today as the University of Auckland registry.
UNIVERSITY OF AUCKLAND

up shop on the Auckland waterfront, L.D. Nathan & Co merged with Brown & Campbell's corporate descendant, Lion Corporation, to form Lion Nathan. This merger, more accurately a Lion takeover, was one of the more controversial of the 1980s because it rewarded the dominant shareholder in L.D. Nathan & Co, merchant bank Fay Richwhite & Co, for warehousing shares for Lion while minority shareholders received a lesser offer of Lion scrip. It highlighted the absence of proper takeover law in New Zealand and led to a campaign — ultimately unsuccessful — for a takeovers code.

Auckland's development in the first years of European settlement was slower than it should have been, held back by recessions and the Waikato War. It was only by the late 1860s, when the impact of the Thames gold boom was felt, that Auckland town (as distinct from the huge Auckland province) started to make headway against its southern rivals. By this time, as we shall see, Campbell was in the company of a small but confident commercial elite ready to invest in a variety of financial and development ventures, and willing to use

Shortland Cr, Auckland, in 1841, the town's principal thoroughfare until Queen St was developed. It was home to several trading houses including Nathan & Co, Brown & Campbell and Gibson & Mitchell.
COURTESY ASB BANK

whatever political influence and inside knowledge it could in the pursuit of profit. This was crony capitalism of the type we condemn these days in Japan and Southeast Asia.

In the 1840s the greatest sin (at least in the colonial government's view) was land speculation. Yet it was conducted to varying degrees by virtually every nineteenth-century settler who could later be described as rich and a number of public servants to boot. In the first Crown auction in Auckland in April 1841, where 116 town lots were put up for sale, some of the highest prices were paid by Lt-Governor Hobson's right-hand man, the pompous colonial secretary Lt Willoughby Shortland — £319 16s for one lot of less than 2000 sq m (half an acre) and £315 13s for another of 1340 sq m (a third of an acre). Shortland, a Royal Navy officer like Hobson who had accompanied the lieutenant-governor from Sydney, served as the colony's administrator for fifteen months following Hobson's death in September 1842. He was sacked by the incoming governor, Robert FitzRoy, in December 1843. His land investments, although small, were purely speculative and smacked of jobbery in the same way as his conduct over the ill-fated purchase of James Clendon's Okiato property as the site for the first seat of government.

Today, free from capital gains tax, property investment remains the dominant feature of New Zealand's savings and investment market. This did not happen by chance. Campbell recalled in 1841 that he and Brown had 'one fixed determination ... to become purchasers of town lots in the new capital and settle down there, acting as very small landsharks.' In a letter to his father at about that time, Campbell remarked: 'The whole and entire object of everyone out here is making money.' Campbell adopted a high moral tone in later life but he was little different in principle from Johnny Jones or the Weller brothers when it came to speculating in property.

Speculation, in the absence of banks or official financiers, also proved a godsend for opportunists like Henry Keesing (1791–1879). A Dutch Jew who served as a conscript in the Napoleonic army, he went to England in 1813, anglicised his name from Hartog Tobias Keesing, married and set up a clothing shop in London. He and his wife went to Auckland in 1843, joining a son there, and soon established a business in Shortland Cr which became a thriving store, London House. By 1844 Keesing was acquiring property by lending money on security of the borrower's land, and he soon owned a number of important sites in the town centre. Four of Keesing's properties were destroyed by fire in 1858 but he continued to prosper nonetheless. He was one of the earliest of Auckland's richer citizens to move to a country property, in 1849 taking up residence at Bird Grove, in Manukau Rd, Epsom. In later years he continued to buy and sell land as well as investing in the sharemarket. A friend of Sir George Grey, he was the first president of Auckland's tiny Hebrew congregation.

To Edward Gibbon Wakefield, the chief promoter of organised settlement in New Zealand, middle-class or commercially driven land speculation was tolerable, if not desirable. What was intolerable was the extension of the practice to the labouring classes. Auckland was outside his orbit — it was a free-fall settlement with little hint of organisation until Hobson moved the capital there in 1841 — but Nelson, Port Nicholson, Petre (now Wanganui), New Plymouth and, after 1850, Canterbury, had no choice but to deal with Wakefield's controversial land-price policy. A beguiling rogue, Wakefield developed his grand colonising plan while serving a three-year sentence in Newgate jail, London, for abducting an under-age heiress and tricking her into marrying him. Although the conviction barred him from standing for the British House of Commons, it did not prevent him engaging in colonial social engineering, and he was able to win considerable support for his plan for the organised settlement of New Zealand.

In reality, Wakefield was a victim of his class — his plan to replicate English

Edward Gibbon Wakefield (1796–1862) tried hard to transplant a modified form of the English class system in New Zealand. Only in Canterbury did it succeed and not in the way he had intended.
ALEXANDER TURNBULL LIBRARY, F-131790-1/2

society and structures failed to work in his New Zealand Company settlements and made limited progress only in Canterbury. The essence of Wakefield's plan was the principle of maintaining a proper balance between land, labour and capital. Settlers should pay a 'sufficient price' for government wasteland to ensure labourers would continue to work for wages and not immediately become landowners. Profits from the sale of land would be used to assist immigration. The plan offered British radicals a plausible alternative to the discredited system of providing assisted passages to paupers or transporting felons; for the speculators it held the prospect of large profits.

Even if the New Zealand Company had obtained the land it had promised would-be settlers and investors, it is unlikely Wakefield's organised settlement would have developed along English lines. In the absence of capital and demand in settlements devoid of basic infrastructure, artisans and labourers were forced to use their wits to survive. Thus, animal husbandry and food-growing took early precedence over pastoralism; merchants and traders took the place of squires and county folk; servants quickly realised they could prosper as well as their masters. In a strange way, Wakefield's vision for a better society succeeded, but for different reasons and by a different set of rules and processes than he had envisaged.

If Wellington's labourers were forced to turn Wakefieldian theory on its head, the town's merchants at least were able to prosper in a similar fashion to their Auckland counterparts. Prominent pioneers were the Jewish traders Nathaniel Levin (1818–1903) and Abraham Hort jnr (1819–62). Hort first arrived in Port Nicholson in 1840 and Levin, whom he later met in Sydney, the following May. Hort set up a trading business with Solomon Mocatta (Hort Mocatta & Co) and Levin established a drapery, hosiery and haberdashery business on Lambton Quay (Levin & Co). In 1843, Levin opened a food, liquor, whale oil and whalebone business in Willis St. He also bought a shore whaling station at Cloudy Bay, at the top of the South Island. Success came quickly. Levin was a founder member of the Wellington Club in 1841 and was soon highly respected in the town's commercial community. (By comparison, the Auckland Club, which was formed in 1856, had few Jewish members in its early years, although the nearby Northern Club, formed in 1869 — opposite the former Auckland synagogue — has a long tradition of Jewish membership.)

Hort's father, the philanthropist Abraham Hort snr (1799?–1869), came to Wellington in 1843 to establish New Zealand's first Jewish congregation, and Levin successfully petitioned Governor FitzRoy for land for a Jewish cemetery and synagogue. He married Hort snr's daughter in 1844, and with Hort jnr, now his brother-in-law, started a business shipping goods and passengers to Tahiti. Business grew and Levin & Co became a well-established shipping and land agency. It expanded to general merchandising and a stock-and-station agency with the development of sheepfarming and the decline in whaling. In 1862 Levin was joined in partnership by Charles Pharazyn (1802–1903), a merchant-turned-Wairarapa pastoralist, but Levin was fast tiring of colonial life, especially the depressed economy of the mid-1860s, and decided to retire to Britain. In 1868 the partnership with Pharazyn was dissolved. The business was carried on by Levin's eldest son, Willie (1845–93), Pharazyn and Walter Johnston (1839?–1907), a wealthy Wellington merchant who later became an

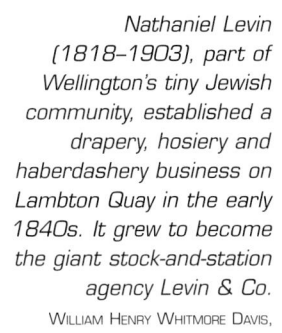

> Nathaniel Levin
> (1818–1903), part of
> Wellington's tiny Jewish
> community, established a
> drapery, hosiery and
> haberdashery business on
> Lambton Quay in the early
> 1840s. It grew to become
> the giant stock-and-station
> agency Levin & Co.
> WILLIAM HENRY WHITMORE DAVIS,
> ALEXANDER TURNBULL LIBRARY,
> F-94430-1/2

MP, a minister in the Hall, Whitaker and Atkinson ministries, and an extensive rural landowner. Nathaniel Levin retained a small involvement only in Levin & Co. Pharazyn retired from the firm in 1871 and Johnston quit in 1878 to join a family concern, Johnston & Co, leaving Willie in charge (with the help of a competent manager) from 1878–91.

The Levins, Pharazyns and Johnstons formed the core of Wellington's commercial elite. The Johnston home in Tinakori Rd, Thorndon, known for its large ballroom, was adjacent to those of the Levins and Pharazyns. Johnston, like Pharazyn, had land in the Wairarapa (Castlepoint station, acquired in 1876) and extensive family interests in Hawke's Bay. The crowning glory of his personal wealth was a 485-ha (1200-acre) estate near Awahuri in the Manawatu where he built a large country house, Highden, in 1897–98. Johnston was also a director of the Bank of New Zealand in 1888 and 1894–98, and served on the committee appointed by shareholders in 1888 to explain how the bank had lost £800,000 of its capital to bad loans. He died leaving an estate worth nearly £500,000.

As for Nathaniel Levin, in 1869 he became the first Jew appointed to the Legislative Council, but he hated politics and never made a speech in the House. As he was preparing to go to England in 1869 he became involved in a messy court case after an English investor, Richard Beaumont, accused him of conspiring with Marlborough grazier Joseph Tetley (1825–78) to cheat him. The recently widowed Tetley, a member of the Legislative Council, had absconded without trace to Uruguay, costing Beaumont his money, Levin & Co £15,000 and Levin £6000 personally. Levin, Tetley's friend, adviser and financier for many years, sued for slander, seeking £5000, but the jury at the Nelson trial could not agree, so the parties agreed to its discharge without a verdict. Levin, his wife and daughter left Wellington for England at the end of 1869. They at least had the satisfaction that the Wellington Club, the centre of the province's business community, stood firmly behind them.

Levin died in England in 1903, with assets worth more than £100,000. This was after generous charitable endowments and the passing of much of his New Zealand property to his son, Willie (who predeceased him by ten years), and others in the family. The Manawatu town of Levin is named after Willie — perhaps the richest young man in Wellington in the 1870s — who was a director of the Wellington & Manawatu Railway Co, an MHR and, like his father, a highly successful businessman and a public benefactor.

The Levins and Horts thrived not simply on their business acumen and public-spiritedness but also through their ability to network through family alliances, Jewish and gentile alike. Nathaniel Levin's wife, Jessie (née Hort), was a sister of Margaret Bell, wife of the wealthy Anglican runholder-politician Sir Francis Dillon Bell (1822–98), and mother of a top-flight lawyer and future prime minister, Sir Francis Henry Dillon Bell (1851–1936). (Bell snr's pastoral holdings in Otago exceeded 91,459 ha [226,000 acres] in 1874 and he had nearly 80,000 sheep — a sizeable flock for someone more interested in gardening than wool.) Willie Levin also married a non-Jew, Amy FitzGerald, daughter of the eccentric Canterbury political leader James FitzGerald, and Willie's sister, Anne, married the rich Wairarapa pastoralist and parliamentarian George Beetham (also gentile). As for Levin & Co, it became a limited liability company in 1896, associated with London-based stock-and-station agency the National Mortgage & Agency Co of New Zealand (NMA). The Levin & Co name disappeared within three years of NMA's merger with rival Wright Stephenson & Co in 1972, but the name has since been acquired by a great-great-grandson of Nathaniel Levin, Peter Levin (born 1932), for his private business interests.

John Plimmer (1812–1905), known as the 'father of Wellington' in the same way as Logan Campbell is the 'father of Auckland', was, like the Levins and Horts, an establishment figure in Wellington business. The eleventh of twelve children of an English builder and timber merchant, Plimmer arrived in Port Nicholson in 1841 and settled at Te Aro, where he established a timber and charcoal-burning business and a small limeworks. In 1850 he bought the 571-tonne *Inconstant*, which had been wrecked at Pencarrow Head. He towed the hull to the Lambton foreshore opposite Barrett's Hotel and converted it to a wharf, business offices and a bonded warehouse. 'Noah's Ark', as it became known, proved highly profitable and was in use until 1883.

Plimmer invested his profits in many local companies and after the huge 1855 earthquake in Wellington — New Zealand's biggest shake — he devoted himself to building and contracting. He was a founding member of the Chamber of Commerce, and active in town and provincial politics. But business was his driving force, and his powerful lobbying for land reclamation, railways and improved harbour facilities contributed greatly to Wellington's emergence from a provincial backwater into an economic centre in its own right. Plimmer died in 1905 at the age of 92. A son, Isaac (1834–1908), worked in the business with him and served on the Wellington Provincial Council, while a grandson, William Plimmer (1874–1959), was a noted music and drama critic on the *Dominion* newspaper for many years. A great-grandson, Sir Clifford Plimmer (1905–88), was a professional company director who is best remembered for his development of former pastoral giant Wright Stephenson & Co (now Wrightson). Sir Clifford was inducted posthumously into the Business Hall of Fame in 1995.

Another pioneer Wellington businessman who enjoyed early success was Dicky Barrett (1807?–47), an English sailor best known for his hotel, Barrett's. Barrett visited New Zealand in 1828 as mate and shareholder in the 61-tonne schooner *Adventure*, bartering Sydney produce for New Zealand pigs, flax and potatoes. He developed good relations with Maori, taking a Maori wife in 1828. The *Adventure* (renamed the *Tohora*) was wrecked at her moorings at Ngamotu (now part of New Plymouth) in May 1828 after a return voyage from Sydney, and Barrett sold her cargo to a passing English trader in the first direct shipment of goods from Taranaki to England.

Barrett and his captain, Jacky Love, were drawn into a protracted tribal war when Waikato Maori besieged their trading colleagues, Te Ati Awa, at Otaka pa, Ngamotu, in 1832. Barrett, using cannon salvaged from the *Tohora*, helped raise the siege. He continued trading, buying a new schooner, and later starting a whaling station at Queen Charlotte Sound. When the *Tory* arrived in Port Nicholson in 1839 with the first New Zealand Company settlers, Barrett was appointed interpreter and piloted the ship to Petone. He played a key role in Wellington's first days, although whaling losses deprived him of his hotel in 1841 and he was forced to return to Taranaki. Many of his land purchases in Port Nicholson, Taranaki and Queen Charlotte Sound were also disallowed by the government after 1840. Barrett died in 1847 after a whaling accident. Barrett Reef at the entrance to Wellington Harbour is named after him.

But no pioneer was to have greater influence on the early colonial economy than Captain William Rhodes (1807?–78), who was born in Epworth, in Lincolnshire, England, the son of a prosperous tenant farmer. Rhodes gained his first command in a ship he partly owned at the age of nineteen, sailing to South America, Africa and India. He later sold his interest in the ship, using the proceeds to speculate on land and stock before taking command in 1836 of the whaling barque *Australian*, which visited New Zealand waters. He joined a Sydney firm in 1839 to buy land from Maori and set up trading stations, acquiring deeds to around 800,000 ha (nearly two million acres) in the North and South islands. In 1840 he escorted the first New Zealand Company immigrant vessel *Aurora* into Port Nicholson. He established his business premises in Te Aro later that year, and the settlement's first wharf in 1841. Rhodes' enterprise, W.B. Rhodes & Co, thrived and within a decade he was able to buy out his Sydney partners. By 1853 he was being described as 'the millionaire of Wellington', with extensive shipping, insurance and finance interests. Many of his pre-1840 land claims were rejected or scaled back by the government, but options on unexercised New Zealand Company entitlements gave him extensive freehold estates including Highland Park on the western Wellington hills and the 12,140-ha (30,000-acre) Heaton Park in the Rangitikei. He acquired or controlled many thousands of hectares more by private purchases and illegal grazing.

In partnership with his brothers Robert (1815–84) and George (1816–64), Rhodes obtained a string of South Island pastoral runs extending from Banks Peninsula to North Otago. Another brother, Joseph (1826–1905), independently established extensive pastoral holdings in Hawke's Bay and the East Coast of the North Island. William Rhodes had no children from either of his marriages, although there was a daughter from an unknown Maori woman. Before his death in 1878 he was probably New Zealand's richest individual. Certainly, in terms of landed wealth, the Rhodes' collective riches outstripped allcomers. Robert Rhodes, for instance, left £572,849 in 1884, and five of the brothers' offspring left six-figure fortunes.

The Rhodes brothers' rural land speculating helped to keep control of the pastoral industry out of the hands of Wakefield and the Canterbury settlement's resident chief agent, John Robert Godley. By the time the Canterbury settlement started in 1850, the Rhodes and others had established the principle that pastoralism should develop in line with the market price for land, not what professional colonisers considered a fair price. If that meant making 'cheap'

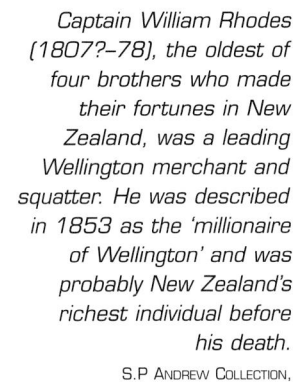

Captain William Rhodes (1807?–78), the oldest of four brothers who made their fortunes in New Zealand, was a leading Wellington merchant and squatter. He was described in 1853 as the 'millionaire of Wellington' and was probably New Zealand's richest individual before his death.
S.P ANDREW COLLECTION, ALEXANDER TURNBULL LIBRARY, F-18602-1/1

land available to would-be farmers, so be it. The squatters had a powerful ally in Governor Grey who, while opposed to squatting, detested Godley and Wakefield and their land-price theories. His General Land Regulations of 1853, allowing the sale of Crown land at between 5s and 10s an acre outside the Canterbury block — the area north of the Waipara River and south of Ashburton — effectively enshrined squatting. Godley had already eased the Canterbury Association's restrictive terms on pastoral leases to take advantage of Australian capital pouring into the colony; Grey's regulations ensured there was no turning back.

The Rhodes brothers were not the first to farm sheep in New Zealand — that honour went to a Scot, John Bell, who brought 102 merino sheep and ten head of cattle from Sydney to Mana Island, off Porirua Harbour, in 1833. But they were among the first to see the big picture and recognise the dominance wool would have in the Canterbury and New Zealand economies. They were also among the first to become rich by it. William Rhodes had established a cattle station in Akaroa in 1839, and he was well aware of the potential wealth extensive pastoralism could generate. The brothers' successful application in December 1850 to squat on three runs in South Canterbury totalling 64,345 ha (159,000 acres), pending the issue of a grazing licence, was the first outside the Canterbury Association's block and proved a watershed in the development of sheepfarming. Their station, the Levels — named after the place near Doncaster, in Yorkshire, where the family had farmed — prospered. Reduced in size after survey, it was carrying 30,000 sheep as early as 1858 — about two per cent of the colony's sheep numbers — and the flock eventually grew to more than 100,000. It survived early setbacks, including the loss in 1855 of 1000 head to sheepstealer James Mackenzie, and contributed to the development of the Timaru area from the late 1880s. The Rhodes brothers also profited handsomely from selling sections in downtown Timaru from 50 ha (126 acres) they had earlier freeholded.

George Rhodes, who managed the Levels on behalf of the brothers until his death from typhoid in 1864, lived initially in a wattle-and-daub hut on the beach at Timaru. He later moved to a totara-slab, thatched cottage, lined with cob, which survives near Washdyke. (One of his earlier homes, built at Purau on Lyttelton Harbour from local reddish volcanic stone in 1853–55, and once

The Levels station, South Canterbury, pictured in 1865, was the role model for southern squattocracy. The Rhodes brothers' successful application in December 1850 to squat on the land, pending the issue of a grazing licence, was the first outside the Canterbury Association's regulated block.
McGregor Collection, Canterbury Museum, Ref: 8699

described as the 'handsomest house in New Zealand', also survives.) One of George's sons, lawyer A.E.G. Rhodes, was MHR for Gladstone from 1887–90 and Geraldine from 1890 until his defeat in 1893, following in the steps of his late uncle, William Rhodes, who had represented Wellington constituencies in Parliament from 1853–66. A.E.G. Rhodes was also mayor of Christchurch in 1901. (He also maintained his share of the family fortune, leaving £216,096 in his will.) But the real political success went to Robert Rhodes' energetic eldest son, the wealthy landowner, stockbreeder and lawyer Sir (Robert) Heaton Rhodes (1861–1956). He was MP for Ellesmere from 1899 to 1925, serving as a Reform minister from 1912–15 and 1920–26. He was a member of the Legislative Council from 1925–32 (and leader in 1926 during Sir Francis Bell's absence) and 1934–41, and a member of the Executive Council without portfolio from 1926–28.

Oxford-educated Sir Heaton bred pedigree stock at Otahuna, Taitapu, at the western foot of the Port Hills, where his imposing 3-storey, 40-room country house, built in 1895, remains as one of the largest and most complete Queen Anne houses in New Zealand. Otahuna, which had extensive lawns, gardens and an artificial lake, was a venue for Canterbury's top garden parties and polo matches. It was also famous for its daffodils, grown for Sir Heaton by

Otahuna, Taitapu, at the western foot of Canterbury's Port Hills, was built in 1895 for Sir Heaton Rhodes. The 3-storey, 40-room home is one of the largest and most complete Queen Anne houses in New Zealand. In its day it was the centre for top garden parties and polo matches.

NEW ZEALAND HISTORIC PLACES TRUST

an expert gardener, A.E. Lowe. Sir Heaton also owned the finest collection of New Zealand postage stamps, and was one of only three New Zealanders to have his name on the Roll of Distinguished Philatelists. In 1930 he had St Paul's Anglican Church built at Taitapu as a memorial to his late wife, Jessie, Lady Rhodes (née Clark), including Australian stone to recognise her Australian origins. In one wall he even incorporated a stone from St Paul's Cathedral, London.

As in Australia, pastoralism was the major engine of wealth-creation in nineteenth-century New Zealand. Wool and then frozen meat were the foundation of the great fortunes of southern runholders. Ironically, however, the origins of this pastoralism were firmly in the north of the colony. In many cases it was born out of settler disenchantment with Wellington in the early years of settlement. Scots settler William Deans (1817?–51) was a classic example. He arrived in Port Nicholson in January 1840 and, unhappy that not all the land promised to him was available, farmed at Petone beach. He later explored other parts of the lower North Island and considered squatting in the Wairarapa. Still not satisfied, he explored the east coast of the South Island in 1842, including travelling some distance up the Otagaro (now Avon) River on the Port Cooper Plains — the site of present-day Christchurch. He liked what he saw and persuaded his younger brother, John, who had arrived in Nelson in 1842 and was unhappy with what that settlement had to offer, to join him.

The brothers sought a lease for land that William Deans had earlier set his sights on, a swampy, bush-covered area at Potoringamotu. A farm was soon established, John Deans imported their first sheep from Australia in 1843, and a 21-year lease for land running 7.2 km (4.5 miles) in every direction from Potoringamotu (13,354 ha or 33,000 acres), at £8 a year, was granted in 1846. The Deans freeholded a 161-ha (400-acre) farm in 1848 after negotiations with the New Zealand Company, which was planning to colonise the Port Cooper Plains. No further land purchases were allowed but the Potoringamotu bush — now Deans Bush — was protected.

They named the farm Riccarton, after their home town in Scotland, and the nearby river the Avon. Pressure from the Canterbury Association forced the Deans to exchange their native lease for one outside the planned town and after much haggling they settled for the 13,354-ha Homebush run, on the Canterbury Plains between the Hawkins and Selwyn rivers. In 1851, however, before the arrangements were completed, William Deans was drowned when the *Maria*, on which he was travelling to Australia to buy stock, was wrecked near Cape Terawhiti. John Deans died of consumption at Riccarton in 1854, leaving a widow and an infant son, also John. John Deans II (1853–1902) produced eight sons and four daughters, providing the basis for the extensive Deans clan which remains in Canterbury today. Homebush was divided among the family in 1910, and many Deans still farm there.

The Deans' second home, Deans Cottage, built at Riccarton in 1844, survives as does much of the original bush — a testimony to their conservation-minded descendants, who gifted it to the people of Christchurch. Part of the Deans' third home, completed in 1856 after William and John's premature deaths, survives as the east wing of the Deans' massive Riccarton House, which is preserved by the Riccarton Trust Board. These days the Deans are known less for their widely dispersed wealth and more for family members who have made other contributions to Canterbury, notably:

- John Deans I's grandson, Bob Deans (1884–1908), a Riccarton farmer; he scored a try for the All Blacks against Wales at Cardiff on 16 December 1905, only to be hauled back by the defence and have it disallowed by a dawdling referee. The setback cost the All Blacks the test and blemished an otherwise undefeated scorecard on their 33-match tour of the UK and France. Bob Deans died at the age of 24 of complications following an appendectomy just two months after playing a test against the touring Anglo-Welsh rugby team in 1908;

- John Deans I's great-grandson, Austen Deans (born 1915), of Peel Forest, Canterbury, a prolific artist of the traditional school whose World War II pictures, many painted or sketched while he was a prisoner-of-war in Greece, Poland, Germany and Austria, are held in high regard. His mother was a great-niece of the novelist Jane Austen, and there were five artists on his father's side; and

- John Deans I's great-great-grandsons, Robbie Deans (born 1959) and Bruce Deans (born 1960), who have also brought credit to their province and country in rugby. Robbie, who lives in Christchurch, was a Canterbury fullback from 1982–85 during the province's Ranfurly Shield pre-eminence, where he scored record shield points. He was an All Black fullback from 1983–85, playing 19 matches and scoring 252 points. He is now the coach of the Canterbury Crusaders Super 12 side and assistant coach of the All Blacks. Bruce Deans, a halfback, played 116 times for Canterbury until his retirement in 1990. After 1987 he played 23 times for the All Blacks as halfback, 10 of them in tests. (Maintaining the sporting connection, in 1983 Bruce and Robbie's elder sister, Nicola, married Jock Hobbs, an All Black flanker who played 21 tests and was a successful team captain.)

The Deans were the most prominent of the 'pre-adamites' — the pastoralists who owned or leased land before the establishment of the Canterbury settlement in 1850 and the arrival of the so-called 'pilgrims' (Canterbury Association settlers). Later Canterbury pastoralists like the Rhodes family, who occupied large tracts of land outside the Canterbury block, were called squatters. If they were Australian — and many Australian sheepfarmers squatted in Canterbury after a bad drought across the Tasman in 1850 — they were more likely to be known as 'shagroons' (from Irish Gaelic) or 'prophets', the latter name arising because they prophesied ruin for the farming pilgrims.

A handful of other South Island settlers also farmed sheep in the pre-adamite period. The Greenwood brothers — James, Joseph and Edward — had a 500-strong flock and 50 head of cattle at Purau, Port Cooper (Lyttelton Harbour), in 1844. The brothers, like the Deans originally New Zealand Company settlers, came from the Brontes' home parish of Haworth, in West Yorkshire, England. They sold their Purau land — leased from local Maori at £8 a year — to their neighbours, the Rhodes, in 1847 and took up land at Motunau, in North Canterbury. Another brother, George, bought the large Teviotdale station, 9 km southeast of Waipara, from a failed runholder in 1867. In 1844, whaler-trader Johnny Jones (see chapter 1), who in January 1840 was the richest New Zealander (if that term could be used then to describe the rough Sydney-born wheeler-dealer), had at least 1000 sheep on his farm at Matanaka, near Waikouaiti, Otago.

The big action, however, took place in the lower North Island through the efforts of three Roman Catholic aristocrat-adventurers, cousins (Sir) Charles Clifford (1813–93), William Vavasour (1822–1860) and Henry Petre (1820–89), products of England's leading Jesuit college, Stonyhurst, in Lancashire. They were joined by Charles Bidwill (1820–84), who had arrived in New Zealand in 1843 from Sydney on the schooner *Posthumous*, with 1600 sheep and some horses. Bidwill suffered losses on the voyage and further losses at Nelson, the first landfall, where many sheep were sold for as little as 15s to 17s each. Bidwill brought about 350 of the healthier sheep to Wellington and grazed them in the Hutt Valley before going in search of land in the Wairarapa with the gentlemen-cousins and an interpreter, naturalist William Swainson (not to be confused with the attorney-general of the same name). Clifford and Vavasour had earlier made contact with Wairarapa Maori who seemed keen to attract Europeans to their area, but government restrictions prevented squatters from buying land and the cousins instead leased more than 12,000 ha (about 30,000 acres) at Wharekaka in the Ruamahanga Valley, near present-day Martinborough — much of it in flax-covered swamp, manuka scrub and bush.

MERCHANT MIGHT, RUNHOLDER WEALTH — 49

Charles Bidwill I (1820–84) of Pihautea, Wairarapa, brought the first sheep into the Wairarapa in 1844, helping establish pastoralism. Pictured here in 1862.
Courtesy Anna Bidwill

Bidwill leased land at Kopungarara (now Pihautea), about 9 km further north. The rent in each case was £12 a year.

In April 1844 Bidwill, accompanied by Swainson, two helpers, two pack mares and two pig dogs, drove his sheep from the Hutt Valley to Okiwi Bay, then via a ridge track on to the mouth of the Wainuiomata River and around the coast to Palliser Bay and Lake Onoke, the mouth of the Ruamahanga River. This incredible journey, through which all the sheep survived, gave Bidwill the undisputed honour of bringing the first sheep into the Wairarapa. Unable to canoe the sheep across the lake because of the rush of water going out to sea, he returned to the Hutt Valley to bring up some cattle. While he was away, twenty-year-old (Sir) Frederick Weld (1823–91) arrived with Clifford, Vavasour and Petre's 500-strong flock of merinos and Southdowns, following the track cut by Bidwill. The shy and delicate Weld, also a cousin of Clifford, Vavasour and Petre and a Stonyhurst old boy (his grandfather had endowed the school), had arrived in the colony only days earlier and knew nothing of the outdoor life. Weld brought his cousins' sheep to Wharekaka — New Zealand's first true sheep station — and Bidwill, following Weld's tracks, reached Wharekaka shortly after with all his stock. He and Swainson stayed there until a track was cut to Kopungarara.

Clifford offered Weld a share in the venture after Petre, whose father, the eleventh Baron Petre, was a director of the New Zealand Company, withdrew his capital, preferring to speculate on horses rather than sheep. Vavasour returned to England in 1845, and died in 1860; Petre to business in Wellington (he was colonial treasurer of the shortlived New Munster province in 1848 and colonial treasurer and postmaster-general in the central government in 1851 and 1853 respectively). In 1847 Clifford and Weld took up a grazing licence for some 23,000 ha (more than 56,800 acres) near present-day Ward in Marlborough, which they called Flaxbourne. An experienced Scots manager, Thomas Caverhill, ran Wharekaka on their behalf from 1844 until he was drowned in December 1848.

In 1850 the partners abandoned Wharekaka and, retaining Flaxbourne, moved into North Canterbury, establishing Stonyhurst on a squatter's licence for 23,714 ha (58,600 acres) applied for in December 1850 (two days after the Rhodes' application for the Levels). The partnership lasted until 1884, earning Clifford and Weld large profits in the early years, unsurpassed standing in pastoralism and an entree into national politics; Clifford was the first speaker of the House of Representatives, from 1854–60, and Weld the country's seventh premier, from 1864–65. Weld even published a bestselling pamphlet in England for would-be pastoralists, *Hints to Intending Sheep-farmers in New Zealand*, but he was always the junior partner to Clifford, owning no more than a quarter of the assets.

This imbalance caused problems when Clifford tried in 1873–74 to include his son, George (1847–1930), in the partnership. Clifford snr decided to dissolve the partnership and buy Weld out, but Weld, by this time governor of Western Australia, rejected the offer and countered with a takeover offer of £240,000. In the event, a compromise was reached over George's involvement and the partnership endured for another ten years. Clifford snr was made a baronet in 1887 and George, who succeeded to the baronetcy after his father's death in 1893, managed Flaxbourne and Stonyhurst after 1874 and was a noted sheepbreeder and horseracer. The seventh baronet, property consultant Sir Roger Clifford (born 1936), succeeded to the title in 1982 and lives in Christchurch.

Clifford snr and Weld's outstanding success at sheepfarming, coming not long after failure in the Wairarapa, is a case study of vision and perseverance. They had Flaxbourne producing healthy profits by 1850, providing a return on capital, according to the disapproving J.R. Godley, of 30 per cent. 'Mr Weld

Fern Hill, the Dunedin home of Johnny Jones (1808/09?–69). It was acquired by the Dunedin Club from Jones' estate in 1874 and serves as the clubrooms to this day.
HOCKEN LIBRARY/UARE TAOKA O HĀKENA, UNIVERSITY OF OTAGO, DUNEDIN

Deptford, or Horeke, on the Hokianga, where Lt Thomas McDonnell (1788–1864) earned his New Zealand fortune. He acquired the bankrupt sawmilling and shipyard business at auction in Sydney in 1831.
NATIONAL LIBRARY OF AUSTRALIA

Captain James Clendon (1800–72), pictured on the Hokianga River in 1834. US consul from 1838–41 and the richest North Islander in January 1840, Clendon lost much of his business when Britain assumed sovereignty of New Zealand.
From O.C.M. Montage, Early Traders: The New Zealand Company, Auckland City Libraries, N.Z., A11633

Clendon succeeded in selling his overpriced Okiato estate in the Bay of Islands, above, to the government as the capital for the new British colony. But New South Wales Governor Sir George Gipps baulked at the £15,000 deal, paying only part of the settlement in cash and denying Clendon the chance to speculate on adjoining land.
Felton Mathew, Alexander Turnbull Library, F-29204-1/2

Former ship's carpenter Gilbert Mair (1799?–1857) set up a trading station/shipyard, above, in Te Wahapu Inlet, Bay of Islands, in the 1830s. He sold up in 1842 when whaling was on the wane and trouble was brewing with northern Maori.
FROM A DRAWING BY MAJOR CYPRIAN BRIDGE, C-030-016, ALEXANDER TURNBULL LIBRARY, F-626-1/1

Samuel Williams (1822–1907), the second son of Anglican missionary Henry Williams, established the East Coast North Island fortune of the Williams family through his skills as a grazier. A missionary and educationalist, he died at Te Aute, Hawke's Bay, with an estate worth nearly £430,000.
WILLIAMS FAMILY COLLECTION, ALEXANDER TURNBULL LIBRARY, F-29569-1/2

Gisborne grazier H.B. Williams (1868–1961), who financed (Sir) Robert Kerridge into the cinema industry in 1923. The Williams family remained partners in Kerridge's business until Kerridge Odeon Corporation's ill-fated merger with Pacer Pacific Corporation in 1987.
COURTESY TE RAU PRESS

Willie Levin (1845–93), eldest son of trader Nathaniel Levin, was an astute businessman and politician — perhaps the richest man in Wellington in the 1870s. A public benefactor and a director of the Wellington & Manawatu Railway Co, he had the Manawatu town of Levin named after him.
SUPPLEMENT TO THE *DAILY ADVERTISER*, WELLINGTON, 8 OCTOBER 1881, ALEXANDER TURNBULL LIBRARY, A-095-004

Sir Clifford Plimmer (1905–88), a great-grandson of 'father of Wellington' John Plimmer, was a professional company director of note, best remembered for his development of the former pastoral giant Wright Stephenson & Co.
COURTESY *NBR*

Barrett's Hotel, Wellington, named after English sailor-of-fortune Dicky Barrett (1807?–47).
HAND-COLOURED ENGRAVING FROM THE ORIGINAL WATERCOLOUR BY SAMUEL BREES, ALEXANDER TURNBULL LIBRARY, A-109-027

Sir Heaton Rhodes (1861–1956), an Oxford-educated lawyer who became a rich gentleman farmer-stockbreeder after his father's death in 1884. He later entered national politics, serving periods in the cabinet and on the Legislative Council.

W.A. BOWRING, COLLECTION OF THE ROBERT MCDOUGALL ART GALLERY; PRESENTED BY THE CANTERBURY SOCIETY OF ARTS, 1932

John Deans II (1853–1902) of Riccarton, Christchurch, fathered eight sons and four daughters, creating the large Deans dynasty in Canterbury. He was the only child of pioneer John Deans (1820–54), who died when he was an infant. His uncle, William (1817?–51), who first identified farming opportunities on the Port Cooper Plains (present-day Christchurch), was drowned in 1851.

CANTERBURY MUSEUM, REF: 6669-1/4

Deans Cottage, centre, was the most prominent of the houses in Riccarton, Christchurch, in 1850. It was the Deans family's second house, built in 1844, two years after William Deans identified the Port Cooper Plains as suitable for farming.
HENRY JOHN CRIDLAND, CANTERBURY MUSEUM, REF: 9752

Riccarton House, Christchurch, pictured in the 1890s, was the third home of the Deans family. Parts of the building date back to 1856.
H.N. WHITEHEAD COLLECTION, ALEXANDER TURNBULL LIBRARY, G-4415-1/1

The shy and delicate (Sir) Frederick Weld (1823–91) joined cousins (Sir) Charles Clifford, William Vavasour and Henry Petre in a venture to bring sheep into the Wairarapa in 1844. Within a few years he was an expert on pastoralism, publishing a book for intending sheepfarmers. Like Clifford and Petre he entered politics, serving as New Zealand's seventh premier, from 1864 to 1865. Pictured with his wife, Mena (née Phillipps), about 1859.
ALEXANDER TURNBULL LIBRARY, F-45100-1/2

Bidwill family members at the back of the Bidwill home, Pihautea, pictured about 1889. The twenty-room house was built in 1876 but lacked curtains and carpets and initially had primitive cooking facilities.
COURTESY ANNA BIDWILL

(Sir) Charles Clifford (1813–93), from a prominent Roman Catholic family in Lancashire, England, was a pioneer in the New Zealand sheep industry. He was later Parliament's first speaker. Pictured in 1860.
ALEXANDER TURNBULL LIBRARY, F-12450-1/2

considers that the gross profit from his 12,000 sheep this year [1850] will be £6000, from which are to be deducted for expenses and contingencies £2000 leaving £4000 net profit on a flock which represents (at 15s a sheep) a capital of only £9000,' Godley wrote, adding that Weld or any other sheepfarmer would consider 12 or 15 per cent too high a rate of interest for money to invest in sheep. At its peak, Flaxbourne covered about 26,600 ha (more than 65,700 acres). It also provided the late William Vavasour's youngest son, Henry (1850–1927), with an entree into New Zealand pastoralism when he arrived from England in 1871 to renew his family's links with the colony. He worked there for three years or so before joining his brother, Ned (1855–95), in Taranaki. He later returned to the South Island, managing Flaxbourne from 1882 until 1897 when he acquired a nearby property, Ugbrooke, from William Clifford (later Baron Clifford of Chudleigh, from the English branch of the Clifford family). Flaxbourne was bought by the government in the early 1900s and broken up for closer settlement. The 30-room, 930-sq m (about 10,000-sq ft) Ugbrooke homestead, built from 75,000 bricks and dating from 1885, was owned by the Vavasour family until 1993.

As for Charles Bidwill, he survived early difficulties in the Wairarapa by converting his flock from merino to Romney (merinos proving unsuited to the swampy conditions), running Red Devon cattle and breeding horses. At the time of the devastating 1855 earthquake he held about 4046 ha (10,000 acres), of which nearly 800 ha (1970 acres) was freehold. Sheep numbers totalled only 500. But Bidwill battled on to become a leading sheepfarmer. His first home was a totara-bark whare but this was soon replaced by a single-storey wooden house, added to as the family grew. A new homestead, a two-storey wooden building with 20 rooms, was built some distance away in 1876. It lacked curtains and carpets and initially had primitive cooking and laundry facilities, but it acquired grandeur over time. Three years later Bidwill leased the run to two of his sons, John and William. The youngest son, Charles, was at college at the time. When Bidwill died in 1884 the sons decided to pay off the legacies due to the daughters and run the station as a single unit. Bidwill's widow, Catherine (the eldest daughter of John Orbell of Waikouaiti, Otago), died in 1894 and two years later the land was subdivided between the brothers. Some

Catherine Bidwill (née Orbell) (1825/26?–94), wife of Charles Bidwill I, and their son, Will, at Pihautea, Wairarapa, in 1862.
COURTESY ANNA BIDWILL

of it was acquired by the government in 1906 for dairy farms under the Land for Settlements Act, and in 1919 for an ex-soldier settlement.

Five of Bidwill's six daughters married pastoralists, most of them rich. The remaining one married a bank manager. The list that follows provides a snapshot of the rural *Who's Who*: Catherine married Richard Barton, owner of Pirinoa station, Lower Wairarapa, and after his death George Hutton; Charlotte married Thomas Balfour, manager of the Bank of New Zealand in Greytown and later in Napier; Ruth married Hugh Beetham, a partner in Brancepeth station near Masterton; Elizabeth married Holmes Warren, managing partner of Tiraumea station, Alfredton, Northern Wairarapa; Laila married Joseph Rhodes of Springhill, Ongaonga, Hawke's Bay, who was a son of Joseph Rhodes, an independent member of the super-rich Rhodes family and owner of the Clive Grange and Milton Grange estates, Hawke's Bay; and Jessy married the even wealthier Robert Heaton Rhodes of Blue Cliffs, St Andrews, South Canterbury, the eldest surviving son of George Rhodes of the Levels (not to be confused with his cousin, farmer-politician Sir [Robert] Heaton Rhodes). Bidwill's sons also married well, notably William, who married Mildred Rhodes, youngest daughter of Joseph Rhodes of Hawke's Bay. William shared his father's passion for horseracing, founding his own stud in 1903 with the purchase of Stepfeldt from the dispersal sale of the Sylvia Park stud farm in Mt Wellington, Auckland. Stepfeldt's progeny won many classic races.

Charles Bidwill snr's eldest brother, the botanist-explorer John Bidwill (1815–53), who inspired him to move to New Zealand, is probably the only member of a wealthy New Zealand family to have plants he discovered named after him. His name survives in the bog pine *Dacrydium bidwilli*, the alpine perennial *Forstera bidwilli* and many others.

The present Charles Bidwill (born 1939), the fourth in the line of Wairarapa Bidwills, has long been counted among New Zealand's rich. But it was his impressive career, not his wealth or breeding, that persuaded the *National Business Review* to make him its inaugural New Zealander of the Year in 1992. Educated at Christ's College, Christchurch, and Auckland University College, Bidwill originally planned a career in the services. He passed the entry examination for Sandhurst Military College in England, but his father disapproved and he settled instead for a management cadetship with the meat company Thos Borthwick & Sons. He later moved to accountancy and sharebroking and, at the age of 25, became the youngest member of a New Zealand stock exchange.

Bidwill remained a member of the exchange for sixteen years before retiring as senior partner with Bidwill Wakeman Paine & Co to form his own financial consultancy with friend and fellow millionaire Alan Gibbs. His more unusual jobs included underwriting New Zealand's first legalised private radio station, Radio Hauraki. He is a keen sportsman and a founding member of the New Zealand Sports Foundation, and competed creditably in the world triathlon championships in 1990. Bidwill is remembered, not always lovingly, as a former managing director of Ceramco Corporation (now Bendon Group). The association with the company dates back to when he and fellow director and former Ceramco chairman Gibbs were financial consultants to Atlas Corporation, which merged with Ceramco in 1985. Bidwill and Gibbs led Ceramco's restructuring, including the merger with lingerie maker Bendon Industries in 1987, the closure of the pottery business in New Lynn, West Auckland, and the sale of accompanying land held for its clay deposits. At the end of the exercise, Ceramco was left with just two main operations, Bendon and Northland-based New Zealand China Clays (the latter sold to a French company in 2000). Bidwill, worth a minimum of $130 million according to *NBR*'s 2003 *Rich List*, is no longer associated with Bendon Group and also quit as a director of Baycorp Holdings (now Baycorp Advantage). He has been in London since 1998, living in a fashionable pad with his second wife. In 1998 he sold his elegant mansion in Godden Cr, St Heliers, Auckland, and in 2001 he sold his 'bach', the historic Matheson Homestead (built 1859), near Leigh, north of Auckland. The latter sale netted him $2 million.

Bidwills still farm in the Wairarapa, as do members of the Beetham family whose impressive Victorian homestead at Brancepeth station, 22 km east of Masterton, survives. Dating from 1886, the homestead and accompanying farm buildings, including a pitsawn whare built in 1856, tell the story of the Beethams' struggle and ultimate success in pastoral farming. William Beetham (1809–88), a portrait painter from Doncaster in Yorkshire, England, took up 4046 ha (10,000 acres) in partnership with John Hutton in 1856, on which he settled his sons, Richmond, William, George and Hugh. He named it Brancepeth, from the Old English 'brawn's path' meaning the path of the pig — a reference to a large boar that came out of the fern and circled Beetham's whare.

Beetham's eldest daughter, Anne, married T.C. Williams, a son of missionary Henry Williams, in 1858. T.C. worked in partnership with the Beethams, expanding the station and bringing in new capital. At its height, Brancepeth covered 66,000 ha (more than 163,000 acres). Like Charles Bidwill, the Beethams found merino sheep ill-suited to the lush English grasses that grew prolifically on the huge areas brought into production every year. The flock was converted to Lincoln–merino cross, then to Romney–Lincoln,

Brancepeth, the Beetham family homestead near Masterton, dates from 1886 and is one of the most impressive homes in the Wairarapa.
NEW ZEALAND HISTORIC PLACES TRUST

and later to Romney. To cope with surplus stock the Beethams built a large boiling-down works at Waingawa, and after the freezing industry started in 1882 they froze their own meat and shipped it to London under the Brancepeth brand. Around 1900 the partnership was shearing 108,000 sheep on Brancepeth and the balance on the 6070-ha (15,000-acre) Annedale block (named after Anne Williams, née Beetham), 64 km away. Brancepeth was subdivided in 1905. Neighbouring Te Parae station, home of the Williams family, was carved out of the original estate and for many years has specialised in breeding thoroughbred racehorses — Straight Draw, ex-Te Parae stud, won the 1957 Melbourne Cup.

The most public nineteenth-century member of the Beetham family was the third son, George (1840–1915), who was MHR for Wairarapa from 1877–81, Wairarapa North 1881–87 and Masterton 1887–90. He was also a leading alpinist. These days the Beetham remembered is George's older brother, William (1837–1925), who was Wairarapa's pioneer winegrower. He planted vines beside his Masterton townhouse in 1883 to please his new French wife, Hermance, who made the first vintage. They later established another vineyard and by 1897 were producing more than eight thousand litres.

Politics was also integral to the Riddiford family from the start of organised settlement of the colony, when Daniel Riddiford (1814–75) and his stepfather, London headmaster-turned-barrister Dr G.S. Evans (1800–68), organised the visit of the *Tory* to New Zealand as an advance party for Wakefield's colonising plans. Evans was the secretary of the New Zealand Company and Riddiford, then about 25, the company's emigration agent in Port Nicholson. With his pregnant mother and Evans, Riddiford travelled on the *Adelaide*, arriving in Port Nicholson in March 1840 to take up his official duties. But he followed others in squatting on land in the Wairarapa, occupying what became the Orongorongo station in the Rimutaka Range where he obtained a lease from Maori in 1848 over some 2832 ha (7000 acres). But the property was not ideal and he looked further afield in 1848–49, leasing the 12,140-ha (30,000-acre) Te Awaiti block from Maori.

Riddiford and his family lived at Orongorongo station until a tidal wave caused by the 1855 earthquake damaged the home and persuaded them to move to a newly acquired 17-ha (44-acre) property, Woburn, in the Hutt Valley. After Riddiford's death his eldest son, Edward (1841–1911) — nicknamed 'King' Riddiford on account of his Wairarapa 'kingdom' — took over the properties. He was well suited to the task, having been well educated and gained experience in sheep- and cattle-grazing in Australia. He had been managing Te Awaiti from the age of twenty and Orongorongo for six years. By 1882 he owned 20,966 ha (51,810 acres) in Hutt county, the Wairarapa and the Manawatu. 'King' Riddiford died in the arms of his Maori mistress, leaving a wife, their three sons and three daughters, and another son by his mistress. His estates were valued at £584,622, although some land had to be sold to pay death duties. One of his sons, Daniel, a one-time Grenadier Guardsman, was a director and major shareholder in the Wellington Publishing Co, publisher of the *Dominion* newspaper, from the time it started in 1907. He was also president of the New Zealand Polo Association for 30 years and was selected for the New Zealand team. One of Daniel's sons, Oxford-educated farmer-turned-lawyer Daniel (1914–74), was minister of justice and attorney-general in the 1969–72 National government.

The 2968-ha (7334-acre) Orongorongo station, one of several Wairarapa runs owned by the family, was sold to outside interests in 1985; according to its owners, lawyer-mountaineer Earle Riddiford (1921–89) — a member of the 1953 British Everest Expedition — and his wife, Rosemary, it was 'too big to look after'. Dating from Edwardian times, the elegant homestead complex — eight bedrooms, two bathrooms, two kitchens, a ballroom, swimming pool, tennis court, croquet green and six workers' houses — served briefly as a country lodge and reception rooms before it was destroyed in a spectacular fire in 1990. Its demise seemed to symbolise the Riddifords' declining fortunes, not least those of investment company Riddiford Holdings (not involved in Orongorongo) which had taken a bath in the property slump following the 1987 sharemarket crash.

Riddiford Holdings had pulled off a spectacular coup in the 1980s when it acquired the Weekly News building in Queen St, Auckland, from Wilson & Horton and promptly onsold it at a healthy profit to merchant bank Fay Richwhite & Co. Riddiford Holdings would have folded after the crash had not shareholder Hugh Riddiford (born 1948), a great-great-grandson of the first Daniel Riddiford in New Zealand, stood behind it. Today it is inactive — the casualty of a matrimonial split — but Hugh is a successful forestry investor who readily accepts that financial setbacks are sometimes the price of entrepreneurship. He is proof that entrepreneurial families, landed or not, are capable of rebirth, as is another fifth-generation Riddiford, Richard (born 1950), who is managing director of Palliser Estate Wines of Martinborough. The founder of the winery was accountant-farmer Wyatt Creech (born 1946), later an MP and deputy prime minister in the Shipley National government, who planted the first vines in his Om Santi vineyard in 1984 and four years later formed an unlisted public company to take it over and build a winery. It was renamed Palliser Estate, and produced its first vintage in 1989. It was an appropriate investment for Creech who, although born in California, had a blue-blood Wairarapa mother, Ellanora Sophia Creech (née Beetham). Palliser Estate has about a hundred shareholders, including Richard Riddiford, one of the original investors. Riddiford is not from a winegrowing background but his marketing experience, gained largely from the meat industry, has been put to good use: Palliser Estate is one of the country's leading boutique wineries.

Richard Riddiford outwardly shares few of the characteristics of his larger-than-life great-grandfather, 'King' Riddiford, who typified the second-generation pastoralist made good. 'King' Riddiford had an abundance of education and wealth — and a large degree of confidence to strut it — but he was no aristocrat. Aristocrat-farmers, contrary to the myth perpetuated by the social climbers of Canterbury and elsewhere, were few although Clifford, Weld, thrice-premier Sir Edward Stafford and John Acland were notable exceptions. The Rhodes brothers, rich and influential in New Zealand, would have struggled for acceptance in the upper echelons of British society in the 1850s, not as a result of their squatting or questionable ethics but because of their involvement in trade.

Much of the capital and stock that developed woolgrowing into New Zealand's number one export earner by the mid-1850s, producing 'reasonable'

Richard Riddiford (born 1950), winemaker of Martinborough, is a fifth-generation member of the Riddiford family in New Zealand. The family's large pastoral fortune had evaporated by the time he started work.
COURTESY NBR

returns to runholders of 25 per cent, came from Australia. The shagroons, hard-bitten but worldly wise when it came to pastoralism, also provided the language New Zealanders soon took for granted in the meat and wool industry — words like station, stockman, old chum, outstation, woolshed, stockwhip and store sheep. But they were forced to deal with two problems of their own making that came close to destroying the industry — scab, a contagious sheep disease resembling mange, and later, rabbits.

The first scab came into Canterbury via sheep from Nelson in about 1854. The disease was able to spread rapidly and ruined many runholders before wire fencing was introduced to stop infected sheep crossing station boundaries, yet fines imposed on the owners of infected flocks proved ineffective. Indeed, the country's richest man in the mid-1880s, George Moore (1812–1905), owner of the wealthy Glenmark station near Waipara, North Canterbury, was the last of the province's runholders to rid his station of scab. In 1864 alone he faced fines of £2400, although it is not clear whether he paid them. Historian L.G.D. Acland, a member of the prominent Canterbury farming family, was certain the maintenance of scab at Glenmark was a calculated move on 'Scabby' Moore's part. 'There can be little doubt,' Acland wrote, 'that he deliberately kept his country scabby for two reasons: this

Glenmark station, Waipara, North Canterbury, the country seat of wealthy Manxman George Moore (1812–1905), had perhaps the finest mansion of any New Zealand sheep run. Completed in 1888 at a cost of £78,000, the home was gutted by fire in 1891.
CANTERBURY MUSEUM, REF: 1959

enabled him to buy out his partners more cheaply and by frightening off prospective purchasers allowed him time to freehold his station.' Scab was certainly a problem at Glenmark until at least 1875 — a runholder described Moore that year as the 'King of Scab' — but it did not affect his ultimate farming success.

Notoriously mean-spirited and at times downright callous, Moore nonetheless built one of the country's finest mansions on a station that at its height covered more than 60,000 ha (150,000 acres) and carried more than 90,000 sheep. The castellated home, set among fine gardens and overlooking an artificial lake, took seven years to build. It was completed in 1888 at a cost of £78,000 but was gutted by fire in 1891. All that remains of Moore's kingdom are a Gothic gatehouse (damaged by fire in 1999 and rebuilt), the former manager's house and huge concrete stables dating from 1881. Nearby is St Paul's Anglican Church, built in 1911 from a £30,000 endowment from Moore's married daughter and principal heir, Annie Townend, in memory of her father. Townend's own mansion, Mona Vale, was built on the Karewa estate in Riccarton, Christchurch, in 1905 and named after her mother's Tasmanian home. (She also kept another home at Sumner.) Mona Vale survives with its beautiful gardens and restored fernery as testimony to Moore's wool and property fortune. Townend, who married secretly in 1900 to avoid the wrath of her father, died a childless widow in 1914. For some years she had been the dominion's wealthiest citizen; her estate was worth nearly £800,000 gross on her death.

While it is easy to find ways to dislike Townend's father, George Moore was no greenhorn in sheepfarming matters or the ways of business. He had emigrated from the Isle of Man to Van Diemen's Land in 1830 with a friend, Robert Kermode, and worked as a cadet on Kermode's father's sheep run. He married Robert's sister, Annie, in 1839, a loveless union that ended in separation in the early 1850s, and ventured with Robert to Canterbury to investigate prospects. Glenmark was acquired by a partnership comprising Moore, his son, William, Robert Kermode and Dr James Lillie, a retired Presbyterian minister, also from Tasmania. Moore was made manager while his senior partners put up the bulk of the capital.

Kermode became Moore's sole partner in 1866 after the deaths of William and Lillie. Kermode died four years later and the station was put up for auction in 1873, in what was then New Zealand's largest private run sale. The flock was free of scab at the time and the sale attracted strong bids from Moore's neighbour, the wealthy runholder William Robinson (1813/14?–1889), and from the former premier, (Sir) Edward Stafford (1819–1901), who had acquired the 1454-ha (3593-acre) Lansdown(e) run, which stretched from the Halswell River to the Port Hills. Moore acquired 15,756 ha (38,935 acres) of freehold land and an accompanying 31,755 ha (78,470 acres) of leasehold. He financed this with the help of a £90,000 mortgage from the Union Bank of Australia, a huge sum for the times. In 1882 Glenmark was the most valuable run in the colony, worth an estimated £362,780. Moore sold off much of his land after 1893 to forestall death duties as well as moves by the government to acquire it for closer settlement. The sale proceeds, placed in his daughter Annie's bank account, led to a major court case after his death (his estate won).

Government acquisition was the fate that befell the Cheviot Hills run of Moore's neighbour, William Robinson, who died in Christchurch in 1889 with an estate valued at £324,729. He had no male heir and a large debt to the Union Bank of Australia. Under his will it was left to his five daughters to agree unanimously on disposing of the 43,299-ha (84,755-acre) Cheviot Hills — the second-richest New Zealand estate in 1882 and probably the richest at the time of Robinson's death.

John Ballance's Liberal government was promising legislation to provide for compulsory purchase of large estates. Cheviot Hills, which carried 105,000 sheep at its 1886 peak and a wool clip that sold for more than £20,000 in 1884, was a prime target for breaking up. The issue came to a head in 1892 when the estate trustees challenged the government's land tax valuation of £304,626 against their own assessment of £260,220. The government assessment was reduced slightly on review but the parties could not reach a compromise. Under the law, if the government refused to accept the lower assessment it could be compelled to buy the estate at the higher price. The trustees, led by Wellington lawyer (Sir) Francis Henry Dillon Bell — who was married to Robinson's third daughter, Caroline — agreed to sell in April 1893 and Lands Minister Thomas McKenzie was able to trumpet the purchase as a coup for the government's closer-settlement policy. In reality, with the economy depressed, pastoral returns down and a pressing debt on the property, the trustees were keen to quit Cheviot Hills. But the symbolism of the purchase, a few months before the government's compulsory-purchase Land for Settlements Act came into force, was not lost on pastoralism or farming as a whole. (Among the first settlers when the estate was broken up was a future prime minister, George Forbes.)

Like Glenmark, Cheviot Hills had been a pastoral kingdom, and Robinson the undisputed monarch. He was a better farmer than Moore — he worked hard to rid Cheviot Hills of scab — but he shared a similar passion for luxury. His stark 40-room Mansion House, built in 1867 and destroyed by fire in 1937, was surrounded by extensive gardens and plantations. An impression of the grandeur of Cheviot Hills can be obtained by inspecting the former estate manager's house, which survives today.

Robinson, a tenant farmer's son from Warrington, in Lancashire, England, was the runholders' de facto advocate in the Legislative Council. He had plenty of experience. After arriving in South Australia in 1839 he established a reputation as a stock dealer and overlander before buying the huge Hill River run in 1844 with a brother, Samuel. Proceeds from the sale of this in 1855 (£44,000) enabled Robinson to front up to the office of the Nelson commissioner of Crown lands with a £10,000 deposit to acquire land under Grey's 1853 cheap-land regulations. It was an audacious step, adding currency to his well-earned nickname, 'Ready Money' Robinson. He soon acquired land between the Hurunui and Waiau rivers from the run of a pre-adamite Scots settler, John Caverhill, freeholding as much as possible. This became Cheviot Hills. Robinson proved to be a talented stockman and breeder, and he was a dominant figure in Canterbury horseracing. He was also a heavy investor in the land, and the barbed-wire fence he had erected along the western edge of the run in 1865 — the so-called 'Great Wall of Cheviot' — is largely intact today.

Despite his undoubted skills, Robinson had a mixed reputation — which was not helped by a murder at his rented townhouse in Cambridge Tce, Christchurch, in 1871, in which his Latin American butler, Simon Cedeno, stabbed the cook to death. Robinson's wife was injured when she intervened and an undermaid was also stabbed. In the murder trial that followed, the deranged Cedeno — said to be of mixed Negro-Indian blood — said he would have killed Robinson had he been at home. He claimed Robinson had insulted him fourteen months earlier at Cheviot Hills, calling him 'black Nigger, black heart', and had not paid him his full wages when he quit in protest. Whatever the cause of Cedeno's grievance, Robinson had brought him to New Zealand and given him a job after they met in a Panama hotel when Robinson was on his way home from England in 1867.

Robinson, Moore, the Rhodes and other wealthy graziers formed the core of the Canterbury 'gentry'. But most were not gentry in the English sense. They were speculator-farmers, gentrified by a Wakefieldian social order that started with the arrival of the pilgrims in Canterbury in 1850, and buoyed by successive generations of Cantabrians keen to maintain their imagined social ascendancy. In 1948 historian J.P. Morrison wrote that Canterbury was so successful in attracting a good class of immigrant that it was 'regarded by the other New Zealand provinces as a very aristocratic settlement'. This gentrification remains alive today — from the learned to the Jade Stadium rabble — and is replicated among the landed families of the North Island's East Coast, the Wairarapa, Hawke's Bay and Otago.

Not all observers have fallen prey to the New Zealand gentry myth. A study of probate records from 1890–1914 by Jim McAloon, a lecturer with the department of human and leisure sciences at Lincoln University, reveals that while 56 per cent of Canterbury's wealth and 39 per cent of Otago's came from agriculture and grazing, the very wealthy tended to be merchants, manufacturers and professionals. This is true for the second half of the nineteenth century at least. While the absentee aristocrat-landlord, living in England off the sweat of others, might have existed it was certainly not the norm. Sheepfarming was as precarious a business then as it is now. Some of the biggest fortunes, like that of John Ritchie (1842–1912), came from servicing pastoralism rather than working in it. As a Dunedin merchant, shipping agent, financier and stock-and-station agent, he was the essential link between Auckland and foreign capitalists and rural borrowers. After 1884, when his firm Russell Ritchie & Co was taken over by the National Mortgage & Agency Co of New Zealand (NMA) — a subsidiary of the National Bank of New Zealand — he wielded even greater influence. He was initially joint managing director of NMA, and after 1884 virtually ran the company, steering it through a crucial period of New Zealand development. Ritchie's estate on his death in 1912 was valued at £134,047, of which £19,047 was held in Britain. Ritchie's grandson, James Ritchie (1907–81), was the last member of the family to control NMA, which merged with competitor Wright Stephenson & Co in 1972. He was the first chairman of NMA Wright Stephenson Holdings, which in 1974 became Challenge Corporation and in 1980 one of the three pillars of the newly created super-conglomerate, Fletcher Challenge (then New Zealand's largest company).

Like Ritchie, London-born brothers Henry and Frederic Le Cren, whose father was a French exile, made their money from servicing the pastoral sector rather than being a direct part of it. Henry (1828?–95), a London-trained merchant banker, was an agent for the Canterbury Association but found a far more lucrative job helping land stores at the new settlement of Timaru. It was the start of a merchant career that would create a £120,000 fortune by the time of his death. Frederic Le Cren (1835–1902), who shared many business interests with his brother, earned a similarly good living although he was less than popular as NMA's Timaru branch manager because of his hard-nosed approach to borrowers during the downturn in the 1880s.

William Boag snr (1827/28?–1904) started farming in New Zealand by leasing 40 ha (100 acres) from John Deans in 1853. He died with an estate valued at £110,229, based on a main holding of 687 ha (1700 acres) of drained swampland at Burnside — the closeness of the land to Christchurch accounting for its value. Another success story is that of Irish-born Hugh Cassidy (1840–1922), whose Cobb & Co coach and mail service between Christchurch and Hokitika earned him a fortune in the last quarter of the nineteenth century. He also owned a grainstore and a farm (in Springfield, Canterbury) and is said to have had 100 horses in full work, with 70 on the road. On his death his estate was worth £56,000, and that was long after the heyday of horse-drawn coaching.

Compare Cassidy's fortune with that of Canterbury blue-blood John Grigg (1828?–1901). Despite the magnitude of Grigg's Longbeach operation, described as 'the best farm in the world', he left just £90,000 in his will and, like so many southern graziers, owed his success to others outside the province. The son of a yeoman farmer from Cornwall, England, he farmed leased land at Otahuhu, South Auckland, for nine years — first growing potatoes then breeding sheep and cattle before venturing south. It was only in partnership with, and with finance from, his brother-in-law, Auckland commercial lawyer Thomas Russell, that he was able to acquire land between the Rangitata and

Canterbury blue-blood John Grigg (1828?–1901) got his start in farming in Auckland where he initially grew potatoes on leased land at Otahuhu. His large Longbeach run in Mid Canterbury, 'the best farm in the world', was financed for many years by his brother-in-law, Auckland commercial lawyer Thomas Russell.
PHOTOGRAPHER: FRANK MCGREGOR, CANTERBURY MUSEUM, REF: 16551

Ashburton rivers in Mid Canterbury, where he developed the Longbeach run into a truly great station. The partnership bought the first sections on Longbeach, totalling 864 ha (2135 acres), in 1863. By 1865 it had freeholded more than 4856 ha (12,000 acres) and by 1873 12,950 ha (32,000 acres). Longbeach was originally a cattle run but eventually carried sheep and pigs as well as growing significant quantities of wheat and oats. At its height it employed 200 permanent hands (future prime minister William Massey was a stationhand) and worked 150 to 300 draught horses.

After financial problems forced Russell to withdraw from the partnership in 1882, 6070 ha (15,000 acres) were sold and the stock was offered at a massive clearing sale. Grigg bought two-thirds of it. Even at its reduced size Longbeach remained a superb venture. Having drained the boggy land, Grigg was able to switch to intensive farming and was one of the first farmers to see the potential for exporting frozen meat. He founded the Canterbury Frozen Meat Co and the

Dairy Produce Export Co, and carcasses from Longbeach were among the first shipments of frozen meat to Britain in 1882. 'Canterbury lamb', the toast of London's Smithfield market for many years, had its origins here, thanks to Grigg's Southdown flock. Today Longbeach, much reduced in size, contains some of the country's most historic farm buildings. The homestead, which is still owned by the Grigg family, was built in 1937. It is the third house on the site. Nearby is Longbeach Chapel, the family's private church, which was moved from Prebbleton to Longbeach in 1973. It is set among 6.8 ha of gardens as a memorial to Grigg.

Grigg outranks Matamata's Josiah Firth (see chapter 3) as the most innovative and scientific farmer of the second half of the nineteenth century. More to the point, his business survived; Firth's did not.

Fortunes from pastoralism's golden age

The short but spectacular golden age of pastoralism — the period before scab, rabbits and debt slashed profitability and productivity — produced substantial fortunes in both islands. Some examples:

▶ Sir John Hall (1824–1907) was a shipowner's son from Hull, England, who owned the Terrace station near Hororata on the Canterbury Plains, acquired in 1853. The leading conservative politician in nineteenth-century New Zealand, Hall was premier from 1879–82, a term remembered for his decision to use force to end the Parihaka dispute in North Taranaki in 1881. He retired from the House of Representatives in 1883 but later returned to politics to fight government threats to private property and to champion votes for women. He unwisely advised Premier Sir Harry Atkinson to stack the Legislative Council with conservatives in 1890.

Hall was wealthy, having freeholded his run as early as 1878 (it was worth more than £90,000 in 1883). A few months before his death he sold nearly 8100 ha (20,000 acres) to a syndicate for subdivision, but he left his two sons fine freehold properties. His estate was worth more than £216,271 on his death. An Anglican layman, vestryman and Sunday school teacher, Hall left generous bequests including £30,000 to Canterbury charitable institutions; £10,000 to the Boys' Gordon Hall Trust, Christchurch; and £10,000 for a brick or stone church at Hororata. Hall's Hororata homestead, dating from 1853, and today classified category 1 by the New Zealand Historic Places Trust, is still used by the family.

▶ John McLean (1819–1902), known as 'Big Jock' McLean, came from the Isle of Coll in Scotland's Inner Hebrides. McLean developed the huge Morven Hills run in the Lindis Valley, Central Otago, from a pasturage licence for 200,000 ha (nearly half a million acres) that he obtained in 1858. At its height the run carried at least 160,000 sheep, possibly as many as 250,000, and in area and stock numbers was probably the largest in New Zealand. With his brothers Allan (1822–1907) and Robertson (1825–71) he also owned the 19,424-ha (48,000-acre) Lagmhor station near Ashburton; the similar-sized Waikakahi station near Waimate, South Canterbury; Waitaki Plains, North Otago; and Redcastle, near Oamaru. Robertson retired after a few years and the partnership later took in a brother-in-law, politician George Buckley, who sold out in 1875. When the partnership was dissolved in 1880, Allan retained Waikakahi and John the other stations. The partnership had earlier owned Ashfield station on the south bank of the Waimakariri River, North Canterbury.

John McLean and Buckley served briefly as directors of the Bank of New Zealand (1888–89), during which time Buckley was president and with McLean

The Valley, Waikakahi, South Canterbury, the 21-room home of runholder Allan McLean. When the estate was compulsorily acquired by the government in 1898 for closer settlement, a distressed McLean moved to Christchurch where he built the huge Holly Lea mansion (now McLeans Mansion).
PHOTOGRAPHER: A. MCLEAN, CANTERBURY MUSEUM, REF: 230

served on the committee charged with the unhappy task of explaining how the bank had lost £800,000 of its capital to land speculators.

Allan McLean, one of Canterbury's more eccentric runholders, preferred the country life and entertained at Waikakahi in grand style. His 21-room former homestead, the Valley — still in use — was a centre of South Canterbury social life, reflecting the high standing of his well-managed station (he leased up to 1600 ha [4000 acres] to contract croppers and ran more than 70,000 sheep). But the run also attracted the attention of the Liberal government, keen to break up large freehold stations for closer settlement. In 1898 it was compulsorily acquired for £323,090 and subdivided into 154 freehold farms, 14 grazing runs and 140 farms on lease-in-perpetuity.

McLean, distressed at being forced off Waikakahi, left the district for good and retired to his late sister's Christchurch home, Holly Lea, in Manchester St. Beside this in 1899–1900 he built a new and many times larger Holly Lea (now known as McLeans Mansion) with a floor area of 2136 sq m (23,000 sq ft), at the time probably the largest wooden residence in New Zealand. Today the peculiar Jacobean-style mansion, designed by Lyttelton-born architect Robert West England jnr, is home to the Christchurch Academy. When McLean lived there it had 53 rooms. Among these were nineteen bedrooms (six for servants), six bathrooms and nine toilets; in the grounds was a large glass conservatory (since demolished).

Allan McLean (1822–1907), a Scot from a humble background in the Inner Hebrides, built up a huge fortune as a sheepfarmer. He died a bachelor with an estate worth nearly £600,000 gross.
CANTERBURY MUSEUM, REF: 16553

McLeans Mansion bore no relation to the rough stone cottage of McLean's humble youth in the Inner Hebrides. It was the epitome of runholder wealth, although its size was surprising given it was built for a 78-year-old bachelor. McLean lived well, sparing no expense, but he also had a strong sense of public and family duty. He had genuine concern for the poor, and his will provided for the establishment of the charitable McLean Institute in memory of his widowed mother, Mary, who had left Scotland with her sons in 1840 to escape poverty. (She died in Christchurch in 1871, aged 85.) The institute's main job, as specified in the will, was to maintain and manage the mansion as a home for poor gentlewomen, and McLeans Mansion served that function until it was sold to the government in 1955. The institute, endowed in 1908 with an estate worth nearly £600,000 gross, continues its work today at another Holly Lea in Fendalton Rd, Christchurch.

John McLean, who predeceased Allan by four years, and was also unmarried, left an estate worth £213,000; his nephew and heir, St John McLean Buckley, left £166,884 in 1915.

▶ John Acland (1823–1904) and Charles Tripp (1820–97), both members of the English bar, founded the Mt Peel station between the Rangitata and Orari rivers, South Canterbury, in 1856. They increased their holding to about

Charles Tripp (1820–97), pictured in May 1891. Together with fellow lawyer John Acland (1823–1904), Tripp founded Mt Peel station, South Canterbury.
CANTERBURY MUSEUM, REF: 4203

101,000 ha (250,000 acres), including Mt Somers, Mt Possession and Orari Gorge, and were the first runholders in Canterbury to conceive that the hill country could be successfully stocked with sheep. Acland, the sixth son of a baronet from Devon, England, died with an estate valued at £44,519. He founded a New Zealand dynasty of Aclands including such notables as his youngest son, surgeon Sir Hugh Acland; his grandson, Sir Jack Acland, who was MP for Temuka 1942–46, chairman of the New Zealand Wool Board 1960–72 and one-time vice-chairman of the International Wool Secretariat; his great-grandson, John Acland, chairman of Meat New Zealand (the former New Zealand Meat Producers Board) since 1995; and a great-nephew, historian-farmer-explorer L.G.D. Acland. The brick Mt Peel homestead (built in 1865–66) is still in private use. Original buildings dating from 1859 at Orari Gorge — the station Tripp bought back from the original John Acland — have been restored by the New Zealand Historic Places Trust.

▶ Duncan Cameron (1840/41?–1908) with limited means joined forces with merchant and financial agent George Gould (1823–89) to save the struggling 8093-ha (20,000-acre) Springfield run near Methven, Mid Canterbury. Cameron, a sheepfarmer's son from Inverness, Scotland, was manager of neighbouring Winchmore station when Gould, who had taken the property over with a view to selling it after a failed auction in 1869, advertised for a manager. Cameron persuaded Gould to take him on as a partner, and by the time of Gould's death in 1889 the run had been largely freeholded. Borrowing heavily from the Australian Mutual Provident Society, Cameron paid the executors £65,000 for Gould's share. Like Grigg's Longbeach, Springfield was converted from a sheep run to a mixed farm, growing wheat and breeding lambs for the frozen export trade. In 1894 Cameron had 2225 ha (5500 acres) under wheat — an Australasian record for a single property. Springfield was reduced in size by land sales in 1902, 1907, 1908 and 1909. Cameron died in 1908 leaving £209,658 — a huge fortune for a one-time farm manager. He is credited with being the first person to introduce systemic irrigation into Mid Canterbury. His two daughters married English army officers, and Duncan Sandys (1908–87), a member of Sir Winston Churchill's last cabinet (and married to Churchill's daughter, Diana), was a grandson.

▶ John Studholme (1829–1903) and his brothers Paul (1831–99) and Michael (1834–86) were from Cumberland, England. They acquired the 30,553-ha (75,500-acre) Waimate (or Te Waimate) station in South Canterbury in 1854, in the first step toward building up nearly 400,000 ha (close to a million acres) of pastoral holdings in both islands. These included sheep and cattle runs at Hororata on the Canterbury Plains; Riverton, Southland; and in Central Otago. A key run in their portfolio was the 20,234-ha (50,000-acre) Coldstream station, Mid Canterbury, acquired in 1867. In 1879, after a shocking drought and low prices, the debt-laden partnership was dissolved (Paul had already sold out, in 1858, and gone to live in Ireland). Waimate went to Michael and Coldstream, 7284 ha (18,000 acres) of which had been freeholded, to John, with some other properties in part-payment. Coldstream was transferred to John's son, Lt-Col John Studholme (1863–1934), in 1890 and later subdivided.

John snr nearly came unstuck in the late 1880s through the failure of the partly developed Lockerbie estate in Matamata, for which he paid £30,738 for a half share in 1879 (it ruined his partner, Auckland ironmonger-turned-speculator Thomas Morrin). Lockerbie and other problems aside, the Studholmes cut quite a dash in South Island grazier society. They helped organise the first race meeting in South Canterbury in 1859, and Michael brought the first hares to South Canterbury in 1865. Waimate in 1880 comprised 18,615 ha (46,000 acres) of freehold and just over 8000 ha (20,000 acres) leasehold. It was carrying 82,000 sheep, including lambs, 2500 head of cattle and 350 horses. About 1618 ha (4000 acres) were under crop each year. Historian L.G.D. Acland noted that Waimate's tradition for 'boundless hospitality and unlimited sport, and the grand scale on which its operations were carried on [make it] perhaps the most interesting station in the province'. He added: 'Its history is the history of Canterbury squatting in a nutshell.'

▶ Edward Elworthy (1836–99), born in Wellington, Somerset, England, acquired the 16,996-ha (42,000-acre) Holme station in South Canterbury in 1864–65 from proceeds from the sale of land at Toowoomba, Queensland. During the next 20 years he developed the station, progressively freeholding it. Although wool provided the bulk of the income, it was also a major grain producer. In 1872 the run, by now 33,184 ha (82,000 acres), was carrying 42,000 sheep. By 1892 Elworthy, a director of the South Canterbury Refrigerating Co, and his family owned 180,827 ha (446,833 acres) of freehold land — more than anyone else in South Canterbury. The land was divided among his three sons after his death in 1899 and by 1914 much of the original freehold land had been sold.

Many Elworthys still farm in the area and several have made their names in society, including Edward's grandson, Baron Elworthy of Timaru, New Zealand, and Elworthy, County Somerset (1911–93), who at various times held the posts of marshal of the Royal Air Force, chief of air staff (UK), chief of defence staff (UK), governor and constable of Windsor Castle, and lord-lieutenant of Greater London; and Edward's great-grandsons, Jonathan Elworthy (born 1936), minister of lands and forests in the 1981–84 National government, and his elder brother, Sir Peter Elworthy (born 1935), first president of the New Zealand Deer Farmers' Association, chairman of Ravensdown Fertiliser (1977–82) and national president of Federated Farmers of New Zealand (1984–87). Sir Peter is also a prominent independent company director. The Elworthys are active investors. Richard Elworthy (born 1945) is managing director of finance and investment company Pyne Gould Corporation, which took over Christchurch-based power lines company South Eastern Utilities (formerly Amuri Corporation). At the end of 1998 South Eastern Utilities was sitting on a $62 million 'war chest' after selling Wairarapa Energy as part of the power reforms. South Eastern Utilities was liquidated in 2001.

▶ John Ormond (1831–1917), an Englishman from Wallingford, Berkshire, acquired a Crown grant in 1857 for 7719 ha (19,075 acres) in the Porangahau block, in Southern Hawke's Bay, which he named Wallingford. He had earlier leased land in the area, and the acquisition was the start to building extensive pastoral holdings. On his death in 1917 his estate of about 14,000 ha (35,000 acres) was valued at nearly £450,000. His stud farm, Karamu, in the Heretaunga block, was one of the finest racing studs in Australasia. In 1876 he built a large mansion here, surrounded by gardens, an orchard, shelter belts and plantations. When his wife tired of the country he built another family home, Tintagel, in Napier.

Ormond, who owed much of his political success to his close friendship with politician (Sir) Donald McLean, was a staunch defender of runholders' rights and Hawke's Bay provincialism. He served as deputy superintendent of Hawke's Bay to McLean, was later superintendent, then was minister of works in the central government in 1871–72, and again in 1877. He was appointed to the Legislative Council in 1891. Ormond also invested heavily in mining, freezing works and boiling-down works. He married well — his wife, Hannah, was a sister of Napier merchant and shipowner George Richardson. Their eldest son, George, married Maraea Kiwiwharekete, founding the Mahia branch of the family. The youngest son, John, took over Wallingford after his father's death, and a daughter, Ada, married Hamish Wilson of Bulls, son of the farmer-MP Sir James Wilson (1849–1929), a promoter of agricultural science and research. The most prominent member of this union was Ormond Wilson (1907–88), the left-wing politician and writer who was the political antithesis of his pampered farming background. Educated at Christ's College

(Christchurch) and Oxford, where he obtained an MA, he farmed at Bulls briefly before being elected Labour MP for Rangitikei in 1935. He was defeated in 1938 and spent the war years in London with the BBC before returning to New Zealand politics, becoming the Labour MP for Palmerston North from 1946 to 1949.

A grandson of the first John Ormond in Hawke's Bay, Sir John Ormond (1905–95), was chairman of the New Zealand Meat Producers Board from 1952–72 and a chairman of the Shipping Corporation of New Zealand. He was awarded the British Empire Medal for gallantry on active military service during World War II. He also represented Hawke's Bay at polo. His sister, Katherine, married the prominent Canterbury farmer and public figure, Sir Jack Acland. His son, John (born 1945), is active in Act New Zealand and a member of the party's board. He was selected in tenth place on the Act party list for the 1996 general election, and was two places off becoming an MP.

▶ Sir Donald McLean (1820–77) was born into a well-to-do family in the Scottish Highlands, and built up a significant Hawke's Bay farming estate which on his death was worth more than £100,000. McLean was one of the more influential second-tier career administrators and politicians of the

Administrator-politician Sir Donald McLean (1820–77), who carved out a Hawke's Bay farming empire worth more than £100,000 on his death.
ALEXANDER TURNBULL LIBRARY, F-22067-1/2

nineteenth century. Appointed Governor Grey's chief land-purchase commissioner in 1853, McLean advanced European settlement, sometimes at the cost of conflict between settler and Maori.

Some observers blame his controversial land-settlement policy for the outbreak of the Taranaki War in 1860. Yet despite this and his personal enrichment, smacking of corruption, he was popular with many Maori and settlers, especially in Hawke's Bay. He was elected provincial superintendent there in 1863 and in 1869 became native and defence minister in the central government. This was his finest hour, and he is credited with contributing to the peace that endured after the war with Te Kooti. McLean's key run was Maraekakaho station in Hawke's Bay, where he bought the first block in 1855, adding to it in 1862. He slowly acquired Akito, on the Wellington provincial border, and also held Run 333 in Central Otago for a time. His only son, (Sir) Douglas Maclean, who preferred to use a different spelling of the surname to his father, trained as a lawyer in England but never practised. He proved a born farmer and developed Maraekakaho, breeding English Lincoln and Leicester sheep, shorthorn cattle and thoroughbred horses. By 1895, after years of toil, the station was in tip-top condition. Land was progressively sold off — the biggest sales were in 1910 and 1930 (the latter after Sir Douglas' death) — and by 1949 only around 242 ha (600 acres) was held by the family. By 1972 some 62 farms had been established on the former station.

Sir Douglas was a director of the North British Freezing Co, Hawke's Bay Farmers' Co-operative Association and the New Zealand Freezing Co, and served as MHR for Napier from 1896 until his defeat in 1899. His only son, Algernon, a captain in the Cameron Highlanders, died at age 30 in 1923 of kidney disease contracted in World War I. There are no other direct descendants on the male line. The cavernous woolshed at Maraekakaho, dating from 1883 and capable of holding 5000 sheep under cover, survives as a reminder of the station's importance; it was one of the first in New Zealand to be fitted with shearing machinery, in 1895. The Cottage, dating from 1869 and used by Sir Donald and later Sir Douglas as a retreat from public life, also survives.

▶ George Duppa (1819–88), born near Maidstone in Kent, England, developed the Birch Hill run in the Upper Wairau Valley, Marlborough, and St Leonards run, Amuri, North Canterbury. In 1862 he sold up and returned to Kent, where he bought his ancestral home from a nephew and lived the life of a country squire. Despite a history of sharp business practices in New Zealand — grazing sheep on others' land without consent, cheating the commissioner of Crown lands out of licence fees, refusing to pay wages legally due and bidding for land on neighbours' runs — he served as a magistrate and high sheriff of Kent. Among the first New Zealand runholders to return to Britain with a fortune, Duppa was described as an 'Australian millionaire' in 1870. His older brother, Bryan, a close friend of Edward Gibbon Wakefield, originally suggested the formation of the Nelson settlement.

▶ George Rutherford (1815–85) was originally from Jedburgh in the Scottish Borders. From 1859 he developed the Leslie Hills run in Amuri, North Canterbury, near present-day Culverden. His half-brother and seven sons followed his example, all eventually farming in their own right on runs stretching from north of Kaikoura to inland of Timaru. Leslie Hills, the station most often associated with the Rutherfords, was an amalgam of two leasehold runs, Addington and Leslie, which Rutherford acquired after selling his interest in a large sheep station, Kulnine, in South Australia and working briefly as a stock-and-station agent in Adelaide.

In 1860 Rutherford joined forces with the poet Alfred Domett (1811–87) to take over what became the Mendip Hills station in North Canterbury. Domett, surprisingly, became premier in 1862 and Rutherford's first and second sons, Andrew and William, took joint tenure of Mendip Hills, while Rutherford snr continued to buy land to extend it (it was eventually some 14,164 ha [35,000 acres]). Andrew bought out William's interest in 1871 and ran Mendip Hills on his own. In about 1876 William took over Montrose station, adjoining Leslie Hills, which his father had acquired in 1871 — some 17,000 ha (more than 44,000 acres) freehold and 1618 ha (4000 acres) leasehold. Rutherford snr's half-brother Walter leased the 6070-ha (15,000-acre) Sherwood run in North Canterbury from 1885 or 1886.

After Rutherford snr was drowned in 1885, Mendip Hills passed to Andrew and William as tenants-in-common and Leslie Hills went to another of Rutherford snr's sons, Duncan, the most successful of the family runholders. He built the 40-room Leslie Hills homestead in 1900, an impressive building with many gables and a central tower that is still used by the family. Andrew followed in his father's footsteps, representing Amuri on the Nelson Provincial Council from 1870–71. He also served for many years in local government and was MP for Hurunui from 1902–08. Another son, John, in partnership with his brother Robert, bought Opawa station, South Canterbury in 1873 — some 14,164 ha (35,000 acres) of leasehold land. A year earlier another son, George, bought Dalethorpe, one of the oldest stations in Mid Canterbury (6474 ha [16,000 acres] and 16,000 sheep), for £13,500. In 1884 he bought the struggling Benmore (or Ben More) station on the south side of Porters Pass. He held Dalethorpe until 1911. Duncan, in partnership with Andrew, bought Highpeak, a difficult station at the source of the Selwyn River, Mid Canterbury, in 1881 and an 80,937-ha (200,000-acre) Amuri run, Glynn Wye, in 1883. Highpeak was transferred to George jnr in 1885. The youngest son, Edmund, farmed Mt Nessing, South Canterbury, from 1873, and from 1899 Kekerengu station in Marlborough (11,416 ha [28,210 acres] freehold and about 30,500 [75,400 acres] leasehold), which he sold in 1911. Other stations farmed by the family include Molesworth, in Marlborough, and adjoining Rainbow and Tarndale, and Godley Peaks in the Mackenzie Country, South Canterbury. Molesworth and the neighbouring stations were acquired by Duncan in 1911 but they never paid their way and were sold after his death in 1918 to pay some £60,000 in death duties. Rutherfords are still prominent farmers today, as well as significant shareholders in the investment house Pyne Gould Corporation.

▶ Robert Campbell (1843–89), an Eton-educated trader and retailer from New South Wales, became one of the largest runholders in New Zealand. He came to New Zealand in 1860 to buy or lease land on his wealthy family's behalf, and the same year was in partnership with William Low in the Galloway run in Central Otago. In 1863 he acquired the Benmore station in North Otago (not to be confused with Benmore in Canterbury); Otekaieke, North Otago, in 1865; and Rocky Pt and Station Peak in South Canterbury in 1869. In 1870 he leased the Southland runs of Burwood, Mararoa and Mavora. Campbell worked hard to freehold his properties in the 1870s, selling land profitably within a few years. He also developed and onsold land in the Manawatu, his big holding there being Oroua Downs near Sanson. Although he was a speculator, Campbell and his brothers were also excellent farmers and he was active in the Otago and North Otago Agricultural and Pastoral associations, education and politics (MHR for Oamaru from 1866–69 and later on the Legislative Council). His business interests, always paramount, included coastal shipping, railways and woollen mills (in Mosgiel and Oamaru). In 1882 his London-based company, Robert Campbell & Sons, was the country's seventh-largest corporate landowner. Many of the properties had earlier been jointly owned by Campbell and his father. Other land was leased in the names of agents or managers, associating Campbell with the sharp practice of 'dummyism' — circumventing the law limiting land aggregation. Campbell's Scottish baronial-style mansion at Campbell Park, Otekaieke, built in 1876, was a centre of North Otago social life for many years. Campbell was much affected by drink, however, and died childless in 1889; his wife died the following year. His

Eton-educated trader-retailer Robert Campbell (1843–89) had a Scottish baronial-style mansion built on his Campbell Park estate at Otekaieke, North Otago, in 1876. Campbell's London-based company, Robert Campbell & Sons, was the seventh-largest landowner in the colony in 1882. But Campbell was accused of 'dummyism' — a practice of leasing land in the names of agents or managers to circumvent the law limiting land aggregation.
NEW ZEALAND HISTORIC PLACES TRUST, NEG: 718, 2881, OTEKAIEKE 5

company ceased trading in 1920 as a result of low wool prices, rabbit plagues and the reduced carrying capacity caused by the rabbits. The Campbell Park mansion, one of the finest homes of its era, survives. From 1908 it served for many years as a residential school for wayward boys before passing to local body control. It later returned to private ownership.

▶ Sir (John) Cracroft Wilson (1808–81), a former magistrate and collector in British India (known as the 'Nabob'), caused a sensation in 1854 by arriving at Lyttelton on the *Akhbar*, his Noah's ark of sheep, cattle and horses (1200 sheep had to be jettisoned during the voyage from Australia). He bought a swamp at the bottom of the Port Hills, naming the property Cashmere after his Indian connections, and leased the Culverton, Broadlands, Cracroft and Highpeak stations. He returned to India in 1854 and was a judge at Moradabad when the Indian Mutiny broke out, playing a key role in rescuing English fugitives and later being knighted for his services. Wilson and his wife returned

Sir (John) Cracroft Wilson (1808–81) stunned Canterbury in 1854 by arriving in Lyttelton with a Noah's ark of sheep, cattle and horses. The former magistrate and collector in British India became a politician and a significant runholder.
CANTERBURY MUSEUM, REF: 16554

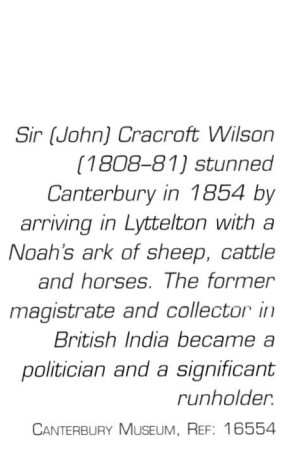

to Canterbury in 1859 with their servants, 52 horses, 2 hares and a Bokhara jackass. Wilson immediately became involved in politics, serving as MHR for Christchurch (1861–66), Coleridge (1866–70) and Heathcote (1872–75). He also served for many years on the Canterbury Provincial Council. Although a colonial servant rather than an aristocrat, he represented the conservative heart of Canterbury. He had impeccable connections, not least through his daughter, Emma, who married wealthy Auckland businessman Dr John Logan Campbell, whom she met aboard ship while returning to India in 1857 (Campbell was on his way to Europe). Wilson's first home, the mud-brick and plaster Cracroft House, was built in 1854–56 in Cashmere Rd, Christchurch, and restored in the early 1990s. Today it houses the Canterbury regional office of the Girl Guides' Association. A stone farm building, built in 1870 to house Wilson's Indian servants and farmworkers, has been restored after being gutted by fire in 1971. A later and far grander Cracroft home nearby burned down during World War II.

The Rich List
January 1855*

Top ten families/individuals with their main sources of wealth

1. **Rhodes brothers**
   Wool, trading, finance, property, speculation
   William Rhodes (1807?-78), Robert Rhodes (1815-84) and George Rhodes (1816-64). The interests of another brother, Joseph Rhodes (1826-1905), were separate from the family partnership and have not been included.

=2. **Campbell, Dr John Logan** (1817-1912)
   Trading, property speculation
   John Logan Campbell and William Brown were the richest Aucklanders by the mid-1850s. Their joint assets in 1856 totalled £110,000.

=2. **Brown, William** (1809/10?-98)
   Trading, property speculation

4. **Jones, John** (1808/09?-69)
   Shipping, food, farming

=5. **Levin, Nathaniel William** (1818-1903)
   Trading, shipping agency, stock-and-station agency

=5. **Hort, Abraham jnr** (1819-62)
   Trading, shipping agency, stock-and-station agency

=7. **Nathan family**
   Trading, property speculation
   David Nathan (1816-86) and his sons, Laurence and Alfred Nathan.

=7. **Henderson, Thomas** (1810-86)
   Timber, shipping

9. **Clifford, Charles** (1813-93)
   Wool
   Clifford's business partner, (Sir) Frederick Weld (1823-91), was worth much less since he held only a quarter of the assets of the partnership.

10. **Maning, Frederick Edward** (1811/12?-83)
    Timber, kauri gum

* Before the 1855 earthquake.

▶ Scobie Mackenzie (1845–1901), who was born at Tain, in northern Scotland, became a substantial Otago runholder but is better remembered for his free-market politics. He arrived in Otago from Australia in 1870 and, after managing the large Deepdell run, bought the 44,864-ha (110,863-acre) Kyeburn station with assistance from Francis Rich and Charles Stewart in 1876. The run prospered and Mackenzie became a member of Otago's elite. An admirer of the imperialism of British politician Benjamin Disraeli, he was a keen supporter of Sir Julius Vogel, entering the House of Representatives in 1884. He moved into Dunedin, building a large house, Melness, above Andersons Bay. In the late 1880s his run got into difficulties because of falling wool prices, rabbits and neglect, and financial difficulties forced him to resign from the Dunedin Club. Mackenzie's political career, which promised so much, was cut short by ill health. He was survived by his wife, Jessy, only daughter of Sir Francis Bell snr, three sons and two daughters.

▶ Major-General George Whitmore (1829–1903), leader of the colonial forces against Maori rebels on seven occasions, acquired a large sheep run near Napier in 1861 which he named Rissington. The run was enlarged to 44,515 ha (110,000 acres) within ten years but was mostly leasehold. Whitmore, who was born in Malta (the son of a lieutenant in the Royal Engineers), raised sheep and thoroughbred shorthorn cattle and ran the run efficiently in between a visit to England and operations against Te Kooti and Titokowaru.

▶ John Reid (1835–1912), owner of the celebrated North Otago estate, Elderslie, was a Scots-born engineer by professsion. He arrived in Otago in 1863, after a period in Victoria, to represent commercial firms. In 1865 he started buying land in North Otago. He moved into Elderslie in 1874 and later bought the neighbouring property, Balruddery, to become the largest freeholder in North Otago. The two estates carried some 33,000 sheep. Reid was a pioneer in the frozen meat industry, arranging with a Glasgow firm to build a steamer, the *Elderslie*, to trade directly between Oamaru and Britain. Reid's other achievements included being a founder of the Colonial Bank of New Zealand and the co-author of a major report on the conservation of New Zealand forests.

3

Crony capitalism

Financial recklessness is one of the characteristics of modern times and experience shows banks are almost as apt to catch the infection as traders and speculators.

THE SOUTHLAND TIMES ON THE BANK OF NEW ZEALAND'S PROBLEMS, 1889

On 7 June 1859 a modest advertisement appeared in Auckland's newspaper, the *Southern Cross*, from the newly formed New Zealand Insurance Co (NZI) offering comprehensive fire and marine cover. It listed as its chairman the respected Auckland timbermiller and shipowner, Thomas Henderson, heading a thirteen-member board of prominent citizens. Its capital was £100,000 (of which £5000 was subscribed by Henderson) with the liability of the directors unlimited. In fact, NZI had been formed barely two and a half weeks earlier in an office on the corner of Queen and Shortland streets. It followed a disastrous fire the previous year which, in less than two hours, had destroyed 50 houses and business premises in the town's commercial heart at a total loss of more than £30,000. Only part of the loss had been covered by the three English insurance companies then represented in Auckland, leading to calls for a better firefighting service and increased protection against ruinous loss.

For 29-year-old commercial lawyer Thomas Russell it was an opportunity too good to miss. He investigated entering the underwriting business and on 21 May 1859, largely at his initiative, NZI came into being. It was the first underwriting company in the colony, with the largest nominal capital of any company then in New Zealand. Russell, the company solicitor, drew up the deed of settlement. The directors, in addition to Russell and Henderson, were David Graham (deputy chairman), Samuel Browning, William Buckland, William

Lawyer Thomas Russell. (1830–1904) was the undisputed leader of the 'Limited Circle' of speculator-investors which established New Zealand's fledgling domestic capital market. He is partly blamed for the severity of the banking crisis that hit the colony in the late 1880s.
Courtesy *NBR*

Connell, Hugh Coolahan, Captain William Daldy, Walter Graham, John Oliver, Captain Stone (Captain was his Christian name), James Williamson and William Wilson. The auditors were Alfred Buckland and George Owen. The secretary was William Hansard and Daldy, a master mariner and merchant shipper, was also the marine surveyor. The names are important because no fewer than six of them became intimately associated with Auckland's rise as a financial capital. For the next 25 years Russell was the effective head of this so-called 'Limited Circle' of capitalists — an investors' elite that expanded to include prominents such as (Sir) Frederick Whitaker, Dr John Logan Campbell, (Sir) Edward Stafford, Josiah Firth and McCosh Clark. It was the group that gave New Zealand its own form of crony capitalism.

Russell (1830–1904) is described by historian Professor Russell Stone as 'arguably the outstanding commercial figure of nineteenth-century New Zealand'. He achieved this prominence through a powerful combination of natural talent, entrepreneurship and roguishness. Born in Cork, Ireland, he came to Kororareka with his parents in 1840. A few months later they moved to Auckland where his father, who was reputedly trained as an architect, worked as a farmer then a carpenter and his mother ran a drapery store to supplement the family income. The young Thomas was educated by his parents at home and in 1844 articled to lawyer Thomas Outhwaite, a former registrar of the Supreme Court. After admission as a barrister and solicitor in 1851 Russell set up on his own — reportedly because Outhwaite refused him a partnership. He was just 21 years old. Although more interested in conveyancing and commercial law than the bar — 'businessman first, lawyer second', Stone wrote — his contribution to the legal profession was huge, not least because of his sense of duty to his brothers, whom he employed and trained as lawyers. Thomas Russell himself founded what is now the Wellington-based law firm of Bell Gully; his brother John Benjamin (1834–94) founded the Auckland firm, Russell McVeagh, in 1863 (now New Zealand's largest commercial law practice); James (1840?–1905) was a founding partner in the Auckland firm of Jackson Russell; and William (1841–1915) founded Preston Russell in Invercargill (he was also Invercargill's first district land registrar).

Thomas Russell became involved in politics early on — as an activist in the Progress Party, promoting Auckland provincial business interests; MHR for Auckland City East and minister of defence 1863–64; and supporting confiscation of rebel Maori lands and military settlement — but business, especially land speculation, was his unrelenting love. He carried out his business activities through his law practice, using initially his Wesleyan network and later various politico-business friendships and family alliances to great advantage. One example of this was his association with John Grigg, a leasehold farmer at Otahuhu, South Auckland, who married Russell's wife's sister in 1855. Grigg, these days considered a pioneer Cantabrian, was president of the Otahuhu Agricultural Association in 1861 and the New Zealand Agricultural Society in 1863–64 (both organisations now part of the Auckland Agricultural & Pastoral Association). Russell financed Grigg into acquiring the Longbeach run in Mid Canterbury in 1863, the partnership lasting until financial problems forced Russell to quit in 1882. In the meantime it gave him the confidence, in 1873, to form a highly speculative, and ultimately disastrous, syndicate to drain the 35,006-ha (86,502-acre) Piako swamp in the northern Waikato. (Swamp drainage had worked well at Longbeach.)

Russell's best business partnership, however, was with (Sir) Frederick Whitaker (1812–91), whose new law firm he joined in 1861. Whitaker, eighteen years Russell's senior, had already displayed great talents as an advocate and speculator, and the partnership, Whitaker & Russell, soon became the richest

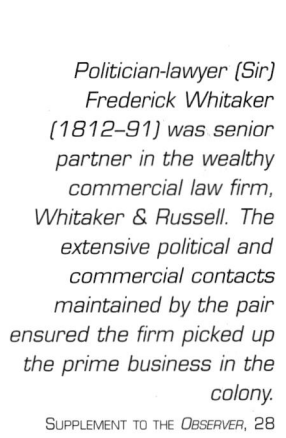

Politician-lawyer (Sir) Frederick Whitaker (1812–91) was senior partner in the wealthy commercial law firm, Whitaker & Russell. The extensive political and commercial contacts maintained by the pair ensured the firm picked up the prime business in the colony.
SUPPLEMENT TO THE *OBSERVER*, 28 JANUARY 1882, ALEXANDER TURNBULL LIBRARY, PUBL-0142-1882-1

practice in the colony. The lack of strong rules in the nineteenth century covering conflict of interest and jobbery allowed the pair to prosper on inside knowledge and turn political policymaking into personal gain. Whitaker was far more the politician than Russell — he was premier in 1863–64 and again in 1882–83 — and championed causes other than private profit, notably electoral reform (supporting unsuccessful campaigns for an elected Legislative Council and single transferable voting for the House of Representatives). But he was equally a crony capitalist who, with Russell, speculated on mining and confiscated Maori land.

However, passing judgment on the commercial behaviour of Russell, Whitaker and others, like assessing the practices and ethics of investment bankers in the mid-1980s, is highly subjective. There is little doubt the speculative greed of Russell's group contributed to, and possibly extended, the depression of the 1880s, but without it and and similar demonstrations of greed further south (such as the unscrupulous behaviour of William Larnach in Dunedin), New Zealand's tiny capital market might never have got off the ground. In addition, infrastructural development, much of it financed by British capital, could have been delayed for years without the skills of people like Russell to harness it. It is hard, for instance, to imagine New Zealand without the New Zealand Insurance Co, or Russell's second creation, the Bank of New Zealand (BNZ). The latter, formed in 1861 by Act of Parliament (from a private member's bill moved by Russell and seconded by Josiah Firth), played a huge role in the development of the colony. Before this New Zealand had been plagued with banking problems, not least a currency problem and lending restrictions by Australian banks on New Zealand businesses in times of monetary stringency. While it was not New Zealand's first bank it was the first of any size and, as with the development of banking in Australia, it was an essential adjunct to the gold industry (a major new gold find was made by Gabriel Read near Lawrence, Otago, in May 1861, a few days after the Melbourne-based Oriental Bank Corporation closed its doors in New Zealand).

On 16 October 1861 the first offices of the BNZ opened in a former drapery in Queen St, Auckland. Its capital was £500,000 in £10 shares, half of which was called up, and the board comprised the five original trustees — James Williamson (president), Thomas Russell and Thomas Henderson (all directors of the New Zealand Insurance Co), Logan Campbell, and businessman and Auckland Provincial Council member James O'Neill — plus two additional members, George Owen, co-auditor of the New Zealand Insurance Co, and Charles Taylor, a prominent citizen. Scots-born Alexander Kennedy, a former manager of the New Zealand Banking Co and immediate past Auckland branch manager of the Union Bank of Australia, was appointed the BNZ's general manager and inspector on a salary of £1200 a year. The bank's law firm was none other than Whitaker & Russell. Other members of Russell's Limited Circle would later serve as directors, including Samuel Browning, William Buckland, David Graham, Captain Stone, Whitaker, William Wilson and his son, Scott Wilson. William Daldy, one of the BNZ's first auditors, played a key role in selling the benefits of a national bank to the southern provinces.

Russell's personal motives for setting up the BNZ are unclear although Falconer Larkworthy (1833–1928), the bank's London-based managing director from 1862–88 — and no friend of Russell — suggested years later it stemmed from the reluctance of the Bank of New South Wales to accept his account following the closure of the Oriental Bank. Whether or not this is the case, there is little doubt that Russell treated the BNZ as a private fiefdom and secured advances incommensurate with the risk and nature of his speculative ventures. As visionary as he was in creating a national bank from nothing, he paid limited attention to detail — in later years he exposed the BNZ to undue risk by a series of investments which became the hallmark of a bad-lending policy, bringing the bank to its knees in 1894. The BNZ was not alone in its suffering. Its allied mortgage lender, the New Zealand Loan & Mercantile Agency Co (the Loan Co), incorporated in England in 1865, was similarly entwined in the affairs of Russell and his Limited Circle. As a lender of second resort its exposure was much greater and its losses commensurately higher.

Many of the failures the BNZ and the Loan Co had to bear related to confiscated Maori land sold to entrepreneurs or land bought or leased from Maori owners. The speculative frenzy among prominent Aucklanders keen to acquire large tracts of rural land in the province was akin to that of squatters in Canterbury and the Wairarapa a generation earlier, and the profits were initially no less substantial. It was fostered by a general pick-up in the Auckland economy as a result of the Thames gold boom in the late 1860s. Auckland became what today we would call an emerging market — with profits and pitfalls in equal measure.

Josiah Firth (1826–97), a successful flourmiller, was the first to venture south, leasing thousands of acres at Matamata in 1866 as the first step toward establishing a country kingdom. Others to follow included Russell, Whitaker, James Williamson, Alfred Cox, William Aitken, brothers Robert and Every Maclean, John Whyte, Edwin Walker, brothers Thomas and Samuel Morrin, Francis Rich, and absentee buyers Larkworthy and Sir James Fergusson (also a BNZ director and the eighth governor of New Zealand, 1873–74). Sometimes the newly acquired land was sold at great profit. Russell Stone quotes the example of James Farmer, a former manager of Brown & Campbell's One Tree Hill estate in Auckland, who bought the confiscated 8093-ha (20,000-acre) Moanatuatua swamp near Cambridge from the government in 1867 and sold it within a year for £5000 — a profit of 250 per cent.

It is hardly surprising, perhaps, that the most blatant example of speculation directly involved Russell. He headed the syndicate that bought the Piako swamp from the government in 1873 at 5s an acre (at a deposit of 2s 6d per acre). The other members were Whitaker, BNZ general manager David Murdoch (who as inspector of the Bank of New South Wales in 1861 had demurred over accepting Russell's account), Waikato land agent Captain William Steele, and later Steele's son-in-law, Henry Reynolds. The deal, suspect from the start, was subject to a parliamentary inquiry in 1875, not least because it had not been advertised in the *Gazette* as required by the regulations covering confiscated Maori land. The same year Russell was criticised over another controversial purchase from the Crown at Te Aroha. He then moved to London and between 1879 and 1883, the most dangerous period of a highly speculative career, floated a number of enterprises including two major companies:

▶ The Waikato (later New Zealand) Land Association (1879), with a nominal capital of £600,000, to acquire the Piako Land Association (the swamp syndicate); and

▶ The Auckland Agricultural Co (1882), with a capital of £800,000 to take over 43,301 ha (107,000 acres) stretching from Cambridge to Okoroire (the Maclean & Co interest).

He also advised on the New Zealand Thames Valley Land Co, a company formed in 1882 with a capital of £500,000 to take over about 121,400 ha (300,000 acres) extending from Okoroire to Atiamuri.

Russell did not hide his motives for such ambitious investments. 'Lock them up, and some years hence, when this land is reclaimed, this will be a splendid investment — it will double or treble,' he said of the Waikato Land Association holdings. But Russell seriously overestimated the likely rise in land values. The three companies, heavily indebted to the BNZ and the Loan Co, were virtually insolvent by the mid-1880s as a result of falling prices, production problems on the land and the general economic downturn. However, Russell's network of friends and business associates, including fellow BNZ and Loan Co directors who had bought discounted shares from him, proved to be his lifeline, continuing to support him against economic good sense. Russell was a London director of the bank until 1888, and remained a director of the Loan Co after that. Whitaker was a New Zealand director of the BNZ until 1888, and president that year. Others associated with Russell's ventures, including Sir James Fergusson, Stafford, Sir George Russell and British Liberal politician and president of the (UK) Board of Trade Anthony Mundella (for many years on the London boards of the BNZ and the Loan Co), were also part of his elaborate shield against bankruptcy.

Russell's recovery was slow but masterful. In 1887 he persuaded the bank to take over the Auckland Agricultural Co on condition that he assume responsibility for the debts of the Waikato Land Association. He then persuaded the colonial board of the Loan Co to advance him £40,000 to pay a call on his Waikato Land Co shares to meet debentures that were falling due. (Had the board not done so, the company would have collapsed on the spot.) In 1891 the Loan Co agreed to an even riskier scheme whereby Russell could be released from the swamp company debts of £162,000 — a surprising degree of confidence given that he was begging Logan Campbell to lend him £3000 so that his wife and daughters could meet calls on their shares in the Waihi Gold Mining Co, which he had floated in London in 1887. It was even more astonishing that the Loan Co took over the Waikato Land Association and reconstructed it as a new company, allowing Russell and David Murdoch, the only other solvent member of the original syndicate, to exchange their debt-ridden shares for fully paid shares carrying no liability. This sleight of hand all but destroyed the Loan Co, and Russell and others narrowly escaped prosecution for fraud after an investigation in 1894. Russell recovered part of his fortune, although not his reputation, through the spectacular turnaround of the Waihi Gold Mining Co after a cyanide plant was installed in 1893, and investment in Australian cement. He died at Normanswood, in Surrey, England, in 1904 with an estate valued at £160,778 — still £100,000 less than his net worth seventeen years earlier.

Logan Campbell, who suffered similar tribulations to Russell in the 1880s, died rich and respected in Auckland in 1912 — untainted by membership of Russell's Limited Circle (an expression Campbell himself coined) or the dirty deals that went with it. His former partner, William Brown, was not so fortunate. By 1894, when the Loan Co made heavy calls on its shareholders, Brown was under heavy financial pressure and was forced to forfeit his shares. He later sold his London house and moved in with his daughter, dying virtually penniless in 1898. To be sure, Brown had squandered his payout from Brown Campbell & Co, but his former partner's financial survival had little to do with business morality.

Campbell was as much a speculator as Russell and, despite cultivating a benign image, could be unforgiving if crossed. Campbell was also a snob, and believed he was more worldly wise than other successful Auckland merchants and speculators. That he stayed in Auckland owed more to chance than planning. Had he been able to find a reliable manager for Brown Campbell & Co, or persuade Brown to return from London to run the business, he might well have ended his days in his beloved Italy. But after he bought out Brown's interest in the business in 1871 he busied himself in public and commercial matters. His directorships included the New Zealand Insurance Co (1877–99) and the BNZ (1872–87, including two terms as president). He also found time to write about his life and establish Auckland's first school of art. In 1878 he bought a timber mill in the Northern Wairoa, north of Auckland, a large cattle station in Whakatane, and extended his Domain brewery in Newmarket, Auckland.

Kilbryde, Campbell's Pt, Auckland, the third home of Dr John Logan Campbell, pictured in 1885. Campbell struggled to maintain his gentlemanly lifestyle in the 1880s depression, but came right after his liquor company, Brown Campbell & Co, merged with brewer Ehrenfried Bros in 1897. The home was demolished by the Auckland City Council in 1924.
AUCKLAND INSTITUTE AND MUSEUM

Like the other speculators, however, Campbell was caught in the squeeze in the late 1880s, struggling to pay creditors and mounting interest bills, and survived only by the sale of his timber mill in 1888 and the Whakatane farm in 1890. Had the Whakatane sale not gone ahead, he would probably have been forced to sell the One Tree Hill estate. As it was, in 1889 Campbell was compelled to borrow £15,000 from the Auckland Savings Bank, of which he was a former trustee, just to meet his debts. The garden of his magnificent home, Kilbryde, on Campbell's Pt, Parnell (completed in 1881), became a wilderness after he was forced to sack the gardeners and the coachman and reduce the servant staff to two maids. But Campbell maintained his capital, and when the Thames-based brewer Ehrenfried Bros merged with Brown Campbell & Co in 1897 his money worries were over. He gave the cream of his One Tree Hill estate to the people of New Zealand in 1901 (it was renamed Cornwall Park in honour of the visit of the Duke and Duchess of Cornwall and of York), and through the sale of house lots on the edge of the park was able to clear the mortgage and make further endowments before his death. Campbell also gave generously to a variety of charities and causes. He was knighted in 1902.

Campbell's funeral cortège, from Kilbryde to his burial place on the summit of One Tree Hill, was then the largest in Auckland's history. (His first home, Acacia Cottage, survives but his second, Logan Bank, in what was formerly Official Bay, has long gone. Kilbryde was demolished in 1924 by the Auckland City Council as part of its campaign to extinguish riparian rights and to excavate Campbell's Pt for the Westfield railway deviation.)

Unlike Campbell, the fortunes of Josiah Firth and Thomas Morrin (1838–1915) did not survive the 1880s. Their heavily indebted estates in Matamata and Morrinsville (Matamata and Lockerbie respectively) were taken over by the Loan Co in 1887, later reverting to the BNZ, and they were each bankrupted in 1889. Firth, a scientific farmer, land developer and exporter on a par with John Grigg in Canterbury, was allowed a modest living allowance and to keep his castellated concrete-and-wooden house on the slopes of Mt Eden, Auckland. He made a modest recovery but never forgave the Loan Co for foreclosing on his Eight Hours mill in 1889, then the most advanced flour mill in the colony. (The mill was later merged by the BNZ with John Lamb's mill to become the Northern Roller Milling Co, these days part of Goodman Fielder Milling & Baking New Zealand.) Fortunately, Firth's innovative spirit lived on. A son, Ned (1867–1951), was an inventor-manufacturer who was responsible for a domestic laundry boiler made from pumice concrete. A plant was set up in Rangiriri, in the Waikato, in 1925 and a company named Ironclad Products established. Two of Ned Firth's sons, aviators Ted (1905–78) and Tony (1907–80), worked in the business, changing the name to Firth Concrete Co in 1934 and expanding its product range. This became the basis of the highly successful Firth Industries group which was taken over by Fletcher Holdings in 1979. The Firth name is still used.

Thomas Morrin, a successful ironmonger and noted stockbreeder before his failure, formed the Sylvia Park and Wellington Park studs, at Mt Wellington, Auckland. He was allowed by his creditors to retain £150 worth of furniture and his heavily mortgaged Wellington Park, on the slopes of the extinct

Josiah Firth (1826–97) accepted reluctantly the loss of his Matamata estate to the New Zealand Loan & Mercantile Agency Co in 1887 but never forgave the Loan Co for foreclosing on his Eight Hours mill in Auckland.
OBSERVER AND FREE LANCE, COURTESY DIANNE DRIVER

volcano. He made some recovery through horsebreeding and an investment in the Waihi Gold Mining Co but never regained his former business status, although in racing circles his reputation as a promoter and long-time chairman of the Auckland Racing Club was untarnished. (In 1886, when Sylvia Park was in his charge, it produced one of the great champions of Australian racing, Carbine, which recorded 33 wins, 6 seconds and 3 thirds from 43 starts.) Morrin returned to his native Canada in 1905 and died in Vancouver. His equal partner in Lockerbie, South Canterbury runholder John Studholme — also a partner in land elsewhere with Thomas Russell — survived the ordeal. But Morrin's brother, Samuel, an equal but subservient partner in the joint-stock family company holding a half share in Lockerbie, died in 1886, aged about 44, when the Lockerbie problems were hitting home. The Morrin brothers' financial fall was a sad end for a pair who had arrived from Montreal in 1865 with little capital but had prospered through their Scottish-Canadian diligence and hard work. Another brother, William, and a cousin, John Morrin, who were well established as grocers and wine and spirit merchants in Auckland, survived the depression. William farmed in what is now the Auckland suburb of Meadowbank. He is said by the family to have named his holding Meadowbank after the original family farm in County of Two Mountains, Montreal, although the origin of the name Meadowbank, Auckland, is disputed. Morrinsville, orginally Morrins Landing, was named after Thomas and Samuel — a cruel reminder of the property deal that brought them down.

James Williamson (1814–88), who was one of Russell's closest associates and a founding director of the BNZ and the Loan Co, was the most prominent member of the Limited Circle to fail. An Irish-born merchant and former ship's officer, he had made spectacular gains from trading and land speculating after arriving in New Zealand in 1839. By the 1860s he was, in historian Russell Stone's words, 'a man of substance'. He lived in style in an impressive home on the slopes of Mt St John which stood out to travellers on the Epsom road (now Manukau Rd). In 1877 he bought the 126-ha (313-acre) Pah Farm estate near

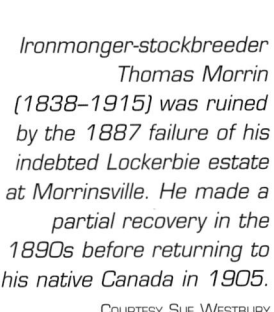

Ironmonger-stockbreeder Thomas Morrin (1838–1915) was ruined by the 1887 failure of his indebted Lockerbie estate at Morrinsville. He made a partial recovery in the 1890s before returning to his native Canada in 1905.
COURTESY SUE WESTBURY

James Williamson (1814–88) was said to have died of heart disease but suicide was suspected following the failure of the Auckland Agriculture Co in which he had invested heavily. A man of substance before the depession hit, Williamson was the first president of Auckland's Northern Club.
Courtesy *NBR*

Onehunga from Russell, and built a palatial Italianate home in plastered brick, the Pah, which could be seen for miles. It was adorned with magnificent gardens and outbuildings and was easily Auckland's grandest residence. Eight gardeners were employed to maintain the grounds. But the collapse in rural land prices weakened Williamson's investments. Some years earlier he had acquired Surrey Hills estate — 127 ha (314 acres) on Auckland's urban fringe (now Westmere) — from the sons of his late business partner, Thomas Crummer, and he now sold this to the Auckland Agricultural Co for £100,000, but even this failed to restore his fortunes. The big hit came in 1887 with the failure of the Auckland Agricultural Co, in which he had invested heavily. Worried sick about his parlous financial state, he died in March 1888 when the depression was at its height. The official cause of death was heart disease but it was speculated that he had committed suicide. (Whitaker's eldest son Frederick, a lawyer, former MHR and a land-buying agent for Russell, had committed suicide in the Auckland Club nine months earlier, depressed at losses from land speculating. He was just 40.)

Monte Cecilia, Auckland, formerly the Pah and the one-time mansion of failed speculator James Williamson. Williamson was the most prominent failure in Thomas Russell's 'Limited Circle' of speculator-investors.
sNew Zealand Historic Places Trust

Williamson's sons mortgaged the Pah to the BNZ fourteen months after his death. Its expensive furnishings were sold in the 1890s and in 1908, after a series of short-term tenacies, it was sold. The house was acquired by the Sisters of Mercy in 1913 for use as a convent and renamed Monte Cecilia. It had a variety of uses over the years and in 2002 was acquired by Auckland City Council for restoration and incorporation in a public park.

Williamson had been president of the BNZ for almost half of its 27 years and his untimely death and the retirement of Whitaker snr — ruined by the failure of the Waikato Land Association — created two vacancies on the BNZ's board. These were taken up by 'clean' directors outside Russell's circle — the rich Wellington merchant, landowner and member of the Legislative Council,

Walter Johnston, and George Buckley, a principal of Dalgety & Co and brother-in-law of another new board member, wealthy South Island runholder John McLean. Buckley became the new president. One of the board's first steps was to set up a committee to try to explain to shareholders how the bank had lost £800,000 of its capital. Another key decision was to dismiss Whitaker & Russell as the bank's law firm — action that should have been taken years earlier on the grounds of conflict of interest alone.

Even if the bank had been better managed, it is unlikely it would have come through the depression unscathed. Although Auckland speculators were the most seriously affected by the depression, especially in 1887–89, the colony as a whole struggled, with businesses as diverse as timbermilling, ironworks and shipping failing at an alarming rate. Unemployment rose sharply, wages fell and tradesmen and investors, including public figures like former Auckland mayor McCosh Clark (1833–98), left New Zealand in droves. Clark, a Russell associate, was managing director of warehouse company Archibald Clark & Sons, and an inveterate company promoter. He had been a popular civic leader — his 1880–83 term coincided with the tail end of Auckland's property boom — but a series of land and company failures left him penniless and he quit the colony a broken man in 1889.

Thomas Henderson, founding chairman of the New Zealand Insurance Co and co-founder of timbermilling-shipping firm Henderson & Macfarlane, came close to ruin, but not through land speculation (although he had been guilty of this in the past). Like Logan Campbell and David Nathan, Henderson had made his money in Auckland's early years and by the late 1850s was a key figure in the town's commercial elite. He had lost his initial business partners — Henry Macfarlane went to live permanently overseas early on and his brother, John Macfarlane, died of a heart attack in 1860 — but by 1861 Henderson was confident enough to let others of lesser experience run the business. Management passed to his eldest son, George, and another Macfarlane brother, Thomas, who came out from Scotland after John's death. Other Henderson sons, Thomas jnr and Henry, also became partners, and in about 1863 Henderson's son-in-law, German-born Pacific trader Gustav von der Heyde, joined the business.

The new management team allowed Henderson to concentrate on outside directorships such as NZI, BNZ and, after 1865, the New Zealand Loan & Mercantile Agency Co, as well as national politics (he was an MHR from 1855 to 1874 and a member without portfolio of the 1861–62 Fox cabinet). But the economic slump in Auckland that followed the departure of British troops after victory in the Waikato War left many Henderson & Macfarlane vessels idle and made it difficult at times to sell inward cargoes. This persuaded Henderson to call in some of his assets, and in 1864 the firm's 4046-ha (10,000-acre) timbermill estate west of Auckland, Henderson's Mill, was put up for sale. The mill did not sell, however, in part because of a questionmark over its legal title, and it closed in 1867. Most of the machinery was dismantled and sold but it was some years before the land could be auctioned. It was the end of Henderson & Macfarlane's golden era and a portent of worse things to come. A fire in January 1865 destroyed the firm's new Queen St warehouse and offices, causing £30,000 worth of damage, and two months later two cutters were damaged beyond repair when a storm hit Auckland.

Henderson's wife died in 1867, his own health suffered and he took leave overseas. While he was away Thomas Macfarlane decided to quit to take up a government post as official assignee — a position he was eminently qualified for. In 1868 Henderson returned to take over the running of Henderson & Macfarlane and rescue the Circular Saw Line, struggling under intense competition from steam. Despite his intervention and the purchase of three steamers the line never regained its old strength. Two of its fastest ships were lost in 1869–70 and the firm suffered another disastrous fire in 1873. Henderson received a further blow in 1876 when retired shipowner John Sangster Macfarlane (1818–80) — no relation to Henderson's late business partner — defeated him in the parliamentary election for the Waitemata seat. The campaign centred on Henderson's opposition to legislation giving timbermillers free rein to float timber down rivers irrespective of the environmental damage caused. Henderson received some recompense for his parliamentary service when Premier Sir George Grey appointed him to the Legislative Council in 1879. He also received a belated payment of £500 from the government for the *Lucy Dunn*, a schooner Governor FitzRoy had forced him to surrender to Ngati Whatua Maori in 1845 to settle a disputed claim for Waitakere cutting rights. John Macfarlane, like Henderson a prominent company director (including serving on the NZI board from 1862–79), died leaving his widow with an interest in Logan Campbell's troubled Whakatane Cattle Co syndicate. She was forced to forfeit this, however, after she was unable to meet her share of the interest charges in 1885.

Henderson's outspoken opposition to the Timber Floating Bill represented a strong sense of duty to the wider community which was by no means unusual among Victorian capitalists. He was a believer in universal public education, evidenced in 1873 when he made available the former library-reading room at Henderson's Mill for the district's first primary school lessons long after his business interests had ended there. He followed this up in 1878 by persuading the New Zealand Loan & Mercantile Agency Co (of which he was a director) to donate 1.6 ha (four acres) for a school site; a new school was opened there in 1880, and served until it was demolished in 1969. The land is incorporated within the present Henderson Primary School which acknowledged Thomas Henderson's generosity at its 125th anniversary celebrations in 1998.

Farmer-speculator James Dilworth (1815–94) also took a keen interest in the welfare of young people. Long before his death he had planned to provide boys of good character with quality education of the type he had received at the Royal School of Dungannon in his native County Tyrone, in Ireland. Dilworth started work as a banker but he made his money through the skilful acquisition of prime urban and farm land and reputedly valuable contracts to supply British and colonial troops during the 1860s land wars. In 1882 his properties were conservatively worth more than £80,000. But Dilworth suffered heavy losses in a number of investments that went awry in the years that followed, not least in the New Zealand Thames Valley Land Co, which acquired land owned by a syndicate which included Dilworth (this alone is said to have cost him £40,000). He survived because of the wide spread of his investments, and by the time of his death in 1894 his estate was worth £104,521. Childless, he left most of it to the Dilworth Ulster Institute Trust to establish a charitable boarding school for destitute orphaned boys or boys of parents in straitened circumstances. They had to be resident in the Auckland provincial district or the province of Ulster in Ireland, and had to submit, at school at least, to the Anglican faith — in keeping with Dilworth's Church of Ireland upbringing. The school opened in 1906 and today straddles two sites that are part of Dilworth's original farm between Mt St John, Epsom, and Mt Hobson, Remuera — some of Auckland's most valuable real estate. Dilworth's last home — a stark wooden mansion built in the early 1860s, the third built for him in Auckland — was used as a school building until its demolition in 1962. The Dilworth Trust, a wealthy and astute institution, earns income from a variety of sources including leases on house lots in Epsom and Remuera. It sold a portion of its land (Hobson Park) to Fletcher Construction in 1986 but bought it back at a substantial discount after the 1987 sharemarket crash. The trust has since built a junior school on the site.

Far less charitable than Dilworth but more prominent in Auckland public life was Glaswegian Robert Graham (1820–85). The third son of a farmer and coalmine owner, he went into partnership with his brother, David (later a member of Russell's Limited Circle), as a general merchant in Kororareka and Auckland in 1842. As a result of developing good relations with the Maori leader Hone Heke, the Grahams were able to evacuate their stock from

James Dilworth (1815–94), a successful Auckland farmer, reputedly made his money from contracts to supply British and colonial troops during the 1860s land wars. Childless, he left most of his fortune to establish a boarding school for destitute orphaned boys.
COURTESY DILWORTH TRUST BOARD

Kororareka without loss at the start of the Northern War. In 1845 Robert Graham bought 8 ha (20 acres) of land, including hot springs, on the foreshore at Waiwera, north of Auckland, the start of a long career of tourism investment and promotion. In 1848 he bought about 228 ha (565 acres) on the Great South Rd, Auckland where, after a three-year business trip to California, he built a mansion for his growing family. Named after his home in Scotland, Ellerslie House included spectacular gardens and a zoo. Some 40 ha (101 acres) were sold in 1881 to the Auckland Racing Club to form Ellerslie racecourse. David Graham's impressive home, the Towers in neighbouring Remuera, later became part of King's School, a preparatory institution for the sons of the rich.

The partnership between Robert and David was dissolved in 1850 and during the next few years Robert Graham acquired and developed more rural land. He established a pedigree cattle and sheep farm on Motutapu Island in the Hauraki Gulf, a farm on neighbouring Motuihe Island with another brother, John, and Lamb Hill, a 910-ha (2250-acre) farm near Waiuku. Graham was a strong pro-Auckland lobbyist on the Auckland Provincial Council — he was provincial superintendent from 1862–65 — and in the central government, opposing the decision to move the capital to Wellington. He was a keen speculator in the Thames goldfield which opened in 1867, acquiring land at Kauaeranga which he subdivided, and laid out a settlement known as Grahamstown (now part of Thames township). At Tararu, 1.6 km north of Thames, he established public gardens and a racecourse, and built a hotel.

Graham's key strength in developing his tourism interests was his ability to speak fluent Maori. In return for settling a tribal dispute at Maketu in 1878, he was offered land at Te Koutu by Rotorua Maori and at Wairakei by Taupo Maori. Wairakei proved a godsend but the 1700 ha (4200 acres) he secured, including the thermal area and the Huka Falls, was a highly controversial acquisition in the light of legislation passed to stop such transfers. He was involved in an equally contentious dispute in 1879–82 when he manoeuvred to gain control of the Ohinemutu Hotel, Rotorua — then one of the leading tourism resorts in Australasia. The Terrace Hotel, which he operated at Te Wairoa, a favourite stopping-off place for people visiting the Pink and White Terraces, was destroyed in the Tarawera eruption in 1886. Like Sir Donald McLean, a similarly skilled negotiator who was fluent in Maori, his success sits awkwardly in history in the light of subsequent Maori land grievances.

Ironically, Graham's great-grandson, Sir Douglas Graham (born 1942), is the politician who has probably done more than any other to address Maori land grievances. An Auckland lawyer, he was a senior minister in the Bolger and Shipley National governments, holding the all-important treaty negotiations portfolio. From a business perspective, however, there is no questionmark over Robert Graham's performance. He speculated in a growth sector with proven demand and unlimited potential, knew his market well and went for it. His contribution to business and the nation was finally recognised in 1999 when he was inducted posthumously in the Business Hall of Fame.

Auckland landlord Edward Costley (1794/95?–1883), who left £135,000 to various Auckland charities, was similarly focused in his business dealings: he earned the lion's share of his income from moneys invested on mortgage, yielding a comfortable nine per cent return. Costley died before the Auckland property crash but his philanthropic projects went ahead regardless.

Among the more curious survivors of the depression were the Wilson family, three members of whom were part of Russell's Limited Circle. William Wilson (1810–76), founder of the *New Zealand Herald*, was a founding director of NZI and a BNZ director for eight years. His sons were also linked to the Limited Circle: Liston (1837–1902) was an NZI director, and Scott

ABOVE: *Glenmark station, North Canterbury, once the richest run in the colony, covered more than 60,000 ha (150,000 acres). With its reputation for scab until 1875, it earned runholder George Moore (1812–1905) the nickname 'Scabby'.*
CANTERBURY MUSEUM, REF: 4118

RIGHT: *Annie Townend (1844/45?–1914) became the richest New Zealander in 1905 after inheriting the bulk of the estate of her late father, George Moore. She died a childless widow worth nearly £800,000.*
CANTERBURY MUSEUM, REF: 16589

BELOW: *John Acland and family in the 1870s at Mt Peel station, the South Canterbury station Acland founded with Charles Tripp.*
PHOTOGRAPHER: BARKER, HAWKINS COLLECTION, CANTERBURY MUSEUM, REF: 2810

Mansion House, Cheviot Hills, the stark former home of 'Ready Money' Robinson, built in 1867. The estate was sold to the government for closer settlement after Robinson's death and the 40-room home, pictured in 1890, burned down in 1937.
ALEXANDER TURNBULL LIBRARY, F-20723-1/2

'Ready Money' Robinson (1813/14?–89) was a talented stockman and breeder but also an uncompromising wheeler-dealer, never more so than when establishing his Cheviot Hills 'kingdom' in North Canterbury. Pictured about 1865.
C. JOHNSTON COLLECTION, ALEXANDER TURNBULL LIBRARY, F-96548-1/2

Scots runholder John Caverhill, who lost out to 'Ready Money' Robinson in the battle to freehold land between the Hurunui and Waiau rivers, North Canterbury.
CANTERBURY MUSEUM, REF: 6598

RIGHT: *Shipowner's son Sir John Hall (1824–1907), who was the leading New Zealand conservative politician of the nineteenth century. His Terrace station near Hororata on the Canterbury Plains earned him a large fortune, worth £216,271 on his death.*
CANTERBURY MUSEUM, REF: 16552

BELOW: *Holly Lea, the retirement home of rich former runholder Allan McLean, was built in Manchester St, Christchurch, between 1899–1900. It was probably the largest wooden residence of its time in New Zealand, with a floor area of 2136 sq m (23,000 sq ft) and 53 rooms, including 19 bedrooms.*
NEW ZEALAND FREE LANCE COLLECTION, ALEXANDER TURNBULL LIBRARY, F-106730-1/2

Thomas Henderson (1810–86), pictured in 1860, co-founder of timbermilling and shipping firm Henderson & Macfarlane, was one of Auckland's more prosperous citizens by the late 1850s. His business subsequently suffered from competition and disasters and much of the family fortune was lost.
ALEXANDER TURNBULL LIBRARY, F-12449-1/2

Dr John Logan Campbell (1817–1912) never practised medicine but used the 'Dr' honorific until he was knighted in 1902. Despite his penchant for property speculation, Campbell considered himself a step above Auckland's other merchants.
ALEXANDER TURNBULL LIBRARY, F-65556-1/2

James Dilworth's third and last home, a plain wooden mansion built near Mt St John, Auckland, in the early 1860s, served as a school building until its demolition in 1962.
ALEXANDER TURNBULL LIBRARY, G-3157-1/1

Larnach Castle, formerly the Camp, was built with materials William Larnach plundered from Guthrie & Larnach. It is said to have cost £100,000 to build and £50,000 to finish.
COURTESY BARKER FAMILY TRUUST

Glaswegian Robert Graham (1820–85) earned the title of New Zealand's first tourism entrepreneur with the acquisition of Waiwera hot springs, north of Auckland, in 1845.
COURTESY *NBR*

'Betrayed.' The near failure of the Bank of New Zealand in the late 1880s — caused by a mixture of depression and bad lending — led to widespread media criticism. Cartoonists were especially savage.
OBSERVER AND FREE LANCE, 22 JUNE 1889, COURTESY DIANNE DRIVER

'Prosperity.' In the wake of the economic tribulations of 1889, the Observer and Free Lance looked forward to 'a healthy and vigorous prosperity'.
OBSERVER AND FREE LANCE, 1 JANUARY 1890, COURTESY DIANNE DRIVER

Ulster-born shoemaker Robert Hannah (1846–1930), who was one of the colony's wealthiest businessmen by the early 1900s.
ALEXANDER TURNBULL LIBRARY, F-116725-1/2

The deeply religious Henry Shacklock (1839–1902), who designed and built a coal range capable of burning New Zealand brown coal. He committed suicide following bouts of ill-health and depression.
COURTESY FISHER & PAYKEL

Olveston, the 35-room Jacobean townhouse of Jewish merchant-benefactor David Theomin (1852–1933) in Royal Tce, Dunedin. It was built between 1904–1906 and contains a rare New Zealand collection of European and Oriental treasures.
ALEXANDER TURNBULL LIBRARY, F-363-1/4-MNZ

(1835–1902) served on the board of the BNZ. The brothers were also directors of the New Zealand Land Mortgage Co (after 1888 the New Zealand & River Plate Land Mortgage Co), a Russell company that survived the crash. It is ironic, therefore, that a businessman with strong ties to the Wilsons, BNZ shareholder Alfred Horton (1842–1903), should play a leading role in recapitalising the ailing bank. In 1888 Horton was sent to England with a BNZ director, Walter Johnson, and a senior bank officer, J.M. Butt, to pacify angry British shareholders and arrange a share placement. It seems not to have bothered the shareholders' committee appointed to investigate the bank's grave state that Horton had years earlier merged his *Southern Cross* newspaper with the Wilson-owned *Herald* to form a major publishing partnership, or that Scott Wilson, a fellow director of Wilson & Horton, was still on the BNZ's board.

Austere newspaper proprietor Alfred Horton (1842–1903) played a key role in recapitalising the Bank of New Zealand. He is credited with introducing web presses into New Zealand.
COURTESY MICHAEL HORTON

William Larnach (1833–98) epitomised crony capitalism in late nineteenth-century New Zealand. His abuse of public office, speculative ventures and high living undid much of the good he did as a member of the House of Representatives and cabinet minister. Overwrought by family and financial problems, he committed suicide in a committee room of Parliament.
OTAGO SETTLERS MUSEUM

his extensive Southland pastoral runs of Eyre Creek, Middle Dome and Longridge, and Conical Hill in South Otago, were acquired in partnership with a bankrupt American-born speculator, Henry Driver (1831–93) — a failed client of Larnach's old employer, the Bank of New South Wales. The money for these deals came from an Australian speculator, Joseph Clarke, the youngest son of the richest Australian landowner, W.J.T. Clarke (1801?–74) — better known as 'Monied' Clarke or 'Big' Clarke. Larnach had made the Clarkes' acquaintance in 1871 when he acted as W.J.T. Clarke's agent for the purchase of the valuable Moa Flat run, 80 km west of Dunedin, from the near-bankrupt Dunedin provincial government. Larnach took a hefty commission from the deal although he was still chief manager of the Bank of Otago at the time.

With its chief manager doing private deals with bankrupts and speculators rather than his job, it is not surprising that the Bank of Otago got into trouble. It was absorbed by the London-registered National Bank of New Zealand in July 1873 and Larnach came under immediate attack from the London directors. He quit that December, to their great pleasure, but remained a customer through his new partnership with Walter Guthrie. In 1875 he sparred publicly with a visiting National Bank inspector from London, John Bridges, who accused him in the prestigious Dunedin Club of dishonest conduct over his departure from the bank. Larnach successfully defended the charge by playing on the National Bank's unpopularity in Otago, but there were a few wiser heads, including Dunedin merchant John Ritchie, who knew that Bridges was right.

Larnach did many things of public benefit as a politician but they were often equally self-serving. In 1878 he went to England, officially to negotiate a loan for the hapless Grey government (which he achieved), but his real purpose was to float the New Zealand Agricultural Co. This bubble company aimed to offload the rabbit-infested Southland runs he held with Driver at inflated prices to British investors. But the company failed when land prices fell — it was wound up in 1890 — embarrassing the New Zealand government and destroying Larnach's relationship with Sir Julius Vogel, the New Zealand agent-general in London and former premier, who had helped Larnach promote the venture. (Vogel was forced to resign as agent-general in 1880 because the government rightly considered his business interests incompatible with his role as colonial representative.) Another victim of the Agricultural Co was the wealthy Southland wheatgrower George Bell.

Despite his business shenanigans, Larnach was awarded the CMG (companion of the Order of St Michael and St George) while he was overseas for his efforts in securing the government loan, but he complained to Premier Richard Seddon years later that he should have got a knighthood. Self-serving as ever, he also grumbled that he had never received true recognition for negotiating the loan.

Larnach's business prospects continued to deteriorate when it became obvious the Agricultural Co was doomed, and with the demise of Guthrie & Larnach's New Zealand Timber & Woodware Factories Co he headed for Australia. Here he entered into a short-term partnership with Vogel's brother-in-law, Montague Pym. He returned to New Zealand luckless and dejected,

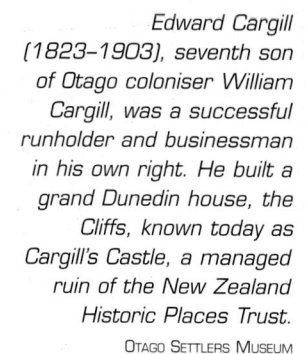

Edward Cargill (1823–1903), seventh son of Otago coloniser William Cargill, was a successful runholder and businessman in his own right. He built a grand Dunedin house, the Cliffs, known today as Cargill's Castle, a managed ruin of the New Zealand Historic Places Trust.
OTAGO SETTLERS MUSEUM

then. Cargill's Castle is now a managed ruin in the care of the New Zealand Historic Places Trust.

▶ Robert Hannah (1846–1930) was born near Belfast in Ireland. He took over a footwear business in Charleston, Westland, in 1868, the first step toward establishing a shoe-manufacturing and retailing empire that is still with us today. Hannah (originally spelled Hanna) moved to Wellington in 1874, setting up the firm R. Hannah & Co, which would eventually have stores from Whangarei to Invercargill. He became one of the country's wealthiest businessmen, building Antrim House (named after his home province in Ireland), an Italianate mansion in Boulcott St, Wellington, in 1905; today it is the headquarters of the New Zealand Historic Places Trust. Notwithstanding his business prowess, Hannah's own life was complicated. In addition to being married with a large family, he kept a mistress but did not adequately provide

Robert Hannah's Italianate Wellington mansion, Antrim House, built in 1905, was a symbol of the former West Coast shoemaker's spiralling fortunes. It is now the home of the New Zealand Historic Places Trust.
NEW ZEALAND HISTORIC PLACES TRUST

for her or the children she had by him, a situation that was revealed publicly in 1997 when he was posthumously inducted into the Business Hall of Fame. Film-maker Jane Campion (born 1954) is part of the Hannah family (her actress mother, Edith, was a Hannah). Hannah was not the only shoemaker-retailer to achieve long-term success. Nathaniel Suckling set up in Christchurch in 1864. He joined with his brother, John, to form Suckling Bros in 1871, and the business they founded (later the listed company Suckling Industries) survived until its takeover by Brierley Investments in 1986.

▶ Choie Sew Hoy (1836/38?–1901), or Charles Sew Hoy as he was known to English speakers, was born in the Upper Panyu district near Canton (now Guangzhou), China. He came to Otago in about 1868 in search of gold and became a prosperous merchant, opening a store in Dunedin in 1869, importing Chinese goods and assisting Chinese miners. Like Chew Chong in Taranaki

he was active in the Congregational Church and other organisations. He committed suicide following bouts of ill health and depression and the business, a limited liability company after 1900, was owned and run by his four surviving sons, John (mayor of Dunedin 1914–15), Henry, Percival and Francis. Francis' youngest child, Jack (1913–99), was the company's last managing director, and saved it from extinction in the 1950s by linking up with Auckland-based whiteware manufacturer Fisher & Paykel. This came about after he sought help from F&P's co-founder and managing director, (Sir) Woolf Fisher. Jack Shacklock became deputy chairman of Fisher & Paykel after H.E. Shacklock became part of F&P in 1971. Jack was blessed with exceptional talents, as well as a love of the good life. He collected classic cars, adored boating and was a keen farmer and pilot. For some years he maintained a flat in Knightsbridge, London, below that of dancer Ginger Rogers, and he enjoyed telling people he 'used to sleep under Ginger Rogers'.

▶ Bendix Hallenstein (1835–1905), a German-Jewish merchant, and James Robertson (1826–76) established Otago's first flour mill at the mouth of the Kawarau River, near Queenstown, in 1867. They called it New Brunswick. With his brothers Hallenstein opened the country's first clothing factory in Dunedin in 1873 — the business later became the retail menswear chain Hallenstein Bros, which thrives today. Since 1987 it has been part of Hallenstein Glasson Holdings. Bendix Hallenstein also founded the Dunedin-based retailer Drapery & General Importing Co (DIC) in 1884, initially as a co-operative store. It lasted until its acquisition by Brierley Investments in the 1980s. He established a successful and generous family and served the Otago community in many ways, including terms as a mayor of Queenstown (1869–72), member of Parliament (1872–73) and Otago provincial councillor (1872–75).

▶ Sir Percy Sargood (1865–1940), an Australian-born clothing and textile importer and manufacturer, led and developed Sargood Son & Ewen into a major New Zealand company. He had been apprenticed to the Melbourne branch of Sargood, a firm founded by his grandfather, and trained in London, and came to New Zealand in 1891 as manager of the Dunedin and Christchurch branches of Sargood's Standard Footwear Co. In 1892 he became a junior partner of Sargood and in 1902, after his father's death, took control of the New Zealand company. Sargood Son & Ewen was formed in 1907 and he was governing director. An enlightened employer, Sargood introduced one of the first staff provident funds in New Zealand. He was also a generous benefactor, contributing to the Dunedin and National art galleries from his personal collection, and he worked for years to bring irrigation to Central Otago. Sargood was a keen supporter of youth organisations, especially the Scout movement which he helped found in New Zealand, and in 1937 received the Silver Wolf, the highest distinction of the Scout movement. He was knighted in 1935 for services to the community. Sargood was a wealthy man with extensive interests, including Wanaka station, purchased in 1912. He also married into wealth; his wife, Lucy, was a member of the landed Ormond family of Hawke's Bay. Sargood directed that after his death the bulk of his estate be converted into a trust to benefit the arts and youth. The Sargoods' fine Dunedin home, Marinoto, acquired in 1902, survives but Sargood Son & Ewen does not. It merged with rival Bing Harris & Co in 1972 to form Bing Harris Sargood, which was in turn acquired by Brierley Investments in 1981 and broken up in 1984.

▶ Sir John Ross (1834–1927) and Robert Glendining (1841–1917) were fellow Scots who set up in Dunedin in 1862 as importers and retailers of softgoods, paving the way for a major manufacturing business. Ross returned permanently to England after his marriage in 1870, leaving Glendining to run the local operation. By 1879 Ross & Glendining was manufacturing woollen goods at the Roslyn mill, Kaikorai. In 1900 it became a limited liability company with a capital of £500,000 and branches in Christchurch, Wellington, Invercargill and Napier. An Auckland branch opened in 1904. Glendining, who died in 1917 at the height of the company's fortunes, left an estate valued at £360,000. Ross, who was knighted in 1922 for services to industry and the community, died in 1927 with an estate valued at £280,000. He and Glendining were public benefactors and recognised as good employers.

▶ William Gregg (1836–1901), an Irish-born coffee and spice manufacturer, set up in Dunedin in 1862. His Gregg's Club Coffee became a national institution, winning medals at exhibitions throughout Australasia. After being hurt by speculation in gold shares and slap-dash accounting, he was bankrupted in 1894. With the help of Australian credit, however, he was able to rebuild his business, laying the foundations of a large and successful merchant house which in 1984 became part of the listed company Cerebos Gregg's, which is controlled by Cerebos Pacific, a subsidiary of UK-based Ranks Hovis McDougall.

▶ Richard Hudson (1841–1903), born in Chippenham in England, founded a biscuit, cake and confectionery factory in Dunedin in 1873. The former sailor, goldminer and pastry cook, who had been orphaned at the age of eleven, was

its gardens), on the shores of Lake Takapuna (now Lake Pupuke) from 1886, and a townhouse, which is still standing, in Princes St in the inner city (at one time the University Club). He was knighted in 1926 for services to the public and the newspaper industry. The successor to his company, New Zealand Newspapers, years later became part of a larger listed holding company, NZ News, which acquired a range of newspapers and magazines. It was taken over by Brierley Investments in the early 1980s. The *Auckland Star*, sold to Wellington-based Independent Newspapers (INL) in 1988 as part of the dismembering of NZ News, suffered heavy losses before finally shutting its doors in 1991. Other NZ News interests were acquired by the group's former opposition, Wilson & Horton, publisher of the *New Zealand Herald*.

▶ Alexander Burt (1840–1920) and Thomas Burt (1842–84) were Scots plumbers and metalworkers who founded A. & T. Burt. After success in the gold rush in Dunstan, Otago, the brothers established a plumbing, gas-fitting and metal-finishing business in the Octagon, Dunedin. In 1865 the firm installed gas lighting for the Dunedin Exhibition, and it later made drinking fountains, rabbit-exterminating equipment, pumps, winches, engines, water-works parts, boilers, machinery, meat-preserving plant and gold dredges. By 1900, A. & T. Burt had branches throughout the country. Family members carried on the business after the deaths of Alexander and Thomas.

▶ John McGlashan (1802–64) was an academic lawyer from Edinburgh whose family home and estate in Dunedin formed the basis of John McGlashan College, founded in 1918. He became Otago provincial treasurer and solicitor in 1854 shortly after arriving in Dunedin, but his best work was in promoting the Free Presbyterian Church and an education system linked to the church. He died from injuries caused by a riding accident.

▶ John Anderson (1820–97), a Scottish blacksmith, became a leading Christchurch citizen and has been described as the 'father of New Zealand engineering'. Arriving on one of the first four ships to the province in 1850, Anderson set up shop on the plains at Riccarton 'amidst the fern, flax and tussock'. His business grew to become the huge Canterbury Foundry — the first in the province to make iron lamp posts, screw wool presses, flax-stripping machinery, gas machinery, boilers, dredges and railway bridges. Anderson was a member of Christchurch's first town board. In 1869 he became the borough's second mayor, and he served on a number of public bodies. He was also a director of the New Zealand Shipping Co until shortly before his death.

Scots-born blacksmith John Anderson (1820–97), pictured here in the 1880s, set up shop in Riccarton, Christchurch, in 1850, establishing what became the Canterbury Foundry. He is today described as the 'father of New Zealand engineering'.
THE CYLCOPEDIA OF NEW ZEALAND

▶ Henry Blundell (1813?–78), a printer from Dublin, Ireland, founded Wellington's first evening newspaper, the *Evening Post*, in 1865. He had earlier worked for the *Evening News* in Dublin, the *Lyttelton Times* and the *Otago Daily Times* before founding the *Havelock Mail* during the Wakamarina gold rush. The *Evening Post*, New Zealand's last surviving metropolitan evening daily until its merger with the *Dominion* in 2002, was run by Blundell's three sons, Henry, Louis and John, in partnership from 1874. Henry jnr's death in 1894 led to the formation of a joint-stock company, Blundell Bros, in 1897. The business was consolidated under Louis and John Blundell, and for many years through John's son, Percy (1872–1961). Percy Blundell, an outspoken defender of the rights and liberties of the press, became a director of the firm in 1917, was chairman for many years and was a director until his death. Henry jnr's son, Ernest, served as chairman, as did Louis' son, Leonard, and

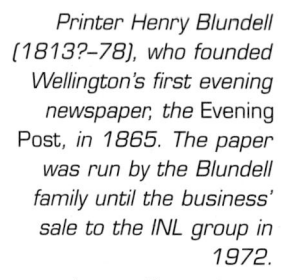

Printer Henry Blundell (1813?–78), who founded Wellington's first evening newspaper, the Evening Post, *in 1865. The paper was run by the Blundell family until the business' sale to the INL group in 1972.*
ALEXANDER TURNBULL LIBRARY, F-105036-1/2

Ernest's son, Neil. The company became part of the Independent Newspapers group in 1972. INL's newspaper assets were sold to Australian publisher John Fairfax Holdings in 2003 for nearly $1.2 billion.

▶   Thomas Kempthorne (1834?–1915), from Cornwall, and Welsh chemist Evan Prosser established drug firm Kempthorne Prosser in Dunedin in 1870. The partnership became a limited-liability company in 1879, supplying a wide range of pharmaceutical and medical supplies, and by the 1880s was a major chemicals manufacturer. Prosser quit the company in 1886 to move to Sydney but Kempthorne continued to play a major role in the business (managing director 1879–1904, chairman 1903–04). He imported Dunedin's first steam car in 1901. In 1977 the company was dismembered after a complicated series of market moves involving Ravensdown Fertiliser Co-operative, the New Zealand Farmers' Fertilizer Co and Brierley Investments. Kempthorne Prosser's fertiliser division became a co-operative, with 60 per cent owned by Ravensdown and

40 per cent by New Zealand Farmers' Fertilizer. The pharmaceutical business, including Kempthorne Medical Supplies (KMS) and dental supplier Shalfoon Bros, was left with New Zealand Farmers' Fertilizer (later Fernz Corporation), eventually becoming part of listed pharmaceutical wholesaler Stevens KMS Corporation in 1985. KMS was sold and no longer exists as a separate entity, and Shalfoon became part of Stevens' new owner, Swiss-owned Zuellig Group.

▶ George Whitcombe (1855–1917), a bookseller who was born in Brittany, France, and George Tombs, a printer-publisher, formed the publishing partnership Whitcombe & Tombs in Christchurch in 1882. Tombs retired in 1889 and the business, although trading as a public company, became a virtual Whitcombe fiefdom after that. Whitcombe died suddenly (while writing out a cheque), and his son, Bertie (1875–1963), took over as managing director, serving until 1958, and was chairman from 1943–62.

Whitcombe & Tombs had no major competition until Dunedin-based bookseller A.H. & A.W. Reed branched into publishing in 1932. In 1971 the listed Printing & Packaging Corporation was formed to facilitate the merger of Whitcombe & Tombs and Christchurch-based printer and packager Coulls Somerville Wilkie to become Whitcoulls. Brierley Investments acquired control of Printpac in 1982 and in 1985 Whitcoulls' non-retail assets were spun off to a BIL-Carter Holt Harvey joint venture, Printpac (later Printpac-UEB). In 1988 Whitcoulls' publishing business was sold to Penguin Books, leaving the company as a bookseller and stationer. In 1991 BIL sold Whitcoulls to Graeme Hart's Rank Group for $71 million. In 1996 it was sold to Blue Star Group, a New Zealand company acquired by United States-owned US Office Products, for $320 million. US Office Products struggled to make the acquisition work and in 2001 sold Whitcoulls to UK book retailer W.H. Smith. The son of Whitcoulls co-founder George Tombs, Harry Tombs (1874–1966), became a boutique printer of note, trading as Harry H. Tombs and later Wingfield Press, the first fine arts press in New Zealand.

▶ Sir Harold Beauchamp (1858–1938), the self-made son of an auctioneer from Victoria, Australia, became a key figure in Wellington business circles and a prominent company director. Beauchamp left school at the age of thirteen or fourteen to work for his father but later took a job with importer W.M. Bannatyne & Co, a firm he eventually took over. By 1889 he was starting to make money and his business skills were being sought elsewhere. Beauchamp was variously a director of the New Zealand Candle Co, the Gear Meat Preserving & Freezing Co, Wellington Gas Co, the Australian Mutual Provident

Society, ICI (NZ) and Berlei (NZ) but his most important directorship was that of the troubled Bank of New Zealand from 1898–1936 (he was chairman from 1907–22 and again in 1934). The appointment, at Premier Richard Seddon's behest, contributed to the bank's recovery. Beauchamp is better known, however, as the father of writer Katherine Mansfield — born Kathleen Mansfield Beauchamp. Kathleen was by far the most difficult of his six children and father and daughter shared a testy relationship, especially after Beauchamp was depicted in her writings. She once described him as 'the richest man in New Zealand and the meanest', but history shows him to have been a generous donor to worthy cases. These included a memorial to his daughter at the southern end of Fitzherbert Tce, Thorndon, Wellington, near the grand house the family moved to in 1907 when Beauchamp became chairman of the BNZ. That home still stands, as does Mansfield's birthplace in nearby Tinakori Rd.

Writer Katherine Mansfield (1888–1923) had a comfortable Wellington upbringing courtesy of the wealth and status of her father, Sir Harold Beauchamp (1858–1938). Beauchamp played a key role in the Bank of New Zealand's recovery, serving as a director from 1898–1936 and chairman from 1907–22 and again in 1934.
B. BENNET ALDER, ALEXANDER TURNBULL LIBRARY, D-P018011

▶ Thomas Cawthron (1833?–1915), the son of a London oil and paint dealer, created Nelson's Cawthron Institute by a £231,000 bequest from his £240,000 estate. A contractor, businessman and later shipping agent, Cawthron dominated maritime shipping from the Port of Nelson. He was an astute investor with a frugal lifestyle but was a generous donor to the people of Nelson, providing land and money for a variety of causes (such as the Cathedral Steps leading up to Nelson Cathedral) and assisting in individual cases of hardship. The Cawthron Institute, Cawthron's last and largest benefaction, conducts scientific research into primary industries with special reference to those of the Nelson area. Indirectly, the Cawthron Institute has helped preserve two of the city's finest homes, Fellworth House, which became the institute's first home in 1921, and Harley House, built in 1868 and bought by the institute in 1960 to house its museum. (The collection has since been transferred to the Nelson Museum.)

Cawthron's contribution to the pursuit of knowledge was not uncommon for capitalists of his time. Alexander Turnbull (1868–1918), a Wellington general merchant, used his ample inheritance to collect some 55,000 artefacts and books. He donated the former to the Dominion Museum in 1913 and bequeathed the latter (along with his brick townhouse in Bowen St) to the Crown, creating what later became the Alexander Turnbull Library. Turnbull's Dunedin equivalent was Thomas Hocken (1836–1910), a talented physician from Rutland, England, who gifted his huge collection of books, pamphlets, manuscripts, newspapers, maps, paintings and photographs to the nation in 1908, forming the basis of the Hocken Library. Auckland had received its own rewards years earlier from several well-heeled donors. Glaswegian James Mackelvie (1824–85), a one-time junior partner in Brown Campbell & Co who later made a fortune from Thames' Golden Crown goldmine, made a series of gifts to the city of Auckland including a collection of English coins, 500 books and several works of art. A bachelor, on his death he left £40,000 to the Auckland City Art Gallery. McCosh Clark, mayor from 1880–83 (and later ruined by the property crash), devoted a large part of his honorarium to the Auckland Public Library. In 1882 former governor and premier Sir George Grey (1812–98), a noted antiquarian, made a large gift to the library of early prints and books, including 36 titles printed before 1501 — by far the most valuable of the library's special collections. Between 1904 and 1928 the library also received some 2300 volumes of manuscripts and early printed books from investors in Thames' Waiotahi goldmine, brothers Henry Shaw (1850–1928) and Fred Shaw (1849–1927). Their gift included 65 books printed before 1501. In 1905 the Leys Institute, a free library and mechanics' institute, was built in

The Rich List*
January 1876

Top ten families/individuals with their main sources of wealth

1. **Rhodes, William Barnard** (1807?–78)
   Wool, trading, shipping, finance
   Described in 1853 as the 'millionaire of Wellington'.

2. **Levin, William Hort** (1845–93)
   Trading, stock-and-station agency
   Running Levin & Co after his father's retirement and move to England. Probably the richest young Wellingtonian in the 1870s.

3. **Rhodes, Robert Heaton** (1815–84)
   Wool
   Left estate worth £572,849.

4. **Moore, George Henry** (1812–1905)
   Wool

5. **Robinson, William** (1813/14?–89)
   Wool

6. **Campbell, Robert** (1843–89)
   Wool

---

*   Ignores absentee runholders and those who had returned to Britain (e.g. George Duppa [1819–88], described as an 'Australian millionaire' in 1870).

Ponsonby, Auckland, with a bequest from bookbinder William Leys (1852–99) and assistance from his surviving brother, T.W. Leys, editor and co-owner of the *Auckland Star*.

Canterbury also benefited from the philanthropy of its better-off citizens. A notable benefactor was Australian-born biscuit magnate Robert McDougall (1861–1942) who presented an art gallery to the city of Christchurch in 1928 (opened in 1932). McDougall made his fortune through Aulsebrook & Co. He had joined John Aulsebrook as a partner in the business in 1882, and became sole proprietor a decade later. McDougall inaugurated a welfare league for his

=7. **Studholme brothers**
Wool
Collective interests of John Studholme snr (1829–1903), Paul Studholme (1831–99) and Michael Studholme (1834–86).

=7. **McLean brothers**
Wool
Partnership of John McLean (1819–1902) and Allan McLean (1822-1907) after their brother-in-law, George Buckley, sold out in 1875.

9. **Clifford family**
Wool
(Sir) Charles Clifford (1813-93) and his eldest son, (Sir) George Clifford (1847–1930), who managed the Flaxbourne and Stonyhurst runs after 1874. (Sir) Frederick Weld (1823–91) was a minority shareholder.

=10. **Reid, John** (1835–1912)
Wool

=10. **Deans, John II** (1853–1902)
Wool

=10. **Whitaker, Frederick** (1812–91)
Finance, property speculation

=10. **Russell, Thomas** (1830–1904)
Finance, property speculation

=10. **Grigg, John** (1828?–1901)
Wool, meat, wheat, oats

staff and set up Temperance & General Group life assurance. He owned the Brookdale sheep station, North Canterbury, and was a founder of the Shirley Golf Club, Christchurch. Aulsebrook's merged with Bycroft Macintosh in 1961 to become AB Consolidated Holdings and was at the centre of a bitter battle for control in 1978 between flourmiller-baker A.S. Paterson & Co and corporate raider Brierley Investments (BIL), won by the latter.

▶ Walter Prince popularised electricity in New Zealand as agent, salesman and installation electrician for Sir Julius Vogel's Australasian Electric Light,

Power & Storage Co and its New Zealand subsidiary, the New Zealand Electric Light Co. He arrived in the colony in 1882 and spent much of the next six years promoting the benefits of electricity to prospective industrial and municipal investors. He demonstrated electricity at the 1885 Industrial Exhibition in Wellington on behalf of R.E. Fletcher & Co, which had taken over New Zealand Electric Light, and installed the equipment in Bullendale, Central Otago, in 1885–86 — the first significant generation and transmission of electric power in New Zealand and the first major hydroelectric generation. He then persuaded people in Reefton to set up a company to build and run the country's first electrical system selling power to the public. This became operational in 1888. But his ventures elsewhere were less successful and after Reefton, where he forfeited his shares in the company because of problems with the system, he tried his luck on the Thames goldfield. Electricity was first used for lighting — the first house lit up was said to be that of wealthy brewer Moss Davis in Princes St, Auckland, in 1882 — but after 1919 it became a steady competitor with gas for heating and cooking. Hydroelectricity became popular after 1884 when a Thames engineering firm heavily involved in mining, A. & G. Price, obtained the rights for the Pelton wheel, which was used widely in early hydro schemes.

▶ Donald Reid (1833–1919), a farmer's son from Strathtay, Perthshire, Scotland, founded the stock-and-station firm Donald Reid & Co in Dunedin in 1878. It grew rapidly with farmers supporting the land-reform policies he had helped steer through Parliament. The business became Reid Farmers, merging with Otago Farmers' Co-operative Association of New Zealand in 1984, and in 2001 merged with Christchurch-based Pyne Gould Guinness, a subsidiary of Pyne Gould Corporation.

4

Brave new world

The principle that regulation of industry and promotion of enterprise conducive to the public welfare were not only prerogatives of the state but also its bounden duty had gained wide acceptance.

R.M. BURDON, HISTORIAN, ON THE POLITICAL ORDER
AFTER PRIME MINISTER RICHARD SEDDON'S DEATH IN 1906

If there had been philosophical debate over the role of the state in New Zealand when the Liberals came to power in 1890, it had well and truly ended with Richard Seddon's thirteen years as premier. A government's right to intervene in the economy or direct social policy was no longer in question; politics centred on the quality of that intervention and whether another government, politician or party could do it better. Thus, even in the drawn-out and often heated debate over whether Crown land should be sold or leased to would-be farmers, the two main political parties shared a common aim: to get as many young men on the land as possible. Few MPs questioned the desirability of the state actively encouraging closer settlement. By the time the new century dawned, the defenders of the big estates had largely disappeared. The government used its compulsory-purchase powers sparingly, preferring to let tax, changing land use and economic reality encourage the big landowners to break up their holdings. This happened relatively quickly. In areas where dairying was on the rise, the estates of failed speculators like Josiah Firth (Matamata) and Thomas and Samuel Morrin (Lockerbie) became the source of prime dairy farms — 117 came from the Matamata estate alone — offering efficiency and productivity greater than that achieved by their former owners.

If this was socialism — what historian Michael Bassett describes cynically as 'the essential goodness of state action' — it was not too bad.

State encouragement of closer settlement, along with a host of other government interventions in people's lives, was acceptable because Seddon had achieved something no premier except his Liberal predecessor, John Ballance, had managed: political stability. Seddon was not by nature a socialist but the economic problems the Liberals inherited when they took office — not least the financial mess that led to the near collapse of the Bank of New Zealand in 1894 — had led a government that espoused liberal sympathies to adopt Fabian socialism by default. The private sector had let New Zealand down; it was the state's turn to have a go, and the Liberals were fortunate that their intervention was assisted by a general rise in commodity prices from the late 1890s.

If the age of wool kings like William Robinson and George Moore had passed, that of the meat barons and the dairy co-operatives had arrived. John

Christ's College, Christchurch, was the school of choice for some of the South Island's wealthiest runholders and their sons. Today, many of the country's leading businessmen are Christ's old boys.
Courtesy Christ's College

Grigg in Canterbury was among the first of the southern pastoralists to realise that the future for extensive farming lay as much with meat — exporting refrigerated sheep carcasses to Smithfield market in London — as with wool. He was followed by other enlightened farmers, but the southern lifestyles based on the wool cheque continued. Young men lined up for Christ's College, while horseracing and garden parties occupied their parents' social calendars even if their incomes were rarely large enough for pastoralists to give up work altogether. The land was rough and the soils poor by English standards, requiring constant attention, and early experiments with imported fauna and flora had resulted in some notable ecological disasters. Rabbits were by far the greatest problem, literally eating sheep out of their homes, and depleting the productivity of once-valuable runs.

The stock-and-station industry, the main link between town and country and the banker for many farmers, prospered on its ability to stay abreast of farming trends. One of the best examples is Wright Stephenson & Co, founded in Dunedin in October 1861 by John Wright (1828–1913) and Robert Robertson as Wright Robertson & Co, 'auctioneers and general commission merchants'. This was three months after the start of the Otago gold rush and the partnership, joined in 1868 by auctioneer John Stephenson (1830–1901), boomed. It was incorporated in 1906 with £250,000 authorised capital, and in its first full year as a company (1907) made a tax-paid profit of £18,143 and paid out £10,620 in dividends. Today it struggles on as a listed company, Wrightson, and despite having gobbled up its erstwhile rival, the National Mortgage & Agency Co of New Zealand (NMA, incorporating Levin & Co), is a shadow of its former self. In its heyday it made huge fortunes for its principals — Wright and Stephenson had magnificent homes in Dunedin — and provided opportunities for enterprising staff. One example is Auckland-born Sir William Hunt (1867–1939), a former fleeceaway-turned-shepherd who joined the firm in Gore in 1891 as a stand-in sheep auctioneer. After showing early talent he was quickly promoted, becoming the architect of Wright Stephenson's dominance in the stock-and-station business. He was chairman and managing director from 1906–39 and held outside directorships including Abraham & Williams (Palmerston North) and the Wairarapa Frozen Meat Co. Hunt was the epitome of the self-made man.

But it was the frozen meat industry, a late entrant to the primary sector, that enjoyed the fastest growth and provided some of the biggest fortunes. It blossomed, with occasional glitches, within a decade of the first shipment of frozen meat from New Zealand to Britain in 1882. Unlike dairying, which seemed better suited to the Scandinavian or Irish co-operative models, meat killing, freezing and processing proved as attractive to foreign corporates as to colonials. From the outset the industry tended to be vertically integrated, with most companies' processing, shipping and retailing operations run as a single entity. The Edinburgh-based New Zealand & Australia Land Co, under general manager William Davidson (1846–1924), pioneered the first refrigerated shipment to the United Kingdom in February 1882, using the sailing ship *Dunedin*, to freeze and transport about 130 tonnes of mutton and lamb carcasses. Slaughtering and dressing had been done on the company's Totara Estate station in Otago. The New Zealand Refrigerating Co followed with a shipment to Britain in May that year, although its meat was sold at a loss, and in August 1882 it opened New Zealand's first land-based freezing works at Burnside, Dunedin.

Among the New Zealand operators who hankered for a share of the meat wealth were two business adventurers from Derbyshire, England — Richard Hellaby (1849–1902) and his brother William (1845–1900). Their partnership, R. & W. Hellaby, began in Shortland St, Auckland, in 1873 (where the one-time NZI building now stands) with the purchase of F.H. Hammond's butcher's shop. Within three years the business was strong enough for R. & W. Hellaby to acquire the freehold of larger premises up the road. But the partners had their hearts set on owning their own works. From 1880 they started buying land at Richmond, 5 km from the centre of Auckland (now part of urban Westmere), and during the next few years established what was reported in 1898 to be the 'largest butchering firm in New Zealand'. (The works' weekly throughput in 1901 was 180 to 200 head of cattle, about 1000 sheep and lambs, 40 to 50 calves and a quantity of pigmeat.)

R. & W. Hellaby became a limited company in October 1900 with an authorised capital of £50,000, but the following month it suffered a major setback with the deaths of William, during a routine operation to cure a troubled shoulder, and his 45-year-old wife, Rosina (née Burdett), who died of shock three weeks later. The family tragedy was compounded in 1902 when Richard died of a heart attack. He and his wife, Amy (née Briscoe), and their six children had been planning to move into their imposing new house, Bramcote (now Florence Court), in Epsom, named after Bramcote Hall, a Hellaby mansion in England. The brothers left substantial estates but the loss of two such talents at relatively young ages left the business rudderless for a time. Its saving grace was its entry into the export trade. In 1899 it had acquired 50 per cent of the Auckland Freezing Co, which had works at King's Wharf and Westfield (Otahuhu) and held the sole meat export licence in the Auckland province. The freezing company had earlier that year been sold to a

Christchurch merchant, A.H. Turnbull, who was associated with British meat importer William Weddel. Its works had once belonged to the New Zealand Frozen Meat & Storage Co but had passed to the Bank of New Zealand after that company's collapse in 1889. The Auckland Freezing Co, under direction of the bank and its associate, the New Zealand Loan & Mercantile Agency Co, had mainly processed stock from Waikato estates the BNZ had foreclosed on during the crash of the 1880s.

R. & W. Hellaby set about revitalising the business, but not without opposition from some in the trade who feared the Hellaby dominance in exporting as well as retailing would force down stock prices. Things came to a head in 1906 when R. & W. Hellaby was obliged to sell King's Wharf to the new Auckland Farmers' Freezing Co-op (Affco) to satisfy farmer lobbying and trustees' concerns and agree not to use its export licence for fifteen years. R. & W. Hellaby agreed not to kill and freeze stock for export, or for clients, except through Affco's works, and in return Affco agreed not to sell meat on the local market, wholesale or retail, or engage in preserving, tinning or canning of meat. R. & W. Hellaby's canned-meat trade with the Pacific islands was not affected but the restraint on the export licence cost it dearly during World War I, when most meat companies boomed. Fortunately the Otahuhu site, on which the Shortland works were built in 1910, turned out to be a sound long-term investment. This was the asset most identified with R. & W. Hellaby's expansion in the twentieth century. Today the Shortland works and the neighbouring meatworks, Vestey-owned Westfield and Affco-owned Southdown, have gone — casualties of an industry old before its time.

In 1985 R. & W. Hellaby fell victim to Ariadne Australia, an investment company of entrepreneur Bruce Judge (born 1942), and was carved up the following year. Judge's motive for the bargain-basement acquisition was property speculation, not meat-processing. Today, R. & W. Hellaby's listed successor, Hellaby Holdings, is an investment shell, with a minor interest only in the meat industry. A former R. & W. Hellaby chairman and managing director, Sir Alan Hellaby (1926–2001), was knighted in 1981 for services to industry. Sadly, the industry he most served is today a skeleton in comparison with the time of his grandfather, Richard, and great-uncle, William.

(Sir) Joseph Ward's huge Ocean Beach freezing works near Campbelltown (now Bluff) got off to a shaky start when it opened in 1892. His decision to build the works was motivated more by parochialism than business sense, and although the works was among the largest and most modern in the world, it initially struggled to pay its way. Ward borrowed heavily through his new farmers' co-operative, the J.G. Ward Farmers' Association, but when

Southlander Sir Joseph Ward (1856–1930) contributed to the failure of the Colonial Bank of New Zealand in 1895 through the debts of his failed company, the J.G. Ward Farmers' Association of New Zealand. But Ward recovered his fortune and political status, serving as prime minister from 1906–12 and 1928–30.
S.C. SMITH COLLECTION, ALEXANDER TURNBULL LIBRARY, G-20342-1/1

commodity prices failed to reach the levels he had hoped for, he was forced in 1893 to sell his interest in Ocean Beach to the works' marketing and shipping agency, Nelson Bros of Hawke's Bay. It too was strapped for money and Ward was paid half in cash and half in shares in Nelson Bros. But Ward's finances and those of the association were too far gone to be rescued. Ward's insolvency, however, was brief — thanks in no small way to support from a group of loyal Southlanders — and with the profitable sale in London of his Nelson Bros shares in 1899 (they had been deemed worthless by the official liquidators), he was able to repay his London creditors and make a full return to political life in New Zealand. He did not re-enter the freezing industry but his new enterprise, Campbelltown-based J.G. Ward & Co, rode on the back of rising meat prices generated by the South African War. The company similarly benefited from generous British meat contracts during World War I and Ward, once a financial disaster, grew rich. The fortune disappeared rapidly after his death in 1930 but J.G. Ward & Co survived until its absorption by NMA in 1960. Until recently its waterfront warehouse in Bluff continued to carry the J.G. Ward & Co name.

James Gear (1837/39?–1911) was another colonial to profit from the freezing industry. A labourer's son from Ilchester, in Somerset, England, he was drawn to the Otago goldfields in 1861 but by 1865 was working as a butcher in Wellington. Three years later he acquired the butcher's shop of Benjamin Ling, one of Wellington's oldest, and went on to buy other butcheries. Gear concentrated on the local market, delivering to Wellington homes, and in 1873 he added a preserving plant and started distributing canned meat. He bought land in Karori and Petone to fatten stock on and built slaughterhouses and a boiling-down plant at Petone in 1874. He also acquired a share in more than 440 ha (1000 acres) at Te Horo, reclaiming swampland for pasture in what some say was an attempt to gentrify his humble origins and homely occupation. He did not live at Te Horo but in 1881–82 bought 170 ha (382 acres) of land overlooking Porirua Harbour where he built a double-storey wooden mansion, Okowai, in the style of a seventeenth-century Italian stone palazzo. In 1882 he incorporated the Gear Meat Preserving & Freezing Co of New Zealand to acquire his butchering and meat-preserving business and use it as a starting-point for entering the frozen-meat trade. But the Petone works, which were to bear his name, were not built until 1889. Gear was a leading

One-time gold prospector James Gear (1837/39?–1911) incorporated the Gear Meat Preserving & Freezing Co of New Zealand in 1882 to acquire his butchering and meat-preserving business and enter the frozen-meat trade. The Petone works bearing his name were built in 1889. They were closed in 1982.
PORIRUA CITY COUNCIL

figure in late nineteenth-century Wellington and Wairapapa business, and when he died in 1911 his estate was worth a little under £75,000 — a remarkable testimony to his foray into the freezing industry. The Gear works closed in 1982 but Okowai (known these days as the Gear Homestead) survives, and was restored between 1977 and 1983 by the Porirua City Council. Set in 4.5 ha of native bushland and magnificent gardens, it is a popular conference and function centre.

The dairy industry also produced significant wealth in the early twentieth century but most of it was dispersed through a large number of small companies, many of them co-operatively owned. But some dairy entrepreneurs did prosper personally, among them Chew Chong (1827/44?–1920), Joseph Nathan (1835–1912) and Sir William Goodfellow (1880–1974).

Chew Chong (Chau Tseung), a pedlar-trader from Canton (now Guangzhou) in China, arrived in New Zealand in 1867 after working in Victoria and Singapore. He came to Taranaki in 1870, setting himself up as a storekeeper in

Shopkeeper Chew Chong (1827/44?–1920) was Taranaki's dairy-factory pioneer and also helped the province's troubled farming industry in the late nineteenth century by creating a market for exporting the Jew's ear fungus to China.
Courtesy NBR

New Plymouth, and creating among other things an export market for Jew's ear fungus (*Auricularia polytricha*) — the so-called 'Taranaki wool' — then common on decaying native trees. This was highly sought after in China for food and medicine, and the trade helped Taranaki farmers augment their incomes during lean times. Chong opened branches in Inglewood and Eltham, trading in a variety of goods including butter, which he exported (with mixed results). But his real dairying success came with his state-of-the-art Jubilee butter factory — named in honour of Queen Victoria's golden jubilee — which opened in Eltham in 1887. Chong later added four creameries and bought the nearby Mangatoki factory. He was also a shareholder in the Egmont Co-op Box Co.

Although his business suffered setbacks in the 1890s, his talent for innovation survived. He installed a Hall's refrigerating machine in his Jubilee factory in 1889 — probably the first freezing machine in a New Zealand butter factory — and introduced sharemilking to Taranaki. Chong, who married a European, died in New Plymouth comfortably off rather than rich, his true reward being the respect he gained from the settler community during a period of widespread discrimination against Chinese. He produced a large and successful family. One prominent Auckland member is his grandson, Trevor Chong (born 1928), proprietor of Chong Press Clipping Bureau.

Joseph Nathan (1835–1912), the sixth of eight children of poor Jewish parents from the East End of London, had already established a substantial merchant business in Wellington (Joseph Nathan & Co) and other commercial interests before he and his sons negotiated the rights between 1901 and 1903 to manufacture dried milk in New Zealand. Milk-drying machinery was installed in the Nathans' Makino dairy factory near Feilding, and in 1904 they built a purpose-designed dried-milk factory at Bunnythorpe. Their venture met with initial opposition, including sabotage, but by 1907 they had organised the marketing of Glaxo dried milk in Britain. In 1937 control of New Zealand dairy-product manufacturing was transferred to Glaxo, by then a separate company. London-registered Joseph Nathan & Co continued to expand after Nathan's death in 1912, in line with the growth of dairying. (In 2000 Glaxo's successor, GlaxoWellcome — brought about by a merger in 1995 — merged with SmithKline Beecham to create Britain's largest company and the world's largest drugs group, Glaxo SmithKline.)

Like Joseph Nathan, the austere Sir William Goodfellow was blessed with the vision and energy to make the dairy industry the best in the world. But he deserves an equal place in New Zealand as a pioneer of radio broadcasting. As managing director of the New Zealand Co-operative Dairy Co, he applied in the

Sir William Goodfellow (1880–1974) entered the dairy industry by chance and revolutionised it through mergers and new technology. He was also a pioneer in radio broadcasting in New Zealand.
Courtesy *NBR*

1920s for a licence to broadcast to dairyfarmers in the Waikato. Although his application was refused he was later approached by the government to set up a central radio broadcasting organisation with a radio station in each of the broadcast zones. In partnership with A.R. Harris, a contractor who had once worked with Thomas Edison, he incorporated the Radio Broadcasting Co in 1925. But his doubts about the state's commitment to broadcasting were borne out in 1931 when the government nationalised the company. By then, however, it had established a range of services that are still maintained by radio today, such as outside sports broadcasts, and its stations were the first to provide regular weather forecasts and programme schedules.

Radio was an unusual turn in a spectacular career path for a man born to a conventional farming family in the Waikato. Goodfellow was educated in Auckland where his Scots-born paternal grandfather, William (1806–90), had been a pioneer flourmiller and baker, and he entered dairying more by chance than design. Goodfellow's school record was undistinguished and on leaving school he joined the hardware trade. By the age of 21 he was a partner in an Onehunga ironmongery firm. Two years later, in 1904, taking advantage of the dairying boom, he set up a base for the firm in Hamilton. Goodfellow entered the dairy industry directly after a buyer of dairy equipment defaulted, leaving him with plant and machinery on his hands. Anticipating greater mechanisation, he formed the Waikato Dairy Co in 1909 (converted into the Waikato Co-operative Dairy Co the following year) through which he pioneered home separation in the Waikato and developed effective pasteurisation. In 1915 he formed the Waikato Co-operative Cheese Co.

Goodfellow was the first managing director of the Waikato Co-operative Dairy Co's successor, the New Zealand Co-operative Dairy Co (formed from Waikato's merger with the rival New Zealand Dairy Association, owner of the Anchor brand), from 1919–32, and an advisory director of the company from 1932–47. Under his stewardship the New Zealand Co-operative Dairy Co (now part of the country's dominant dairy company, Fonterra Co-operative Group) became an industry leader, providing a quality premium on cream, establishing milk grading, the country's first dairy company laboratory, and a farm dairy instruction service, and promoting herd-testing. The company

Around the turn of the century, dairy factories were the centre of rural life in much of the North Island. Amalgamations started in the first quarter of the twentieth century and have been a feature of dairying ever since. This photo shows carts lined up to transport dairy produce to market. Courtesy *NBR*

acquired its own colliery and box factory under his leadership, and in 1927 he was responsible for bringing lower fertiliser costs to farmers by establishing Challenge Phosphate Co in partnership with Wright Stephenson & Co.

Nationally, Goodfellow is best remembered as an advocate of strong international marketing of dairy produce, and for playing a key role in the government's decision in 1923 to set up the New Zealand Dairy Control Board, the forerunner of the New Zealand Dairy Board. He served on the board and it was only when interested parties rejected the principle of board control that he formed Amalgamated Dairies and, in 1929, Empire Dairies, a partnership between Amalgamated and the Australian Producers' Co-op Federation. The New Zealand Co-op Dairy Co, as the main shareholder in Amalgamated Dairies, also had a substantial shareholding in Empire Dairies, which handled sales of all the company's butter.

In 1954 Empire Dairies, which handled more than a third of New Zealand butter sales to the United Kingdom, was acquired for the dairy industry by the Dairy Products Marketing Commission. Goodfellow and his family retained Amalgamated Dairies whose subsidiary, Amalgamated Marketing, was prominent in major independent meat deals with the Soviet Union in the 1970s. Amalgamated Marketing also benefited from one of the biggest trading coups in New Zealand history — the Dairy Board's bold move in 1982 to recycle 100,000 tonnes of United States butter for the Soviet market when commodity prices were low and US–Russian relations strained. Amalgamated helped set up Sovenz, a joint-venture company, to promote two-way trade between New Zealand and the Soviet Union, which led to Lada cars, Russian tractors and fertiliser entering New Zealand in return for the Russians taking New Zealand butter.

Respect for Goodfellow's contribution to dairying led to his being created a freeman of London in 1951. He was knighted in 1953 for services to New Zealand — the first person knighted by a reigning monarch on New Zealand soil — and in 1963 the University of Auckland conferred on him an honorary LLD degree. He was a generous benefactor to Auckland, supporting many causes including the Auckland War Memorial Museum, and donating 70 ha of land to Auckland Centennial Memorial Park. The Goodfellow name and fortune lives on. One of his five sons, Douglas Goodfellow (born 1917), is among the oldest entrants on the *NBR Rich List* and was, until 1994, the wealthiest. That year the *Rich List* estimated his wealth at a minimum $290 million — earned, among other sources, from long-term holdings in blue-chip companies such as Fernz Corporation (chemicals) and Sanford (fishing), and through the family-owned Amalgamated companies. In 1995 his lawyer said

Goodfellow had given away most of his riches to a range of charitable trusts including the St Kentigern Trust, associated with the elite Presbyterian boys' college in Pakuranga, Auckland, co-founded by his father in 1953. This reduced his minimum net worth to an estimated $15 million (said to be at least $20 million in 2002) — more than enough for him to live on in his remaining years in Auckland. However, in 2002 a court case revealed that the Goodfellow family wealth had been grossly undervalued. The court was told that their company, Amalgamated Dairies, had been valued at $359 million in 2000 and had declared a $70 million dividend the previous year.

Sir William Goodfellow, like Wright Stephenson's Sir William Hunt, is a first-class example of a diligent, hardworking New Zealander who prospered in the brave new world that emerged after the 1890s. He seized opportunities in a commodities boom that started in 1896 and was to establish New Zealand's reputation for agricultural excellence. It has been said many times that World War I was the making of New Zealand agriculture — and the war certainly created a huge demand in Britain for food — but it came at a large cost to the top business and farming families and created unreal expectations for New Zealand's post-war farm-based economy. The sons of the rich were among the first to enlist and they departed overseas, in most cases, with the overwhelming support of their parents. 'Ardour of war was so potent that all sets of the rich united politically for the first time in the history of the [dominion],' wrote historian Stevan Eldred-Grigg. 'The ... dominion army was commanded in large part by wealthy merchants, landowners and industrialists.' All communities rallied to the call for war but support was especially strong among the better heeled in rural areas, notably pastoralists who gave not only their sons to the service of the empire but money as well. Many of the volunteers, especially native-born New Zealanders, joined British regiments related to their heritage. Eldred-Grigg noted of Canterbury: 'Few landed families of the province failed to send at least one son into a British regiment.' But it would be wrong to view the sacrifice of war as falling on farmers alone. Sir William Goodfellow, for instance, lost two brothers, Eric and Gordon, in the Great War and a son, Richard Maclaurin Goodfellow, in World War II (commemorated in the University of Auckland's Maclaurin Chapel, which Sir William funded and which also commemorates his distinguished uncle, academic Richard Cockburn Maclaurin [1870–1920]).

The only son of Dunedin industrialist (Sir) Percy Sargood and his wife, Lucy (née Ormond), Lt Cedric Rolfe Sargood, died at Gallipoli in 1915 aged just 22. Their loss could hardly have been any less than that suffered by Hawke's Bay pastoralist and company director Douglas Maclean and his wife, whose only son, Captain Algernon Maclean (only grandson of the nineteenth-century politician-speculator Sir Donald McLean), died in 1923 of a war-related illness.

The volunteers, wrote Ormond Burton, were 'like young gods in a new world of romance', imbued with a fatal mixture of patriotism, enthusiasm and adventure. They were also under huge social pressure to enlist lest they be labelled cowards. Few weighed up the cost of military service to their family companies or farms, although the impact on the rural sector, where labour had been short before the war, was immediate and dramatic. Conscription was introduced in 1916 as much to sort out the problems of domestic manpower caused by the war as to ensnare shirkers or would-be conscientious objectors.

Even where the soldier sons of the rich escaped death, their absence overseas caused hardship at home. Such was the case with R. & W. Hellaby, where the three sons of the late Richard Hellaby (Fred, Syd and Jack) and the two sons of his late brother William (William and Arthur) all volunteered and all served overseas. This left the company, already bereft of management following the premature deaths of its founders, seriously short of talent. Richard Hellaby's widow, Amy (1864–1955), had two families to look after and in 1914 she sold her elegant Auckland home, Bramcote, and took her two younger unmarried daughters to London for three years, buying a house in Bayswater to provide a home for her sons and nephews when they were on leave. She returned to Auckland to find R. & W. Hellaby in decline but under her direction its fortunes steadily improved.

Those who chose to stay behind to carry out what they considered essential jobs faced military sanction and public censure. Auckland mail-order merchant Robert Laidlaw (1885–1971) appealed against military service on the grounds his firm, Laidlaw Leeds, could not do without him. A Scots-born Christian fundamentalist (Plymouth Brethren), Laidlaw had launched his business in Fort St, Auckland, in 1909, along the lines of the US mail-order companies Montgomery Ward and Sears Roebuck. It had boomed with the growth in dairying and the expansion of the railways, dealing wholesale and on a cash basis with the farming community only, but wartime shortages, delays and fluctuating prices had slashed profits and in 1916/17 it suffered its worst year. Laidlaw had lost his younger brother (and Laidlaw Leeds' first employee), Jack Laidlaw, in a solo flying accident at Hendon in England in 1916, while he was training for a commission in the Royal Naval Air Service. Another brother (and former employee), 2/Lt Arthur Laidlaw, was serving with the New Zealand Division in France. On top of all this, Robert Laidlaw was conscripted for military service. He argued before a military service appeal board in 1918 that

Christian fundamentalist Robert Laidlaw (1885–1971), who set up as a mail-order merchant in Fort St, Auckland, in 1909. His business, Laidlaw Leeds, became the dominion's largest department-store retailer, the Farmers' Trading Co, from 1926.
Courtesy Wentforth Press

his company, employing 189 people and supplying more than £300,000 worth of goods to farmers, would close if he were forced to serve, leaving family and creditors in the lurch. The board was sympathetic — other prominent businessmen and professionals such as James Borthwick, Australasian head of meat company Thos Borthwick & Sons, and Crown solicitor John Tole had been granted exemptions — and it adjourned Laidlaw's appeal sine die, granting him a de facto exemption. One MP remarked at the time that the 'wealthy men are left in this country while the poor have to go' and the newspaper *Truth*, an advocate of conscription without exemption, asked why Laidlaw's brother-in-law could not run the firm as he presumably had during Laidlaw's recent trip to the United States. The newspaper went so far as to find someone to buy Laidlaw Leeds, persuading the appeal board to reconvene. But before the board could sit, fate intervened: news came through that Arthur Laidlaw had been killed in the German Spring Offensive on the Somme —

Robert Laidlaw, as the sole surviving son with two brothers killed on military service, was granted an automatic exemption.

Whatever the merits of his case, Laidlaw's success in fighting conscription paid dividends. He had been prepared to sell his business and, even without the prompting of *Truth*, had entered into an agreement with Laidlaw Leeds' main rival, the Auckland-based co-operative the Farmers' Union Trading Co (FUT). But the sale to FUT in the third quarter of 1918 was effectively a reverse takeover, leaving Laidlaw in the driving seat. It laid the foundation for the country's largest department-store operator, known after 1926 as the Farmers' Trading Co. The turnaround of the business owed much to Laidlaw's ability to persuade the board of directors in 1919 to introduce credit selling and go retail. The passing of the Chattels Transfer Act in 1924 opened the door to non-registered hire-purchase agreements, further increasing business. Laidlaw, once morally opposed to selling goods on terms, dismissed suggestions that the Act would lead to 'wild extravagance' by purchasers. For Farmers, at least, it

The Farmers' Trading Co department store in Hobson St, Auckland, famous to generations of city shoppers. The company was taken over by Chase Corporation in 1986 and the Hobson St store closed in 1992. The building, now the Heritage Auckland hotel, was developed by interests of former Chase executive chairman Colin Reynolds.
COURTESY WENTFORTH PRESS

was a godsend — by 1938 it was claiming to dominate the time-payment business 'in the Auckland province and further afield'. It is doubtful the company would have enjoyed such dramatic growth had Laidlaw suffered the fate of his brothers in Europe. In World War II, however, Laidlaw — by then well past military age — did his duty, serving as field director of the Soldiers' & Airmen's Christian Association in Britain and Europe. This was in spite of a multitude of war-induced problems at home including shortages of stock, lack of manpower and the rigours of the Price Tribunal.

The Farmers' Trading Co survived the war and increased its dominance, despite odd hiccups, acquiring competitors and leading the market with the introduction of credit cards and point-of-sale computer terminals. By 1984, its seventy-fifth birthday, Farmers was employing 3769 people directly in stores and factories throughout the country, earning a profit of $16.5 million on sales exceeding $337.6 million. It was taken over by property developer Chase Corporation in 1986 but the new owner brought few benefits and was a victim of the sharemarket crash the following year, finally succumbing in 1990 with its shares worth just 5c. Chase was placed under statutory management and Farmers was pulled from the corporate wreckage. The last chairman of the pre-Chase Farmers was Laidlaw's son, Lincoln (born 1921), a paratrooper in World War II and a toy manufacturer (chairman and managing director of Auckland-based Lincoln Industries). Lincoln Laidlaw was president of the Auckland Manufacturers' Association in 1972 and the New Zealand Manufacturers' Federation in 1974–75. He lives in Murrays Bay, Auckland. Lincoln's sister, architect Lillian Chrystall, became the first female president of the ASB Bank in 1983. She and Lincoln attended the 1999 launch of a book about their father's life, *Man for Our Time: Robert A. Laidlaw*, which was held, appropriately, in the Robert Laidlaw Room of the Heritage Auckland hotel — the former Hobson St department store and head office of the Farmers' Trading Co.

Farmers was in many ways a barometer of New Zealand's economic health and development. Its launch and spectacular growth before World War I underscored the arrival of consumerism — the age of spending for spending's sake. Its rape by Chase 70-odd years later was but one example of a family-influenced company falling to a corporate raider more interested in property development than traditional business. McKenzies (NZ), a New Zealand variant of a US nickel-and-dime chainstore, suffered a kinder fate. Its business, comprising 75 stores employing 1800 people, was at least taken over by a retailer, L.D. Nathan & Co, in 1980. The name disappeared, ending the McKenzie family's association with retailing, started by Australian-born (Sir) John McKenzie (1876–1955) in Dunedin in 1910. McKenzie, son of a

Australian Sir John McKenzie (1876–1955) founded the nationwide McKenzies department-store chain in Dunedin in 1910. At the height of its success it had 75 stores employing 1800 people.
Courtesy *NBR*

Melbourne customs officer, was a veteran of the South African War who had never planned to set up in New Zealand. He had earlier started and sold a successful fancy-goods business in Melbourne and was prevented by a restraint-of-trade agreement from carrying on business in that city. He ran stores in Tasmania and Sydney, but a holiday visit to New Zealand in 1909 convinced him of the need for a fancy-goods chain in the dominion. The business grew rapidly and in 1936 it became a public company, with 50 per cent of Sir John's shares being transferred to Rangatira, a private investment company formed the following year.

Most young people today would not know the McKenzies (NZ) name, but the family name lives on in the charitable endeavours of McKenzie himself — the J.R. McKenzie Youth Education Fund, established in 1938 with a gift of £10,000, and the J.R. McKenzie Trust, set up in 1940 with £100,000. The trust shareholding in Rangatira was restructured in 1954, a year before McKenzie's death, and today holds 10 million of the 17 million shares in Rangatira. McKenzie, a staunch Rotarian, involved Rotary International in his charitable work. He was also one of the nation's most successful breeders of trotting horses, at his Roydon Lodge stud near Christchurch, to which he retired. McKenzie did not die a particularly wealthy man because, according to his surviving son, philanthropist Sir Roy McKenzie (born 1922), 'he believed in helping others and returning something to the people and country where he had settled.' His estate, worth about £80,000, was left to the Salvation Army, YMCA, Presbyterian Social Services (now Presbyterian Support Services) and the Blind Institute. Sir Roy has continued the work of his father's charitable trusts and established two of his own, the McKenzie Education Foundation and the Roy McKenzie Foundation.

Like McKenzies (NZ), most of the larger longstanding family companies have now gone, but not all. Smith & Caughey, an upmarket Auckland department store, has survived intact, not least because it remains firmly under family control and its shares are not listed. It was founded as a general

Marianne Smith (née Caughey), who founded the drapery store that was to grow into Smith & Caughey, the upmarket Auckland retailer that is still the epitome of the family-owned department store. Similar family-owned department stores in other regions included Kirkcaldie & Stains (1863, Wellington), J. Ballantyne & Co (1854, Christchurch) and Arthur Barnett (1903, Dunedin).
COURTESY *NBR*

drapery in Alexandra St (now Airedale St) in 1880 by Irish-born Marianne Smith (née Caughey, 1851–1938). A year later she was joined by her husband, Methodist philanthropist William Smith (1850/51?–1912), and the firm traded as Wm H. Smith until Marianne's brother, Methodist preacher and former draper Andrew Caughey (1849–1928), joined the business in 1882, creating the Caughey dynasty in Auckland. In 1884 Smith & Caughey bought rival James Smith and with it the valuable Queen St site that is Smith & Caughey's principal store and headquarters today. The firm aimed at the 'good-middle to better-end' of the market, establishing a reputation for quality merchandise and genteel custom. Today Smith & Caughey is property rich, operating a store on Broadway, Newmarket, in addition to its Queen St site. Both sites are freehold, debt free and extremely valuable. The board of the company is made up entirely of Caugheys — eight directors chaired by prominent businessman Simon Caughey (born 1940), a great-grandson of Andrew Caughey and a son of Sir Harcourt Caughey (better known as Pat) who worked for Smith & Caughey for 63 years, 30 of them as chairman and managing director. An All Black from 1932–37, Sir Harcourt served for 25 years on the Auckland Hospital Board, including fifteen as chairman. In 1998 he was inducted posthumously into the Business Hall of Fame in a ceremony attended by several family members including his widow, Mary, Lady Caughey (née Finlay, born 1917) and Simon Caughey.

The Caugheys were first included in the *Rich List* in 1994 with an estimated minimum wealth of $30 million; in 2003 they were listed at $45 million. They do not flaunt their wealth, however. A charity associated with the family is the Marianne Caughey Smith-Preston Memorial Rest Homes Trust, which Simon Caughey chairs. The trust runs homes and a hospital for the elderly (originally for women only) and was set up on the death of Marianne Smith, who left most of her estate and her 47 per cent shareholding in Smith & Caughey to the trust. She outlived her first husband, William, and in 1932 married retired Methodist minister Raymond Preston. She had no children, but she and her first husband brought up Reginald Caughey Seymour Smith (1907?-84), an English-born orphan, although he was never formally adopted. He sued unsuccessfully to gain a share of Marianne Preston's estate.

Smith & Caughey is an oddity — a successful old-world department-store retailer specialising in expensive clothes in an age of swank shopping malls and boutiques. Most businesses dating from the late nineteenth century or early twentieth century have not been so fortunate. In general two common factors have determined their fate:

▶ Family members have moved from direct control of the operations their forebears founded, and their ability and will to resist takeovers has correspondingly dissipated;

▶ The attraction of a share of family wealth long locked up in businesses has proved too great to the grandchildren and great-grandchildren of the founders.

Smith & Caughey is special for another reason: it represents 'trade' wealth. A book by Angela Caughey, *An Auckland Network*, provides the genealogy linking family members in a range of prominent Auckland businesses. This illustrates the ties of blood and marriage that bound an important and clearly delineated section of Auckland's wealthy commercial community in the late nineteenth and early twentieth centuries — a tradesman's equivalent of Thomas Russell's Limited Circle, although the common threads were not property speculation and financial manipulation but religion and business. Companies linked in this way include publisher Wilson & Horton (established 1876, now no longer a family business), builders' supplier and contractor Winstone (1864, now part of Fletcher Building plus a separate pulp company), hardware and machinery merchant John Burns & Co (1881, gone), department store retailer George Court & Sons (1886, gone), meat processor R. & W. Hellaby (1873, gone), fabric retailer Rendells (1882, still a family business), Smith & Caughey, and seed merchant Arthur Yates & Co (1883, now Yates New Zealand, no longer a family business). The two groups tended to be self-contained and mutually exclusive, with the exception of some early Wilsons, who were part of the Limited Circle, and Russell himself. There were, of course, other Methodists who became wealthy outside trade, such as ship's captain-turned-farmer William Potter (1801?–78), but generally Non-Conformists fared better in the urban environment where they could mix work and proselytising with ease.

Most of the Methodist businesses that have disappeared were victims of takeovers in the early to mid-1980s. The biggest loss by far was Winstone, which was started by a twenty-year-old Englishman, William Winstone (1843–1924), at the end of the Waikato War. He had been attached to the militia and his skill with horses had proved invaluable in taking food and supplies from Auckland to army outposts at Drury and Mercer (he even carried the iron ship *Gymnotus* piece-by-piece overland via the Bombay Hills to Mercer). With his younger brother, George (1848–1932), who joined him in 1869, he established a solid business quarrying scoria on Auckland's volcanic hills for use as a base for roads and railway ballast, and stone for harbour reclamation and road cuttings. The firm continued to expand over the next century. In 1982 interests associated with corporate high-flier Bruce Judge acquired more than ten per cent of the company. At that point there were still Winstone family members holding shares. Judge increased his holding but in 1984 his stake passed to corporate raider Brierley Investments with BIL's takeover of the Judge-controlled Christchurch brushmaker, Bunting & Co. In 1987, the year Winstone ceased to be listed on the Stock Exchange, it was ranked New Zealand's ninth-largest company by shareholders' funds, fifteenth by earnings, and twenty-seventh by market capitalisation. It employed more than 5000 people. Among Winstone's many assets was a pulp mill at Karioi in the Central North Island, and Winstone Samsung Industries, a joint venture with the Korean *chaebol*. The Winstone group was among a group of assets BIL sold to Fletcher Challenge in 1988 to ease its problems after the sharemarket crash. It accounted for a third of BIL's trading base. Just two divisions bearing the Winstone name remain under Fletcher Building. The pulp and forestry interests, now called Winstone Pulp International, have operated as a separate company since 1988 and are owned by Asian interests.

A business network that was never part of Russell's Limited Circle or the Methodist-dominated traders was Auckland's Jewish community. It had its own alliances, and its members tended to marry within their faith. This is true, for example, of L.D. Nathan & Co, which can be traced back to the business established by Orthodox Jew David Nathan in 1841. Angela Caughey made this plain in *An Auckland Network*: 'The reason I did not bring [the Nathans] into this book is that, being Jewish, they seek to marry into other Jewish families and are therefore not likely to be an integral part of this network,' she wrote. The same cannot be said of Wellington's Jewish pioneers, the Levins, several of whom married into the Christian establishment. Indeed, Peter Levin, a great-grandson of Levin dynasty founder Nathaniel Levin, married Gael Horton, a sister of Michael, the last Horton to manage Wilson & Horton.

New Zealand's richest family, the billionaire Todds of Wellington, are also in a class of their own. Their empire started in West Otago in 1884 when Scots-born Charles Todd, who had managed a fellmongery and goldmines, opened his own fellmongery at Heriot. His son, also Charles (1868–1942), joined him in the venture and was soon running it. Charles jnr became a storekeeper and auctioneer in 1892 and took up farming in Lawrence and Heriot. In 1908 he imported a 1904 De Dion Bouton car (thought to be a first in West Otago) and in 1912, with his brother, James, opened a small repairs garage at Heriot. His big move came in 1915 when he founded stock-and-station agency Todd Bros in Dunedin, securing the local franchise for Ford cars, and established a thriving business with branches throughout Otago.

A national dealership, the Todd Motor Co, based in Christchurch, was formed by Charles jnr's son, (Sir) Desmond (1897–1970), in 1923 to distribute the United States-made Gray car. Desmond's brothers, (Sir) Bryan (1902–87) and Andrew (1904–76), took over managing the Canterbury and Otago areas respectively. Another brother, Charles (1896–1965), who had served overseas in World War I with the Royal Flying Corps and the Royal Navy, also worked for the company. The Todd Motor Co was forced to drop the Otago Ford franchise in 1923 and after Gray cars ceased manufacture in 1926 it took on the Chrysler franchise. In 1929 it added Rootes Motors (Hillman, Humber and Commer) and, finally, Mitsubishi in 1970.

In 1925 the stock-and-station part of the family business was sold to Dalgety & Co, and the following year the Todds moved to Wellington where the dealership was incorporated as Todd Motors. In 1935 assembly of completely knocked-down (CKD) cars started under the guidance of Andrew Todd at Petone (Todd Motor Industries) — the first of four assembly plants the

Sir Bryan Todd (1902–87) changed the face of the oil industry in New Zealand, first by importing Russian petrol in 1933 and a generation later by spearheading oil exploration. His family is the richest in New Zealand.
Courtesy NBR

Oil finds in Taranaki have been a major contributor to the Todd family's fortune. The private sector rather than the government pioneered exploration.
REED PUBLISHING PHOTO LIBRARY

company would own — and in 1937 the Todd Motor Corporation (now the Todd Corporation) was formed as a holding company for the family's interests. Todd Motor Industries was sold to Mitsubishi in 1987.

Running parallel to motor-vehicle assembly was the Todds' interest in the oil business — ultimately the greatest source of their wealth. It started when Bryan Todd entered the petroleum industry after being denied supplies because of a price war in Christchurch in 1929. In 1931 he formed the Associated Motorists' Petrol Co (AMPC) with the help of friends, the New Zealand Farmers' Union (now Federated Farmers of New Zealand) and car clubs. Its imports of Russian petrol — the first shipment arriving in March 1933 — substantially reduced the price of petrol in New Zealand. AMPC's survival against the majors was guaranteed in late 1933 by government price control, and the company became highly successful and profitable. From 1954 it was known as Europa Oil. In 1972 it was sold to British Petroleum, which also bought the company's 26-strong service station network after deregulation of the industry in 1988. During Europa's independent years, Sir Bryan Todd used his standing to challenge scientific advice to the government that oil exploration would be fruitless. He pressed ahead with a joint venture with Shell and BP (Shell BP & Todd Oil Services), striking oil at Kapuni, Taranaki, on the first try in 1959. In 1969, offshore drilling by the consortium off the Taranaki coast (Maui) discovered one of the world's largest gas/condensate fields. Bryan's brother, Charles, also played a key role in the Todds' oil exploration.

The family's diverse interests, which include energy, communications and property, are held by the family-owned Todd Corporation. The estimation of the Todds' minimum net worth at $2 billion in the 2003 *Rich List* has not been challenged.

Like the Caugheys, the Todds hold firm to old-fashioned values of duty to family and society. They are extremely private, although the activities of the Todd Charitable Trust, established in 1960, and the Todd Foundation, set up in 1972, attract publicity from time to time. These funds, additional to other family benefactions, have made substantial grants to education, research, welfare, medicine, the arts and humanities. The family patriarch, Todd Corporation chairman John Todd (son of Sir Desmond, born 1927), rarely talks about family matters publicly, although in 1988 he told Wellington's *Evening Post*: 'I suppose I'm comfortably off. I'm not really as rich as many of the people on the *Rich List*. If you take the total value of our corporate assets and family assets and things, when you split it up among the number of entities there are, each one, individually, is not hugely wealthy.' John Todd has been more forthcoming in recent years on the activities of the Todd Corporation. In the 1999 *Rich List* he reiterated the old dictum common to many family companies, 'cash is king', adding that 'borrowings should be done only conservatively' and noting that the Todd Corporation had 'worked on that basis ... since the early 1930s'. 'When [we] get a situation like 1987 [the sharemarket crash], we're not in trouble,' he said.

History is on his side. The Todd group flirted briefly with sharemarket dandy Judge Corporation (another Bruce Judge creation, this time from unlisted shell company J. Mercer Industries) in June 1987, taking ten million shares in the company in a 'bargain' placement. Four months later the market collapsed, taking Judge Corporation and other shonky investment companies with it, yet the Todd group lived to tell the tale. Other major corporate investors in Judge were not so fortunate.

No New Zealand family comes close to matching the Todds' wealth; it is the only one qualifying for New Zealand billionaire status. Like the Caugheys, the Todds tend to be straight-laced. Charles Todd jnr was an ardent temperance worker, serving as president of the prohibition lobby the New Zealand Alliance, and of the Otago branch of the United Temperance Reform Council. In 1919, during the national debate over the future of the liquor industry, he wrote a pamphlet entitled *Catholics and Prohibition*. Fortunately, there is more to Todd family history than work and wowserism. Charles jnr was a keen cricketer and rugby player in his youth, and his sons had varied sporting interests: Sir Bryan liked skiing, sailing, golf and shooting; Charles enjoyed horseracing and tennis; Andrew was a keen golfer, and Sir Desmond is credited with bringing the first water skis into New Zealand in 1936.

Similar innovation in business probably played as great a part in the Todds' success as their financial prudence. Early in the twentieth century Charles Todd jnr identified New Zealanders' love for the motor car, and his sons showed equal foresight in their investment in the motor and oil industries. Even in the depths of the Depression, the demand for cars (especially American ones) continued, albeit at a slower pace. The Wellington-based Colonial Motor Co, run if no longer controlled by the Gibbons family, is testimony to this. It produced large fortunes over many years for its shareholders and is among the last of the larger listed companies still operating out of the capital, having survived raids from BIL (1986) and Guinness Peat Group (1996).

The Colonial Motor Co was founded by William Black in 1859 as the Empire Carriage Factory. By 1879 it had become the Empire Steam Carriage Works, and was producing about 40 different styles of horse-drawn carriages from its Courtenay Pl plant. It later became Rouse & Hurrell, converting to a limited liability company in 1902; it issued its first shares the following year to (Sir) Charles Norwood (1871–1966), a Wellington Gas Co executive who later founded Dominion Motors. In 1908 Rouse & Hurrell acquired the Ford agency for New Zealand and in 1910 it sold out of coachbuilding altogether, changing its name the following year to the Colonial Motor Co.

On Ford Canada's recommendation R.J. Larmour acquired a dominant shareholding, and in 1916 this was bought by Tasmanian-born merchant Hopeful Gibbons (1856–1946) and his family. Gibbons became managing director two years later and in 1919 the company was reconstituted with control vested in his four sons. It became New Zealand's first car assembler in 1921, and was so efficient at marketing Ford vehicles and products that the Ford Motor Co deferred establishing its own assembly plant here until 1936. One of Colonial's key Ford franchises was John W. Andrew (later John W.

Andrew & Sons, now John Andrew Ford), one of three appointed in Auckland in 1917. Founded by Papatoetoe-born engineer John Watson Andrew (1869–1949), the business merged with Colonial's Universal Motor Co subsidiary in 1927, giving John W. Andrew & Sons complete control of the Ford franchise in Auckland for many years. Wealthy car dealer-boat builder Neville Crichton (born 1945) acquired the business in 1983 with the help of motor industry magnate Colin Giltrap (born 1940), centring its activities on a single site (first Khyber Pass Rd, then the corner of Great North and Newton roads). Crichton sold John Andrew Ford in 1987 for more than $11 million to Nelson-born car dealer Stuart Bowater (1947–98), who developed it into New Zealand's largest and most successful Ford dealership. It was acquired after Bowater's premature death (from cancer) by the Ford Motor Co of New Zealand.

Hopeful Gibbons, had he been alive, would probably not have approved of the sale of the franchise in the first place. He was a very proper man, proud of the national company Colonial had become but modest in success. He had been awarded the MBE for patriotic work in World War I, been made a commander of the Order of St John for ambulance services, and served as mayor of Wanganui from 1924–28. He would have been similarly upset at the virtual demise of a parallel company to Colonial, cycles and accessories (and, for a period, car parts) wholesaler Hope Gibbons. Hopeful and his sons had bought the business, then Palmerston North-based J. Clarkson & Co, in 1906.

The former Newmans Group, which was started as a carrier and coach operator by Nelson-born Harry Newman (1850–1919) and his brother, Tom (1859–1944), in 1879, was for many years the dominant player in the motor transport industry. When Harry died Tom purchased the shares held by Harry's sons and brought his eldest son, (Sir) Jack Newman (1902–96), into the business, then known as Newman Bros. Jack became manager in 1927, managing director in 1935, and founded Transport (Nelson) Ltd in 1938. In 1952 the business went public with the formation of Transport (Nelson) Holdings — later TNL Group and, after 1984, Newmans Group — to acquire the shares of Transport (Nelson) and Highways Construction Co (Nelson). Jack, the first chairman of TNL, became president in 1981. He was also a founding member, former president and life member of the New Zealand Travel Association, and was similarly active in the New Zealand Passenger Transport Federation and the Pacific Area Travel Association. Newmans, the company he had guided through its greatest period of growth, lost its way in the 1980s, in no small part due to its disastrous foray into commercial aviation with the launch of Newmans Airways in 1985. Newmans tried unsuccessfully to buy the

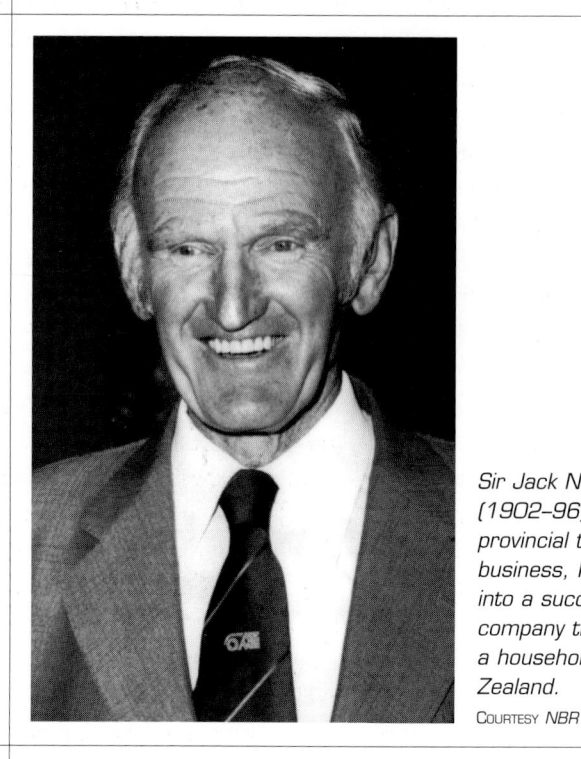

Sir Jack Newman (1902–96) transformed a provincial transport business, Newman Bros, into a successful public company that for years was a household name in New Zealand.
COURTESY *NBR*

Mount Cook airline 'to protect and extend Newmans Airways as a leading tourist airline'. When this failed — Air New Zealand gained control of Mount Cook instead — Newmans developed links with Ansett and Brierley Investments to tackle Air New Zealand head on. Newmans Airways did not survive but its assets, principally two Dash-8 aircraft, were acquired by Ansett New Zealand, providing a base for its national launch in 1987. Newmans also left an important legacy in Nelson — a huge pine forest and Nelson Forest Industries' fibreboard plant — but little survives of the group today other than the Newmans coach brand, now owned by Tourism Holdings.

The story of the Mount Cook Group is not dissimilar to Newmans'. It owes its existence to the foresight of Rodolph Wigley (1881–1946), the son of a South Canterbury sheepfarmer and legislative councillor. He was educated at Christ's College, Christchurch, but was not interested in classical studies and later studied electrical engineering by correspondence. He built a steam engine and experimented with electricity in a workshop on the family's Opuha Gorge station. Not content to be a farmer, Wigley sold his interest in the family property and in 1904, with Samuel Thornley of Waitohi, formed a company specialising in traction-engine haulage and contract harvesting. After investing in Timaru's first Stanley Steamer car, he bought a two-seater De Dion Bouton and in 1906 made the first car journey to the Hermitage, Mt Cook. The trip whetted his appetite for tourism and that year he formed a company to buy Darracq service cars, establishing the Mount Cook Motor Service, providing what is believed to be the first bus business in Australasia to deliver mail.

The firm failed in 1907 due to high running costs but, undaunted, Wigley took over the assets and in 1912 formed the Mount Cook Motor Co. The company acquired the lease of the Hermitage in 1922 and held it until 1944. Wigley revamped the complex, installing electricity and the telegraph, and building facilities for trampers, skaters and skiers. A keen outdoorsman, he made the first winter ascent of Mt Cook in 1923. A related company, in partnership with (Sir) James Fletcher snr, built the Chateau Tongariro at the foot of Mt Ruapehu in 1929, and Wigley also bought hotels in Auckland, Rotorua and Queenstown. He also established the country's first rental car business, Mutual Rental Cars. Keen to enter commercial aviation, he formed the New Zealand Aero Transport Co in 1920, comprising seven war-surplus aircraft. The business failed in 1923, but was later resuscitated as Queenstown–Mount Cook Airways. In 1928 his road transport business, by now called Mount Cook Tourist Co of New Zealand, became a public company. By 1930 it was the largest tourism organisation in New Zealand, and in 1976 it became the Mount Cook Group (now part of Air New Zealand).

Wigley's wife, Jessie, and sons, Harry and Sandy, helped expand the business. Harry (1913–1980), who took over running the business in 1945, was knighted in 1976 for his contribution to travel and aviation — an honour denied his father because of his early business failures. Rodolph Wigley's recognition came posthumously, in 1999, when he was inducted into the Business Hall of Fame.

Rodolph was not the father of New Zealand aviation — that honour belongs to fellow Cantabrian (Sir) Henry Wigram (1857–1934) — but he was the first to identify its tourism potential. Unlike Wigley, Wigram was wealthy, and had a proven business record and the capital to develop aviation. The son of a well-heeled London barrister, he was a substantial businessman and public figure before joining with business and professional friends to form the Canterbury (NZ) Aviation Co flying school at Sockburn, Christchurch, in 1916 (renamed Wigram Aerodrome in 1923). The school aimed to train pilots for war, promote aviation in local defence and pioneer commercial aviation, and it did this without government funding. Training was in two-seater Caudron biplanes, the first two provided by Wigram, and by 1919 182 pilots had been trained and all but one had joined the Royal Flying Corps in England.

Wigram's New Zealand business career had started in 1886 when he and his brother, William, bought a malthouse and brickworks in the Heathcote Valley near Christchurch. Henry went on to found the Canterbury (NZ) Seed Co and a nail factory, and then took over the South Malvern pipeworks and another brickworks at Woolston, Christchurch. In public service, as in business, he excelled — as a leading supporter of patriotic groups during the South African War, as a commissioner for the visit of the Duke and Duchess of Cornwall and of York in 1901, and as mayor of Christchurch (1902–1904) where he revamped the transport system and advanced local body amalgamation. He also presented the Wigram Shield for competition among surf lifesaving teams.

Wigram died childless, but his widow, Agnes (née Sullivan), carried on his activities in public life, and in 1949 presented the Lady Wigram Trophy for an international motor-racing competition that used to be held annually at Wigram. She died in 1957. Wigram's contribution to New Zealand's economic development in the first half of the twentieth century, like that of Rodolph Wigley, Sir Jack Newman and the Todds, was huge.

Two other Todd families — originally from Scotland but not related to the billionaire dynasty — also deserve mention in New Zealand's wealth and enterprise stakes. Glaswegian William Todd (1842–1912), described as a 'man of infinite and dynamic energy', started one of Invercargill's longest-lasting businesses. He pitched a tent there after landing at New River, Southland, in 1863 but was soon off to Queenstown where he opened a store at the height of the gold rush. Before long he returned to Invercargill, where he started work with an auctioneer. Todd got his auctioneer's licence in 1865 and three years later was drawn to Hokitika, the centre of the West Coast gold rush, where he set up another auctioneering firm, got married and became involved in local politics (he was mayor of Hokitika and a Westland provincial councillor).

Todd returned to Invercargill in 1878, resuming the auctioneering business, but his love of minerals remained strong. He led prospective investors to Stewart Island in the 1889 tin rush and later to Preservation Inlet, southwest Southland, where gold had been discovered. In 1896 he joined the gold rush in Coolgardie, Western Australia, but stayed only a year before returning to auctioneering in Invercargill. Todd was noted for his spirited auctioneering style and good humour. He always wore a frock suit and silk belltopper — the Belltopper Falls near Pegasus, Stewart Island, were so named after Todd's hat got caught in a tree above the falls.

The other Todd family, also Southland based, is that of Thomas Todd

(1823–1908), a pious peasant farmer's son from Craighall, Mauchline, in Scotland. He established a brick-and-tile business (Todd & Sons) on the Woodlands clayfield north of Invercargill in 1878, and in 1890, when the clay started to run out, acquired a substantial brickworks at Waikiwi, now a suburb of Invercargill. In 1917 the Todd interests merged with those of the Lambert and McSkimming families to form an enterprise that eventually became McSkimming Industries.

A grandson of Thomas Todd, Sir Garfield Todd (1908–2002), was prime minister of Southern Rhodesia from 1946–58. A minister of the Church of Christ, he opposed Ian Smith's Unilateral Declaration of Independence in 1965 and was placed under house arrest on and off for several years by the Smith government. Sir Garfield's nephew, Jeff Todd (born 1942), is a prominent former chartered accountant and public figure. He was director of the Goods and Services Tax Co-ordinating Office in 1985–86 and chairman of the controversial 1991–92 Taskforce on Private Provision for Retirement, an inquiry that recommended against the introduction of compulsory private superannuation. He is the former New Zealand head of accounting practice Price Waterhouse (now part of PricewaterhouseCoopers). A granddaughter of Thomas Todd, Louisa Todd (1902–92), settled in Russia in the 1930s where she married, brought up a family, compiled schoolbooks, taught, and worked as a translator.

In West Auckland a substantial brick-and-tile business was established by (Rice) Owen Clark (1816–96), who shared Thomas Todd's pious nature, although that is where the similarities end. Clark was from an established family in Great Marlow, Buckinghamshire, England. He had received a good education, including three years in France, and had worked for a London wine merchant and Lloyd's of London before settling in Port Nicholson. His initial foray into farming failed and a teaching career at a Wesleyan school was cut short when the schoolroom was damaged in the 1848 earthquake. He and his wife and one-year-old daughter moved to Auckland and in 1854 bought 56 ha (139 acres) of 'sterile and desolate' Crown land at Hobsonville, on the upper reaches of the Waitemata Harbour. They were the first settlers there, and Clark soon discovered that the thin topsoil and heavy clay made farming difficult, if not impossible. He set out to capitalise on his misfortune, experimenting with field tiles and draining sufficient land to establish a market garden. His business, which would form the basis of a large twentieth-century public company, started in 1862.

Over time the business expanded into a full pottery, involving his growing family — first his eldest son, Eddie (1852–1929), then another son, Rice Owen

II (1855–1905), who took charge in 1876 when his father went on a trip to England. By 1885 the pottery, then one of about sixteen in West Auckland, was producing up to 60,000 bricks a week, shipping them to Auckland, where an office and yard were established. The Clarks proudly promoted their wares as the 'hardest bricks in Auckland'. The business survived the vicissitudes of the depression of the late 1880s, and by 1898 R.O. Clark II was billing the works as the largest in New Zealand and the Hobsonville clay the 'finest in the colony'. In 1902 he built what was then West Auckland's grandest house — an impressive two-storey country home made from ceramic building blocks with a decorative tile relief. Ironwork imported from Australia, stained-glass windows and mosaic-tiled floors gave the house an Australian 'Federation' look, yet the native-timber ceilings made it distinctly New Zealand. It was among the first houses in Auckland to have central heating and remains in good shape today; it is now owned by the Royal New Zealand Air Force and used as a medical centre for the adjacent Hobsonville air base.

When R.O. Clark II died in 1905, his Australian-born widow, Mary, and their two eldest sons, Thomas (1887–1964) and (Rice) Owen III (1881–1969), took over. Thomas became factory manager and Owen business manager. The product range increased steadily, including from 1906 Clark's patent hollow building blocks, but pipemaking remained the core business. From the early 1900s the business came under increased competition from a group of potteries operating a few kilometres away near the Whau River in New Lynn–Avondale, the most serious being Albert Crum's NZ Brick, Tile & Pottery Co.

An English-born stonemason, Crum (1863–1951) had already proved his worth in Ashburton. With capital from the entrepreneurial former mayor of Ashburton, grain speculator Hugo Friedlander (1850–1928), he installed the country's most modern plant and was determined to take the Auckland market by storm. Owen Clark countered by forming an industry combine in 1906 with nine competitors (excluding Crum) to end price cutting and ensure orderly tendering. Two years later he converted the family business into a limited liability company, R.O. Clark Ltd, with provision for other companies to join. It was the start of a slow process of industry rationalisation. In 1927 R.O. Clark Ltd took over the NZ Brick, Tile & Pottery Co, retaining Crum as works manager, and by 1929 the four remaining companies of the West Auckland clay industry had formed a single combine, the Amalgamated Brick & Pipe Co, with R.O. Clark Ltd the largest shareholder. A £150,000 debenture issue was made to finance the deal. Two other companies closed and R.O. Clark Ltd's Hobsonville pottery was shut down and dismantled, with salvageable items being taken to New Lynn. Other closures followed with the onset of the

Depression, and the industry faced a new challenge from Crum who had grown restless working for the strong-willed joint managing director of the new company, Thomas Clark.

According to historian Dick Scott in *Fire on the Clay*, the breaking-point in the relationship between Crum and Clark was the company's recognition of union rights. This proved too much for Crum and he set about re-establishing his business, financing his sons into a greenfields pottery in New Lynn in 1929, the Crum Brick & Tile Co. (It was to last until 1975 when Crum's sons rejoined Amalgamated Brick & Pipe.) The effects of the Depression and the government's decision after the 1931 Napier earthquake not to use bricks in public buildings reduced demand for bricks to a trickle. Amalgamated had anticipated changes, buying an Auckland reinforced-concrete pipe manufacturer in 1930, and in 1932 Crum patented the 'Quakeproof Brick' and sold the sole manufacturing rights to Amalgamated. But the industry's problems were such that Thomas Clark's second son, Tom Clark jnr (born 1916), was taken out of King's College in 1931 to join his older brother, Malcolm (1910–87), at Amalgamated. Staff numbers had dropped from 250 to 7.

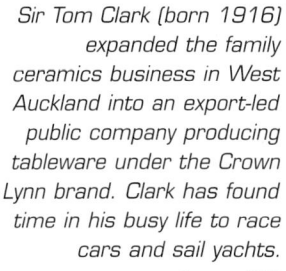

Sir Tom Clark (born 1916) expanded the family ceramics business in West Auckland into an export-led public company producing tableware under the Crown Lynn brand. Clark has found time in his busy life to race cars and sail yachts.
Courtesy *NBR*

Tom used his ground-floor start at the New Lynn pottery to experiment with new products, preparing the company for opportunities provided by World War II to branch into crockery manufacturing. By the war's end a new name, Crown Lynn — stamped on a growing range of utility china — was becoming known throughout New Zealand. The post-war boom was not without problems but new technology and expert staff recruited from Staffordshire, England, enabled Crown Lynn tableware to match international standards. Tom and Malcolm became joint managing directors in 1964 and the company embarked on a bold set of acquisitions. Tom became sole managing director in 1973 and the following year Consolidated Brick & Pipe Investments, the parent company of Amalgamated and Crown Lynn Potteries, was renamed Ceramco (Ceramco Corporation after 1987). Tom, who was knighted in 1985, stepped down as a director in 1993 after more than 62 years with the group, by then shed of much of its traditional business. Today, following the divestment of its fine-clay export operation in Matauri Bay, Northland, and a small microsilica mine in Rotorua, the group is no longer in the pottery business. It is now called Bendon Group, reflecting the success of its apparel division, formed after Ceramco merged with lingerie maker Bendon in 1987. In 1999 the group transferred the bulk of its manufacturing offshore.

As for Sir Tom Clark, he is probably as well known for his sporting prowess as his business success. A prominent racing-car driver in the 1950s, he was seriously injured when his Ferrari Super Squalo crashed in the 1956 Australian Grand Prix at Bathhurst. He was also a superb yachtsman and owned racing yachts including *Saracen*, *Infidel* and *Buccaneer*. The last, a black-hulled 73-ft sloop, took line honours in the 1970 Sydney to Hobart Race. Sir Tom and his wife, Patricia (née France), were for years keen gardeners and hobby farmers, and in 1984 established a 200-ha model farm at South Head on the Kaipara Harbour.

Brewing, like the pottery business, is an ancient trade and, at times, an extremely profitable one. In the nineteenth century it attracted colourful and sometimes powerful figures such as James Speight (1834–87), the son of an English dyer, who worked variously as a debt-collector, bookkeeper, clerk, boarding-house owner and commercial traveller before moving into brewing. In 1876 he led a partnership to take over a redundant malthouse in Dunedin to form a brewery that was to become a city landmark. Speight died of cirrhosis of the liver in his early fifties, leaving his shareholding in James Speight & Co to his widow. His eldest son, Charles (1865–1928), who worked for the firm, inherited his mother's shares and became head of the brewery after Speight's became a limited-liability company in 1897. Charles steered the

Hugh Speight (1904–69), grandson of Speight's Brewery founder James Speight, who became a director of New Zealand Breweries.
SPEIGHT'S BREWERY

brewery through a difficult period of increased state regulation, higher beer duty and pressure from the prohibition lobby. In 1923 he persuaded fellow directors to agree to Speight's amalgamating with competitors to form a giant combine, New Zealand Breweries, to fight the threat of prohibition. His third son, Hugh (1904–69), also worked for Speight's, and after his father's death became a director of New Zealand Breweries. Speight's beer, once a minor brand threatened with extinction, has made a comeback in recent years and in 1999 was New Zealand's best-selling regional beer.

Another Englishman of varied background (sheep and cattle farming) who made a success out of brewing was Charles Louisson (1842–1924). He and his brother, Cecil, took over Christchurch's Crown brewery, the city's biggest, in 1871. Louisson was also a prominent public figure in Christchurch (mayor 1888–89, 1898–99), a founder of the city's Jewish congregation, and a legislative councillor from 1900 until his death (excluding the years 1915–18). His main passion was trotting. He was a member of the committee of the New Zealand Metropolitan Trotting Club from 1893–1907 and thereafter president, and a member of the Canterbury Jockey Club.

Brewing still has the capacity to create and maintain wealth, but much less than in the past. It made Douglas Myers (born 1938), the driving force behind Lion Nathan, New Zealand's richest individual from 1990–93 and 1995–2001. His net worth in 2003 was at least $600 million. A third-generation member of a brewing dynasty, Douglas Myers turned his head start in life into an unassailable lead, barely putting a foot wrong after gaining effective control of Lion Breweries (the company that became Lion Corporation and later Lion Nathan) in 1981. The industry might not be the rich man's club it was when Myers' politician-grandfather, Sir Arthur Myers (1867–1926), was in charge, but Myers has left his mark on it nonetheless. In 1998 he sold his shareholding to Japanese brewer Kirin for $473 million — a sign that foreigners value the trans-Tasman company more than New Zealand or Australian investors — but he stayed on as chairman until 2001. The sale was a turning point for the Myers family, who had entered the industry by chance 115 years earlier.

Arthur Myers was born in Ballarat, on the Victorian goldfields, where his German–Jewish father, Louis, was working as a trader-pawnbroker. The family

Sir Kenneth Myers (1907–98) had never wanted to join the liquor industry, but was forced to take over the family company after the managing director, Sir Alfred Bankart (1870–1933), died suddenly. Myers' father, brewer-politician Sir Arthur Myers, had died in 1926.
COURTESY *NBR*

returned to New Zealand in 1869 where Louis' brother-in-law, Thames brewer Louis Ehrenfried (also a German Jew), got him a job as a travelling jewellery salesman. Louis Myers was drowned in 1870, leaving his wife, Catherine, to provide for five children under the age of eight. Fortunately Louis Ehrenfried, who had lost his brother, Bernard, a year earlier and had no children from his own marriage, was keen to look after his sister's family. Arthur Myers, the third child, joined Ehrenfried Bros in Thames in 1883 as a sixteen-year-old. By the age of twenty he had demonstrated his business talent and had been designated the successor to the firm.

In 1897 Ehrenfried Bros, which had been brewing in Auckland since 1885, merged with Logan Campbell's Brown Campbell & Co to form the Campbell & Ehrenfried Co (C&E). The greater part of Louis Ehrenfried's holding in the new company was left to Arthur Myers, who became managing director of the new company. 'Although only 30, he had become a wealthy and powerful man,' historian Russell Stone wrote in *The Dictionary of New Zealand Biography*. Myers set about reshaping the company and, after marrying wealthy Jewish socialite Vera Levy in England in 1903, the Auckland political landscape as well. He built a mansion, Cintra, which soon became a centre of Auckland society life, and in 1905 he was elected mayor of Auckland. Among other things, he was responsible for the building of the concrete-span Grafton Bridge, the Town Hall, and improved electricity, water supply and drainage. Myers Park, established after he had quit the mayoralty, was created from slum-clearance land he gifted to the city in 1913. Also named after him is the free kindergarten he had built in the park.

Myers failed in his 'Greater Auckland' campaign — an early attempt to encourage local body amalgamation — but proved highly successful in national politics, serving as an MP from 1910–21 and a first-class cabinet minister in two administrations. After quitting politics he took his family to England, leaving Campbell & Ehrenfried in the hands of managing director Sir Alfred Bankart. Myers' premature death, after a series of heart attacks, and that of Bankart in the midst of the Depression, left the company leaderless, and Myers' accountant son, (Sir) Kenneth (1907–98), was forced to pick up the pieces. Indeed, Kenneth Myers had no plans to enter the liquor industry at all but, like his father, did his duty when called upon. He and his new English wife, Margaret (née Pirie), had been holidaying in San Francisco on their way to New Zealand when they received news of Bankart's death. Kenneth Myers had a promising career ahead of him, working in London with international accounting practice Whinney Smith & Whinney after being educated at Cambridge, but his shareholding in C&E left him little choice but to take over running the company. Arriving in a depressed Auckland, he and Margaret set about revitalising the company and setting standards for a disorganised and rundown industry. He did this with characteristic firmness, upgrading hotels and facilities and introducing a rebuilding programme.

Kenneth Myers was appointed to the board of New Zealand Breweries, the brewing conglomerate partly put together by his father, soon after his return to New Zealand, and later became chairman. He joined the board of the South British Insurance Co in 1938, became its chairman in 1945 and served as a director for 47 years. It was one of numerous outside directorships he held. After distinguished war service with the army in the Middle East and Italy (after which he was awarded the MBE), he set about further modernisation at C&E. He introduced bulk-beer dispensing systems from tanks (at the Edinburgh Castle Hotel, Auckland), the first beer garden in New Zealand (Ellerslie Hotel, Auckland), and à la carte dining and machine accounting (Poenamo Hotel, Northcote, Auckland).

Kenneth Myers' business and charitable interests went ahead at a pace despite two personal setbacks — a throat growth that led to the removal of one of his vocal glands and the partial loss of his voice, and a mucky court case in 1976 where he and his son, Douglas — C&E's managing director — were pitted against other family members over profits arising from trading in the company's shares. Fortunately Kenneth's throat growth turned out to be non-malignant, and the court case was settled in 1978 at Kenneth's and Douglas' expense with a $2 million payout to former C&E shareholders — more than compensated for by the $6 million Douglas earned from trading the C&E shares and the control he gained of the company. On the surface father and son came through the ordeal unscathed — indeed, Kenneth was knighted in 1977 for services to commerce and the community — but the court case soured relations with other family members.

The genesis of the dispute had been Douglas' reorganisation of C&E, not least the sale of a prime block of land in Queen St, Auckland, containing the Coburg Hotel and the Strand Arcade, for $3.5 million. After offloading all but one of C&E's aging hotels to Lion in 1971, Douglas became managing director of New Zealand Wines & Spirits, a joint venture with Lion. Under the deal C&E held a 50 per cent stake in the new company, based on its initial $2 million contribution, and ran the business. It proved a highly profitable union, if not an especially happy one. By 1973 C&E's interest was estimated to be worth $5.1 million, and eight years later it was the springboard for Douglas' $27 million raid on Lion, courtesy of a clever put option by which Douglas was able to force Lion to buy C&E's half share in New Zealand Wines & Spirits. This made Douglas' acquisition of nearly a fifth of Lion's capital virtually self-funding.

Lion had its problems when Douglas Myers took over as managing director in 1982 but it had dominated the liquor industry since it was formed as New Zealand Breweries in the 1923 industry merger. Although Myers was not a brewer by personality and education (a BA in history at Cambridge, management training at Harvard), he was very much one by genealogy. The 1923 merger made the Myers family more than kissing cousins of Lion, given that the merger had brought C&E's brewing interests (the Lion Brewery Co, formed in 1916) together with (Sir) Ernest Davis' powerful Hancock & Co and a number of others (including Staples & Co in Wellington and Speight's in Dunedin).

Auckland-based Hancock & Co, with initial capital of £250,000, was the dominant player in New Zealand Breweries from its inception, and Davis (1872–1962), philanthropic and shrewd in equal measure, its undisputed master. He was well equipped for his new role, being the son of London-born entrepreneur Moss Davis (1847–1933), a Jew who had helped save the liquor trade from destruction by turning the 1919 referendum vote narrowly favouring prohibition into a narrow vote for continuance. Moss Davis had done this by leading a campaign in Britain to persuade New Zealand troops waiting to return home to reject a 'dry' New Zealand. The troops voted four to one for continuance.

Ernest Davis had joined his father at Hancock & Co in 1892, and with his brother, Eliot (1871–1954), had taken over running the company after Moss' retirement in 1910. With a controlling shareholding, Ernest had become managing director, building the company into the largest brewing and liquor operation in the country. This was despite sustained pressure from the prohibition lobby, including the loss of fourteen Auckland hotels without compensation after the 1908 liquor referendum. Through Hancock & Co the Davis family controlled New Zealand Breweries from day one but Ernest also wielded commercial power in other industries including shipping, road transport, food-processing and manufacturing. He was also a founding director and dominant shareholder in the New Zealand Distillery Co, formed in 1960. He was easily one of the richest New Zealanders of his time, enjoying a lifestyle and influence unknown to most New Zealanders.

Ernest Davis was surprisingly popular in Labour Party circles, despite Labour's traditional hostility toward wealth and big business. It was a Labour government that knighted him in 1937, honouring a long association with the party dating back to his support for agitators in the Waihi miners' strike in

1912, his regular donations to Labour candidates' election funds and his relief work for the unemployed during the Depression. Davis' financing of the painting of Prime Minister Michael Savage's portrait in London in 1936, when the Labour leader was there for the Coronation, was a measure of his influence in high places. He commissioned several other fine portraits during his busy lifetime, including those of Queen Elizabeth II, the Queen Mother, the Duke of Edinburgh, Baron Freyberg and Sir Edmund Hillary.

Davis' main recreation was yachting — he presented his ketch, *Viking*, to the New Zealand Division of the Royal Navy — but like his brother, Eliot, a member of the Legislative Council, he also shared a passion for horseracing. His horse, Arawa, won the Auckland Cup in 1954, and Bali Ha'i won the St James Cup at Trentham in 1958. The Queen Mother presented him with the cup after the race, and he presented her with Bali Ha'i. It is estimated that Davis held office in some rank in 94 community and sporting organisations, including 11 national bodies. His public service included terms as mayor of Newmarket and of Auckland. A notorious womaniser, he had numerous extramarital affairs over many years. He even left a substantial bequest in his will to actress Vivien Leigh, whom he met and entertained when she visited Auckland in 1962 (he was 90 at the time).

Davis was a complex character, immortalised as Sir Ernest Booze in politician-writer John A. Lee's book, *For Mine Is the Kingdom*. He had taken a shine to Lee, and had even given him a hotel to manage in Rotorua after Lee lost his seat in the 1928 general election. But Davis' alliances went well beyond the parliamentary left. He was close to the secretary of the Hotel and Restaurant Workers' Union, Frederick Young, and the Seamen's Union president (and later Federation of Labour strongman), Fintan Patrick Walsh — characters Lee described as 'gangsters [and] Davis' hirelings'. Ernest Davis was undoubtedly the most powerful member of his family — capable of good and bad. His death brought the Davis brewing dynasty to an end as he was survived by a daughter only, and his brother, Eliot, had died eight years earlier having lost his only son, Trevor, in 1947. Davis' death was genuinely mourned, far more than that of any New Zealand industrialist before or since. 'He was,' wrote Lee, 'a big bad man, a big good man, a son of Adam … His powerhouse activity is an important and unknown part of New Zealand's history.'

Davis' career is as illuminating for the politics of the trade as it is for those of the individual. He was a rich man who supported a Labour Party far left of today's party. Eliot Davis was a Reform member of the upper house. C&E's Sir Arthur Myers was an avowed Liberal, as was Sir Alfred Bankart, who ran C&E after Myers' death. (Sir) Henry Kelliher (1896–1991), who launched New

Zealand Breweries' main competitor, Dominion Breweries, in 1930, had different politics again. Outwardly conservative, he leaned toward Douglas Credit and later Social Credit because of their commitment to monetary reform, yet it was a National government that knighted him in 1963.

Born in Central Otago, Kelliher was anything but a typical brewer. He was a Gallipoli veteran, and had been a hotel owner, Scotch whisky importer and women's magazine publisher and editor before going into partnership in 1930 with the Coutts family who, a year earlier, had opened the Waitemata brewery in Otahuhu, Auckland. Kelliher was confident and rich — he owned a Rolls-Royce by the age of 30 — and despite the Depression he made the struggling brewery a success. Under his leadership Dominion Breweries, a public company, expanded to become a major hotel owner and liquor distributor, challenging New Zealand Breweries in an era of six o'clock closing, prohibitionist pressure and, after 1944, competition from the licensing trust movement. Kelliher retired in 1982, not just a successful and popular businessman but a philanthropist, patron of the arts and supporter of a variety of other causes, among them constitutional reform. His leisure interests included motoring, hunting and travel. Kelliher outlived his wife and son, and was survived by five daughters. His former home on Puketutu Island on the Manukau Harbour survives intact, complete with his extensive library.

The Waitemata brewery remains the flagship (some would say the millstone) of DB Breweries, the corporate successor to Dominion Breweries. The brewery was founded in the face of stiff temperance opposition by (William) Joseph Kuhtze, the son of a pioneer German brewer in New Zealand, Joseph Friedrich Kuhtze (1833–1901). A grandson of J.F. Kuhtze, Morton Coutts (born 1904), directed the brewery under Dominion Breweries' ownership. (The difference in the spelling of the family surname dates back to 1917 when some members chose to anglicise their German name at the time the British royal family changed its name from Saxe-Coburg and Gotha to Windsor. Today, the Kuhtze name has been resurrected as a popular brand of lager in the DB stable.)

Kelliher's entry into brewing in 1930 represented the return of a degree of competition to a trade that had been anti-competitive for years. It came the same year as Albert Crum's re-entry into the brick-and-tile business, and a year before (Sir) Bryan Todd's first move toward petrol retailing. These developments reflected the impact of the depressed economy on business — the need for lower prices to stimulate demand — and partially countered industry rationalisations such as the creation of New Zealand Breweries in 1923 and Amalgamated Brick & Pipe in 1929. The 1920s and early 1930s were hard on business but not all business. New Zealanders had vigorously embraced a range of new technologies over a short period, covering forward-looking sectors such as telegraphic communications, motoring, aviation, dairying and broadcasting. They had even witnessed renewed competition, albeit briefly, in one of the country's pioneering institutions, the fourth estate. The first example was the launch in 1927 of Edward Huie's bold *Sun* newspaper in Auckland, which faced a war of attrition from the *Auckland Star* and the *New Zealand Herald*. It was acquired in 1930 by the majority owner of the *Star*, (Sir) Cecil Leys (1877–1950), along with directors of the *Herald*, and was shut down (not dissimilar to the fate of the latter-day *Auckland Sun* in 1988). In Christchurch the newspaper battle of 1934–35 was even tougher with Huie's 21-year-old afternoon paper, the *Sun*, and the morning *Christchurch Times* (originally the *Lyttelton Times*, founded in 1851) being forced to close after a savage price war. The evening *Christchurch Star*, itself owned by the Leys-controlled Lyttelton Times Co, acquired the goodwill, copyright and business of the *Sun*, and the *Press*, Christchurch's longstanding morning paper, did the same with the *Times*.

The grocery trade had also entered a new phase of competition with the formation of buying companies to help independent grocers battle farmers' co-operatives and price-cutting chains such as Self Help. Auckland's independent buying company, Foodstuffs — later Foodstuffs (Auckland) — was formed in 1925, taking over from the Auckland Master Grocers' Buying Group founded by Heaton Barker (1867–1947) in 1922. Wellington followed with United Buyers in 1929, also taking over from a buying group formed in 1922. Barker founded the Four Square organisation; by 1930 he had persuaded United to adopt it and, by 1935, the Foodstuffs name as well. He ran Foodstuffs (Auckland) from 1922–34 and was a director from 1934–47. In 1936 he launched the industry magazine *Grocers' Review* (still being published), and a son, Phil (1907–82), spent his working life with the Auckland company and was its highly successful managing director from 1934–74. Another son, Reg (1908–82), was secretary of the Auckland Master Grocers' Association from 1935–73 and the National Association of Retail Grocers of New Zealand from 1935–76. Phil's son, Neil (born 1939), was a senior executive with Foodstuffs (Auckland). He left in 1984 after 29 years with the company.

Today Foodstuffs, comprising three regional co-operatives, has about 55 per cent of the national grocery trade and a wholesale turnover of some $4 billion. It covers more than 850 stores under various banner groups — Pak 'N Save, Write Price, New World, Four Square, Four Square Discount and On the Spot service stores — and also services a large number of other outlets through its cash-and-carry wholesale operation, including dairies, service stations, delicatessens, catering establishments, hotels and commercial and industrial businesses.

Foodstuffs' dominance is all the more surprising given the intensity of competition in the grocery trade, not least from Progressive Enterprises which owns the Foodtown Supermarkets chain. The business was established in 1958 when fruiterer's son Tom Ah Chee, Norman Kent and John Brown opened a supermarket near Otahuhu, South Auckland. Ah Chee (1928–2000) was the first managing director and Keith Kemp joined the board soon after. In 1961 Wellington-born Brian Picot (born 1921) became a partner and joint managing director, bringing in family capital and expertise. His father, Frank (1893–1971), a professional company director who had been prominent in the dairy and allied produce business, and cousins David and Peter Picot joined the board of Progressive, now the holding company for the supermarket group, reflecting the Picot family's 50 per cent stake in the restructured business.

A second supermarket was opened at Takanini, near Papakura, in 1961 and others in Kelston, West Auckland, and Pakuranga, Auckland, in 1963 and 1965 respectively. Thereafter new supermarkets were opened on a regular basis,

Craig Heatley (born 1956), whose Rainbow Corporation gained control of Progressive Enterprises in 1986 but lost out to Brierley Investments the following year in a bitter war of attrition. Heatley was to survive the sharemarket crash in better shape than most of his contemporaries. His family wealth, boosted from the sale of his shares in Sky Network Television, exceeded $150 million in 2003. Pictured in 1987.
COURTESY *NBR*

usually about one a year. In 1971 Progressive listed on the Stock Exchange and in 1985 it bought the 3 Guys group of sixteen supermarkets, launched the Georgie Pie Family Restaurant chain and embarked on a $30 million expansion programme, mainly acquiring land for the building of eleven more supermarkets in the North Island. In the ten years to the end of 1986, Progressive's share-price performance was three times the average for New Zealand listed companies. By 1987 Foodtown and 3 Guys had 45 supermarkets in Auckland and other North Island centres, and 5 Georgie Pie restaurants in Auckland.

Craig Heatley's Rainbow Corporation gained control of Progressive in 1986, lifting its shareholding to 43.6 per cent, and the following March Heatley announced plans to merge the two companies into a new holding company, Astral Pacific. Brierley Investments objected strongly, considering the 30-year-old Heatley and his executive director, Gary Lane (born 1950), upstarts. BIL wanted Progressive for itself, not least Progressive's 20 per cent stake in Woolworths Australia, in which BIL also held 20 per cent through its Australia

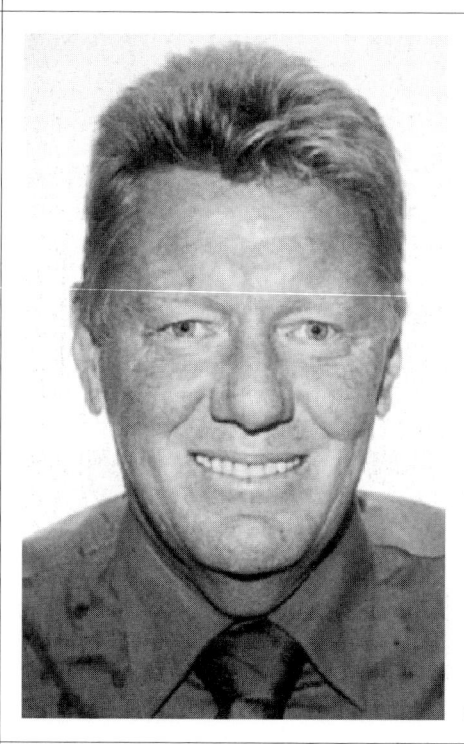

Gary Lane (born 1950) was long attracted to the food industry. His Lanes Food Group controlled the Hansells, Healtheries and Lanes Biscuits brands. In 1986 he was labelled an upstart by Brierley Investments when he was party to Rainbow Corporation gaining control of Progressive Enterprises. His fortune exceeded $170 million in 2003 following the sale of his food business to US food giant Kraft Foods.
Courtesy *NBR*

subsidiary, Industrial Equity (IEL). After a war of attrition, which proved financially debilitating for Rainbow, it was agreed that Rainbow would buy BIL's 13.5 per cent stake in Progressive in return for Brierley Investments taking 30 per cent of Rainbow. In May 1987 Heatley joined the BIL board as a non-executive director but he did not fit the culture there and left after a year to pursue other interests. BIL gained control of Rainbow in August 1987 and set about carving up its assets, just as it had done with Bruce Judge's Bunting & Co three years earlier. Rainbow's prime asset, Progressive, joined the stable of BIL's brewing and retailing subsidiary, Magnum Corporation, but did not stay there for long. BIL was hard hit by the sharemarket crash and in 1988 Progressive was sold to Coles Myer of Australia for $479 million in cash. But Brierley Investments rather than Magnum was the true winner, extracting a staggering $244 million from the cash-rich Magnum by way of a $1.25-a-share special dividend in 1989.

Progressive relisted on the Stock Exchange in 1992 when Coles Myer sold 100 million ordinary Progressive shares to the public. In 1993 West Australian

Brian Picot (born 1921), these days acknowledged as a founding father of Progressive Enterprises, owner of the Foodtown Supermarkets chain, actually joined the business in 1961, three years after it was started by fruiterer's son Tom Ah Chee (1928–2000). Picot brought family capital and expertise to the group and remained a director until 1986. Pictured in 1984.
Courtesy *NBR*

The Rich List*
January 1906

Top ten individuals and main sources of wealth

1. **Townend, Anne Quayle** (1844/45?-1914)
   Inheritance (wool/property)
   Heir to fortune of George Moore (1812-1905). Her gross estate in 1914 was sworn at £796,448.

2. **McLean, Allan** (1822-1907)
   Wool
   Value of estate in trustees' hands on McLean's death was about £596,000 gross. McLean's runholder brother, John (1818/19?-1902), left £213,000 to his nephew, St John McLean Buckley (died 1915).

3. **Hannah, Robert** (1846-1930)
   Shoes
   Built Antrim House, Wellington, 1905 (now headquarters of New Zealand Historic Places Trust).

4. **Davis, Moss** (1847-1933)
   Brewing

5. **Riddiford, Edward Joshua** (1841-1911)
   Wool
   Estate valued at £584,622 gross on his death.

6. **Johnston, Walter Woods** (1839?-1907)
   Trading, wool
   Built Highden mansion in the Manawatu, 1897-98.
   Left estate worth nearly £500,000.

7. **Acton-Adams, William Acton Blakeway** (1843-1924)
   Wool, property
   Estate on death worth £460,000 in New Zealand and England, in property and shares.

retailer Foodland Associated, through its New Zealand subsidiary, Foodland (NZ) Holdings, became a major shareholder, and by the following January had completed its $128.2 million acquisition of Coles Myer's stake, giving it 57.4 per cent of the company. As part of the deal Progressive acquired Foodland's New Zealand interests, principally the Countdown supermarket chain.

8. **Williams, Samuel** (1822–1907)
   Wool
   Estate valued at £429,566 on his death.

9. **Ormond, John Davies** (1831–1917)
   Wool
   Estate valued at nearly £450,000 on his death.

=10. **Rhodes, (Robert) Heaton** (1861–1956)
   Inheritance (wool), farming
   Wealth stems from inheritance from father, Robert Rhodes (1815-84). Built Otahuna mansion, Taitapu, 1895.

=10. **Reid, John** (1835–1912)
   Wool, meat
   Became largest freeholder in North Otago. He later sold part of his land to the government (1908), realising £79,758 from that transaction alone. Twelve children.

=10. **Macarthy, Thomas George** (1833/34?–1912)
   Brewing, investment
   His estate on death was worth £369,689, most of it left to the T.G. Macarthy Trust to offer assistance for 'charitable or educational purposes or institutions' in the Wellington provincial district. His widow, Mary Ellen Macarthy (née Fitzsimons) (1896/97?–1934), remarried but as she was childless, the bulk of her estate passed to the T.G. Macarthy Trust on her death in accordance with her first husband's will.

=10. **Myers, Arthur Mielziner** (1867–1926)
   Inheritance (brewing), brewing, hotels
   His uncle, Louis Ehrenfried (died 1897), left Myers the greater part of his holding in the newly formed Campbell & Ehrenfried Co. Myers built Cinta mansion, Auckland, about 1905.

---

* Dunedin-based clothing and footwear manufacturer (Sir) Percy Sargood (1865–1940) possibly qualifies for the top ten. He acquired his fine Dunedin home, Marinoto, in 1902 and Wanaka station in 1912.

Brian Picot, who these days is acknowledged as a founding father of Progressive, had quit as a director in December 1986. He was less than thrilled at being included in the 1987 *Rich List*, complaining that he was worth much less than the $33 million attributed to the Picot family, and adding that he and his wife, Suzanne (née Brown), held only about 3.5 per cent of Progressive's shares when the *Rich List* did its calculations. (Ah Chee, whose motto was 'excellence not extravagance', had stepped down in 1982 to take up other interests including commercial mushroom-growing and property development.) Picot, a graduate of the advanced management programme at Harvard in 1973, is perhaps better known as chairman of the government-appointed Taskforce to Review Education Administration in 1987–88, whose wide-ranging *Tomorrow's Schools* report was the basis of the biggest shake-up in the running of the country's schools in more than a century. It was one of several public duties Picot undertook, most of which had little in common with retailing.

Picot's contribution to business and public life was recognised publicly in 2001 by his induction into the *National Business Review* Business Hall of Fame. Ah Chee's pivotal role in the business was honoured the following year — two years after his death.

Picot's success in the grocery business did not herald a new age of competition but rather continued a trend that had started in the first quarter of the twentieth century. By 1925, New Zealanders had experienced a taste of consumer choice and credit. Middle-class families had long been able to buy houses, albeit through an antiquated and inefficient banking system, but they could now buy an ever-widening range of consumer goods, on either layby or hire-purchase. What they could not count on after 1922 was economic stability. They would have to experience a shocking depression in the 1930s and put their faith in a left-leaning Labour government before confidence would return. This would mean a change in mindset not just for the public but for the new-age creators of wealth. Some, like the wily Sir Ernest Davis, had guaranteed their interests by snuggling up to the left. Others were soon to discover that doing business with the enemy — a Labour Party founded on the principles of militant trade unionism and Bolshevism — could be not only successful but highly profitable to boot.

5

Wealth and welfare

Whatever the government had done in reforming the economic and social system the majority of the public would have supported: for them the Labour government had brought them from the dark into the light.

DR W.B. SUTCH, ECONOMIST, ON THE POLICIES OF THE FIRST LABOUR GOVERNMENT

Timing was the key to Labour's success in winning the hearts, minds and bank books of the wealth-creators after the party's landslide win in the 1935 general election. Economic recovery was already under way, and many of the new government's measures to strengthen its control over the economic system had been debated or started by the Depression coalition or earlier administrations. Labour's policies appeared formal, even doctrinaire, but in reality they were more evolutionary than revolutionary. Since the time of Richard Seddon the state had been dominant or had acquired significant interests in a range of sectors, including banking, coalmining, insurance, tourism, railways, hospitals and pensions. Labour chose to codify, rationalise and expand that involvement, adding key new areas such as housing and industrial development. The former was born out of a collapse in house building during the Depression; the latter from a dire need to ration foreign exchange.

Labour's ambitious state-housing programme, the most radical of its policies, was to have a huge impact on the building industry, and on one company in particular — the Fletcher Construction Co. Fearing nationalisation, company founder James Fletcher snr (1886–1974) reluctantly agreed to build houses for the government but the contracts proved to be a

The Labour government's ambitious state-housing programme in the 1930s was said to have been the making of Fletcher Construction, but the contracts were so tight that the company lost £200–£300 a house. It was saved only by a £200,000 government-guaranteed overdraft.
MAKING NEW ZEALAND COLLECTION, ALEXANDER TURNBULL LIBRARY, F-2154MNZ-1/2

nightmare because of bureaucratic inefficiencies and rising wages. From the opening of the first house in Miramar, Wellington, in 1937, the company was losing £200–300 per house. It faced annualised losses that year of £100,000 on the contracts. Its cash reserves diminished rapidly and only a government-guaranteed £200,000 overdraft saved it.

The conventional view is that the state-house contracts were the making of the company. Financially they were not, but Fletcher Construction's ability to deal with a government swamped by officialdom and with no experience in the construction industry earned it the unofficial status of preferred supplier. Indeed, the speed with which Fletcher Construction rebuilt the Social Security Building in Wellington after it was razed by fire so impressed Prime Minister Peter Fraser that James Fletcher was co-opted to the war administration in March 1942 as commissioner of defence construction and, later that year, as controller of shipbuilding. This all-powerful job — entailing virtual control of the building industry — meant Fletcher had to sever his business connections during his term of office. His eldest brother, William (1879–1953), took over as chairman of Fletcher Holdings, by now a public company with a turnover of

The Rich List*
January 1936

Top ten individuals/families and main sources of wealth

1. **Davis, Ernest Hyam** (1872–1962)
   Inheritance (brewing), brewing

2. **Goodfellow, William** (1880–1974)
   Dairying

3. **Kelliher, Henry Joseph** (1896–1991)
   Brewing, liquor distribution
   Millionaire in 1930 (before taking on Dominion Breweries).

4. **Todd family**
   Car dealing, petrol

5. **Gibbons family**
   Car dealing

6. **Seabrook, Philip** (1901–72)
   Car dealing

7. **Ward family**
   Inheritance
   Estate of Sir Joseph Ward (1856–1930), mostly shares and land, sworn at £337,000 and shared among his surviving five children. By 1937 the ravages of the Depression had reduced the estate to £275,921.

8. **Wigram, Lady (Agnes)** (1862?–1957)
   Inheritance (business, investment)

9. **Myers, Kenneth Ben** (1907–98)
   Inheritance (brewing), hotels
   Heir to fortune of Sir Arthur Myers (1867–1926). Kenneth Myers noted that the Campbell & Ehrenfried Co, the main source of the family's wealth, was run down and facing competition from Dominion Breweries when he took it over in 1933.

10. **Winstone family**†
    Quarrying, contracting

---

* Pastoral wealth omitted.
† The Fletcher brothers, builders/constructors of Auckland, possibly also qualify.

£2.2 million; his second son, 27-year-old junior accountant Jim (later Sir James, born 1914), who had less than 5 years' experience in the group, became managing director. Long term, this move was the real making of the company.

A grateful Labour government knighted James snr in 1946. It was overdue recognition for a self-made carpenter from Scotland who had set up a small joinery and housebuilding business in Dunedin in 1909. Fletcher Bros, as the firm became after James snr was joined by his brothers, William, John (1888–1934) and Andrew (1884–1950), had suffered more than its share of ups and downs. But James snr, a relentless expansionist, had steered it through the tough times — at the expense of good relations with his brothers. In 1919 it had become a private company, the Fletcher Construction Co, with a registered capital of £25,000, and in 1925 the head office was moved to Auckland. Anticipating the pace of urbanisation and industrialisation, James had expanded the company nationwide, diversifying into brick-and-tile manufacturing and steel merchandising. Fletcher Construction survived the

(Sir) James Fletcher snr (1886–1974), a tough Scots-born builder, won the heart of the first Labour government and was co-opted to the all-powerful war administration posts of commissioner of defence construction and controller of shipbuilding in 1942. He is pictured speaking at the launch of two towboats in Auckland in 1942.
J.D. Pascoe Collection, Alexander Turnbull Library, F-606-1/4

Depression and the Labour government to go public in 1940 under a new name, Fletcher Holdings. But it remained very much a family business. In 1942 the board comprised James snr, his brothers Andrew and William, and sons John (1913–84) and Jim jnr (or J.C. as he was better known). Over time management would revert to James snr's immediate family.

The post-war period was kind to Fletcher Holdings, not least because of the huge construction backlog created by the war and the Depression. The company's ability to deal with the state extended to the National governments of (Sir) Sidney Holland, elected in 1949 and 1951. In 1952 Fletcher Holdings joined forces with the government to form Tasman Pulp & Paper Co, with the aim of utilising pulp from radiata pine for kraft papermaking in the central North Island. This was a huge venture in New Zealand terms, involving the construction of a newsprint mill at Kawerau in the Eastern Bay of Plenty. The initiative rested largely with Sir James Fletcher, although a cocky young Wellington sharebroker, (Sir) Frank Renouf, arranged the underwriting of the 1954 prospectus for the issue of 500,000 £1 shares at par and £2,000,000 in 5 per cent registered debentures — the first private underwriting in New Zealand history.

Sir James stepped down as Fletcher Holdings' chairman in 1968 and became founder president. J.C., managing director from 1942–79 and chairman from 1972–81, made the business truly international when he brought Tasman, Fletcher Holdings and (Sir) Ron Trotter's Challenge Corporation together in 1980 to form what was then New Zealand's largest company, Fletcher Challenge (FCL). J.C.'s middle son, Hugh (born 1947), married to Chief Justice Dame Sian Elias, was chief executive from 1987–97. The eldest son, Jim (1944–93), a former managing director of Dominion Breweries, was executive chairman of Fletcher Construction until he was stabbed to death by a burglar in his Bay of Plenty holiday home. J.C.'s third son, Angus (born 1950), married to former Auckland mayor and former National MP Christine Fletcher (née Lees), was FCL's corporate relations director.

The Fletcher dynasty, worth at least $50 million according to the 2003 *NBR Rich List*, retains a relatively small interest in today's remaining Fletcher operations — perhaps just as well given the former group's poor performance and muddled strategy in the 1990s. FCL was formed as a conglomerate when conglomerates were in vogue. As conglomerates fell out of favour the group tried to reinvent itself, floating or selling a range of businesses that no longer fitted (such as retail property and the stock-and-station business), and introducing letter stocks to enable international investors to place their money directly in sectors of interest rather than in an amorphous corporate. This any-which-way approach fooled the equities market for a time but could not overcome the long-term slump in commodity prices or the effects of poor-quality acquisitions by the group.

By the late 1990s Fletcher Challenge, one of the few New Zealand companies to internationalise and stay in New Zealand hands, was starting to break up. It announced in late 1999 plans to dismantle its letter stocks and in 2000 it sold Fletcher Challenge Paper to a Norwegian paper producer, Norske Skog. This was followed in 2001 by the creation of Fletcher Building and Fletcher Challenge Forests as standalone companies (the latter being the new name for FCL), the sale of Fletcher Challenge Energy to Shell New Zealand and Apache Corporation, and the creation of a new company Rubicon. Rubicon, listed on the Stock Exchange like Fletcher Building and Fletcher Challenge Forests, aimed to 'commercialise emerging technologies'.

Hugh Fletcher, the most public of J.C.'s three sons, was a reluctant chief executive and, unlike his predecessor at FCL, Sir Ron Trotter (born 1927), never part of the big boys' club, the New Zealand Business Roundtable. Indeed, Hugh demonstrated mildly leftist tendencies more in keeping with those of a history professor than a corporate head. That is not to suggest that he rejected

Hugh Fletcher (born 1947) was a reluctant industrialist. As Fletcher Challenge's chief executive from 1987–97, he transformed the group from New Zealand's largest conglomerate to a slimline resource-based business. It was broken up after his retirement.
Courtesy NBR

his birthright — he has long shared his father's and grandfather's passion for horses, for instance — but a flaunter of wealth he is not. It could be said that he has been influenced by his liberal wife, Sian, or lacks the killer instinct required for modern business. This is not so. Hugh has long been a business thinker — he introduced the latest business and human-resource practices to FCL — but he is a product of the era of the dominant state. His grandfather had been drafted into the war administration before he was born, and his father was holding together a public company during that difficult period. Throughout the 1950s and 1960s much of Fletcher Holdings' expansion was courtesy of the government of the day. It is hardly surprising that Hugh should appear less of a free marketeer than some of his business contemporaries. Neither of his sons is going into the business.

The two Sir James Fletchers have been inducted into the Business Hall of Fame, as has Sir Ron Trotter. That honour is unlikely to extend to Hugh Fletcher and he is probably the last person to have any regrets about that. He made his contribution to the corporate world and then got out on his own terms. Not many top-level CEOs have that opportunity or would choose to take it if they did. In that sense, his superior intelligence shines through.

Forestry played an important part in the Fletcher family's rise, as it did in the country's national development. It is an industry that reflects individual foresight and initiative, in some cases as far back as the mid-nineteenth century. As early as 1858 the Canterbury provincial government passed an ordinance promoting tree-planting, and a similar central government Act was passed in 1871. This was followed by legislation in 1874 to regulate sales of native timber, and further laws in 1885 to provide for the orderly management of state forests. The 1885 Act led to some trial plantings but it was 1896 before these took place on the bleak Kaingaroa Plains in the central North Island. The foresters experimented with exotic species, using prisoners to do the planting, and by the mid-1900s numerous species had been established. As early as 1909/10 foresters noted that radiata pine would 'on account of its rapid growth' yield an early return in timber, but the general view was that the timber was of little value, except for firewood. Plantings went on but public policy on forestry took a back seat during World War I despite a 1913 Royal Commission on Forestry. In 1919 a Forestry Department was created from the forestry branch of the Department of Lands & Survey. The department, later called the State Forest Service and then the New Zealand Forest Service, survived until the formation of the New Zealand Forestry Corporation in 1987. Forestry policymaking is now in the hands of the Ministry of Forestry.

Fortunately, the future for forestry was not the prerogative of the state alone. It owes its commercial success to two enterprising young men, Henry Landon Smith (1893–1983) and Douglas Wylie (1892–1972), who founded a bond-issuing company, New Zealand Perpetual Forests, in 1923. Smith, an Australian-born ex-farmer and Gallipoli veteran, met Wylie in Auckland while working as a commission-based share salesman. The pair got on well and seemed destined to do business together despite their varying backgrounds. Wylie, the son of a Scottish civil engineer, was born in Hong Kong and educated at good schools in England and at Otago University before moving to Auckland in 1914 to work for a public accountant. He passed his accountancy examinations with flying colours and by 1919 was in practice on his own account. Smith was also on the move, rising from commission salesman to real estate agency principal and sharebroker.

Wylie became convinced that afforestation with fast-growing exotics would be a paying commercial proposition. In 1923, armed with an option on 1133 ha (2800 acres) of potential forestry land at Putaruru, he and Smith formed a company, Afforestation, with a view to selling shares to the public. It had an authorised capital of £125,000, comprising 5000 £25 shares. Wylie was the interim secretary and Smith, also a director, was the broker for the new company. For their promotional efforts, Smith and Wylie were each to receive 30 fully paid shares worth £750, and 5s for every £25 of capital subscribed, apart from the cost of brokerage. The Afforestation shares sold so well that the partners concluded there was even greater scope for forestry flotations. Wylie investigated forming a company that would issue debenture bonds entitling the purchaser to an acre of land on which the issuing company would contract to plant 680 trees and maintain them for twenty years. The new company, New Zealand Perpetual Forests, was incorporated in 1923, two months after the Afforestation shares started selling, and a prospectus was issued early the following year. A brokerage operation, Smith Wylie & Co, was incorporated to handle the business. Soon bonds were being sold door to door throughout Australasia with the help of slick promotion from the partners, including a publication, the *Smith Wylie Journal* (later called *Wealth*), which lasted until 1928.

Plantings of radiata pine started almost immediately, to match the growing level of investment. But Smith and Wylie's scheme came in for considerable criticism and in 1928 they faced problems from a new director of New Zealand Perpetual Forests, Melbourne king's counsel (Sir) Robert Menzies. He succeeded in having the pair pushed off the board on the grounds that there was a possible conflict of interest because they were directors of Smith Wylie & Co and the bond-issuing and planting company to which Smith Wylie & Co

Amy Hellaby (née Briscoe, 1864–1955) was left to bring up two families after the untimely deaths of her husband, brother-in-law and sister-in-law. She had to manage the family's Auckland-based meat business and supervise the completion of a new house, Bramcote (now Florence Court)
Courtesy NBR

Smith & Caughey, Auckland's leading department store, has remained under family control since it was founded in 1880. Today the board of the company is made up entirely of Caugheys. Forty-seven per cent of the company's shares are held in a charitable trust.
Alexander Turnbull Library, F-99293-1/2

Rodolph Wigley (1881–1946), 'Wigs' to his friends, turned his back on pastoralism to develop a career in tourism. Although he suffered financial setbacks, Wigley revolutionised domestic travel and aviation.
COURTESY WIGLEY FAMILY

Carrier and coach operator Harry Newman (1850–1919) pictured as the driver of a passenger coach on the West Coast of the South Island, about 1900.
ALEXANDER TURNBULL LIBRARY, F-4402-1/2

A Cadillac V53 that served as Newman Bros' coach from the mid-1930s, pictured in the grounds of Nelson Cathedral. For years, Newman Bros was a household name for providing reliable, long-distance motor transport.
RAILWAYS COLLECTION, ALEXANDER TURNBULL LIBRARY, G-3864-1/1

Tasmanian-born merchant Hopeful Gibbons (1856–1946) took over Wellington's Colonial Motor Co in 1916, making it New Zealand's first car assembler in 1921. Gibbons family members run, if not control, the company today.
S.P. ANDREW COLLECTION, ALEXANDER TURNBULL LIBRARY, F-18208-1/1

TOP LEFT: *One-time debt-collector James Speight (1834–87), who took over a redundant malthouse in Dunedin in 1876 to form a brewery that was to become a city landmark.*
SPEIGHT'S BREWERY

TOP RIGHT: *Wealthy brewer Sir Ernest Davis (1872–1962) charmed women and politicians in equal measure. Writer-MP John A. Lee portrayed him as Sir Ernest Booze in a savage novel,* For Mine is the Kingdom. *Davis is pictured aboard his yacht,* Moerewa, *off Kawau Island, in the Hauraki Gulf.*
AUCKLAND CITY LIBRARIES, N.Z., A14458

LEFT: *Douglas Myers (born 1938) was for many New Zealand's richest individual. Although born to money — a third-generation member of a brewing dynasty — he built on this by demonstrating a level of business acumen and tenacity that has left his business rivals for dead.*
COURTESY *NBR*

Industrialist Sir Woolf Fisher (1912–75) speaking to the Auckland Manufacturers' Association. With his business partner, Maurice Paykel, Fisher set the standard for New Zealand manufacturing during the period of import licensing and import substitution.
COURTESY *NBR*

Maurice Paykel (1914–2002), who went into business with brother-in-law (Sir) Woolf Fisher in 1934 to import Crosley refrigerators from the United States — the start of Fisher and Paykel.
COURTESY *NBR*

Sir Patrick Goodman (born 1929) cultivated a homespun image of 'just a baker'. In reality he was as ruthless in business as he was successful. In 1976 he staged a proxy coup to take control of flourmiller-baker A.S. Paterson & Co, ousting the chairman, Alex Paterson. It was the shape of business dealings to come for Goodman and his brother, Peter (born 1933).
Courtesy *NBR*

Sir James Fletcher jnr (born 1914), J.C. to his family, led the post-World War II expansion of the Fletcher industrial empire. He made the business truly international when he brought the family company, Fletcher Holdings, together with Tasman Pulp & Paper Co and Challenge Corporation in 1980 to form Fletcher Challenge.
Courtesy *NBR*

TOP LEFT: *Sir William Stevenson (1901–83) shunned personal aggrandisement and viewed philanthropy as an extension of business. His Auckland-based contracting and civil engineering business, W. Stevenson & Sons, lives on as a monument to his hard work but he is also remembered for his contribution to sport.*
COURTESY *NBR*

TOP RIGHT: *Hokitika-born Sir Jack Butland (1896–1982) made a fortune in World War II by supplying tinned cheese to British troops. But he returned the profits – all £77,752 17s 2d – to the British government because it was 'unthinkable' he should make money when British soldiers were dying to defend New Zealand.*
COURTESY JOAN, LADY BUTLAND

RIGHT: *Sir Robert Owens (1921–99), whose Bay of Plenty canvas-stitching business — launched with £70 of borrowed capital in 1953 — grew into a stevedoring and shipping empire.*
COURTESY *NBR*

Sir Robert Jones (born 1939) was the doyen of New Zealand property investors for many years until his public company, Robt Jones Investments, overreached itself. He is still wealthy personally and he finds time to write books on a variety of issues that perplex him. His centre-right New Zealand Party helped unseat the National government in the 1984 snap election.
COURTESY *NBR*

Sir Ron Brierley (born 1937), looking his age in 1993, three years after stepping down as chairman of troubled Brierley Investments. However, through his new investment vehicle, Guinness Peat Group, he proved that he still retains some of the magic of a corporate raider.
COURTESY *NBR*

was under contract. The issue, well publicised in the Auckland *Sun* newspaper, undermined public confidence in forestry investment during a difficult economic time. Menzies, having stirred up the trouble, quit soon after to enter Victorian state politics and, after 1934, Australian federal politics (he went on to become Australia's longest-serving prime minister).

New Zealand Perpetual Forests was always expected to have a limited life, and as early as 1925 one of the original trustees put forward a plan for converting bonds to shares in a public company to build a pulp mill at the appropriate time. But the move required special legislation to protect bondholders' rights. In 1934 an Act was passed to give effect to this, and the following year a 'realisation' company, NZ Forest Products (NZFP), was incorporated for the purpose. It was chaired by a 'stiff and sombre' (and teetotal) Scots-born engineer-manufacturer, (Sir) David Henry (1888–1963). But it was 1938 before the legal wrangling was sorted out, the assets handed over to the new company and the bonds converted to shares. Wylie was well out of the picture by then but his much-criticised bond-selling scheme had attracted some 90,000 bondholders, raised about £4 million and set in train an industry that would eventually become one of New Zealand's largest and wealthiest.

Wylie had quit Smith Wylie & Co in 1928 after a dispute with Smith over ventures he had entered into without Smith's knowledge. Wylie sold his shares to Smith and other directors followed suit, leaving Smith the dominant shareholder. Wylie continued to practise as a public accountant before launching an independent forestry company, Putaruru Pine & Pulp Co, along lines similar to New Zealand Perpetual Forests. But the venture struggled during the Depression and the bonds were eventually converted into shares and a 'utilisation' company, Putaruru Pine Products, formed. It suffered various problems, including being unable to get a pulping plant ordered from Germany in 1939, but recovered after World War II. It was taken over by BIL in 1964 and liquidated in 1966. Wylie had also invested in New Guinea with mixed success, including founding a rubber plantation in 1938. The plantation suffered losses during the Japanese wartime occupation and through a volcanic eruption in 1951. Wylie and his wife lived on the plantation from 1953 to 1960, managing it successfully until it was taken over.

Smith, his former business partner and a foundation director of NZFP, enjoyed an equally interesting and varied career. After New Zealand Perpetual Forests took over bond-selling by mutual agreement in 1930/31, Smith Wylie Australia (which had bought out the New Zealand company) entered the oil business as an independent supplier, financing shipments of petrol and oil from Romania for Independent Oil Industries. Smith Wylie was forced to take over Independent Oil when it suffered financial problems during a price war, but the industry eventually stabilised and Smith Wylie launched its own brand, Purr-Pull petrol, and steadily expanded. In 1939/40 Landon Smith negotiated a contract with the new Caltex Oil Co, which had been split off from the Standard Oil Co as a result of American antitrust laws. Smith Wylie, renamed Purr-Pull Oil Industries in about 1950, was taken over by public company H.C. Sleigh in 1954.

As for NZ Forest Products, it blossomed under David Henry's astute and energetic leadership — he was also managing director 1938–63 — despite a number of early difficulties including getting permission to import much-needed heavy machinery. It opened its first wallboard factory in Penrose, Auckland, in 1941 and in 1953 a massive pulp and paper mill near Tokoroa. This was named Kinleith after the Kinleith mill on Water of Leith, Scotland, where Henry had served a papermaking apprenticeship. The company continued to expand, acquiring Whakatane Board Mills in 1961 in what was then the largest and most expensive takeover in New Zealand's commercial history. In 1970 Mataura-based New Zealand Paper Mills, a papermaking pioneer established in 1876, joined the group. By the early 1980s the all-powerful NZFP had changed from hunter to hunted, living in constant fear of being taken over — a fear realised in November 1983 when the Goodman Group, a Nelson-based baker and flourmiller, and Wattie Industries, a food processor, raided it, jointly acquiring nearly 25 per cent of the company.

Wattie's, effectively controlled by Goodman, had been a reluctant co-suitor but it was to bear the full wrath of NZ Forest Products when, two days before Christmas 1983, the forester countered with a partial takeover bid for Wattie's. The offer deliberately excluded the 35 per cent shareholding in Wattie's held by Goodman, in direct breach of company law and the New Zealand Stock Exchange's limp-wristed takeover rules. The exchange suspended NZ Forest Products' shares but NZFP obtained a High Court injunction — the first ever against the Stock Exchange — to lift the suspension. The exchange took the matter to appeal and won, but by that stage NZ Forest Products and Wattie's had resolved their takeover plans through direct dealings. Wattie's holding in NZFP was sold in 1986 to an NZFP investment arm, Rada Corporation, formed a year earlier, and the forester's 24 per cent stake in Wattie's was distributed as a share issue to Wattie Industries' shareholders. Sanity had been restored but it was the beginning of the end for NZFP as an independent company and Rada, its would-be white knight, was to be its undoing. NZ Forest Products' sheer size — it was the third largest company in New Zealand by market capitalisation in 1985, and the second largest by shareholders' funds — made it a highly attractive takeover target. It fought off a strong bid from Fletcher Challenge in 1986 but gained brief stability when it merged with Australia's Elders Resources Group in 1988. Elders, however, was beset with its own problems and in 1990 Elders Resources NZFP, as the new company was known, fell to a long-time rival, Carter Holt Harvey (CHH).

Ironically, CHH's forerunner, Carter Holt Holdings, had made history in 1980 by fighting off a strong takeover bid from Fletcher Holdings, even though the latter, with friendly companies, had amassed a majority stake in the company. It did this by a dirty tricks campaign that resulted in its shares being suspended. The bid was finally rejected in terms of the Commerce Act, and the shares purchased by Fletcher Holdings were sold to Alex Harvey Industries (AHI) and National Mutual (later the AHI stake was placed with institutions). The difference between Carter Holt's takeover defences and those of NZ Forest Products was far more than the passing of the years. Although publicly listed, Carter Holt was very much a family company, led from the top by Alwyn Carter (1909–85), known to many as K.C.A. The family was comfortably off on the basis of its significant shareholding in Carter Holt and any attack on that shareholding, especially from the old enemy, Fletcher Holdings, was as personal as it was painful.

The family business had been started about 1895 when K.C.A.'s father, Francis Carter (1869–1949), J.W. Lee and Arthur Wright opened a sawmill at Koputaroa, 7 km northeast of Levin, processing kahikatea swamp timber. Francis Carter, who was born at nearby Moutoa, had earlier been a contractor on the Wellington–Palmerston North railway line. After clearing the Koputaroa forest, Carter and Wright concentrated on a sash and door factory they had opened in 1897 at Mangaweka, then the northern railhead of the main trunk line. Carter set up a flaxmill with R.W. Smith near Taupo about 1900, and with Wright re-entered sawmilling in 1902. The flax venture failed but Carter's interests in sawmilling gradually extended throughout the North Island, mostly the central and southern regions. They included mills, timber yards and joinery factories. Carter, a tough but fair employer who was noted for his strong work ethic, died at Rangataua near Ohakune, where the family had been living for many years.

K.C.A. Carter joined his father as a clerk at the Rangataua sawmill and helped expand the business to supply a growing home market. Under his direction the business grew dramatically after 1951, when he combined the family's separate milling interests into one public company, Carter Consolidated, using the funds generated to venture into the new exotic radiata pine

Old-world industrialists Sir Richard Carter, right, and his twin brother, Ken. They borrowed heavily in the 1980s to expand the family company, Carter Holt Holdings, into a major industrial and forestry concern. Ultimately the debt burden proved crippling, costing the brothers control of the group. COURTESY *NBR*

industry. In 1969, in the face of strong opposition from NZ Forest Products, Fletcher Holdings and the then independent Tasman Pulp & Paper Co, Carter Consolidated negotiated rights from the government to mill the Kaingaroa State Forest, some six million cubic metres of wood. It was on the strength of this concession that the company negotiated a joint venture with the Japanese partners of Oji Paper Co and Sanyo Pulp to establish a pulp mill (Pan Pac) at Whirinaki, near Napier.

In 1971 the company more than doubled in size by merging with Hawke's Bay-based Robert Holt & Sons, a business formed by timber merchant Robert Holt (1832/33?–1909) in 1859 and converted to a limited company in 1929. Carter Holt later became involved in the near-bankrupt Nelson-based fishing company Sealord Products, turning the company around within five years (it sold this interest in 1992). In 1983 Carter Holt joined forces with Alex Harvey Industries (AHI) in a non-threatening partnership to buy fibreboard manufacturer Canterbury Timber Products and diversified wood-products manufacturer Henderson & Pollard. AHI's origins were in a business started in 1886

> Scots-born Alexander Harvey (1841–1919), who abandoned his Te Puke farm after it was covered by ash from the Mt Tarawera eruption in 1886. He went into business in Auckland with his three sons, making, among other things, cream churns. It was the start of New Zealand's largest diversified manufacturing group.
> COURTESY SWEENEY VESTY

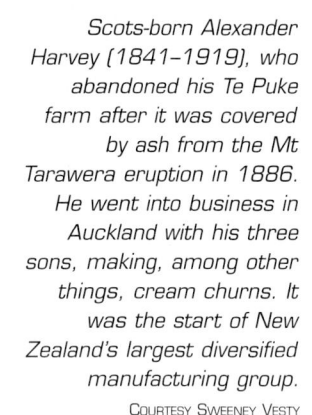

when Scots-born Alexander Harvey (1841–1919) abandoned his farm in Te Puke following the Mt Tarawera eruption and went into business in Auckland with his three sons, making tin cans and later cream churns. Alex Harvey & Sons expanded over the next century into New Zealand's largest diversified manufacturing group, becoming a major corporation in 1969 when it merged with the New Zealand interests of Australian Consolidated Industries (ACI), leaving ACI with a controlling stake in the company. In 1985 New Zealand's fourth-largest public company was created when the executive chairman of Carter Holt Holdings, (Sir) Richard Carter (K.C.A.'s son), paid more than $300 million for the AHI shares owned by ACI International of Australia. The deal gave Carter Holt 86 per cent control of AHI, and followed earlier transactions in which Carter Holt had outlaid $150 million in cash and shares to minority shareholders in AHI. This was just the start of the big deals. Uncertain of the government's intentions over its ownership of state forests, Richard Carter's twin brother, managing director Ken Carter, turned to Chile, and by late 1986 the enlarged company, Carter Holt Harvey, had taken a 30 per cent stake in the forest products conglomerate, Compañia de Petroleos de Chile (Copec). Next came the $300 million acquisition in 1989 of battle-scarred tissue-maker

Caxton Group, owned by reclusive multimillionaire John Spencer. That year also signalled the start of CHH's acquisition of New Zealand's state forests. In 1990 came Elders Resources NZFP.

In buoyant times the debt required to finance these acquisitions and investments might have been manageable but the country had been badly wounded by the 1987 sharemarket crash and the economy remained depressed until well into 1991. Richard and Ken Carter, holding more than 20 per cent of CHH through their debt-laden private company, Krondor Corporation, hung on as other debt-laden companies crashed around them. The apparent solution came in May 1990 during Carter Holt Harvey's long-winded takeover of Elders Resources NZFP. Brierley Investments, which Carter Holt Harvey had joined in a printing and packaging venture five years earlier, took a 4.7 per cent stake in CHH in return for $30.5 million cash. BIL soon topped up its stake with shares from Krondor, with the blessing of the Carter twins (with a put option for more), and by August that year, allowing for its 2–3 per cent holding in Elders Resources NZFP, it had up to 14 per cent of the merged company-to-be. This eased Krondor's debt problem, allowing CHH a free hand in the Elders Resources NZFP takeover, and the Carter twins were at pains to paint BIL's involvement as benign. That it was not. In November 1991 the United States-based forestry giant, International Paper, in a joint venture with BIL, bought a 32 per cent stake in Carter Holt Harvey. In April 1992 Richard and Ken Carter resigned, the ultimate casualties of an overly ambitious acquisition diet.

K.C.A. Carter was not alive to witness his sons' exit from the business he had battled for much of his working life to keep in family hands. He would no more have approved of Americans running Carter Holt Harvey than the Fletcher family. But Sir Richard Carter — he was knighted in 1992 — and Ken Carter, perhaps the last of the homespun corporate executives, cannot be counted as failures. Their gambles with the Alex Harvey takeover and other acquisitions made sense at the time and might have worked had not the sharemarket crash intervened. They were not part of the smart-money set of the 1980s. Indeed, Richard described the merchant bankers and property developers who ditched traditional loyalties and embraced Rogernomics — the free-market economic philosophy of Labour Finance Minister (Sir) Roger Douglas — as 'traitors to the country'. Today Sir Richard has mellowed a little. He has a range of small-business interests, including some in forestry, but his biggest involvement was as chairman of Ports of Auckland, a job he did well in the face of stiff competition from other ports. He and Ken's collective wealth probably exceeds $40 million. Like most twins, they are close. In their case there is an added bond: Richard received a kidney from Ken in the 1970s after Richard's kidneys were damaged by hepatitis.

Sir Richard and Ken are also fortunate to be able to witness their old company playing a major role in the industry it helped mould. Had Sir James Doig (1913–84) been alive today, he would not have been amused. His old group, UEB Industries, was dismembered after an unfortunate takeover in 1987 by investment company New Zealand Equities, lured by the attraction of UEB's overfunded pension scheme. New Zealand Equities proved to be the epitome of the corporate asset-stripper, selling the group off in bits with scant regard for its proud history in packaging and carpetmaking. It would have walked off with $21 million from the pension fund had not the Court of Appeal intervened. The irony is that New Zealand Equities, formed in 1984 after Avon Carpenter and Peter J. Francis gained control of listed Canterbury roading contractor Farrier-Waimak, had itself failed by the time the matter went to court. (The litigation was brought by its hard-nosed receiver, Michael Stiassny, better known as 'the Terminator' or 'Rambo'.) The only asset New Zealand Equities had helped increase during its short involvement with UEB was the pension fund and it did this by sacking staff and closing divisions. When the pension scheme closed in 1988 as part of New Zealand Equities' 'restructuring', the $21 million 'surplus' was shown as an asset in UEB's balance sheet.

This was a far cry from UEB's glory days as a manufacturer committed to taking New Zealand expertise to the world. Even in 1987, when the group was under pressure, there were 40 plants making paperboard and flexible packaging, all-wool carpet and carpet yarn, wall coverings and furniture. Exports were going to some 40 countries. At its peak UEB employed 3300 people and ran smoothly with the benefit of a modern, decentralised management structure. (Two of its top executives in the textile division were to become prominent public figures in their own right — the export manager from 1969–70, Jim Anderton, later Alliance party leader and deputy prime minister; and his boss, general manager (marketing) 1967–72, Gordon Dryden, also a broadcaster and publisher.) In its better days UEB encapsulated the vision of Jim Doig, the hard-drinking Glaswegian and former Merchant Navy officer who founded the company in 1947 as United Empire Box to manufacture cartons and boxes. Doig, who was knighted in 1970, maintained the tradition of Auckland knights of industry (one that is alive to this day) of living at the city's richest address — Paritai Dr, Orakei.

UEB, like many other manufacturers, was a product of the first Labour government's activist industry policy which started with the introduction of the Industrial Efficiency Act in 1936. The Act, which set up a Bureau for

Industry, was vigorously opposed by the opposition amid claims that it would be a shackle on free enterprise. In reality, for those industrialists willing to play the government's game, including prominent ones such as the Todd family (petrol and motor-vehicle assembly), James Fletcher snr (construction) and Ernest Davis (liquor), the long-term benefits were good even if bureaucracy and regulations were frustrating along the way. For small or would-be manufacturers the Labour government offered similar stimulus, if not directly, through its public works and state-housing schemes.

Firth Concrete Co, a tiny Waikato-based business run by the son and grandsons of the failed nineteenth-century businessman-speculator Josiah Firth, owed its expansion to Labour's public spending. Other industries as diverse as whiteware, electrical appliances, tyres and toiletries were to be even more directly affected after 1938 when, in response to a rapid fall in overseas funds, the government introduced comprehensive import and export licensing and embarked on a 'buy New Zealand goods' campaign. Prime Minister Michael Savage spoke of a 'scientific selection of imports', a polite way of telling the world New Zealand had sealed its trade borders. Importers initially howled at the controls but soon discovered that having access to a limited number of import licences had the potential to be far more profitable than the former free market. Consumers would have to accept a limited selection of imported goods, at prices they could not influence. Hence, some of the biggest fortunes were made by those once morally and politically opposed to state intervention in the economy. The heavily regulated liquor industry, notable for its scruffy bars, shabby accommodation and poor work practices, recovered after the Depression to enjoy a level of profitability brewers and hoteliers would kill for today. This was apparent in evidence given to the 1945 Royal Commission on Licensing, and had changed little after the first community-owned liquor franchise, the Invercargill Licensing Trust, opened its doors the previous year. The fact that the liquor trade had not been deemed essential by the government in World War II served only to delay much-needed redevelopment and restrict competition further. After the war it was relatively easy for the two main players, New Zealand Breweries and Dominion Breweries, to increase their market dominance to the point where by 1955 they shared about 82 per cent of New Zealand's beer production. They were simply building on a platform created by the industrial policy of the first Labour government.

Among the manufacturing businesses spawned by this policy was Fisher & Paykel Industries, an innovative group that adapted to change better than most, especially after the removal of tariff protection in the 1980s. It owes its success to the foresight and flexibility of its founders, brothers-in-law (Sir)

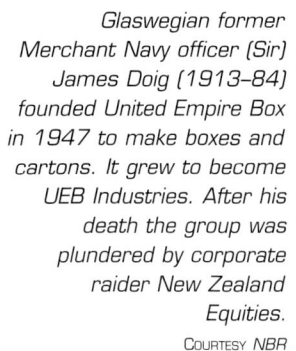

Glaswegian former Merchant Navy officer (Sir) James Doig (1913–84) founded United Empire Box in 1947 to make boxes and cartons. It grew to become UEB Industries. After his death the group was plundered by corporate raider New Zealand Equities.
Courtesy NBR

Woolf Fisher (1912–75) and Maurice Paykel (1914–2002). The pair, prominent members of Auckland's Jewish community, worked for Paykel Bros, a private company co-founded by Maurice's father, George (1886–1945), before setting up on their own in 1934 to import Crosley refrigerators from the United States. The idea came from Maurice's mother, who had imported one of the refrigerators after reading an advertisement in the *Ladies' Home Journal*. Business picked up as the economy shrugged off the Depression, but Fisher & Paykel's big break came in 1938 when it won the Kelvinator franchise which included commercial fridges. By this stage the business was also importing Maytag washing machines and starting to assemble Pilot radios. In December that year, however, the government imposed draconian import controls, virtually killing the business overnight, and Fisher & Paykel had the stark choice of closing down or making its own fridges and washing machines. Without facilities or money it sought local help from manufacturer Alex Harvey & Sons and foundry operator Mason & Porter, and in 1939 it was producing product for the local market. (This was another feather in the cap of Mason & Porter which had produced its first Masport power mower in 1938 and had been asked by the government to meet the whole country's lawnmowing needs.) The war made so-called non-essential manufacturing difficult but Fisher & Paykel survived and by 1945 it was well established, necessitating a move to larger premises. Fisher & Paykel continued to expand by manufacturing under licence and through its acquisition of 50 per cent of troubled Dunedin-based stovemaker H.E. Shacklock, and it moved again, this time to a purpose-built plant in the Auckland suburb of Mt Wellington (beside Mason & Porter). In 1957 the company set up Allied Industries to make Murphy radios, radiograms and, after 1960, television sets. Fisher & Paykel became an exporter of manufactured appliances from 1966, and in 1971 struck a deal with Matsushita Electric Co of Japan which led to local manufacture, import and marketing of electronic products under the National, Panasonic and Technics brands.

Sir Woolf Fisher, the eldest of three sons of a Paraparaumu shopkeeper, had once remarked that 'today's luxuries are tomorrow's necessities' and he was proved right. This great Kiwi success story was controlled by the Fisher and Paykel families until it was floated publicly in 1979. In 2001 Fisher & Paykel Industries was split into Fisher & Paykel Appliances and Fisher & Paykel Healthcare as part of a major restructuring of the group. Maurice Paykel's son, Gary (born 1942), became executive chairman of Fisher & Paykel Appliances and chairman of Fisher & Paykel Healthcare.

Fisher is remembered primarily for his industrial interests (Fisher & Paykel and the formation of New Zealand Steel) but his love of horses — both breeding and racing them — was an equally important part of his life. He established Ra Ora stud in Mt Wellington shortly after World War II, moving it to nearby East Tamaki in 1962. He was president of the Auckland Polo Club from 1957–62 and of the Auckland Racing Club from 1973 until his death. He and his wife, Joyce, Lady Fisher (Maurice Paykel's sister), had no children, but he helped set up the Outward Bound course at Anakiwa and was president of the Outward Bound Trust of New Zealand from 1961–63. His name survives in the Woolf Fisher Trust, a charitable foundation that provides travelling fellowships for teachers and school principals.

In 1934 Fisher's younger brother, Lou (1913–77), established L.J. Fisher & Co, which became a major building supplier, producing Decramastic roofing from 1953. It was sold to Alex Harvey & Sons in 1969 but the Fisher Windows brand remains. Lou created the Sunny Hills estate, Pakuranga, in 1960, by subdividing a 56-ha (138-acre) dairy farm he had bought for about £3000 before serving overseas in World War II. The balance of the estate, some 10.9 ha (26.9 acres), was sold in 1987, a decade after his death, to Auckland property developer-financier Hilton Lowndes (born 1923) for $8.1 million — then an auction record for an Auckland residential property. The nearby mansion of Lou Fisher's son, Stephen Fisher (born 1948), was sold to a Canadian buyer at the same auction for $1.35 million, a huge sum for a house purchase at that time. Lowndes, the free-wheeling nephew of international finance and insurance magnate Noble Lowndes, had planned an exclusive 20-house high-security 'walled village' for the site, but planning problems forced him to settle for a more conventional 78-plot subdivision.

These days Stephen Fisher lives with his wife, Virginia, whom he married in 1976, in a magnificent waterfront home at Herne Bay, Auckland. They have one son, Benjamin (born 1979). Stephen Fisher is managing director of investment company Fisher International and has a range of other business, cultural, charitable and sporting interests. He represented New Zealand at yachting between 1971 and 1978, and is chairman of the Spirit of Adventure Trust (his father donated the 90-ft auxiliary ketch, *Spirit of Adventure*, to the youth of New Zealand in 1973).

Sir Woolf's youngest brother, Gus (born 1920), is an art connoisseur with a collection that includes Hoyte, Gully, Blomfield, Goldie, Hodgkins and Nerli. He made his fortune in the textile and fashion business, notably El-Jay (NZ), a company set up by Lou Fisher in the 1930s. A nephew of Sir Woolf Fisher, Noel Robinson (born 1944), owns Auckland-based manufacturer Robinson Industries. He was on the *Rich List* from 1995 until 1998, when his net worth was reassessed as being less than $10 million — the then threshold for entry to the list. The Fisher family was included collectively in the 1987 and 1988 *Rich Lists* (a minimum net worth of $50 million and $60 million respectively) but has not appeared since. The Paykel family remains on the list at $40 million minimum net worth. Gary Paykel and his wife, Dorothy (née Bone), live in a grand home on Paritai Dr, Orakei.

Sir Woolf Fisher and Maurice Paykel have been inducted into the Business Hall of Fame — Fisher posthumously as an inaugural laureate in 1994 and Paykel in 1998. It was a tribute to two modest achievers who did more than their share for New Zealand. Auckland-born Paykel, who was awarded the CBE, was Outward Bound Trust president, a member of the New Zealand Inventions Development Authority from 1968–74, a member and chairman of the Medical Research Council, and active in the Laura Fergusson Trust for Disabled Persons. Like Fisher, he had a passion for horseracing. Business and benefactions aside, the Fisher and Paykel families have generally escaped the publicity that normally attaches to the rich, as have the Porters of Mason & Porter (Masport).

The same could not be said for canner Sir James Wattie (1902–74) or movie-theatre entrepreneur Sir Robert Kerridge (1901–79). Wattie was accused many times of being a monopolist and profiteer, and the colourful Kerridge was the subject of considerable gossip about his three marriages and glamorous lifestyle.

Wattie's greatest critic was the vocal housewives' lobby, Campaign Against Rising Prices (Carp). As illogical and unsophisticated as its claims might have been, Carp needled Sir James and his business at a time when good corporate citizenship carried weight with the government of the day. Wattie's had benefited greatly from import licensing and tariff protection, and was mindful of any suggestion that it might be abusing its market dominance. During the inflationary 1970s Carp's concerns were echoed by Labour Prime Minister Norman Kirk, contributing to a political climate that later allowed the National government of (Sir) Robert Muldoon to impose nationwide wage and price controls. To be sure, Wattie's had prospered from inflation, but the criticism of Sir James was unfair. He was well off but not rich on the scale of Kenneth

Despite being labelled a monopolist and profiteer by the anti-price rise lobby Carp, food magnate Sir James Wattie was a down-to-earth boss who knew many of his workers by their first names. In this photo from 1972, Wattie, extreme right, is acknowledging the long service of three company employees.
EVENING POST COLLECTION, ALEXANDER TURNBULL LIBRARY, F-147314-1/2

Myers or the late Sir Ernest Davis. 'Sir James and Lady Wattie lived modestly,' wrote former J. Wattie Canneries company secretary David Irving. 'Sir James had few vanities. He owned a few racehorses and his horse, Even Stevens, won the Melbourne Cup in 1962 [it also won the Caulfield Cup that year] ... He acquired a Bentley but would have nothing to do with a chauffeur.'

Today the Wattie name lives on not through Sir James' wealth but as part of Heinz Wattie's, the company created when the American food giant H.J. Heinz Co took over Wattie Foods in 1992. It was not love of rugby that persuaded the Heinz chief executive, former Lions and Irish rugby international Dr Tony O'Reilly, that New Zealand should be the centrepoint for his expansion down under. Rather, it was his confidence in Wattie's, a company he had wanted to buy for twenty years, that won the day. The only regret about the $567 million purchase was that Sir James was not alive to see it — although he and O'Reilly could not have been more different, he would certainly have approved.

James Wattie was a self-made man. He was born at Hawarden, in North Canterbury, and as a thirteen-year-old moved with his parents to Hawke's Bay where they took up a small block of land for farming. He started work running errands at the Hawke's Bay Fruit, Produce & Cool Storage Co before joining the Post & Telegraph Department as a telegraph messenger. But an eye problem stopped him getting a fulltime job there and he joined the Hawke's Bay Farmers' Meat Co as a clerk, studying accountancy part time and rising to assistant accountant. After a brief period as an accountant for a local department store he became secretary of Hawke's Bay Fruitgrowers in 1925 and was soon promoted to manager. While there he developed the idea of setting up a canning factory to handle a jam contract from an Auckland firm. In 1934 it became a reality when, with accountant-partner Harold Carr, he formed a syndicate and leased a small cottage from Hawke's Bay Fruitgrowers for the purpose. J. Wattie Canneries was registered soon after, with Wattie as managing director and Carr as secretary. Success was swift, helped in no small way by World War II contracts to supply dehydrated foods to New Zealand and American forces. In 1947 the company started quick-freezing vegetables, a process that was to lead to spectacular economic development in Hawke's Bay and Poverty Bay. In 1951 a branch factory opened in Gisborne with the idea of using produce from the fertile Poverty Bay flats in the way that had proved so successful with the Heretaunga flats near Hastings. In 1956 the National government, impressed by James Wattie's skills, arranged for him to visit the Cook Islands to investigate setting up a canning industry there. In 1957 his New Zealand operation produced its first cans of Wattie's baby food, a product that was to become as well known in Kiwi households as rugby football.

Size was everything in the food market and in 1968 Wattie's merged with General Foods Corporation (NZ), which had grown from the Tip Top Ice Cream Manufacturing Co formed in 1936. In 1969 the enlarged group absorbed Cropper-NRM, a cereals and starch manufacturer that dated back to an Invercargill flour mill established by Thomas Fleming (1848–1930) in 1879. By the time Wattie Industries was formed as a parent company in 1971, its subsidiaries and interests throughout the country, in Australia, Fiji and Japan, made it the largest New Zealand-owned food-processing group. The company increased its penetration and acquired interests in the meat industry (the ill-fated Waitaki International) and in the 1980s became intertwined with baker/flourmiller Goodman Group (later Goodman Fielder) to become part of a major Australasian company, Goodman Fielder Wattie, in 1987. Fortunately the Wattie name — and the New Zealand identity — survived. When Heinz took over in 1992 Sir James had been dead for eighteen years and his sons, Gordon (former managing director of Wattie Industries) and Ray (former managing director of J. Wattie Foods), had long retired. Yet Sir James' reputation as a benevolent if idiosyncratic employer lived on. Hastings workers remembered how he knew all their first names, and he was admired for looking after retired workers, including making regular payments to some who had not paid into the company superannuation scheme. He was famous for his maxim: 'The only time success comes before work is in the dictionary.' The officiating minister at his funeral described Sir James as a 'tycoon with a common touch'. Tycoon was probably too strong a word, although he could be tough when he wanted to be. A portrait by W.A. Sutton was described by journalist Selwyn Parker as unflattering, 'showing a pair of gimlet eyes, pugnacious jaw, florid complexion and rather large head'. Yet this was the man who, with his company, was the founding sponsor of New Zealand's largest literary contest, the Wattie Book Awards, which ran for 25 years.

If Sir James was a tycoon he was small fry compared with baker brothers Sir Patrick Goodman (born 1929) and Peter Goodman (born 1933), the so-called 'Beagle Boys' from Motueka who founded the Goodman Group. Back in 1968, when Wattie's merged with General Foods, the Wattie family's share-holding in the company bearing their name was less than one per cent. The Goodman brothers were already well on the way to becoming super-rich by then. The Goodmans had started out modestly enough, joining the family bakery in Motueka, a firm dating back to 1843. In 1968 they formed Quality Bakers of New Zealand, a corporate grouping of provincial bakers, to wrest control of the heavily regulated industry from the British-based group George Weston. Quality Bakers steadily acquired bakeries, linking with Lower Hutt flourmiller-baker A.S. Paterson & Co, a firm founded in Dunedin in 1886. In 1976, aided by Nelsonian sharebroker Bob Gunn (born 1930), Pat Goodman staged a proxy coup to take control of A.S. Paterson & Co, ousting its chairman, Alex Paterson (born 1927), a grandson of the founder. This reverse takeover set the scene for the way the Goodmans would do business in future. It also boosted the career of A.S. Paterson & Co's deputy chairman, Wellington sharebroker Peter Shirtcliffe (born 1931). A grandson of Sir George Shirtcliffe, who had been a partner of the original A.S. Paterson from 1898, Peter Shirtcliffe became the company's new executive chairman and later group managing director of the Goodman Group, which A.S. Paterson & Co became in 1979. (Years later Peter Shirtcliffe founded the Campaign for Better Government, which lobbied unsuccessfully for retaining the first-past-the-post electoral system when New Zealanders voted on electoral reform in 1993.)

In time the Goodman Group became a huge company, notably after 1986 when it merged with Australia's Fielder Gillespie Davis and Allied Mills to dominate the Australian food market. The acquisition of Wattie's completed Pat Goodman's vision of controlling the trans-Tasman food chain. But his business strategy was not perfect. Under his control the group made mistakes — it tried to take over the British food group Ranks Hovis McDougall, and unwisely bought into John Elliott's Elders IXL and BIL's Australian subsidiary, Industrial Equity — but he survived. Pat Goodman cultivated his homespun image of 'just a baker' while operating as one of Australasia's toughest businessmen. During the 1980s he enjoyed the use of the Goodman Fielder Wattie corporate jet, and in 1987 paid for extensions to the Nelson runway so it could land there. Today, retired from Goodman Fielder and Heinz Wattie's, he runs a successful Sydney-based family investment house with his three sons, Patrick, Gregory and Craig. Knighted in 1995, Sir Patrick Goodman's heart is still in Motueka where he lives with his wife, former baker Hilary, Lady Goodman. While his major interests are his family and deep-sea fishing, he enjoys the good life. He has also been generous in giving time and money to a range of worthy causes, not least the Business & Parliament Trust, an organisation that aims to bridge the gap between politics and business. His family's minimum worth in 2003 was at least $550 million.

Goodman Fielder, taken over in 2003 by the Graeme Hart-controlled Burns Philp & Co, contained Sir Patrick's spirit well after his departure, when it came to going about its business. In 1999 it cleaned up a long-time competitor, listed Christchurch-based cake-maker Ernest Adams, in a bitter and drawn-out takeover. Ernest Adams, a South Island icon, began in 1921 as a cake and pastry-making partnership between Ernest Adams (1892–1976) and Hugh

The Rich List*
January 1966

Top ten individuals/families and main sources of wealth

1. **Todd family** — *Cars, petrol, oil exploration*

2. **Kerridge, Sir Robert James (1901–79)** — *Cinema, entertainment*

=3. **Butland, Sir Jack Richard (1896–1982)** — *Processed cheese*

=3. **Myers family** — *Hotels, liquor distribution*
Kenneth Myers (1907-98) and son Douglas (born 1938).

5. **Kelliher, Sir Henry Joseph (1896–1991)** — *Brewing, hotels, liquor distribution*

6. **Goodfellow, Sir William (1880–1974)** — *Dairying*

=7. **Fletcher family** — *Construction, pulp & paper*

=7. **Jeffs brothers** — *Construction, property, manufacturing*
Jim (1925-94), Kevin (1928-84) and Vaughan (born 1930).

9. **Brierley, Ronald Alfred (b. 1937)** — *Investment*

=10. **Carter, (Kenneth Clifford) Alwyn (1909–85)** — *Timbermilling*

=10. **Cole, Noel (1892–1975)** — *Building*

=10. **Winstone family** — *Quarrying, contracting*

=10. **Fisher and Paykel families** — *Whiteware, electronics*

=10. **Stevenson, Sir William Alfred (1901-83)** — *Quarrying, contracting*

=10. **Doig, James Nimmo Crawford (1913–84)** — *Packaging*

=10. **Gibbs, Theodore Nisbet (1896–1978)** — *Property development, transport*

---

* Pastoral wealth omitted.

Bruce (died 1930). After Bruce retired in 1929 Adams formed his own company, Ernest Adams, but was forced to sell the Adams Bruce partnership, which served the North Island, to fund his fledgling company through the Depression. He was managing director from 1930–65. In 1970 Adams Bruce was bought back, and in 1973 Ernest Adams went public but with the Adams family firmly in control. It made some strategic acquisitions. In 1994 the New Zealand Dairy Board sold its holding in the company, and Gourmet Direct Investments, a boutique marketer of speciality meat cuts controlled by Wellington entrepreneur Errol Clark (born 1950), completed a raid in early 1995, lifting its stake in Ernest Adams to 22 per cent. At the time of the raid about 50 Adams family members held some 11 per cent of the company. Gourmet Direct mopped up most of the remaining family-owned shares in 1996, lifting its stake to nearly 47 per cent. It then initiated a restructuring programme and introduced a Malaysian company, Mega First Industries, to the share registry; soon Gourmet Direct and Mega First held more than 50 per cent between them. The restructuring programme, which included centralised distribution, failed miserably, costing the company dearly and paving the way for a full Goodman Fielder takeover. The Adams family was removed from the *Rich List* in 1997 at the request of one of Ernest Adams' three surviving sons, former company managing director Hugh Adams (born 1923). Hugh's brother, Neil (1917–85), was a director of Ernest Adams until 1975, and a former Southland branch manager. Hugh's son, Ralph (born 1951), and his nieces, Sarah and Jessica Adams, also held senior positions with the company.

Unlike Sir Patrick Goodman, pioneer food processor-exporter Sir Jack Butland (1896–1982) is remembered as much for his philanthropic streak as his business prowess. Butland was the leading public benefactor of his day, donating at least $500,000 to a variety of worthy causes and charities, but he shunned publicity. 'Money-making's been fun,' he said in a rare interview with the *Auckland Star*. 'I've been lucky and I like to see my earnings spent on causes of my choice in the way I think will help most people.' Butland was a man of great principle, returning to the British government £77,752 17s 2d in profits from wartime contracts supplying tinned cheese to British troops. 'It seemed unthinkable to me,' he said, 'that profits should be made on an essential food for troops when the British people were being bombed to death night and day trying to get weapons to Libya and Burma to defend us and, incidentally, other countries.'

Jack Butland was born and educated in Hokitika and never forgot his southern roots, although today he is remembered as a true-blue Aucklander. His father, Henry Butland, had been a goldminer and an All Black halfback from 1893–94, and Butland retained gold dust and nuggets obtained by his father, bringing them out to show a newspaper reporter when he was knighted in 1966. Butland began his career as a clerk with the Bank of New South Wales. He later sold tyres for Goodyear before moving to Auckland and setting up business collecting agencies for imported foodstuffs. He founded J.R. Butland Pty in 1922, NZ Cheese four years later, organised the orderly marketing of honey in Britain in 1933, founded Butland Tobacco in 1936 (which handled the Rothmans agency) and Butland Industries in 1949. Jack Butland helped establish Rothmans in New Zealand and was a director of Rothmans Industries for many years (Butland Tobacco was the second-largest shareholder in Rothmans when Butland died, holding more than 18 per cent of the company). Butland Industries was famous for manufacturing and exporting the product most associated with Sir Jack Butland — Chesdale processed cheese. He and a friend, Harry Coe, had developed the brand in an Auckland basement before the war. They first experimented with emulsifiers, grated cheese and an egg beater, but had little success until a visiting American suggested they try melting the cheese first.

A son from Butland's first marriage, Jack Malfroy Butland (born 1919), and a grandson, Jack Richard Butland (born 1946), played key roles in the development of the business. In 1981, 49 per cent of Butland Industries was acquired by US food giant Kraft Corporation, which had tried unsuccessfully in 1973 to obtain 60 per cent of the company in the face of opposition from unions and farmers. The business ran as a joint venture until 1989 when Kraft bought the remaining shareholding. It later moved production from Ellerslie to Wiri, South Auckland, and changed the name of the company to Kraft General Foods New Zealand. It put its local brands on the market in 1995, in line with its new strategy of 'selling non-core businesses and reinvesting in selective strategic opportunities around the world'. The New Zealand rights to Chesdale were sold to the New Zealand Dairy Board, returning a New Zealand icon to New Zealand ownership.

The Butland Industries name might have gone but two other reminders of Sir Jack Butland survive — the family launch *Sirdar*, which has been owned by a succession of wealthy businessmen since his time, and Blandford Lodge horsebreeding stud near Matamata. The 1991 *Rich List* assessed the collective wealth of J.M. Butland (Sir Jack's son) and J.R. Butland (his grandson) at more than $50 million. This included the Ellerslie land, much of which was put up for sale in 1993. J.R. Butland, who quit Butland Industries in 1988, unhappy with the direction of the Butland-Kraft joint venture, formed his own company, J.R. Butland & Sons, in 1991. Two years later it was producing Peter Piper pickles and sauces. It is now, primarily, a gift marketer. J.M. Butland was made a member of the New Zealand Order of Merit in the 2000 New Year honours list for services to the community.

Sir Robert Kerridge, born five years after Sir Jack Butland, lived life to the full, seemingly untroubled by the publicity surrounding his business and personal life. Whatever people think of him — and he has his critics to this day — no New Zealand businessman in modern times can have a greater claim to the title entrepreneur. His business career began humbly enough, but before he was 50 he owned and controlled the largest theatre-entertainment organisation in the southern hemisphere. A consummate dealmaker, he reigned unrivalled in entertainment and cinema distribution. He started young — as a five-year-old, when his parents gave him a magic lantern — and he never looked back. Like Sir James Wattie, he was a South Islander who moved to the North Island's East Coast. As a seventeen-year-old staying with his mother's relatives in Gisborne, he set up a small orchard for his parents. Kerridge had earlier worked as a junior accountant in Christchurch, studying accountancy

No New Zealand businessman in modern times can have a greater claim to the title of entrepreneur than Sir Robert Kerridge (1901–79). Before he was 50 he controlled the largest theatre-entertainment organisation in the southern hemisphere. His philandering in private life caused problems to family members and contributed to the break-up of his business after his death.
COURTESY BOB KERRIDGE JNR

at night school, but in Gisborne he sold real estate briefly before starting the Kerridge Commercial College of Poverty Bay, a school where he would recycle mail-order accountancy papers from the United States to paying pupils. That venture failed and in 1923 he became manager and then owner of a coach service between Gisborne and Napier, Wilkinson's Motor Co (later De Luxe Motor Service) — the first to use cars. This barely paid its way, but while in the motor business he also went into partnership in the cinema industry with H.B. Williams, a wealthy grazier and a grandson of missionary William Williams. Their first acquisition was Benjamin Fuller's Palace picture theatre in Gisborne. Kerridge had originally tried to borrow money from H.B. Williams but Williams recognised an entrepreneur when he saw one and became a full partner. Kerridge, the driving force behind the business, soon entered into a distribution agreement with the J.C. Williamson group. In 1937 he acquired the *Gisborne Times* newspaper and brought out an editor from England but he was unable to beat the entrenched opposition, the *Gisborne Herald*, and eventually sold out to the *Herald*.

Kerridge expanded in 1943 by acquiring a controlling interest in New Zealand Theatres and in 1945 by taking over the Fuller–Hayward theatre chain. But his ultimate business achievement came in 1946 when he sold half his business to Odeon Theatres, a subsidiary of the J. Arthur Rank Organisation. This deal filled a gap in Rank's Commonwealth distribution chain, forestalled anti-monopoly moves by the Labour government and guaranteed Kerridge a supply of British movies, adding to agreements with American studios such as Metro-Goldwyn-Mayer, which had already guaranteed their first-release films to the Kerridge chain. The deal was sweet all around and Kerridge was rewarded personally with a Rolls-Royce car from J. Arthur Rank himself, delivered in a packing case to his home in Portland Rd, Remuera, Auckland. (After women, expensive cars were his greatest love.) By 1947 Kerridge had acquired the theatres of the J.C. Williamson Picture Corporation, giving him an unrivalled 130-theatre chain. Under his tight direction Kerridge Odeon Corporation dominated the cinema business — it owned 75 per cent of the country's picture theatres at its height — and diversified into tourism, hotels, advertising, catering, publishing, recordings, merchandising, property and finance. It built the 246 shopping complex in Queen St, Auckland, acquired Pakatoa Island in the Hauraki Gulf, turning it into the country's first island holiday resort, and introduced the first hydrofoil service on the Waitemata Harbour. Kerridge also organised concert tours by overseas stars including the Beatles, the Bolshoi Ballet and pianist Julius Katchen.

In the public domain Kerridge was as conservative as he was powerful, abhorring the trend toward sex and violence in films. In private, he was notoriously unfaithful in marriage. He spoiled his children but could also be stern with them, and was unwilling to groom any to take over the business (although his three sons worked for him at various times). Worse still, he made little effort to plan his estate or sort out complex family problems of his own making. These failings were to seal the fate of Kerridge Odeon Corporation after his death. Kerridge married his first wife, Emslie Malpart, the daughter of a French manufacturer, in Gisborne in 1925. They were divorced in 1935 and two months later, in January 1936, he married Meryl Jones in Palmerston North. She had already borne him a child, Vanessa (later Mrs Tengblat), and in 1938 she gave birth to Bob, who was to become a prominent animal welfarist and Auckland director of the Society for the Prevention of Cruelty to Animals. Kerridge's second marriage ended in divorce in 1955 and the following year he married his housekeeper, Phyllis Calhoun (née Roland), a divorcee with three young children, Rolly, Gail (later Mrs Conder) and John. Phyllis, who was born in Te Aroha and educated in Vienna, had met Kerridge in the 1930s when she was touring the country as a violinist in a family sextet. Her children were legally adopted by Kerridge and after his death in 1979 they successfully contested his estate, with the court declaring them to be his natural children.

The Kerridge Odeon Corporation steadily declined after Kerridge's death and things came to a head in 1987 when Rank decided to get out of its New Zealand theatre interests. However, it indicated it would pay due regard to the Kerridge and Williams families over who the new partner should be (they owned a half share of the business between them). Interest was shown by several parties, including property developer Chase Corporation (owner of Kerridge's long-time rival, Amalgamated Theatres), Mainzeal Group and Unigroup Pacific, Brierley Investments and Triple M, but the winner was an outsider, corporate loner David Phillips (born 1949). With support from the Williams family and Kerridge's 'first family' (Bob Kerridge and Vanessa Tengblat), he merged Kerridge Odeon with his bloodstock company, Pacer Pacific Corporation, to form Pacer Kerridge Corporation. The deal incurred the wrath of Kerridge's 'second family' (Rolly Kerridge, Gail Conder and John Kerridge), and when Pacer Kerridge struggled after the sharemarket crash the Williams family turned on Phillips as well.

Pacer Kerridge, stripped of its non-bloodstock assets, limped on in virtual receivership at the mercy of its bankers. Phillips faced civil action over his management of the group and criminal prosecution on various counts of fraud, being accused among other things of using Pacer Kerridge's current account as a personal cashbox. After a three-month trial in 1997 he was acquitted on a perjury charge and three fraud charges and the jury was unable to agree on four other fraud charges. A retrial on the remaining charges was abandoned after solicitor-general John McGrath QC decided it was not in the public interest. The failure of Pacer Kerridge — which had been reduced to owning just twenty cinemas in 1992 — cost the Williams and Kerridge families dearly; it was a lesson on the pitfalls of selling outside the family. Had Sir Robert Kerridge maintained better family relationships, Phillips would not have been invited in.

Phillips survived Pacer Kerridge, discredited if not destroyed by his disastrous foray into the big time. His plans to marry Angelina Davis, the daughter of controversial former Air New Zealand chief executive Morrie Davis, evaporated with the decline in his business interests, as did any serious political aspirations. But it was his failure to complete an $8 million deal to buy Auckland's finest surviving Edwardian mansion, Florence Court — the price a record for a New Zealand house purchase at the time — that attracted the most publicity. The Epsom house, formerly called Bramcote, had been built for meat baron Richard Hellaby who had died in 1902 before he could take possession.

David Phillips (born 1949) gained control of the property-rich Kerridge Odeon Corporation in 1987. But the sharemarket crash intervened and the cinema empire, once New Zealand's largest, was reduced to a shell of its former self.
Courtesy *NBR*

His widow, Amy Hellaby, supervised its completion and lived there until 1914, when she sold it and moved to London to be nearer her sons and nephews who were serving in the Great War. The house was then sold to electricity entrepreneur and former MP Felix McGuire, who died in 1915, aged 70. His widow, Sarah-Jane McGuire, a daughter of wealthy quarryman, coalminer and brickmaker J.J. Craig (1860–1916), lived there with her family until 1938. The following year it passed to Philip Seabrook (1901–72), a distinguished motor racer and part-owner of Auckland car dealership Seabrook Fowlds (later part of the New Zealand Motor Corporation), which held the valuable Austin franchise.

When David Phillips set his heart on Florence Court in 1987 Philip Seabrook's 83-year-old widow, Lal Seabrook (née Munro Wilson), was still living there. Phillips paid the estate a $1 million deposit to secure the deal,

Florence Court, Auckland's finest surviving Edwardian mansion, was originally called Bramcote and built for meat baron Richard Hellaby. But Hellaby died in 1902 before he could take possession and his widow, Amy, supervised its completion and lived there until 1914. In 1939 it passed to car magnate Philip Seabrook (1901-72) and stayed in the Seabrook family for more than 50 years. Entrepreneur David Phillips tried to buy it in 1987 but the deal fell through.

Courtesy John Sax

which allowed her to live in the house until her death. But the sharemarket crash intervened and Phillips defaulted, losing the deposit which Mrs Seabrook is said to have used to add to her extensive antiques collection. The property had been transferred to her only living child, Diana Robinson (born 1931), and in 1991 Lal Seabrook moved to Christchurch to be near her daughter. She died eleven days later. Since 1997 the house has been owned by interests associated with property developer John Sax (born 1955), a survivor of the 1980s property crash, who makes it available for visiting dignitaries (the former Fijian prime minister, Major-General Sitiveni Rabuka, stayed there when he visited Auckland in 1999).

Phillips has retained his bloodstock interests and in 1999 he made a humorous return to politics, launching an odd-ball political party, NMP. It offered a three-year membership for 5c and Phillips claimed to have 2000 members. NMP (short for New Millennium Party) advocated the abolition of the mixed-member proportional system and the political parties that went with it. If elected it said it would abolish the Inland Revenue Department, ban genetic engineering and make New Zealand wholly organic by 2010.

Phillips was but one of scores of corporate casualties of the over-exuberant 1980s, when share values and land prices rocketed in a newly deregulated financial market and then crashed with similar rapidity. For the first 25 years or so after World War II most fortunes were built from old money, and protected industries such as manufacturing or long-term property holdings. Company investment, such as it was, tended to be conservative, centring on a handful of Australian and New Zealand blue-chip stocks, with the emphasis more on a company's ability to pay dividends than to provide investors with substantial capital gains (Brierley Investments excepted). Hostile takeovers were uncommon — although BIL, the Goodman brothers and Fletcher Holdings tried them — and significant corporate failures rare. Indeed, in the post-war period the first company collapse of any consequence was that of the Dunedin-based Standard Insurance Co in 1961 (the previous failure on a similar scale had been John McArthur's Investment Executive Trust of New Zealand and other interests in the 1930s). All this was to change in May 1972 when the Australia & New Zealand Bank appointed a receiver to what had hitherto been New Zealand's most exciting conglomerate, the JBL group.

JBL's collapse, which was spectacular by any standards, not only damaged the reputation of New Zealand's fledgling entrepreneurial community but marked a decade of miserable economic and business performance for New Zealand — a period that included two other spectacular corporate failures, Cornish Lamphouse (1974) and Securitibank (1976), followed by the near collapse of the Public Service Investment Society (1979). The demise of JBL had ramifications well beyond investors and creditors associated with the companies and syndicates that comprised the diversified group. It had all the ingredients of a soap opera: family rivalry, greed, negligence and malfeasance. Only the government of Prime Minister (Sir) John Marshall and the receiver it appointed, Doug Hazard, came out with any credit.

JBL was established by the sons of a close-knit Roman Catholic farming family from Ruawai, a flat, uninspiring district on the Kaipara Harbour. It began life in 1956 as Jeffs Brothers Ltd, a contracting-manufacturing company owned by Jim (1925–94), Kevin (1928–84) and Vaughan Jeffs (born 1930). By 1959 the company was using the JBL acronym and expanding into a variety of activities, and by the early 1960s construction was becoming a major part of its business. With backing from a group of Ruawai and Auckland businessmen, Kevin and Jim Jeffs moved to Auckland in 1965 to expand into property development. Vaughan Jeffs followed in 1967, the year JBL Consolidated was formed as a parent company for the group. Growth continued at a pace with

Jim Jeffs (1925–94) was rich, arrogant and for a time successful. But his over-ambitious JBL group grew too fast, and its collapse brought Jeffs and his two brothers down with it
AUTHOR'S COLLECTION

JBL expanding into a range of new areas including fishing, cosmetics, mineral exploration and sheep and cattle farming. At its height some 52 companies made up the JBL group, with offices in Australia and Japan. Jim Jeffs was the driving force behind JBL's expansion but by 1971 a shortage of working capital, poor investments and failed special partnerships started to affect the ability of the group to pay its bills.

The Jeffs brothers continued to enjoy a corporate lifestyle that was then largely unknown to New Zealand business executives, while lax accounting and financial reporting systems masked the gravity of JBL's problems to outsiders. The appointment of Richard Dwyer as the ANZ Bank's receiver might not have come as a surprise to the Jeffs but it sent shockwaves through the New Zealand economy. Dwyer acted precipitately, abrogating suppliers' and customers' contracts — in the words of journalist Reg Birchfield, 'tearing the company apart' — and even went on television to warn that other unrelated companies might be dragged under by the JBL collapse. Jim Jeffs, who was in London at the time, suffered a minor heart attack. The matter was so serious that a week after Dwyer's appointment the government intervened, appointing company reconstruction specialist Doug Hazard as its own receiver and winning praise from the hospitalised Jeffs in the process (this was to change over time).

Hazard, a much different character to Dwyer, was determined to save what could be saved in an orderly way and to avoid incurring legal fees. In time, conspiracy to defraud charges were brought against key players in JBL's fall — Jim Jeffs was sent to prison, and Vaughan Jeffs and five others received heavy fines. The Court of Appeal later quashed the convictions against all but the brothers. Jim Jeffs got nine months but was let out in six for good behaviour. He later moved with his family to England where he worked as a freelance financial consultant, dying of cancer in Solihull in 1994. Kevin Jeffs, who was not charged in connection with the JBL collapse, had died in England a decade earlier, also of cancer. Vaughan Jeffs, who was fined $2000 for his part in the JBL saga, is retired and living with his wife in Auckland.

Jim Jeffs, who was noted for his arrogance, was described by Hazard in 1972 as 'dynamic [with] tremendous ambition and personal drive', and appearing to wield absolute control over JBL. Hazard said Jeffs was 'dominated by a conviction that a substantial profit can be made out of inflation' but lived in a dreamworld and had created a structure that was 'highly vulnerable to hiccoughs in the progress of inflation'. Hazard spent the next 25 years unravelling the mess created by Jeffs, in one of the most cost-effective and successful receiverships in New Zealand history. (Accountant Harold Goodman's handling of the Securitibank liquidation was similarly deserving of praise.) During Hazard's quarter century with the JBL receivership he charged just $376,540 in fees, and kept legal expenses to $84,108 and audit fees to $107,261. Management and administration expenses, including wages, totalled just $1,283,700 — a tiny sum compared with receivership costs following the 1987 sharemarket crash. Several operating units of the group were restructured successfully and sold, in many cases for significant gains. These included JBL Seafoods (fishing), JBL Laboratories/Mill Valley (cosmetics) and the listed JBL Minerals (mineral exploration). JBL-Sargent Construction, which was virtually put out of business by the behaviour of the ANZ receiver, Dwyer, in 1972, had much of its equity salvaged by Hazard. In all, about 3500 investors and 2500 creditors were affected by the JBL collapse. Of the 52 companies, 21 were registered overseas. Some 88 commercial properties had been developed or partially developed at the time of the receivership. Twenty-seven fishing boats had been completed or were under construction, and there were 60 settled and nineteen unsettled investment syndicates. Under Hazard's direction, various secured or preferential creditors were paid in full — nearly $19.6 million — and other unsecured creditors and second-debenture interest claimants were paid in part nearly $2.5 million.

Wellington property investor Bob Jones (born 1939), later Sir Robert Jones, who was to suffer business problems of his own years after, said in 1972 that the JBL saga was essentially a story about property. 'It began as a property-dealing operation and died because it failed to graduate into a property-investment concern. The host of other enterprises it undertook were never more than peripheral nonsense.' Jones paid tribute to the 'entrepreneurial drive and vitality' of JBL but accused the management of falling victim to that common weakness of the newly successful — believing its own publicity. To be sure, there were few tears from the old-money brigade at JBL's demise; it was just a little too brash and rough around the edges to be taken seriously by the business establishment.

For his part, Jones, a pushy product of Lower Hutt with a passion for boxing (he was New Zealand universities' lightweight champion in 1957), had battled from the age of nineteen to convince a disbelieving world that he had an uncanny ability to succeed. After local schooling and a stint at Victoria University College he worked from 1958–60 as a self-employed advertising contractor and then from 1960–63 publishing, among other things, building industry directories. Recognising early on that he had special skills for property investing (as distinct from developing), in 1964 he founded the Robt Jones Investment Group, floating Robt Jones Investments as a public company in 1982. His self-appointed role as an authority on property was sealed in 1977 with the publication of his book *Jones on Property*, one of several entertaining books produced during his busy career. A rebel, renowned for his outspoken views on women, parking fines and authority generally, he became a hit in the Wellington establishment. He and National Prime Minister (Sir) Robert Muldoon were great mates until Muldoon imposed the interest clawback on the industry that had made Jones rich — a de facto capital gains tax on investment properties sold within ten years of purchase. Jones never forgave him and in 1983, playing on the country's general disillusionment with National, formed the New Zealand Party with the aim of changing the government. Jones himself stood for Parliament in the 1984 snap election, and although his party failed to win any seats, it attracted 12.3 per cent of the vote. Its success identified a constituency for financial and economic deregulation and propelled the reform-minded Labour Party to the Treasury benches.

Jones took the election result rather well. He did not have the temperament for Parliament, but at least had the satisfaction of seeing Muldoon dumped from office. In 1985, fed up with heading a party that would not die gracefully, Jones declared the organisation in recess and became a political recluse. When a day's fishing at Lake Taupo was interrupted by journalists seeking an explanation for his decision to kill off the New Zealand Party, Jones punched several and was later prosecuted for assault. Jones was nevertheless knighted by the Labour government in 1989 for services to business management, a controversial honour at the very least. For Labour, though, Jones was living proof that a party once steeped in Bolshevism was capable of working with a disciple of the free market. Today Jones, shed of his troubled public company (now part of Trans Tasman Properties) after leading it through less-than-glorious times, is still rich (at least $100 million in 2003), if not on the same scale as before the sharemarket crash. He is one of only two entrants on the *Rich List* to have publicly complained about being undervalued.

Although Jones can be witty when he wants to be, like his former friend the late Sir Robert Muldoon, he has a powerful counterpunch if crossed. In his heyday, when the listed Robt Jones Investments counted for something, he instituted a scale of 'fines' for sharebrokers and journalists who talked down the company. Most paid up rather than face litigation. Even in virtual retirement Jones has remained in the public eye. He niggled the Reserve Bank governor, Dr Don Brash, over monetary policy and the role of the central bank, berated journalists and politicians alike, and was even involved in a bitter dispute with a former gardener at his Western Hutt mansion who was alleged to have poisoned many of his prize plants. Had Jones been born in the East End of London, rather than Lower Hutt, he would by now be running British boxing and almost everything else. Notwithstanding this accident of birth, New Zealand has treated Jones well.

Post-war New Zealand, in spite of regulations and big government, treated immigrants well, and several established businesses that were to generate great fortunes. Sir James Doig of UEB was a shining example, as was fellow former Merchant Navy officer Sir Robert Owens (1921–99). English-born Owens — plain Bob Owens when he arrived in New Zealand — set up a canvas-stitching business in the Bay of Plenty in 1953 with £70 borrowed capital. The company would eventually became the Owens Group. He became the kingpin of stevedoring and shipping at Mt Maunganui. In 1957, with textile importer Owen Rainger (1906–88), he pioneered the export of pine logs to Japan, a trade that is now the mainstay of Mt Maunganui. In 1964, when the shipping division of his business secured the agency for Japanese shipping giant Mitsui OSK Lines, Owens' business entered a new league. In 1970 he spearheaded a consortium of New Zealand business interests to purchase the Union Steam Ship Co from P. & O. The bid failed but Owens succeeded in securing half the company in New Zealand hands. Staunchly loyal to the Bay of Plenty, Owens scored a unique double in local body politics, serving after the 1971 council elections as mayor of both Tauranga and Mt Maunganui. He played a major role in having a bridge built to link the two communities.

In 1981, shortly after retiring from active management in his company, Owens was approached by his old friend, Prime Minister Robert Muldoon, to rescue the state-owned Air New Zealand — at the time struggling with poor returns and low morale in the wake of the Mt Erebus disaster. He turned the company around in his three-year term as chairman, during which time he was instrumental in breaking a trade union ban on trade with Chile, imposed after Augusto Pinochet seized power there in 1973. John McCrystal, who wrote a biography of Owens, said of him: '[He] was extraordinarily generous to his adoptive town and country, to charities, cultural groups and sporting organisations.' This was recognised by both businessmen and politicians: he was awarded the CBE in 1991 and the Chilean Order of Merit in 1994, inducted into the Business Hall of Fame in 1995, and made a knight commander of the New Zealand Order of Merit in 1997. The Owens family's minimum net worth was estimated in the 2000 *Rich List* at $45 million but their entry was removed from the 2001 list.

Jimmy Kirkpatrick (born 1930) is another Englishman who gave up the sea to start a new life in New Zealand. He jumped ship from the *Birchbank* at the age of nineteen, for a period selling cars in Auckland and running his own yard. In the mid-1960s he moved into property investment, where he has stayed and prospered ever since. He is now one of Auckland's largest private landowners, but he shuns publicity and has always been sensitive about his true age. Kirkpatrick lives at Auckland's premier address, Paritai Dr, Orakei, and runs his empire from a thirteen-storey office building, Albert Plaza, in central Auckland, but he has few airs and graces. His net wealth exceeds $65 million. Kirkpatrick is great mates with his lawyer, the Auckland property investor Michael Friedlander (born 1939), but said in a rare interview some years ago there was 'no other business connection' between the two. Friedlander and his wife Harriet (née Nathan, born 1939) have a collective wealth of at least $75 million, according to the 2003 *Rich List*. They are keen patrons of the arts but, like Kirkpatrick, have an aversion to publicity. They have two children. Unlike Kirkpatrick, the genesis of their wealth is birthright. Michael inherited property from his father, Walter, a German-Jewish immigrant and land baron, and Harriet likewise from her father, Auckland investor Peter Nathan. The Friedlanders are significant investors in public companies, and Michael is a prominent company director.

Non-Anglo-Saxon immigrants, despite language difficulties and cultural differences, have long identified business opportunities in New Zealand and several have created sizeable fortunes. Assid Corban (1864–1941) did not start

Lebanese immigrant Assid Corban (1864–1941) did more to commercialise the New Zealand wine industry than anyone else. The family's West Auckland-based company was sold in 1975 but Corbans Wines, now part of Montana Group (NZ), is a leading maker and exporter of premium wines.
COURTESY CORBAN FAMILY

the New Zealand wine industry but he and his industrious family did more than anyone else to commercialise it. Their West Auckland-based company was sold in 1975 but Corbans Wines, now part of Montana Group (NZ), lives on today as one of this country's leading makers and exporters of premium wines. Virtually all the developments that led to Corbans Wines' success can be traced to the Corban family and its New Zealand founder. Born in Lebanon, Assid Corban arrived in New Zealand in 1892 and initially worked as a trader in the mining towns of the Coromandel Peninsula. Within three years he had a shop in Queen St, Auckland, but it was 1902 before he bought a piece of scrubby gumland at Henderson on which to grow grapes. The undercapitalised venture struggled initially — against pests, family crises and prohibition — but by 1909 it was selling wine and by the early 1920s Mt Lebanon vineyards was the centrepoint of Henderson and its wines were finding favour throughout the country. In the 30 years following Corban's death the firm moved from producing mainly sweet fortified wines to meet a growing demand for drier wines and lighter, more subtle wines. It pioneered wine-making technology, set new industry standards and led the way in wine exporting. Family members, still prominent in Henderson, have been active in trade associations and the community. Some examples:

▶ Wadier Corban (1891–1982) MBE (for contrbution to wine industry); second winemaker in family company from about 1920–49; first Corban involved in local government;

▶ Alexander Corban (born 1925) OBE BSc DipOen; winemaker, Corbans Wines, Henderson (1949–76); secretary, New Zealand Wine Council (1949– 52); executive member, Wine Institute of New Zealand (1976–81), fellow (1983); honorary life member, New Zealand Society of Viticulture & Oenology;

▶ Assid Corban (born 1925) OBE; mayor of Waitakere (1989–92); mayor of Henderson for fifteen years; member of the Auckland Regional Authority for twelve years; holder of a variety of other public posts; the most prominent surviving member of the Corban winegrowing family of Henderson;

▶ Brian Corban (born 1946) QSO MA(Hons) LLB; company secretary, Corbans Holdings (which managed Corban family interests in Corbans Wines); foundation partner, Corban Revell law practice, Henderson; chairman, Broadcasting Corporation of New Zealand (1985–88); chairman of the ministerial advisory committee on the restructuring of broadcasting into state-owned enterprises (1988); foundation chairman, Television New

Zealand (as a state-owned enterprise); member, Waitangi Tribunal; director of various energy companies at different times; chairman, Melanesian Mission; chairman and 50 per cent owner of Ngatarawa Wines, Hastings;

▶ Dr Corban Corban (1900–74) MB ChB; specialist in medical disorders and nervous diseases; appointed assistant medical officer, Tokanui Hospital (1927); medical officer, southwestern territory, based in Hokitika Mental Hospital (1941); general practice in Remuera, Auckland (1944); amateur astronomer of national standard;

▶ David Corban (1925–98); chairman, A.A. Corban & Sons; first chairman Corbans Wines (1963–73); active in wholesale wine industry associations;

▶ Joseph Corban (born 1929) MBE (for services to viticulture); third-generation Corban working at Corbans Wines; runs family viticulture and propagation business, J.A. Corban & Family Nurseries; and

▶ Alwyn Corban (born 1952) MS (viticulture and oenology); managing director, chief winemaker and 50 per cent owner of Ngatarawa Wines, Hastings.

George Waldemar Skjellerup (1881–1955), born of Danish and Welsh parents, did not have a language problem confronting him when he sailed for New Zealand in 1902, or a lack of ideas, just a shortage of capital — he had only £3 17s 6d to his name. He had gained a knowledge of the rubber industry while making tyres for the Dunlop Pneumatic Tyre Co in Melbourne and found work in a Dunedin bike shop when he arrived. While there he wrote to his former employer and got a job with Dunlop in Christchurch, where he spent the next six years fitting and repairing tyres and selling rubber goods. Convinced that Dunlop was not providing a sufficiently wide range of products, he left in 1910 to form his own business, the Para Rubber Co, named after Pará state in Brazil, a source of high-quality rubber. Para opened its first store in Manchester St, Christchurch, selling milking-machine rubberware, tyres and rubber components on behalf of Michelin, Dunlop, Continental and North British. By 1918 Para had four retail shops and in 1919 the company floated on the Stock Exchange, enabling it to branch out across the country. Para later manufactured its own rubber items and acquired a number of subsidiaries which made tennis shoes, waterproof coats, gumboots and slabs of latex foam. During World War II, when rubber was scarce, Para opened a plant to reclaim rubber from old car tyres. It also established a solar saltworks at Lake Grassmere, Marlborough.

Skellerup Industries (without the silent 'j') was incorporated as a holding company in 1948 but the Para Rubber trade name remained. After George Skjellerup's death in 1955 his elder son, (Sir) Valdemar Skellerup (1907–82), took over as managing director while his younger son, Peter (born 1918), was assistant managing director. Under their leadership the company acquired more subsidiaries and expanded into Australia and Malaysia. Peter Skellerup, who took over after his brother's death, was a prominent professional company director as well as being active in conservation and community affairs (22 years as a Christchurch city councillor, including six years as deputy mayor). Like his brother he received the CBE (in 1978, for services to the community, industry and horticulture) and he was made a knight of Dannebrogordenen first class in 1981 by Queen Margrethe II of Denmark, in recognition of his many years' service as honorary Danish consul.

In 1987 Skellerup Industries became a Brierley Investments subsidiary after a $20.8 million buyout of the family shareholding. Peter Skellerup retired from the company, as did his son, assistant managing director George Skjellerup (born 1942). Thereafter the group went downhill. It was refloated as part of the 'baby Brierley' Skellerup Group in 1993 by BIL's former New Zealand operations chief executive, baby-faced Murray Bolton (born 1948). The new group, 33 per cent of which was floated, was, to quote *NBR*, 'eclectic in the extreme', including gardening suppliers Palmers Gardenworld and Lanes Industries, lawnmower manufacturer Masport, ink manufacturer Morrison-PIM Holdings, former Cable Price Downer companies, salt manufacturer Dominion Salt and rubber products from Skellerup Industries itself. In 1994 Skellerup Group paid $74 million for home-decorating chain Levene & Co, owned by wealthy Jewish merchant David Levene (born 1919) — $35 million of it for the Levene brand alone. This 70-year-old family business, started by David Levene's father and uncle, immigrant contract painters Lewis and Mark Levene, comprised a paint and wallpaper factory, 44 decorating shops and 4 hyperstores. It turned over about $150 million a year. David Levene retained the properties, said at the time to be worth at least $50 million. Under Bolton's new broom the magic that had made Levene & Co so successful was swept away. In other respects, Skellerup was reported to be performing strongly.

In 1996 Bolton, confident that Skellerup's languishing share price would rocket, staged a $520 million leveraged buyout of the group through Maine Investments. This involved several of his colleagues and a range of leveraged-buyout funds associated with US investment bank Goldman Sachs & Co. Bolton was left with about 10 per cent of the company, and Goldman Sachs' interests 83 per cent. Most of the funds to finance the deal were borrowed, including some $77 million in junk bonds issued at ten per cent. Maine got into difficulties in 1997 when its plan to sell underperforming assets and turn others around failed. Goldman Sachs forced a restructuring and Levene & Co was placed in receivership, followed by contract miner DML Resources and, in early 1998, Palmers. Palmers was, with difficulty, able to trade out of receivership; Levene & Co could not. David Levene took the failure of his old company especially badly. A book written about his business (with his consent) and earmarked for publication in late 1999 was withdrawn because Levene said it 'opened up too many wounds'. As for the Para Rubber Co, the original source of the Skellerup family wealth, it survived as a restructured franchise operation. It was sold in 1997 to leading Australian franchiser Clark Franchising, which operates the Clark Rubber chain in Australia. One of its first moves was to restore the word 'Rubber' to the Para name — it had been removed during BIL's time.

Bolton, the so-called $30 million man, was removed from the *Rich List* in 1998 after his ousting from Maine. Despite having the trappings of wealth — a $2.6 million pad in Remuera, Auckland, including an indoor swimming pool and manicured gardens — Bolton claimed he was not rich enough to stay on the list. Woes aside, he found time to play tennis, compete in half-marathons and duathlons, and ride his Harley-Davidson motorbike (a hobby shared by others on the *Rich List* including Auckland mayor John Banks [born 1946], and former BIL chairmen Bob Matthew [born 1944] and Bruce Hancox [born 1949]). Bolton even took part in the 1997 Speight's Coast to Coast endurance event when it was obvious Maine was in trouble, but he pulled out of the 1998 Coast to Coast. In 1999 Bolton assumed a new title — 'cabbie' — with the purchase of taxi company Corporate Cabs. He sold his minority stake in the troubled Auckland Bridge Climb in 2003.

Fred Turnovsky (1916–94), the son of well-heeled parents from Prague, Czechoslovakia, is another example of a non-Anglo-Saxon immigrant going for the main chance in a new country. A former law student, he and his young wife, Lotte, arrived in New Zealand as refugees on Centennial Day 1940. His parents were to die in concentration camps in Europe two years later. Turnovsky saw an opportunity to manufacture small leather goods, initially watch straps from leather offcuts, after working as a clerk in a small radio manufacturing business called Radio Corporation. He founded a leather company, Tatra Leather Goods (later part of Tatra Industries), in Wellington in 1943, naming it after a mountain range in Czechoslovakia. By 1952 the business was exporting to Australia, manufacturing a range of leather goods under licence to Buxton.

Turnovsky said of his foray into the leather business: 'It was the sort of

Czech refugee Fred Turnovsky (1916–94) founded Tatra Leather Goods in Wellington in 1943 and built the business into Tatra Industries. But his fortune disappeared in 1988 when Cory-Wright & Salmon (CWS), in which Tatra was indirectly the major shareholder, collapsed.
Courtesy NBR

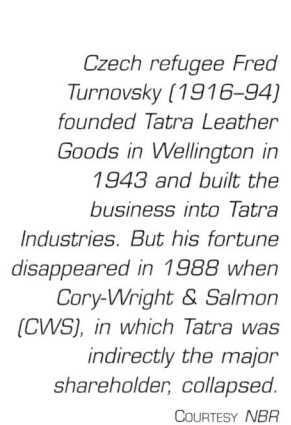

industry you could start with very little money and with a bit of hard work you could get somewhere fairly quickly.' While he proved that to be true, his interests extended well beyond Tatra. He was active in manufacturing organisations, including terms as president of the New Zealand Manufacturers' Federation (1972/73, 1978/79), and held a number of outside directorships. He was chairman of the state-owned Development Finance Corporation from 1973–76, his contribution cut short after newly elected National Prime Minister (Sir) Robert Muldoon branded him a socialist and declined to reappoint him. Turnovsky later railed against Rogernomics, the free-market reforms of Labour Finance Minister (Sir) Roger Douglas, opposing policies that he said crushed manufacturing.

Turnovsky suffered personal heartache when listed engineering and importing company Cory-Wright & Salmon (CWS), in which Tatra was indirectly the major shareholder, collapsed in 1988 with losses of $57 million. CWS' former chief executive, Robert Philpott (born 1948) — Turnovsky's son-in-law and successor — was later jailed for two years for fraud, false accounting and forgery over an unauthorised $1.1 million CWS loan he had arranged for his brother, farmer Bryan Philpott (born 1952). Tatra had held a controlling stake in CWS until 1987 when it transferred it to an Australian listed company, Kia Ora Stud (later called Dapoli Corporation), after acquiring 62 per cent of that company. The Philpott brothers had gained control of Kia Ora in 1986. Robert Philpott, whose wealth was estimated to be at least $25 million in the August 1987 *Rich List*, had been chairman of Tatra after Turnovsky's retirement. Turnovsky's wealth at that time was said to be at least $20 million. Both were removed from the list after the sharemarket crash.

The demise of CWS was a sad end for a company that dated back to a partnership formed in 1919 between Silston Cory-Wright (1888–1976) and Cedric Salmon (1891–1979), two New Zealand Army officers who had met in London during World War I. The business, which became a private company in 1933, initially supplied equipment for roading, quarries, cement works, gasworks, breweries, power stations and railways. It soon extended to handling equipment for gold-dredging, meatworks and dairy factories. Fortunately for Turnovsky, CWS was an interlude in an otherwise outstanding career that extended well beyond business. He had established an early reputation as an arts patron, co-founding the Wellington Chamber Music Society in 1949 and serving on a variety of arts bodies including the New Zealand Federation of Chamber Music Societies (president, 1953–60), New Zealand Opera Company (chairman, 1959–69), the Queen Elizabeth II Arts Council (member, deputy chairman, 1968–73) and the National Music Council of New Zealand (president, 1981–86). He was also active in Unesco, serving on the Paris-based executive board from 1978–83. An economic theorist, Turnovsky produced several books and essays on New Zealand's role in a changing world economy.

Polish-born John Roy (born 1933), who arrived in New Zealand with two sisters in 1944, enjoyed similar success in his adopted home. They were part of a group of 700 displaced children brought here by the New Zealand government after the USSR invaded their homeland. Roy, whose original name was Jan Wojciechowski, came from East Poland, in what is now Belarus. On arrival he could not speak English, and owned only the clothes he was wearing. He lived in a refugee camp at Pahiatua for two years before attending St Patrick's College, Silverstream, and Victoria University College where he obtained an accountancy degree. After a period in commercial accountancy, Roy entered the construction industry in 1983, joining forces with Mainzeal Corporation chief executive Peter Menzies (born 1937) in a management buyout of the company. Roy's involvement with Mainzeal had, in fact, started nine years earlier when he led Atlas Majestic Industries (where he was finance director) to acquire a 49 per cent stake in the listed company, then known as

Mainline Corporation (NZ), after its Australian parent had crashed. There was also another link: Menzies' older brother had been in Roy's class at St Pat's.

Roy later became managing director of the restructured and relisted New Zealand company (renamed Mainzeal Group) and also became involved with leather company Mair Astley Holdings through Mainzeal's 1988 merger with Leyland Growth. But Roy's career was not without its problems. As executive chairman of Mair Astley in 1993 he was involved in allegations of incorrect accounting in the company's leather division, and was criticised for a $13 million loss in the wool division. He was also censured by the New Zealand Stock Exchange market surveillance panel after accusations that he had misled them over the reasons for a fall in the company's share price. But the cheerful, thick-set Roy, a survivor all his life, took the criticism in good grace. He was retiring anyway.

Today Roy lives in Howick, Auckland, with his wife, Valerie (née Young). They have four sons and two daughters. Roy, who loves the sea, builds boats commercially through a company he bought from a receiver. Proud of his Polish roots, he sponsors a Polish studies programme at Auckland University and in 1999 was appointed Poland's first honorary consul to New Zealand. He is worth at least $20 million. Menzies, his former business partner, has retired from Mainzeal and sold his stake in the company, and was valued at a minimum $25 million on the 2003 *NBR Rich List*.

The success of Dutch engineer Jo La Grouw, who was born in Amsterdam in 1913, typifies the opportunities for enterprising tradesmen and entrepreneurs in the post-World War II housing boom. He never looked back after arriving in New Zealand in 1951 with fellow engineer John van Loghem (1919–2000), to sell prefabricated steel-framed houses on behalf of a Dutch company. The pair soon realised the vast potential of New Zealand's timber resources and formed Lockwood Buildings, developing a wooden modular home scheme into a house-building empire comprising the Lockwood and Initial Homes brands. Rotorua-based Lockwood Homes, which has 50 franchises nationwide, has the lion's share of the module-building market and has a proud exporting record. It is controlled by La Grouw Corporation, which became family owned in 1982 when van Loghem was bought out on his retirement — a move aimed at forestalling a possible takeover bid by Fletcher Challenge. Jo La Grouw's first and third sons, Joe jnr (born 1940) and Corgi (born 1946), were for some years joint managing directors of La Grouw Corporation, while the middle son, Sydney-based Tjeerd (born 1944), was also a shareholder. In 1999 Joe jnr gained 100 per cent of the company by acquiring shares held by the family through La Grouw Holdings, which led to Corgi's resignation from the La Grouw Corporation board. He remains managing director of La Grouw Holdings, which has substantial property investments and forests; it also owns the Pacific Pine Industries mill at Putaruru, which supplies La Grouw Corporation with 10–20 per cent of its housebuilding materials. Jo La Grouw, who maintains an active interest in the business, was made a member of the New Zealand Order of Merit in 1999 for services to the community and business. La Grouw family wealth today is likely to exceed $35 million.

The rise of Keith Hay Homes mirrors that of Lockwood. The business was started by Keith Hay (1917–97), the son of a door-to-door National Provident Fund salesman, Scots-born William Hay, who instilled stern Free Presbyterian values in his young family. Keith Hay was a child when prayer started working for him. His mother fell seriously ill during a family visit to Scotland and Hay's father told him and his four sisters to pray as hard as they could to stop their mother dying in the night. She lived and Hay became a staunch Christian. After leaving school at thirteen Hay worked as a farm labourer at Kohukohu on the Hokianga Harbour and Ngatea near Thames, also gaining carpentry experience. He later worked at a box factory in Morningside, Auckland, for a motor bodybuilder in nearby Dominion Rd, and for Fletcher Construction until the age of 21 when he bought a set of tools and started in business on his own as a maintenance carpenter. His first job was repairing the windows at Belmont Presbyterian Church on Auckland's North Shore.

The acute housing shortage after World War II created demand for low-cost housing and Hay saw an opportunity for pre-built houses after tendering successfully for the removal of American army huts. By 1953 he was producing his own ready-made houses in Mt Roskill, Auckland, laying the foundations for a huge nationwide business that continues to flourish after his death. By Hay's own description he was 'a carpenter doing God's work', loyal to Presbyterian values and generous to charities and community organisations. In 1955 he was in charge of organising an outdoor meeting to which 75,000 came to see American evangelist Billy Graham — then the largest Christian gathering in New Zealand history — but he is best remembered as the popular, hard-working mayor of Mt Roskill from 1953–74. His service to Mt Roskill and to the Auckland Regional Authority was honoured by the award of an OBE, and later a CBE.

Keith Hay's son, David (born 1947), an accountant, followed his father into local government, winning the Mt Roskill mayoralty in 1987 and going on to become deputy mayor of the new isthmus-wide Auckland City Council in 1992, a post he held until 1998. He and his brother, Grant (born 1957), are joint managing directors of Keith Hay Homes. Another brother, Ian (born

1944), who was also formerly joint managing director, is on the international board of Habitat for Humanity, a charity that builds low-cost houses using the collective skills of its members to keep costs down. The shares in Keith Hay Homes — worth at least $25 million — are held in four family trusts. The Hays form the core of Mt Roskill's conservative 'Bible belt', the Christian environment that gave rise to the political aspirations of John Banks. They have long promoted family values, opposing abortion on demand and homosexuality. In 1985 Keith Hay lent his support to the 830,000-strong petition against the Homosexual Law Reform Bill after God spoke to him in his garden. At the time he said: 'If a man wants to be a homosexual, that is his business but I don't think … a schoolteacher should have the right by law to interfere with a boy over 16 who gives his consent.' David Hay has been similarly robust in his criticism of homosexuality, campaigning against public money being spent on Auckland's annual gay and lesbian Hero parade and objecting to the presence of *Hero* magazine in city libraries. He and other Auckland city councillors were cleared by the Human Rights Commission in 1998 of discrimination on the grounds of sexual orientation — charges arising from the Hero parade debacle.

Sir William Stevenson (1901–83) was never so public in expressing his Christian or personal views. His entry in the 1978 edition of *Who's Who* is just four lines — a reflection of a man who viewed philanthropy as an extension of business success yet shunned the publicity that went with it. In reality, his life was far more than business and philanthropy. He loved farming and fishing, was an excellent sportsman, and was manager of one of New Zealand's most successful Olympic teams. Born in Auckland and educated at Albany, in what is now North Harbour, he joined the carpentry business of his father, William Stevenson. In 1921 the firm bought a Model T Ford, three wheelbarrows and some picks and shovels and branched out into the construction business. William took over the firm after his father fell ill and later brought in his three sons, William jnr, John and James.

Education might not have played a significant part in William's success but practical skills and personal courage certainly did. Among his first contracts was the driving of drainage tunnels in the volcanic strata of Mt Eden, Auckland, and the hard clay of New Lynn, West Auckland. This involved spending hours underground using the painfully slow hammer-and-tap method. But it was on the outfalls at Devonport and Takapuna on Auckland's North Shore and at New Plymouth that another of his skills — skindiving — came to the fore. He would go down 5 m to place gelignite under sealed rocks without the aid of a snorkel. His 'wetsuit' was a pair of saddle-tweed pants and a generous coating of grease. During World War II W. Stevenson & Sons was awarded several key military contracts and after the war it won major North Island construction contracts, including those for much of Auckland's Southern Motorway, the Greenlane–Penrose bypass, the Glenbrook steelmill site, and the Nihotupu dam in the Waitakere Ranges west of Auckland. The company thrives long after Sir William's death, with a range of enterprises that includes engineering contracting, quarry ownership and management, civil engineering, masonry and building supplies, premixed concrete and mechanical and engineering workshops.

Sir William's other achievements are equally impressive: New Zealand single-sculls rowing champion in 1923, 1924, 1926 and 1927; double-sculls champion 1925 and 1926; manager of the 1950 Empire Games rowing camp at Lake Karapiro (he tried to convert a disused quarry at Lake Pupuke, Takapuna, into an international rowing course but settled for Karapiro); manager of the rowing contingent at the 1954 Empire Games at Vancouver; and manager of the New Zealand team at the 1964 Tokyo Olympics — the team that included world-beating athletes Peter Snell, (Sir) Murray Halberg and John Davies. Sir William's list of private donations and endowments is similarly impressive. It includes financing the rebuilding of St Thomas' Church, St Heliers, Auckland, equipment donations to hospitals, endowing the chairs of orthopaedics and plastic surgery and a lectureship in ophthalmic studies at Auckland University medical school, and helping set up the Laura Fergusson Trust for Disabled Persons. Despite his extensive business interests he found time for local body politics, breeding horses and developing the huge Lochinvar station on the Napier–Taupo Rd. In 1970 he broke a five-year-old world fishing record, catching a black marlin off Cairns that weighed 558.6 kg (1231.5 lb). Sir William never became obsessed with the intricacies of high finance. 'Finance was never one of my greatest worries because I knew what I could do and where I was heading,' he once said. 'Big finance is only a matter of common-sense and sincerity.' Sir William was inducted posthumously into the Business Hall of Fame in 1995.

W. Stevenson & Sons is one of many family-owned contracting and civil engineering businesses that blossomed in the post-World War II economy. Dunedin-based Fulton Hogan Holdings, which employs about 1600 people and has a paid capital of $100 million, is a national roading contractor of note that dates back to 1933, yet its well-heeled shareholders barely rate a mention in the business magazines or the social pages. It was formed as a partnership between Jules Fulton (1901–73) and Bob Hogan (1900–92), who had lost their jobs in the Depression. It became a company, Fulton Hogan, in 1935, and a holding company was formed in 1954. Green & McCahill, formed in Auckland in 1971 by Hughie Green (born 1931) and Barney McCahill (born 1928), has an equally low profile yet the partners' collective wealth, though they have largely gone their own ways, is at least $210 million, much of it earned from property speculation and development. This, along with pastoral and horse-racing success, is a significant achievement for two Irish Catholic navvies who arrived in New Zealand from Australia in 1952 with nothing but a wheelbarrow and a pickaxe. Any publicity surrounding Green & McCahill has centred on the sporting prowess of McCahill's large family (he has nine children and Green has five), notably former All Black Bernie McCahill (born 1964), who is married to New Zealand women's soccer player Michelle Cox. His sister, Terry-Anne, was a New Zealand soccer player. Another four brothers have also achieved representative status of one sort or another in rugby, including Sean, who played for Ireland.

While Sir Ron Brierley (born 1937) has never been short of publicity about his business activities, he is another who has not courted it. He stands out as the true corporate loner of the welfare state and is one of its most successful products. He was born in Wellington and brought up in the suburb of Island Bay. His father, John Brierley, one of nine children, was a taxidriver-turned-civil servant with little interest in business; his mother, May (née Reader), a housewife and former accounts clerk. Ron Brierley showed an early liking for money, something his biographer, Yvonne van Dongen, put down to a genetic inheritance from his English-born grandfather, Thomas, a successful, if tightfisted, baker. But in other respects Ron Brierley was an unremarkable child. He lacked co-ordination, was an average performer at school, and struggled with simple tasks like making his bed, and making toast or tea. Only in stamp-collecting did he show any diligence.

After leaving Wellington College he worked as a clerk for the Sun Insurance Co, studying accountancy part time at Victoria University College. It was at this time that he started to get an inkling of how the sharemarket worked. He started dabbling — the first shares he bought were in the Auckland Gas Co — and with some mates formed a share club. In 1956 he published the first issue of a sharemarket tipsheet, *New Zealand Stocks and Shares*, billing the modest publication as 'The Leading Investment Journal'. Leading or not, *New Zealand Stocks and Shares* sent shockwaves through the sedate investment market of the late 1950s. In 1959, more confident than ever, Brierley joined with Trevor Beyer to form an investment company, Investment Funds New Zealand. In 1961 he incorporated his own company, R.A. Brierley Investments, proclaiming in an advertisement to a mystified public: 'Now you can have Real Adventure on the stock market, even if you've never owned a share in your life.' The company promised to pay a 10 per cent dividend on its first full year of operation.

(Sir) Ron Brierley's greatest skills from his earliest days were research and surprise. The commercial establishment, especially old-style company directors, detested his brashness, but long-suffering shareholders applauded him for 'unlocking value' in poorly performing companies.
Courtesy *NBR*

Adventure it was. Brierley was to send the stuffy sharebroking fraternity into a frenzy and frighten the directors of every poorly performing public company in the land. His mission was simple: R.A. Brierley Investments would take over other companies and reorganise their finances, selling off surplus assets and reinvesting the funds for the more useful development of an existing business. Its first acquisition was *New Zealand Stocks and Shares*, and the first company it bid for was Otago Farmers' Co-operative Association, a sleepy, poorly performing operation on the Stock Exchange's unofficial list. It was the start of long-term corporate raiding, for which Brierley would be cast as a corporate devil. R.A. Brierley Investments (renamed Brierley Investments after 1971) made steady progress in the early years, incurring a loss in 1966 but otherwise living up to its promise. In 1967 the company started to take off and, inflation notwithstanding, broke the $1 million profit mark in 1974. By 1983 its profit exceeded $25 million, and from 1987 the company measured profits in hundreds of millions of dollars. Brierley Investments, or BIL as the market preferred to call it, had joined the list of the largest twenty companies in New Zealand by market capitalisation in 1980/81. But its inclusion with the blue chips was a two-edged sword. It was now part of the establishment, not the disrespectful raider looking on, and would face greater market scrutiny. Most of BIL's loyal shareholders were unaware that the quality of the company's profits had been declining steadily since 1978 even though the gross profit had been rising.

The aftermath of the 1987 sharemarket crash should have brought BIL's problems to a head but the market, cluttered with so many corporate failures, let the company off the hook. BIL had done some things well but had made a number of bad investments. Among the 'dogs' was newspaper group NZ News, publisher of the loss-making *Auckland Star* and the failed *Auckland Sun*, the

---

The Rich List*
August 1987
(two months before the sharemarket crash)

Top ten families, main sources of wealth and minimum amount

1.	Todd	Energy, property	$700m
2.	Goodman	Baking, food	$165m
3.	Butland[†]	Food processing	$140m
4.	Moller[†]	Car dealing	$100m
5.	Turner[†]	Fruit/vegetable auctioneering	$80m
6.	Stevenson[†]	Civil engineering, contracting	$66m
=7.	Abel	Cashed up	$60m
=7.	Baigent[†]	Timber	$60m
=7.	Williams	Farming, property	$60m
=10.	Fisher[†]	Whiteware, electronics	$50m
=10.	Gibbons	Car and truck dealing	$50m

* From *Personal Investor Rich 100*, now part of the *National Business Review*.

[†] Removed from the list in subsequent years for reasons other than the 1987 crash. The Todd, Abel, Williams and Gibbons entries were removed in 1989 and 1990 when the *Rich List* ceased to include family entries, but have been restored. The Goodman family was later listed under its principal member, Sir Patrick Goodman, but in 2003 reverted to a family entry.

The Rich List*
August 1987
(two months before the sharemarket crash)

Top ten individuals, main sources of wealth and minimum amount

1. **Spencer, John Berridge** (b. 1934) $675m
   Pulp and paper
   Suffered heavy losses in the 1987 crash but survived and remained rich.

2. **Hawkins, Allan Robert** (b. 1941)† $361m
   Investment banking

=3. **Judge, Bruce Raymond** (b. 1942)† $300m
   Investment

=3. **McConnell, (Arnot) Malcolm** (1930–95)† $300m
   Construction

=5. **Brierley, Ronald Alfred** (b. 1937) $250m
   Investment

=5. **Myers, (Arthur) Douglas** (b. 1938) $250m
   Brewing

=5. **Reynolds, Colin William** (b. 1945)† $250m
   Property development

=8. **Fay, (Humphrey) Michael Gerard** (b. 1949) $175m
   Merchant banking

=8. **Richwhite, David McKellar** (b. 1948) $175m
   Merchant banking

=10. **Giltrap, Colin John** (b. 1940) $150m
   Car dealing

=10. **Herbert, Colin Francis** (b. 1943)† $150m
   Hotels, liquor

---

* From *Personal Investor Rich 100*, now part of the *National Business Review*.

† Main casualties of the 1987 crash. Hawkins was jailed for fraud. McConnell remained on the *Rich List* until his death in 1995 but at a fraction of his pre-crash high. His net worth in 1995 was listed at the minimum entry level of $10 million. For Bruce Judge, see chapter 6.

fledgling airline Ansett New Zealand, and a range of investments entered into by BIL's Australian subsidiary, Industrial Equity, and its international arm, Industrial Equity (Pacific). Brierley himself had signalled an unusual note of caution in his twenty-seventh chairman's annual review in 1988, noting obliquely that there were 'some uncertainties regarding the long-term role of BIL'. Forces within the board were gathering against him and now the raider, who for years could do no wrong, realised that his days at the top were numbered. He did the decent thing, stepping down as chairman from 1 January 1990 but remaining a director. This allowed him to pursue other interests including a UK investment company linked to BIL, Guinness Peat Group. As BIL sold down its holding in GPG, Brierley stepped up his involvement, taking control of the company in 1991, although holding only about 4 per cent of the shares. Year by year GPG looks more like the BIL of old, preying on underperforming companies and offering its own dose of added value. Among those to feel its presence were Auckland fruit and vegetable auction house Turners & Growers, acquired after a division in the Turner family, and Wellington's Colonial Motor Co, where GPG gained a stake after a split in the Gibbons family (the GPG holding has since been sold to a Malaysian company). Among GPG's successes was the sale of Australian insurance and funds management group Tyndall Australia, and a stake in UK company Bluebird Toys. Among GPG's failures was a bid to overturn the demutualisation plans of Tower Corporation, the former Government Life Office in New Zealand.

Sydney-based Brierley, now an Australian citizen, plays hardball in business but outside work has been a generous supporter of cricket and, from time to time, the arts. A bachelor, he lives frugally, gaining more enjoyment from reading the annual report of some long-suffering company than wining and dining a supermodel or jetting off to a rugby match. When his old company, BIL, was in steady decline, he at least had the satisfaction of being able to do deals with people other than bankers. Of all the Kiwis who became wealthy in the era of the welfare state, Brierley is the most perplexing and least understood. He is worth more than $180 million. As for his old company, Brierley Investments, the least said the better. It changed its name to BIL International in 2001 to put its not-so-glorious past behind it and reflect its Asian ownership and direction.

6

1987's long hangover

> *The economic upheaval of the 1980s has created a major shift in who holds wealth and power in New Zealand.*
>
> BRUCE JESSON, JOURNALIST AND AUTHOR, ON THE PERIOD BEFORE THE 1987 SHAREMARKET CRASH

Most things the late Bruce Jesson wrote contained an element of truth. His critique of wealth-creation in the 1980s was no exception. A socialist, but one not opposed to having fun, he viewed the spate of company takeovers and mergers and the wide-ranging public-sector reforms as an epoch — and not an especially attractive one. Yet Jesson was among the minority of the educated left who understood why New Zealand came out of its cocoon-like existence and embraced globalisation, even if he did not approve of the consequences. Prime Minister (Sir) Robert Muldoon had done his best to hold the line against the effects of the world economy by a mixture of policies that included heavy borrowing, subsidies, Think Big energy projects, an overvalued exchange rate, and wage and price freezes. While this made the country sterile for financial entrepreneurs, it was really only continuing the economic nationalism established by the first Labour government. In the words of millionaire former brewer Douglas Myers: 'New Zealand was Poland with sunshine.'

By the early 1980s Muldoon's economic influence was starting to wane and his government was taking the first steps toward deregulation. With his fall in the 1984 general election, and his unconscionable behaviour in the period between National leaving office and Labour coming in, the floodgates opened. The financial markets were quickly reformed after

Labour took over and the public sector followed in short order, providing monstrous incomes for a rising band of wealthy advisers and hatchet-men — the bankers, consultants and sharebrokers associated with the change process. The long-dormant sharemarket took off, giving investors their greatest range of new flotations since the mining- and land-company booms of the 1870s and early 1880s. Investment reached its peak in 1987, despite interest rates of 20 per cent or more and two market 'corrections' — one in January 1987 after Dennis Conner's *Stars & Stripes* defeated New Zealand's *KZ-7* in the America's Cup challenger final, and a second four months later. Undeterred, most sharebrokers and financial advisers continued to promote investment in equities, disregarding the economic axiom that high interest rates and a rising sharemarket do not mix. It was often said in those heady days that you could float an old tyre and be guaranteed the issue would be heavily oversubscribed.

In 1987 the New Zealand Stock Exchange's official list contained a record 361 New Zealand and 178 overseas companies. It reflected not just the confidence of those peddling shares but a new wave of economic liberalism that pervaded the upper echelons of business and certain sections of academia. The Bible for both groups was *Theory K*, an analysis of New Zealand management published in 1986, loosely based on a highly successful American publication, *In Search of Excellence*. The foreword, by Sir Ron Trotter, chairman of the New Zealand Business Roundtable and organiser of the 1984 economic summit, spelled out the direct relationship between business success and wealth-creation. This was a first for a New Zealand academic-type publication. Trotter praised the Labour government for its 'great boldness' in reducing regulation, tariff protection and subsidies and for encouraging competition. 'If New Zealand can maintain the political will to continue these policies to their conclusion,' he wrote, 'it can ... look forward to an era of dynamic growth that will improve all real incomes. The objective to double our real [gross domestic product] per head between now and the end of the century is not unrealistic. Business is the wealth-producing organ of society. As the government withdraws its regulations and interventions, the opportunities for economic growth and new investment will increase. The responsibility and incentive for taking these opportunities lies with business.'

Although few free-marketeers today would dispute Trotter's dictum, what lets *Theory K* down is its excessive faddism. To be sure, it identified the ingredients of a successful enterprise but from today's viewpoint many of the case studies included — such as Brierley Investments, Chase

The first New Zealand Rich List, published by Personal Investment New Zealand *magazine in December 1986, listed the fortunes of 56 individuals and 12 families collectively worth $5.296 billion.*
Courtesy *NBR*

Corporation, Equiticorp Holdings, Rainbow Corporation, Smiths City Market Group, Newmans Group, Community Pharmacy (CPL) and Wilkins & Davies Construction Co — make it a laughing-stock. In 1986–87, however, *Theory K* provided the intellectual underpinning to the belief that the sharemarket knew no bounds.

When Black Tuesday arrived on 20 October 1987, the true strength of New Zealand's capital market was revealed. Just as it had shrunk to a rump a century before, so too in 1987 it contracted rapidly. The crash was an international phenomenon set off by a plunge on Wall Street but while Japan, the United States and Britain got their equity markets back on track fairly quickly, New Zealand slid into a medium-term recession. In the three weeks following Black Tuesday (Black Monday in the US) New Zealand share values tumbled 37.4 per cent, compared with falls of only 15.5 per cent in New York, 18.3 per cent in Tokyo and 28.3 per cent in London. For Wall Street this was a well-signalled if extreme correction after a five-year bull run. US companies and their investors took their medicine and got on with life, refusing to relive the tragedy of the October 1929 crash. New Zealand's sharemarket, which had waited until 1931 to react to the 1929 collapse, received a sharp lesson this time round on the costs of entering the global economy. But international events and wheeler-dealer investment bankers alone cannot be blamed for the pessimism that pervaded New Zealand business and investment markets until well into 1991 — three and a half years after Black Tuesday. New Zealanders on the whole have never been long-term share investors, no more than they have voted in governments with long-term agendas. Between 1984 and 1987, a period of huge growth in the New Zealand sharemarket, it was nigh impossible for any financial journalist to persuade investors that the market was flawed. People did not read prospectuses, certainly not before seeking their firm allocation of shares from a friendly broker, and were not prepared to tolerate suggestions that large-scale property development or investment banking was out of kilter with the true potential of the domestic economy.

The magnet to investors was not so much the companies on offer but who ran them. Thus Equiticorp Holdings' taciturn Allan Hawkins (born 1941), Chase Corporation's mercurial Colin Reynolds (born 1945), and dozens of others with 'management fundamentals' became the sole reason for people to invest, rather than being part of the investment equation. It

Allan Hawkins (born 1941) could do no wrong when he created merchant bank Equiticorp Holdings in 1984. Although devoid of natural charm, he nonetheless inspired investors by his true-grit approach to business. This Equiticorp annual meeting was no exception.
COURTESY *NBR*

is no surprise that those stocks based on confidence and no small degree of hype were the first to tumble in 1987. Much of the true shareholder value in less glamorous stocks survived, although investors had to wait some time to see share prices bounce back. Of the top-ten wealthy New Zealanders in the 1997 *NBR Rich List*, no fewer than six were in the top-ten list in August 1987, just two months before the crash, and a seventh, investor Alan Gibbs (born 1939), was elsewhere on the 1987 *Personal Investor Rich 100* list. The main top-ten casualties — Hawkins, Reynolds and investors Bruce Judge (born 1942) and Colin Herbert (born 1943) — suffered directly from the collapse in share and property prices, as did many others further down the wealth stakes. But prominent businessmen such as toilet-paper magnate John Spencer (born 1934) and construction king Malcolm McConnell (1930–95), who had strayed outside their areas of expertise, also took a caning.

Luck, or rather bad luck, also had its hand in the state of people's fortunes after the crash. Hawkins' fall was especially cruel. On Monday 19 October 1987, the day before the crash, merchant bank Equiticorp, in which the Hawkins and Bayldon families held 40 per cent of the shares, bought the government's 89 per cent stake in New Zealand Steel for $327 million. It was paid for by issuing the Crown 92.9 million Equiticorp shares at $3.52 each. On the face of it the government was taking a $200 million loss on the deal, but it had insured itself by a complicated arrangement whereby Hawkins would buy back the Equiticorp shares at a fixed price if another buyer could not be found. Equiticorp shares were trading at $3.50 on 19 October. At the end of Black Tuesday they were worth $2.90 and falling. Like most investment stocks they continued to slide in the absence of buyers and by the end of February 1988, when the market was particularly bearish, they were fetching $1. Hawkins, without another buyer in sight, had to buy the shares tendered for New Zealand Steel at the pre-crash price.

After Equiticorp's collapse in 1989, its statutory manager successfully sued the Crown to recoup the losses suffered by shareholders in the New Zealand Steel purchase, and was awarded $328 million by the High Court in 1996 — the most expensive legal suit in New Zealand history. A prolonged battle in the courts seemed likely, but in 1998 the Crown agreed to an out-of-court settlement of $267.5 million after deciding an appeal was too risky. This and other out-of-court settlements brought to $331.5 million the gross proceeds the statutory manager had managed to obtain for thousands of shareholders and creditors — more than Equiticorp's original purchase price for New Zealand Steel. Soon after this the statutory manager agreed to pay the liquidator of Equiticorp Australia $23.5 million, allowing payments to be made to the creditors of Equiticorp Industries Group and debentureholders in Equiticorp Holdings. Equiticorp Australia had been seeking $130 million. Meanwhile Hawkins, the second richest New Zealander in the August 1987 *Rich List* ($361 million minimum net worth), and several of his Equiticorp management team had served jail terms for fraud relating to their running of Equiticorp and the financing of the New Zealand Steel purchase. Hawkins, sent down in 1992, was given the longest term by far — six years — but he was out in fewer than three. While he had to contend with rumours he had stashed millions of dollars of Equiticorp money away in family trusts, the truth was that as the dominant shareholder in Equiticorp he was the biggest loser. Unbowed after his release from prison in 1995, he said: 'I am going to go out there and I am going to earn it again ... [People] are going to say, "he must have something hidden away". All I can say to those people is that they can get stuffed.'

Merchant banker Allan Hawkins pictured at the time of his fraud trial in 1991. He was jailed in 1992 for six years, but was out within three, beaten yet never broken by his ordeal.
Courtesy *NBR*

Equiticorp was the pall that hung over New Zealand after the crash because Hawkins, unlike other failed merchant and investment bankers or property speculators, was no Flash Harry. He was older than most (in his late forties) and had been at the serious end of business for many years, although his career had been far from plain sailing. The Christchurch-educated accountant had all the charm of actor Robert Mitchum on a bad day. If a reporter was lucky enough to get an interview with Hawkins, he or she could expect little more than a 'yep' or a 'nope'. Hawkins might manage a smile if the interviewer happened to share his passion for marathon-running, but that could not be guaranteed. If Hawkins had an X-factor it was in the meticulous way he did business and the confidence he inspired rather than his personality.

The gregarious Chase boys, on the other hand, whose mirror-glazed headquarters in Manukau Rd, Auckland, was within metres of Hawkins' office, courted key journalists and opinion-makers regularly, entertaining them at in-house business lunches and occasionally after work. The 'smoothie' of these property developers was executive chairman Colin Reynolds, who had founded Chase Holdings in 1970 with fellow accountant Rodney Spiers (born 1945) and farm consultant Wilson Jolly (born 1942). But deputy executive chairman Peter E. Francis (born 1945), another accountant, executive directors Adrian Burr (born 1943) and Seph Glew (born 1954), and others did their bit. Their talk over the lunch table was confident, businesslike and inspirational, and they played their guests well. Reynolds was the Te Awamutu bookkeeper made good (worth at least $450 million according to the 1986 *Rich List*); Francis ($45 million) the strategist — the director who had got Chase into bed with the Moodabe family (Amalgamated Theatres) and wooed Lincoln Laidlaw and other Farmers' Trading Co directors to accept Chase's takeover offer; Burr ($95 million), a former wine salesman, demonstrated the haughtiness of someone with natural flair and an ability to pick winners; and Glew ($10 million), the Kaikohe kid who had once worked for the State Advances Corporation and had lived in a state house, who was off to run Chase's operation in the United States.

Compared with Hawkins, in straight business terms Reynolds and his team were Johnny-come-latelies, but during the sharemarket boom they were the cardinals of corporate New Zealand — a class apart from the hatchet-men at Brierley Investments (or so it seemed). The only thing Hawkins and Reynolds had in common was a background in accountancy. Hawkins had started his career conventionally enough as an accounting clerk with Mobil Oil. He then joined Pacific Factors, which became Marac Finance, and moved to Auckland where he met John Bayldon (1942–80), leaving Marac in 1978 to join Bayldon at Transvision Holdings, a listed television rental company and small finance house. He and Bayldon, who was dying of leukaemia, borrowed heavily to acquire a 40 per cent holding in Transvision. In 1980, shortly before Bayldon's death, the Commercial Bank of Australia was persuaded to buy 51 per cent of Transvision with a view to transforming it into a fully fledged finance company and merchant bank. It duly changed its name to CBA Finance Holdings. Hawkins, the chief executive, had expanded the business rapidly after Bayldon's death, selling off the TV-hire operation and developing the finance section. But under Westpac Banking Corporation control, following a merger between the Commercial Bank of Australia and the Bank of New South Wales, Hawkins felt his management style was being cramped. Westpac felt he was 'too flamboyant', so much so that the new bank delayed gracing its subsidiary with the Westpac name. The differences were insurmountable and Hawkins departed in February 1984 to form his own company, Equiticorp Holdings, with the bank acquiring his 15 per cent stake in CBA Finance. Some sixteen CBA Finance staff, six from his old company, Marac, and three from another finance house, Broadbank Corporation, joined him, attracted by his entrepreneurial spirit. Westpac was furious. It sought to restrain Hawkins and former CBA Finance staff from having anything to do with Equiticorp, and filed a $6.5 million writ against Hawkins. Hawkins counterfiled.

Originally Equiticorp was to have been a $20 million dealmaker and merchant bank half owned by Hawkins/Bayldon interests, but that was considered too small and it was capitalised at $35 million. The float of Equiticorp that year was spectacular: the shares traded up to $1.65 on the first day, giving the stags a profit of $1.15 a share. The Hawkins/Bayldon interests earned a paper profit of $22 million in the first hour's trading. Hawkins, although not prone to laughing, could literally laugh his way to the (Equiticorp) bank. He wasted little time establishing Equiticorp's presence in New Zealand and in 1985 he branched out in Australia with attempts to take over ACI International and strategic purchases in Broken Hill Pty (BHP). This was not the stuff of a corporate fly-by-nighter, and Hawkins' master plan might have worked had not the sharemarket crash intervened.

Hawkins' failure was the most dramatic and his 'web of deceit' (as Serious Fraud Office director Charles Sturt described it) contributed to the

Bruce Judge (born 1942), pictured here with his private jet, symbolised the misplaced confidence of investors in the power of management before the 1987 sharemarket crash.
Courtesy *NBR*

fall-off in investor confidence that weakened New Zealand property and financial markets long after overseas markets started to pick up. But he was not alone. The actions of many others had panicked the Labour government, local banks, small businesses and home-owners, and saddled the Bolger National government, elected by a landslide majority in October 1990, with an unexpected massive second bail-out of the partly state-owned Bank of New Zealand.

The Treasury had realised early on that the New Zealand sharemarket was suffering a prolonged period of mourning and in March 1988 it had asked *NBR* editor Nevil Gibson to identify major public and commercial concerns over sharemarket deals and announcements leading up to and following the crash. He was also asked to provide case studies supporting these concerns, and to comment on Securities Commission proposals aimed at greater market disclosure and eliminating insider trading. Gibson provided twelve case studies — some involving the nation's richest businessmen — along with recommendations for greater disclosure, a takeovers code that would enhance minority shareholders' rights, improved financial reporting standards and elimination of conflicts of interest. Gibson's report, produced before the failure of Equiticorp, placed the complicated Judge Corporation-Renouf Corporation-Kupe Group deal at the top of the list. This grouping of companies associated with Bruce Judge, a Christchurch businessman and former New Zealand Olympic hockey representative now living in Brisbane, first raised concern in early 1987 when a deal was announced involving Auckland merchant bank Euro-National Corporation. Euro-National, floated by entrepreneur Rod Petricevic (born 1949) in 1985, had bought 47 per cent of property developer Kupe and later sold it to Judge Corporation, a newly formed investment company controlled by Bruce Judge. Delayed settlement and option agreements meant the deal did not go through before Judge Corporation's collapse, leaving Kupe controlled by Euro-National and Brierley Investments.

Another Bruce Judge deal involved changing control of Renouf Corporation, a listed merchant bank and investment company founded in 1980 by Wellington sharebroker (Sir) Frank Renouf (1918–98), but not disclosing the beneficial owner of Harmony Securities, which had acquired a parcel of Renouf Corporation shares before the sharemarket crash. In late 1987 Euro-National revealed that Harmony was owned by Caxton Group interests — those of John Spencer — and had the right to sell these virtually worthless shares to Euro-National at prices well above the market value. The option had not been exercised at the time of Gibson's report but was provided for in Euro-National's reported sharemarket losses of more than $200 million. Renouf Corporation, under Judge control, also reneged on a takeover of Impala Pacific, a Bruce Judge-controlled Hong Kong company, and was suspended by Hong Kong Stock Exchange officials. Renouf Corporation suffered the ignominy of being described by the *Wall Street Journal* as the world's worst stock (the crash had wiped 90 per cent off its share price). Overall, the New Zealand losses of the companies involved in the Judge-Renouf-Kupe deal exceeded $500 million.

Other deals singled out by Gibson included:

▶ The merger in 1988 of NZ Forest Products, once New Zealand's largest company, with Australia's Elders Resources after a series of expensive share dealings involving NZFP's so-called white knight, one-time investment company Rada Corporation. Rada's defence against a takeover bid from Fletcher Challenge in 1986 — paying over the odds for Wattie Industries' strategic 25 per cent stake in NZ Forest Products — caused heavy losses to Rada shareholders and was to lead to its collapse. It reported a loss in July 1988 of $488.9 million, then the largest for a listed New Zealand company. Much of the responsibility for

Sir Frank Renouf's snobbishness and extreme vanity put him offside with many and when he got his comeuppance after the sharemarket crash, there was little sympathy for his predicament. But before his death in 1998 his unique contribution to merchant banking and sharebroking was honoured by his induction into the Business Hall of Fame.
COURTESY NBR

its demise could be laid at the feet of Rada's and NZ Forest Products' managing director, George Wheeler (born 1947), the former general manager of NZI Corporation's information technology subsidiary, Paxus Corporation;

▶ Pacer Pacific Corporation's merger with Kerridge Odeon Corporation and the gold-plated rights issue Pacer's David Phillips and his brother, Steven, scored from the deal;

▶ The formation of Sydney-based Inter-Pacific Equity from the shareholder-directors of listed New Zealand construction company McConnell Dowell Corporation. Inter-Pacific Equity was geared up to acquire their shareholdings at a hefty premium but minority shareholders in McConnell Dowell were later offered a lesser deal in a full takeover;

▶ The merger of Lion Corporation with L.D. Nathan & Co, in which merchant bank Fay Richwhite & Co received a hefty cash premium for its 35 per cent strategic stake in L.D. Nathan while minorities got Lion scrip only for their shares. This arrangement breached the spirit and intent of the New Zealand Stock Exchange's takeover rules, and a Securities Commission inquiry was held after a complaint from Lion's other major shareholder, Malayan Breweries. The chief participants in this deal: Lion Corporation managing director Douglas Myers; L.D. Nathan shareholders Peter Cooper (born 1951) and Chris Mace (born 1944), and Fay Richwhite principals (Sir) Michael Fay (born 1949) and David Richwhite (born 1948); and

▶ Unexplained dramatic share-price rises in two minor investment stocks, Energycorp Investments and Epicorp Investments, followed by equally rapid receiverships.

Energycorp, which was run by several prominent accountants and former associates of John Spencer, seemed to encapsulate the all-embracing greed of the sharemarket boom. It had managed to get a $15.5 million loan from the Bank of New Zealand, yet after the company failed only $4 million was recovered from its assets which had a book value of $35 million. 'Before the crash,' wrote historian David Grant, 'four Energycorp directors had given themselves salaries of $325,000 apiece, BMWs, Alfa Romeos, Mercedes and Rovers and made use of the company's Lear jet. By 1989, three of the directors — Gerald Henry, Steven Trott and Raymond Joy — were either bankrupt or had reached compromise deals with creditors for debts and personal guarantees of $55.7 million, $22.2 million and $16.7 million respectively.' Henry (born 1955), who was adjudged bankrupt in 1989 on a credit card debt, fled to the United States where he was later jailed for four years and eight months for fraud and conspiracy to defraud. He had been found guilty by the US District Court on eleven charges after his investment company, Madison Company of New York, fraudulently obtained $US1.3 million from private investors.

New Zealand banks' bad lending was blamed for fostering a rash of corporate ill-doings, but the truth was that a broad swathe of New Zealanders had a hand in creating the climate of pre-crash greed, not least financial journalists who had asked too few hard questions of company promoters. The October 1986 cover story of the glossy *Personal Investment New Zealand* magazine was on Ray Smith (born 1949), governing director of the Auckland Coin & Bullion Exchange, and his advice to would-be gold investors. Auckland Coin & Bullion was acquired by Goldcorp Holdings, which floated early the following year with Smith as chairman. The tipsheet, *Headliner*, described the company as a 'glamorous newcomer' to the sharemarket, and Auckland sharebroking house Hendry Hay McIntosh salivated, recommending investors buy the shares because of the 'entrepreneurial flair, professional skill and motivation of the people involved'. The glitter barely lasted beyond the sharemarket crash. Smith was sacked as chairman in March 1988 when the company announced it was suing him and his family trust over their sale of Auckland Coin & Bullion to Goldcorp before the public float. When Goldcorp failed in July 1988, 408 Goldcorp certificate holders tried unsuccessfully to stop the receivers trading their platinum, gold and silver, which was said to have been stored on their behalf in Goldcorp's vaults. In 1995 nearly 200 investors won a partial victory, the Privy Council in London ruling that those who could prove a proprietory interest in gold and silver stored on the actual date of the receivership had a valid claim against the receivers. That entitled them to a share of $525,000 seven years after Goldcorp went into receivership — less than 6 per cent of the original $9 million sought by them. Some claimants bitterly recalled Ray Smith's reassuring comments well before the crash — 'We'd be delighted if there was a run on [the gold in our] bank; we're running out of office space,' and 'We don't trust the banks to store our gold — a gold person doesn't trust the banking system or government.'

Smith showed no remorse for his part in the company's downfall. In 1993 he was jailed for six months after being found guilty on fifteen charges brought under the Insolvency and Companies Acts relating to his business activities while a bankrupt and to concealing assets from creditors. The judge found Smith was involved in the sales of a hot-air balloon and an aviation business for $150,000; helicopter parts for $US67,291; a house in Kohimarama, Auckland, for $110,000; and a Chrysler Le Baron convertible car for $US7500. A feature of the trial was the role of his estranged wife, 25-year-old model Monique McFadden, who had returned from the United States to give evidence against him. Even in jail Smith was not out of the limelight. He made news in 1994 when it was disclosed that he and three other inmates had been let out of the light-security Tongariro-Rangipo prison to play golf at Turangi. In a book released that year Smith wrote in detail of his passion for cars and his tastes in women, and tax-avoidance schemes he had operated in the 1980s. His parting shot: 'I don't have a debt to society.'

Smith was but one of several investor-speculators to have been hyped by the media before the crash. The cover story in the inaugural issue of *Personal Investment New Zealand* magazine in September 1986 featured Bruce Judge, the man who would become the first major New Zealand victim of the crash. The same issue contained profiles of Ron Brierley, Colin Reynolds, Allan Hawkins and Bob Jones. Only Brierley and Jones survived the crash — they were knighted in 1988 and 1989 respectively — but their companies, corporate raider Brierley Investments and property investor Robt Jones Investments, took a pounding longer term. In September 1987, a month before the crash, Reynolds featured in *Personal Investor*'s cover story, which carried the alluring headline: 'Get rich in property — $250 million man Colin Reynolds tells how.' The new boy on the block, 31-year-old Craig Heatley, provided *Personal Investor*'s October cover story. This issue, on sale when Black Tuesday struck, carried the headline: 'Your first steps to a fortune.'

By a strange irony *Personal Investor* was nearer to the mark than it had ever been. Heatley, whose Rainbow Corporation had been gobbled up by Brierley Investments that August for having the temerity to challenge BIL for control of companies like Masport and Progressive Enterprises, was sitting pretty. To be sure, Heatley's paper fortune had been halved to $60 million during the year as a result of the tumble in Rainbow's share price — a decline in part due to bad-mouthing by BIL's New Zealand chief executive, Paul Collins (born 1953), during the battle for Progressive — but he was largely a free agent. As a non-executive director of Brierley Investments, a post more ceremonial than real, Heatley had income, standing and 20 million BIL shares (from the sale of his 25 per cent stake in Rainbow), but no responsibility when the sharemarket crash hit home. With the exception of Rainbow's strategic stakes in Progressive and Woolworths Australia, its assets were not up to much — certainly not a patch on those of Winstone or Magnum, two other companies that joined Brierley Investments' stable in 1987. Rainbow's much-vaunted Rainbow's End fun park in Manukau city — briefly the investment flagship for the diverse group — never paid its way yet Heatley, described by *Personal Investor* in 1987 as the 'fastest of the fast-moving entrepreneurs Rogernomics threw up', had steadfastly believed otherwise.

A year on the BIL board was enough and Heatley was off on a second career. With cricketer and textile trader Terry Jarvis (born 1944) he launched the Sky pay-television UHF network in New Zealand in May 1990. Later that year, when the investment markets were still wallowing in post-crash blues, Sky announced that it had attracted 25,000 subscribers who were paying an average of $14.99 a week, although it was still not making a profit. Heatley's old magic had returned. Soon the trappings of this new phase of wealth were starting to show through. He sold down part of his Sky holding to American interests in 1991, sold his designer mansion in St Heliers, Auckland, and moved with his wife and young family to an even grander mansion (costing $2 million to build) at Milford on Auckland's North Shore. He helped bankroll the right-wing lobby, the Association of Consumers & Taxpayers, which became the political party Act New Zealand, in November 1994.

Heatley and Jarvis sold more of their Sky holdings as part of the float of the company in 1997 and most of the remainder in 1999 when the company was taken over by Independent Newspapers. The Heatleys' minimum net worth, taking into account family trusts in place for many years, was estimated in the 2003 *Rich List* to be at least $150 million. Not a bad return for a one-time Upper Hutt paperboy who reputedly had invested $500 in the sharemarket by the age of eleven.

The secret to Heatley's success is his ability to look forward rather than back, and it was no surprise to find in 1999 that he had linked up with another entrepreneur, the king of office supplies, Eric Watson (born 1959), in an electronic commerce venture. Who knows what he might be doing in twenty years' time? If only Heatley's spirit had been universal after the sharemarket crash. The property sector, whose survival depends far more on confidence than on the level of interest rates, was especially badly hit after 1987. In the 24 months following Black Tuesday, the market capitalisation of public property companies in New Zealand fell by nearly four-fifths to less than $1.3 billion. In October 1987 there were 43 companies in this group. By September 1989 no fewer than fourteen companies had been placed in some form of receivership, three were defunct and five were taken over or subject to takeover. The effect of this clean-out on the paper wealth of prominent New Zealanders was huge. The minimum collective wealth of the 76 individuals and 25 families on the 1987 *Rich List* was more than $8 billion. A decade later, the wealth of 117 individuals and 27 families was less than $7.5 billion. Even in the 2003 *Rich List*, which contained 157 individuals and 37 families, the total value was less than $18.4 billion — about 2.27 times the pre-crash level of personal and family wealth although nearly 16 years had elapsed since Black Tuesday. This suggests that the value of property and investment stocks during the 1985–87 bull run was an aberration, given that most of the long-term rich survived the crash. But such wisdom after the event is of little comfort to principals or key investors in the string of investment and property companies that failed.

Among the more publicised casualties was Auckland's Olly Newland (born 1939), who seemed to epitomise the flakiness of large-scale property speculation. At his business height in 1987 he was conservatively worth $45 million, and was enjoying the good life that came with such wealth. The son of German-Jewish refugees, Newland was nineteen when he first dabbled in property, putting a deposit on a section and selling it at a profit two months later. By the age of 30 he owned 200 residential properties in Auckland. Three years later he bought his first Rolls-Royce (he was to own nine of them) and over time he developed a love for other luxury cars, especially Bentleys, and antiques. Newland switched to commercial property in the 1980s and in 1982 floated a public company, Landmark Properties (later Landmark Corporation). He held 21 per cent of Landmark at the time of the crash as well as a substantial stake in Pacific Metropolitan, a retail property investment company. When Black Tuesday arrived Newland and his companies had no realisable assets to cover their borrowings. They toppled like dominoes. To his credit, Newland took his punishment well, and in his 1994 book, *Lost Property* — one of several he has written — he fully admitted to his bad decision-making before the crash. Newland had moved away from his forte — buying property — and had become obsessed with the Landmark share price. His frank assessment of his own failure was refreshing, as were his parting shots:

1. Never trust bankers;

2. Put everything you own into your wife's or children's name or into a trust so that if disaster befalls you, at least something will be salvaged;

3. Always take a profit when it is offered; and

4. Remember that all too often justice comes through the chequebook. If you can afford the huge costs of a court battle you are far more likely to get a fair go. If you cannot pay you will miss out. Tough luck.

Such homespun advice might have saved property investor David Grose (born 1956) from financial disaster. He had failed to learn his lesson in 1987 when his property portfolio got overheated and he was forced to sell it to Chase Corporation for $30 million. This deal settled a string of debts and allowed him to expand his Australian operation by acquiring a range of well-priced properties following the sharemarket crash. At its peak, Grose's Australian portfolio was worth $A200 million, but high interest rates and the severity of Australia's post-crash recession started taking their toll. Soon he was experiencing problems similar to those he had suffered in New Zealand in the mid-1980s. In late 1990 Grose again turned his attention to New Zealand, making an audacious bid to buy Wellington's Harbour City development for around $43 million on a deposit of $4 million. He was unable to raise the necessary finance, the deal foundered and he lost his deposit. A bid in 1991 to buy the capital's 31-level Plimmer City Centre for a reported $51 million also failed through lack of finance. Grose's failing in New Zealand and Australia was not his inability to close deals but his reluctance to sell and take a loss when under pressure. This ultimately led to his bankruptcy in New South Wales and New Zealand. One result was that his elderly parents, former state-house tenants, lost the home in Glandovey Rd, Fendalton, Christchurch, that Grose had bought for them. Long discharged from bankruptcy, he is still doing property deals in the hope that the 'big one' will come along. It has not yet.

Grose is living proof of the lengths property investors and developers will go to in order to reinvent themselves. In the case of the Chase boys, who bailed Grose out in 1987, it has largely worked. Colin Reynolds, wiser and greyer than in 1987, rejoined the *Rich List* in 1998 on the strength of his Symphony Group's successful redevelopment of the former Farmers' Trading Co building in Hobson St, Auckland — ironically the ex-head office of the company Chase took over in 1986 and nearly destroyed. Compared with Chase's disastrous Finance Plaza in Queen St in the 1980s, the conversion of the old Farmers building into the Heritage Auckland hotel and the construction of adjacent office buildings has drawn wide praise.

These days Reynolds avoids publicity, as does Adrian Burr, who is by far the most successful of the Chase alumni. Burr managed to offload his Chase shares, later worthless, in 1988 and continued to show good form in the property market. In 1998 he staged the coup of coups when he acquired the Viaduct Basin, home of the America's Cup, from Ports of Auckland. His successful bid, through his Westmed Group, was in conjunction with two other victims of the sharemarket crash, Mark Wyborn (born 1949) and David Muller (born 1947) of Tramco Investments (later Tramco Harbour Holdings), a company in which Burr has an interest and which bought the valuable adjacent leasehold site, the former Turners

& Growers produce market. Wyborn and Muller had been principals of Auckland-based Unigroup Pacific (formerly Unity Group and before that D. McL. Wallace) when it crashed in 1988. The centre of their present interests is just down the hill from the ex-Farmers building redeveloped by Reynolds' Symphony Group. Uptown, Peter Francis made his post-crash mark in the entertainment business through his company, Force Corporation. Force took over Amalgamated Theatres, a movie-theatre chain once owned by Chase, and built a multiplex in Newmarket and other suburban multiplexes. His big project involved restoring the Civic Theatre, opening a big-screen Imax theatre and bringing Planet Hollywood to New Zealand. It came on stream in 1999. In 2000 Force was to take over internet service provider Ihug (the Internet Group) — probably the first New Zealand entertainment company to join forces with an internet operation — but the $120 million deal came unstuck when 'dotcom' stocks took a tumble worldwide. This was the second reversal for Ihug. In 1999 plans by company owners the Wood family to sell 30 per cent of Ihug to Sky Network Television for $30 million fell through because Sky directors apparently considered the Woods 'greedy'. The Woods, for their part, suggested the deal foundered over a 'struggle for control'. The estimated worth of the Wood family in the 1999 *Rich List* was $75 million, but fell to $35 million in the 2000 list and was said to be $30 million by 2003.

Force, meanwhile, had its own problems and in 2001 Francis sold his majority stake in the company to casino operator Sky City Entertainment Group, netting him nearly $20 million and guaranteeing his continued inclusion in the *Rich List*. He and Wyborn had returned to the list in 1998 after many years' absence but, like Reynolds', their fortunes are smaller than the paper wealth they enjoyed before the sharemarket crash.

The re-emergence of the failed developers of the 1980s has raised a few eyebrows among older members of Auckland's business community, but for the most part their projects have won support. Compared with the original Britomart scheme, in which the Auckland City Council was to have played a key role, the projects of these born-again developers have gone relatively smoothly. They have had their problems, of course — Symphony Group swapped construction companies mid-stream on the former Farmers building — but nothing like those they faced when the market collapsed in 1987. Their days of having to charm financial journalists and analysts to prop up a wobbly share price are well over.

The reborn developers have had to compete with a handful of smart, young deal makers who either were not around in 1987 or were sufficiently

The Rich List
July 1997
(nearly ten years after the sharemarket crash)

Top ten individuals, main sources of wealth and minimum amount

1. **Myers, (Arthur) Douglas** (b. 1938)* $325m
   Brewing

=2. **Fay, Sir (Humphrey) Michael Gerard** (b. 1949)* $245m
   Merchant banking

=2. **Richwhite, David McKellar** (b. 1948)* $245m
   Merchant banking

4. **Gibbs, Alan Timothy** (b. 1939)† $220m
   Investment

=5. **Giltrap, Colin John** (b. 1940)* $200m
   Car dealing

=5. **Hart, Graeme Richard** (b. 1955) $200m
   Cashed up

=5. **Spencer, John Berridge** (b. 1934)* $200m
   Cashed up, investment

8. **Tindall, Stephen Robert** (b. 1951) $150m
   Retailing

9. **Brierley, Sir Ronald Alfred** (b. 1937)* $120m
   Investment

=10. **Hoggard, Kerrance Mervyn** (b. 1941) $90m
   Chemicals

=10. **Watson, Eric John** (b. 1959) $90m
   Office products

* In the top ten in *Personal Investor Rich 100*, August 1987.

† Elsewhere on the August 1987 list.

The Rich List
July 1997
(nearly ten years after the sharemarket crash)

Top ten families, main sources of wealth and minimum amount

1.	Todd*	Telecommunications, energy, etc.	$1.4b
2.	Horton	Media	$148m
3.	Levene	Property	$95m
=4.	Stewart	Plastics, electrical goods	$80m
=4.	Talley†	Fisheries	$80m
6.	Foreman	Investment	$78m
7.	Huljich	Cashed up	$70m
8.	Abel*	Cashed up	$50m
9.	Vela	Fishing, racehorses	$48m
10.	Fletcher	Pulp, paper, energy, etc.	$45m

* In the top ten in *Personal Investor Rich 100*, August 1987.
† Elsewhere on the August 1987 list.

junior to survive the crash intact. The undisputed leader of this group — affectionately known as the 'brat pack' — is Andrew Krukziener (born 1965). The son of Holocaust survivors Abraham and Vera Krukziener, who are substantial property investors in their own right, he made his mark in the business from age twenty when he managed commercial properties with Landmark Corporation. He left in 1988 and established Krukziener Properties. Krukziener was one of the first developers to find a new use for old buildings as ritzy apartment blocks. In 1996 he bought One Queen Street, arguably one of Auckland's uglier tower blocks, which he refurbished successfully with the help of his friendly banker, HSBC.

Another large project (and one critics said would be his undoing) was the swank 40-storey, 350-apartment Metropolis tower incorporating the former Auckland Magistrates' Court. It was saddled with financial problems from the day it was built, damaging Krukziener's whizz-kid reputation and personal fortune in the process.

Not just property high-fliers of the 1980s have managed a comeback. Corporate raider Bruce Hancox, the gung-ho chief executive of Brierley Investments from 1984–86 and its chairman from 1990–92, has been steadily acquiring businesses from his Nelson base since quitting the BIL board in 1996. His interests include FM radio, a timber company and a printing works. In 1999 he joined another ex-Brierley Investments chief executive, Paul Collins, and a former BIL director, lawyer Patsy Reddy (born 1954), in a Wellington-based venture, Active Equities. The company invests in a range of listed and unlisted companies. Collins returned to the *Rich List* in 1998 after being fired from the struggling Brierley Investments, leaving with a $4 million golden parachute. Former BIL chairman Bob Matthew, a victim of the same boardroom reshuffle, got $750,000. BIL founder Sir Ron Brierley described the payouts as 'scandalous', a criticism that did not go down well with Matthew or Collins. Matthew, whose language is more in keeping with a bar room than a boardroom, has been on the *Rich List* since 1987. He is a former chief executive of Magnum Corporation (now DB Breweries), having joined Magnum's predecessor, Rothmans Industries, in Hawke's Bay as a data processing manager in 1968. By 1977 he was group general manager, and four years later managing director. He made a $34 million killing in 1986 on shares he bought from Rothmans International of London as part of a deal by which Rothmans Industries sold its New Zealand cigarette and tobacco interests to Rothmans Holdings of Australia. He masterminded the restructuring, changing the company's core business to liquor and groceries, and in 1988 was appointed New Zealand chief executive of BIL. His minimum net worth in 2003 was estimated at $40 million.

The ability of highly motivated businesspeople who have had a bad run of luck to bounce back is not something that can be taken for granted. Labour Justice Minister (Sir) Geoffrey Palmer certainly did not when, in October 1988, he established a five-man Ministerial Commission of Inquiry into the sharemarket. The inquiry, better known as the Russell Inquiry after its chairman, former Reserve Bank governor Sir Spencer Russell, was launched a year and eight days after Black Tuesday. It reported in March 1989 after hearing 113 submissions. Its prime task was to ensure an efficient, fair and disciplined sharemarket — one that would address the types of abuses *NBR* editor Nevil Gibson had identified in his March 1988 report to the Treasury. Russell's commission had little time in which to act — the markets were weak and waiting for leadership — and its report was all the bolder for the time constraint. It led to the first major revamp of the New Zealand Stock Exchange since its establishment as a national body in 1983, not the least significant innovation being the creation of a market surveillance panel. More importantly, the committee identified several reasons for the exchange's poor performance, including:

▶ Leveraged investments and property companies whose performance was particularly sensitive to market change;
▶ Administrative and liquidity problems with certain sharebrokers;
▶ Dubious transactions and accounting practices in some listed companies;
▶ Lack of economic growth to provide stimulus for the market;
▶ Uncertainty over taxing of superannuation funds;
▶ Adverse impact of international tax reforms on listed companies; and
▶ Lack of an internationally comparable supervisory structure for the market.

The commission did not get all it wanted — had it done so New Zealand would have been blighted with overregulation like Australia — but its report was the start of the post-crash healing process. That process was as much personal as institutional. By 1991, when the economy was strengthening, small investors were starting to own up to the fact that they shared some responsibility for the crash. But there was no great urge to return to the sharemarket. An *NBR* poll in October 1992 revealed 44 per cent of the public considered the sharemarket was being manipulated, and 77 per cent considered the big players were getting a better deal than small investors.

The crash affected victims in many different ways. There were a few prominent suicides, among them Auckland Club president and prominent lawyer Peter Martelli. People like Bruce Judge and Richmond Paynter (born 1948), executive chairman of Christchurch-based developer-constructor Paynter Corporation, lent heavily on their Christian faith to pull them through. Others never became reconciled to the post-crash investment environment — the 'black-armband brigade'. Fortunately many New Zealanders who had been hurt by the sharemarket crash learned to get on with life and enjoy the fruits of a growing economy during 1992–95, even if their reaction to equity investment was 'never again'.

Pride played a big part in how some of the victims adjusted to their reduced status. Publicity-shy John Spencer and his former business associate Rod Petricevic put their Sydney waterfront mansions on the market in 1988 without fuss or bother. Spencer's Pt Piper home carried a price tag of at least $A15 million (he had bought it the previous year from investment banker Robert Whyte for $A11 million but had apparently never stayed there). Petricevic's Darling Pt home, Callooa — the original Darling family home on Darling Pt — went to auction with a reputed reserve of $A5 million. For Petricevic, a partner in merchant bank Fay Richwhite & Co before setting up Euro-National Finance in 1981, it was the end of a short but indulgent life in the fast lane. Today he is managing director of Bridgecorp Holdings, an Auckland-based finance company that bears little resemblance to Euro-National — and just as well. Still, as the first Kiwi-born member of a Croatian family that maintained links with New Zealand over three generations, he has done better financially than most of his forebears here; they were seamen, gumdiggers and eating-house proprietors.

For Spencer, whose wealth was largely inherited, the sale of his Sydney mansion was an admission that he was wounded if not destroyed by the sharemarket crash. Spencer had topped the 1986 and 1987 *Rich Lists* with an estimated minimum wealth of $650 million and $675 million respectively. His involvement with Petricevic, through Bruce Judge's giant corporate paper shuffle, was a rare direct foray into the public company arena. The origin of his wealth was the Caxton Printing Works, founded in Auckland in 1890 by his grandfather, Albert. His conservationist father, Berridge Spencer (1896–1974), had expanded the business after World War I, opening a mill at Kawerau and a printing works at Henderson, West Auckland, served by 30,000 ha of planted forest in the Bay of Plenty that was leased from Maori landowners. Caxton became a significant exporter and in the local market, aided by import protection, Caxton Pulp & Paper established a monopoly in tissue, toilet paper and other household products. After Berridge's death the business reins passed to John Spencer, who had been working in the company with his younger brother, Peter (born 1936), and Caxton was upgraded and expanded. Its overseas investments included interests in the Finnish pulp and paper industry, the link being John Spencer's Finnish wife, architect Tytti (née Laurola), who died of cancer in 1992, aged 54. In 1989 Caxton was sold to Carter Holt

Harvey for $300 million, ending the Spencer family's almost 99-year involvement with the group. John Spencer then moved into the investment area, although most publicity about him centred on his unsuccessful battle with residents on Waiheke Island who wanted to use a public road that ran through his Stony Batter estate.

Peter Spencer, who had had only a small interest in Caxton, developed a wide range of business interests over a long period including car assembly (Motor Holdings), financial services (Equitable Group), clothing (Alliance Textiles [NZ]), meat (Affco Holdings), communications (Cellular-Vision [NZ]), property and farming. Many of his trading companies were brought under the wing of his private investment vehicle, Caspex Corporation. Reputedly New Zealand's largest farmer, he retains extensive pastoral holdings throughout New Zealand, the largest being the 4856-ha Erewhon station near Taihape, a sheep and cattle run dating back to the 1860s which he bought for $6 million in 1992. (Its name was inspired by Samuel Butler's famous novel, as was the South Island station of the same name.) Despite his commitment to New Zealand, he now lives in Essex, England.

The post-crash tribulations of John Spencer and Rod Petricevic were not a patch on those surrounding Sir Frank Renouf, who was linked to the pair via Bruce Judge's share deals. In April 1988, devastated by the tumble in Renouf Corporation's fortunes, he sold his Pt Piper mansion, Paradis sur Mer, for $A19.2 million, much to the disgust of his estranged wife, Susan, Lady Renouf (better known as Susan Sangster), who had tried to stop the sale and had refused to leave the property. Renouf had bought the mansion, then known as Toison d'Or, from her second husband, British racehorse owner Robert Sangster, for $A8.5 million. He had married the twice-divorced Australian socialite in 1985 after his marriage to Ann Renouf (née Harkin), the mother of his four children, was dissolved after 31 years. But the marriage to Susan Sangster lasted only for the period Renouf was rich. By December 1987 Sangster was claiming in court that Renouf had lost $3.85 million of her trust funds on the sharemarket (Renouf Corporation) and was using her to gain international fame. Despite talk of a reconciliation, the marriage ended and in 1991 Renouf tried marriage again. A heart condition — he had major bypass surgery in 1984 — and personal financial woes notwithstanding, he married the beautiful Michèle, Countess Griaznoff (then aged 44), in a society wedding in London. That union lasted just three months — the countess had reportedly not mentioned that she was the daughter of an Australian truck driver.

Renouf's sharemarket blues and poor judgment in his personal relationships tended to cloud an otherwise spectacular career. Not prepared to work in his father's handkerchief business after returning from a stint at Oxford University and four years as a prisoner-of-war, in 1950 he joined Wellington sharebroker and foreign exchange dealer Duff Daysh (1907–75) at Daysh Longuet & Frethey. His salary was £20 a week. It was the start of a broking career that included the underwriting of £500,000 in shares and £2 million in debentures for the float of Tasman Pulp & Paper Co in 1954 — the first of its kind in New Zealand — creating the first New Zealand share index in 1957, and establishing the country's first merchant bank in 1960. His firm, Daysh Renouf & Frethey (later Daysh Renouf & Co), became the training ground for countless talented brokers over the next generation, including Bryan Johnson (born 1941) and Kevin O'Connor (born 1940).

Renouf's much-dreamed-of merchant bank came into being in 1960 as New Zealand United Corporation (NZUC) with an issued capital of £250,000. It was neither welcomed by the stock exchange nor encouraged by the government, but it paved the way for a home-grown merchant banking industry. Renouf sought to replicate NZUC's success with the float of Renouf Corporation but, following an initial boom, came unstuck after getting involved with Bruce Judge. Outside business, Renouf was a generous man who endowed a number of Wellington interests including the capital's tennis centre, which bears his name. He was inducted into the *NBR* Business Hall of Fame in Wellington on his seventy-ninth birthday, 31 July 1997. Weak after a stroke and unable to speak clearly, he was accompanied by a daughter, Frances Underwood, and greeted by a spirited rendition of *Happy Birthday*. The former grand old man of the equity markets had been forgiven. As Renouf noted in his autobiography: 'In view of the vicissitudes of a busy, sometimes complicated career, [my induction into the Business Hall of Fame] was an exciting and satisfying culmination to a major part of my life's mission.' He died the following year.

Although Renouf mixed with royalty at Wimbledon (where he had once played) and was seen hobnobbing with the beautiful people at grand occasions here and overseas, he was a loner in business terms. He was considered snobbish by many in the Wellington sharebroking community and his extreme vanity did not help. He was a very different character to Ron Jarden (1929–77) whose sharebroking firm, Jarden & Co, was another that nurtured many fine brokers. Jarden was a man of exceptional talent who achieved a tremendous amount in a variety of spheres during his short life. He came from a modest background in Wellington, and started his career as a history teacher before working as an executive trainee with Shell Oil. His extracurricular activities, spread over many years — top athlete, All Black wing three-quarter, Admiral's Cup yachtsman, company director and, shortly before his premature death, chairman of the Broadcasting Council of New Zealand — provide a snapshot of this bold and energetic Kiwi. He was a true renaissance man. He shook up the Wellington sharebroking establishment, building a strong business and becoming the country's first specialist in odd-lot shares.

The network that grew out of Jarden & Co, known as the 'Jarden Boys', has proved one of the more enduring in business circles. In 1967 Bryan Johnson left Daysh Renouf & Co to join Ron Jarden, then a sole practitioner, and helped develop Jarden & Co into New Zealand's largest sharebroker. He became the senior partner on Ron Jarden's death, responsible for developing the firm's corporate and equity service in New Zealand. The merchant banking and related activities became a public company, Jarden Corporation, in 1983, merging with Deak Morgan in 1988 to become Jarden Morgan. Following the sale of Jarden Morgan to Credit Suisse First Boston in 1991, Johnson became chairman of Credit Suisse

Ron Jarden (1929–77), a man of many talents who was an All Black wing three-quarter and international yachtsman, established Wellington sharebroking house Jarden & Co. It became the country's first specialist in odd-lot shares.
COURTESY *NBR*

First Boston NZ Holdings and Jarden Corporation. His fortune survived the sharemarket crash and in the 2003 *Rich List* he was conservatively valued at $60 million. One of his former colleagues claims his wealth exceeds $150 million.

Other Jarden Boys who have become rich include:

▶ Paul Baines (born 1950), a former New Zealand chief executive of Credit Suisse First Boston who is in strong demand as a company director. He is the former chairman of the Enterprise New Zealand Trust, a body that promotes enterprise education in schools and organises the Business Hall of Fame. Baines' wealth was estimated in 2003 to be at least $17 million;

▶ John Benton (born 1945), who looks after what is left of the Jarden interests within Jarden Corporation. Personal wealth: at least $25 million;

▶ Lloyd Morrison (born 1957), who lives in Wellington and is an investment banker, came close to selling his infrastructural investment

Lloyd Morrison (born 1957), a former 'Jarden Boy', became a New Zealand leader in infrastructural investment. His fortune, which includes an art collection, exceeded $70 million in 2003.
COURTESY *NBR*

business, H.R.L. Morrison & Co Group, to Australia's Macquarie Bank in 2000. Though the deal fell through, the bid earned him an immediate (and overdue) place on the *Rich List*, based on the 65 per cent of the shares held by him and related interests. Personal wealth, which includes an impressive art collection: at least $70 million;

▶ Keith Taylor (1942–97), who returned to rural life after the sale of Jarden Morgan. His family interests own Waimanu station in the Manawatu, raising beef and breeding horses, and the high-profile Trelawney stud in Cambridge. Taylor joined forces with the Preston butchery family in Wellington to form Taylor Preston, acquiring the former Wellington city abattoir and meatworks, Ngauranga Meat Processors, from Lowe Walker NZ in 1991. He soon had it making money. Family wealth: at least $40 million;

▶ Dr Ray Thomson (born 1952), who has the most diverse background of any former sharebroker. A physicist, he has earned a healthy living from Strathmore Group, an investment company that survived the sharemarket crash as a cashed-up shell. He and his magazine publisher

Howard Paterson [1952–2003] started making money as an arts student at the University of Otago. He became the South Island's most successful property developer, with his estate valued at a conservative $170 million in the National Business Review's *2003* Rich List.
Courtesy *NBR*

wife, Lorraine Thomson (née Hunt), are keen racegoers and bloodstock owners. Personal wealth: about $10 million; and

▶ David Wale (born 1941), who lives on a lifestyle block in rural Ohariu, near Wellington, and has been a quiet private investor since leaving his old company. Personal wealth: at least $20 million.

Another Jarden Boy not on the list is Irish-born economist Brian Gaynor (born 1948), a former senior partner with Jarden Corporation, who has been a keen defender of minority shareholders' rights through a regular column he writes in the *New Zealand Herald* (and before that in *NBR*). He denies he qualifies for entry to the *Rich List* but is a keen and regular share buyer.

The South Island equivalent of the Jarden Boys' network is the 'Tartan Mafia', an affectionate name for a group of investor-dealmakers with loosely Dunedin roots and a hint of Scottish ancestry. The 'Godfather' of this business network is the highly respectable, dapper Eion Edgar (born 1945), former chairman of the New Zealand Stock Exchange, chancellor of the University of Otago, and independent company director. As the principal of Dunedin-based sharebroking house Forsyth Barr, Edgar has for years been at the centre of sharemarket deals and flotations big and small. At times Forsyth Barr has been criticised for backing a number of penny-dreadful stocks, including Mr Chips Holdings, Iddison Group Vietnam and Waipuna International, but Edgar has on most occasions successfully defended his company's conduct. Edgar has been on the *Rich List* for many years, but not by choice. In 2003 his personal wealth was valued at a conservative $35 million.

Edgar might be the head of the Tartan Mafia, or Edinburgh Trust as it is more genteelly known, but the wealthiest member was Howard Paterson (1952–2003), the South Island's most successful property developer and one of its richest residents. The son of a spec builder from Dunedin, he started making money as an arts student at the University of Otago and was worth at least $170 million when he died suddenly in Fiji in July 2003. Paterson had survived the 1987 crash, earlier selling his Christchurch commercial property interests to Chase Corporation. He bought his first farm near Gore in 1988 and became a substantial rural landowner through various trusts, ventures and investments. Recent ventures included the biotechnology area — A2 Corporation, Blis Technologies, PharmaZen and Botry-Zen — though most of his fortune came from property investment.

Like others of the Tartan Mafia set, Paterson spent much of his time in the Southern Lakes region. He had a holiday home in Wanaka, not far from the hilltop mansion of fellow *Rich List* entrant, Dunedin accountant, investor and professional company director Ian Farrant (born 1941), who won respect for helping Dunedin-based Primary Producers' Co-operative Society (PPCS) become a leader in the meat industry. Other names likely to turn up in Tartan Mafia deals include tourism magnate Chris Alpe (born 1950) and property developer John Martin (born 1952) — both *Rich List* entrants — chartered accountant Murray Valentine, landscape architect/property developer John Darby, executive Dougal Rillstone, lawyer Bernie O'Donnell and consultant David Smallbone.

Wanaka, said to have the highest density of multimillionaires per capita of any New Zealand town, is also home to a *Rich List* survivor of a crash of a different sort, Christ's College old boy Sir Tim Wallis (born 1938). This vintage aircraft enthusiast is lucky to be alive after crashing his $1.5 million Supermarine Spitfire in 1996 — his fifth aviation accident, the third involving injury and by far the most serious. Wallis, who founded the

Sir Tim Wallis' luck almost ran out in 1996 when he crashed his $1.5 million Supermarine Spitfire. It was his fifth aviation accident, the third involving injury, but by far the most serious for the founder of the Warbirds Over Wanaka international air show and a pioneer in helicopter live-deer recovery.
COURTESY *NBR*

Warbirds Over Wanaka international air show, made his fortune (estimated in 2003 to be at least $50 million) from the deer industry, in particular using helicopters for live-deer recovery through his company, Alpine Helicopters. He also founded the Helicopter Line (now Tourism Holdings) which listed on the stock exchange in 1986 after a public float. It acquired Alpine Helicopters and other assets. In 2002 he was inducted into the *NBR* Business Hall of Fame.

Auckland's wealth-creating networks are less obvious than those in the south because of the size and cosmopolitan nature of the region, but they exist nonetheless. After the fall of Thomas Russell's Limited Circle in the 1880s business cliques fell from grace, although from the 1920s to the 1940s Auckland played host to a second-generation Limited Circle — the notorious 'Kelly Gang'. This group of financiers and lawyers associated with the Limited Circle's spiritual home, the Northern Club, and linked originally to the Reform Party, was said to control £180 million of the country's funds and assets and have a hand in every nefarious business deal going. Among its prize scalps was the colourful Canadian-born entrepreneur, forestry promoter and speculator John McArthur (1883–1963), whom it helped destroy in the 1930s. McArthur was no angel but his worst crime in the eyes of the Kelly Gang was to challenge the Auckland business establishment — the Kelly Gang's establishment.

Canadian-born wheeler-dealer Dr F.J. Rayner (1876–1931) was more fortunate than McArthur, if no more honest. A dentist by profession but a businessman by blood, he was always one step ahead of his adversaries, earning a good living in Auckland through questionable forestry, night club and picture theatre ventures. His early death perhaps saved him from the attentions of the Kelly Gang. It was Rayner who helped make (Sir) Noel Cole (1892–1975) one of Auckland's richest builders.

These days Auckland business networks tend to be based more on pragmatism than professional association, blood lines or the old school tie. Just as Jarden & Co in Wellington proved the hothouse for a generation of successful sharebrokers, so too did key Auckland-based companies nurture a team of budding entrepreneurs. Marac Finance, once Auckland's smartest finance company, spawned John Bayldon and Allan Hawkins. Atlas Majestic Industries (later Atlas Corporation) sharpened the skills of John Roy, Charles Bidwill and Alan Gibbs. Through a private investment company, Tappenden Holdings, Gibbs also linked up with publicity-shy transport operator Trevor Farmer (born 1935) — a connection originating from the 1979 acquisition of Auckland's ailing Tappenden Motors by Gibbs,

Alan Gibbs (born 1939), unofficial high priest of the New Right, proved to be a skilled investor — his minimum net worth in 2003 was $300 million.
Courtesy *NBR*

Bidwill, lawyer John Fernyhough (1938–2003) and car dealer-turned-sharebroker Warren Paine (born 1937), Bidwill's former broking partner. With the exception of Bayldon (who died before the New Zealand *Rich List* was invented), Farmer and Paine, these Auckland entrepreneurs were all entrants on the inaugural *Rich List* in 1986. And apart from the disgraced Hawkins, and Paine, all are listed in the wealth stakes today. Gibbs, who spends much of his time in England these days, was named the eighth-equal richest Kiwi in 2003 with a minimum net worth of $300 million. Farmer was valued at a conservative $120 million and Bidwill, who also lives in England, was worth at least $130 million.

Gibbs, a former diplomat and unofficial high priest of the New Right, made his mark through corporate restructuring, initially acting with Bidwill as a financial consultant to Atlas Corporation, a company whose interests once included whiteware, appliances, poultry processing and property investment. Atlas merged with crockery and brickmaker Ceramco in 1985 and Gibbs and Bidwill had a field day knocking Ceramco into shape. Like Bidwill, Gibbs was involved in the private radio station operator Radio Hauraki (NZ) in its early days. In 1985 he and Farmer borrowed $120 million to acquire the listed transport operator, Freightways Holdings, in what was then one of the largest management buyouts in Australasia. Ironically, it was a homecoming of sorts for Gibbs. Freightways, originally called Allied Freightways, was a conglomerate of four regional transport companies created by Gibbs' late father, accountant and property developer T.N. Gibbs (1896–1978). T.N. had been elbowed out of the chairmanship by insiders in 1967.

Alan Gibbs continued to make lots of money, earning his reputation as one of New Zealand's most astute businessmen, if not always its most affable. He and Farmer bought heavily into the privatised Telecom Corporation of New Zealand in 1991. They sold part of their holding in 1993, effectively paying for the purchase and netting a huge profit. But Gibbs was always much more than an entrepreneurial investor. He was an early backer of Rogernomics, the free-market policies of former Labour finance minister and Act New Zealand founder Sir Roger Douglas, and strongly supported their continuation under National's feisty finance minister, Ruth Richardson. In 1992 he established the BBC World Service permanently in New Zealand, partly in protest at the sometimes negative and anti-business stance of National Radio's *Morning Report* programme. But the station struggled financially and he sold it in 1994 in the first move toward divesting himself of his New Zealand interests. Like others on the right, Gibbs had become frustrated by the slowdown in the economic-reform process under Prime Minister Jim Bolger. He steadily severed his links with New Zealand, selling down shares owned with Farmer in Freightways and offloading his Telecom stake. He quit the Telecom board in 1999, citing a conflict of interest because of a large chunk of shares owned by Gibbs family interests in Sky Network Television. (The year before he had doubled his stake in the listed pay-TV network through associated interests to 12.7 per cent.) Gibbs had been involved with Sky since 1990.

Just when it looked as if he and Farmer had all but given up on New Zealand's economic prospects, their investment vehicle, Tappenden Holdings, emerged in early 2000 as part of the ill-fated New Zealand consortium that acquired 72 per cent of airline Ansett New Zealand from its Australian owner, News Ltd. The consortium, put together by Auckland merchant bank Clavell Capital, included *Rich List* colleagues Sir Clifford Skeggs (born 1931) through his Dunedin-based Skeggs Group; and Ian

Hendry (born 1946) and Chris Coon (born 1944) who made their money through Auckland-based life insurer Sovereign.

This Ansett acquisition reminded observers of Gibbs' ability to surprise. Belying his calculated approach to business, Gibbs has an eclectic mix of private interests. He is a keen yachtsman and hunter, collects armaments (he is said to own an inoperative ex-Australian armoured personnel carrier) and has a passion for war games. In 1998 Gibbs commissioned the building of a pyramid on his 107-ha farm at Kaukapakapa, north of Auckland, adding to an already impressive sculpture collection there. He was not showing off but rather reflecting his love of art, cultivated during 35 years of marriage to Jenny Gibbs (née Gore, born 1940). The couple split in 1996 and Jenny Gibbs, an art collector in her own right, was propelled onto the *Rich List* in 1997 with an estimated minimum wealth of $35 million, based on a gold-plated marital settlement. She retained the couple's stunning mansion in Paritai Dr, Orakei,

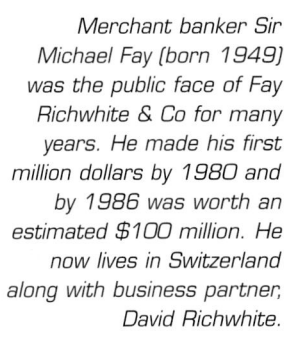

Merchant banker Sir Michael Fay (born 1949) was the public face of Fay Richwhite & Co for many years. He made his first million dollars by 1980 and by 1986 was worth an estimated $100 million. He now lives in Switzerland along with business partner, David Richwhite.
Courtesy *NBR*

Auckland, acquired in 1988 from the chairman of failed ferry operator Fullers Corporation, Harry Julian, for $1.7 million. After being upgraded it is said to be worth more than $12 million. Jenny Gibbs made the headlines in 1998 when she negotiated the return of the stolen Colin McCahon painting, *Urewera Mural*, from her friend, tattooed Maori nationalist Te Kaha. She stood by Te Kaha when he was sentenced to 200 hours' community service, but rejected media reports that suggested there was more to their relationship.

Alan Gibbs' non-business activities after the marriage breakup were far less controversial: he spent considerable time working on his family history, commissioning three books that were published in 2002 and a fourth about the Maori chief Te Hemara Tauhia. The Gibbs books started with an account of Gibbs' ex-convict great-great-grandfather, William Spickman (1800–81), who arrived in New Zealand in 1823, and ended with the death of Gibbs' father, T.N. Gibbs, in 1978. Gibbs jnr appears to have inherited his father's entrepreneurial genes. T.N. Gibbs and his eldest son, Ian (born 1928), developed Kinloch on the western bay of Lake Taupo from the early 1950s with prime minister-to-be (Sir) Keith Holyoake, resulting in the building of the country's first marina in 1961.

No business network or partnership in the late 1980s or early 1990s, in Auckland or elsewhere, has bettered that of Sir Michael Fay and David Richwhite, principals in merchant bank Fay Richwhite & Co. For them, the sharemarket crash was good news; it cleaned out competitors and paved the way for their company to pick up gold-plated government restructuring contracts. Fay and Richwhite first met as employees of the newly formed Auckland merchant bank Securitibank. Fay, a law graduate from Victoria University, had worked as a law clerk in the capital and briefly for Freightways before applying for a job at Securitibank in 1972 on the recommendation of Wellington sharebroker Ron Jarden. He showed early talent and established a solid friendship with two later Securitibank recruits, Richwhite and Rod Petricevic. Fay left after an office row in 1974 and set up on his own account in rented rooms in O'Connell St, in central Auckland. The natty Petricevic soon followed. Fay offered him half the office for half the rent, which he willingly accepted. In 1975 Richwhite also quit Securitibank and immediately joined forces with Fay. Their merchant bank steadily picked up business, and in 1978 Petricevic became a third principal after selling his company, Security Discounters, into Fay Richwhite. (This was not long after the partners' old employer, Securitibank, had collapsed owing outside creditors more than $30 million.) Petricevic

Widower John Spencer (born 1934), perhaps the most reclusive of New Zealand's super-rich, took a battering during the sharemarket crash but still makes the Rich List's top ten. There are few public photographs of him and he would like to keep it that way.
Courtesy *NBR*

Colin Giltrap (born 1940), affectionately known as 'Lord Hubcap', has dominated the Auckland car sales market since the 1960s, amassing a fortune exceeding $220 million.
Courtesy *NBR*

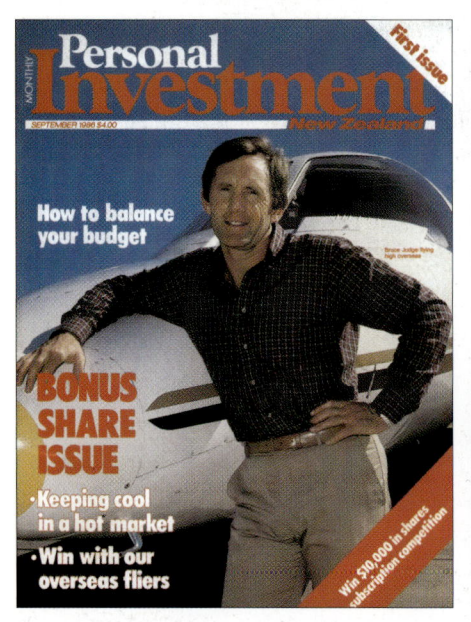

Personal Investment New Zealand
Bruce Judge.

Personal Investment New Zealand
Ray Smith.

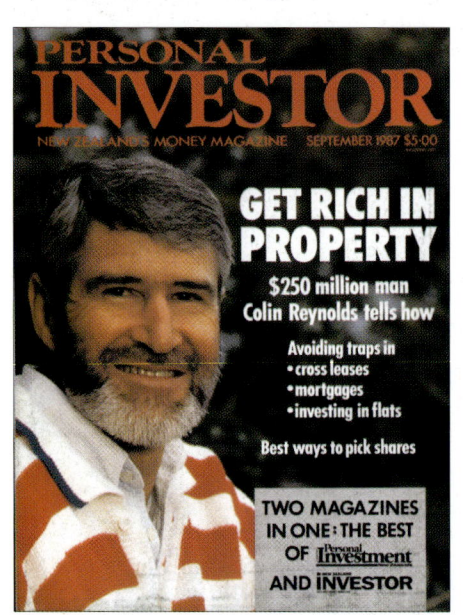

Personal Investor
Colin Reynolds.

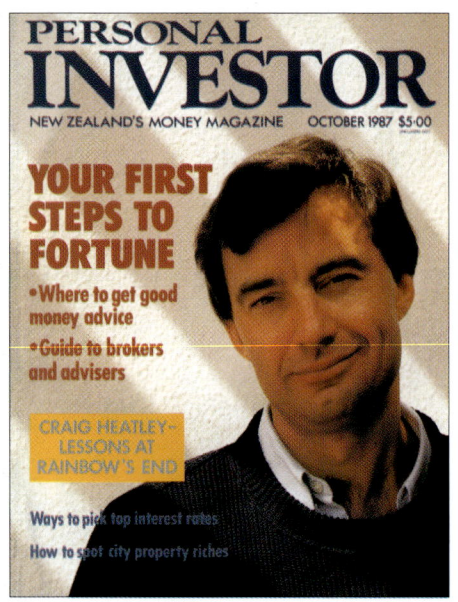

Personal Investor
Craig Heatley.

The high-fliers got star treatment from the New Zealand financial media in the 1986–87 bull run, but of the four 'coverboys' above only Craig Heatley came through the sharemarket crash unscathed. Bruce Judge was the biggest corporate disaster; Ray Smith's company failed and he was later jailed; and Colin Reynolds' property empire sank (though he was one of several property developers to make a comeback in the 1990s).

Courtesy *NBR*

Eric Watson (born 1959) proved to be the perfect rich and good-looking 'coverboy' for the late 1990s. Watson left school in Christchurch at age fifteen and at nineteen was managing a Whitcoulls store. Today his interests are extensive. In 2003 his minimum net worth was $275 million.
Courtesy *Metro*

Filmmaker Peter Jackson (born 1961) entered the Rich List *in 2001 with the release of part one of his* Lord of the Rings *trilogy. He was valued at $70 million in the 2003* Rich List *but could be worth several times that. The UK* Sunday Times *valued Harry Potter author J.K. Rowling in 2003 at £280 million.*
Courtesy *NBR*

Problems in 1997–98 with Graeme Hart's principal investment, Australian spice company Burns Philp & Co, did not stop him completing his mansion in Glendowie, Auckland, or having 49-m superyacht *Ulysses* built at a cost of $US20 million.

VAUGHAN JAMES

This clifftop home at Takapuna on Auckland's North Shore was completed for Craig Heatley in 1994 at a reputed cost — land, building and furnishings — of $13 million. It contains a cinema, swimming pool and steamroom and has five bedrooms.

VAUGHAN JAMES

National Business Review publisher Barry Colman (born 1947) and wife Cushla Martini completed a multimillion-dollar redevelopment of their clifftop home in Glendowie, Auckland, in 1998.

VAUGHAN JAMES

The striking Herne Bay, Auckland, home of Stephen Fisher (born 1948), son of building supplies merchant Lou Fisher (1913–77). He lives there with his wife, Virginia (née Fenton), and son, Benjamin.

VAUGHAN JAMES

Paritai Dr, Orakei, Auckland, has for three generations been the city's most exclusive address. It probably houses more millionaires than any other street in the country.
COURTESY DAVID HALLETT

Wentworth House, Kohimarama, Auckland, the home built for cashed-up former smallgoods manufacturer Paul Huljich (born 1952) at a reputed cost of $20 million. It is said to be the most expensive house built in New Zealand; it is certainly one of the biggest.
COURTESY DAVID HALLETT

The National Business Review *voted Robin and Erika Congreve's home at Takapuna, Auckland, as New Zealand's best in 2001. Designed by Pip Cheshire of Jasmax and built in 1994, it had a government valuation in 2001 of $4.5 million.*
COURTESY JASMAX

Property investor Olly Newland (born 1939) was one of the first casualties of the sharemarket crash. At his business height he was worth at least $45 million.
COURTESY *NBR*

West Australian-born Wendy Pye (born 1943) carved out a healthy fortune from the international children's book market after parting company with Brierley Investments-controlled NZ News in the 1980s. She was worth at least $35 million according to the 2003 Rich List. Pictured left is the invitation for her sixtieth birthday celebration on 7 June 2003 in the Whitford town hall, south of Auckland.
AUTHOR'S COLLECTION

Actor-producer Sam Neill (born 1947), despite his star status, has never taken kindly to publicity about his wealth or private life. In spite of that, there are numerous websites devoted to him, reporting among other things that his favourite foods are macaroni cheese and boysenberry ice cream. Born in Northern Ireland, the second son of an Irish Guards officer who was later a director of Dunedin liquor company Wilson Neill, Neill joined the Rich List *in 1994 with an estimated minimum net worth of $8 million. In the 2003 list he was listed at a minimum $25 million.*

COURTESY NEW ZEALAND MAGAZINES ARCHIVE

Sharon Hunter (born 1966) entered the Rich List *in 1996 on the strength of the success of PC Direct, a computer company she and Maurice Bryham (born 1965) started in a warehouse in Ponsonby, Auckland, in 1989. The business enjoyed spectacular growth and in 1995 they sold 25 per cent of it to Direct Capital Partners for $4.16 million; the remaining 75 per cent was sold in 1997 to US Office Products for $30 million.*

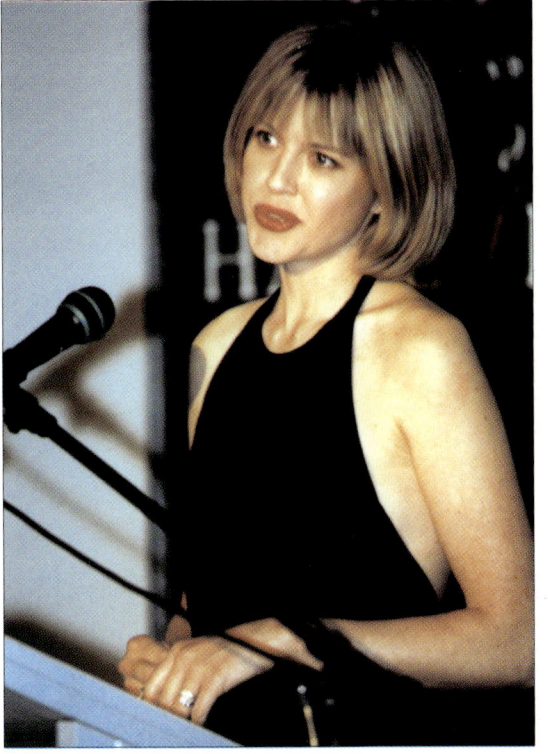

COURTESY *NBR*

Aucklander Andrew Krukziener (born 1965), leader of the 'brat pack' of young rich, went into business on his own in 1988 but has had his share of problems. He has a passion for fast and expensive cars. Minimum net worth: $20 million.
Courtesy *NBR*

Kidney disease might have put his career on hold, but Jonah Lomu (born 1975) remains the country's richest rugby player. His minimum wealth in 2003 was estimated at $10 million.
Courtesy *NBR*

left Fay Richwhite three years later to form Euro-National Finance, to take advantage of the boom in financial services.

Fay and Richwhite are said to have made their first million dollars each before 1980. True or not, they certainly prospered in the restrictive financial climate created by the Muldoon National government. Their speciality in those early years, when the top marginal tax rate was 66c in the dollar, was tax avoidance for high-net-worth individuals. This involved intricate tax planning and investment schemes, including bloodstock and film-making partnerships. Deregulation of the financial markets after Labour's win in the 1984 general election opened up a whole new horizon for Fay Richwhite. Not only did the deals get bigger but Fay Richwhite also developed a public profile through its listed vehicle, Capital Markets, a former oil-exploration company Fay Richwhite had floated in 1983. This was to launch Fay and Richwhite into the big time. By 1986 the partners' personal fortunes were estimated at $100 million each, and there seemed no stopping them. Fay was instrumental in New Zealand challenging for the 1986/87 America's Cup in Fremantle, heading the Bank of New Zealand-sponsored challenge. New Zealand lost narrowly in the challenger final in January that year, taking Capital Markets' shares and the New Zealand sharemarket generally off the boil for a time. But Fay was back again, telling the media he was 'not after the America's Cup [but] after the America's Cup industry'. Using a little-known clause in the America's Cup deed of gift, which allowed anyone to force the cupholder to defend within ten months, he and Richwhite mounted a multimillion-dollar challenge for the cup off San Diego, California, in 1988. The challenge, in the name of the Mercury Bay Boating Club, did not restrict the challenger to the standard 12-m America's Cup specification — the challenger could specify any yacht up to a 90-ft waterline. Fay and Richwhite chose a large monohull yacht. The cupholder, the San Diego Yacht Club, initially ignored the challenge, then countered with a two-hulled catamaran. Fay, furious at the defender's sharp tactics, went to the New York Supreme Court but in the meantime the challenge went ahead with San Diego winning 2–nil. Fay returned to court claiming a mismatch, and San Diego was ordered to forfeit the cup. On appeal the New York State Court of Appeals ruled 5–2 in San Diego's favour. Undeterred, Fay made a commitment to compete in the next America's Cup regatta in San Diego in 1992. By early 1992 it was reported that Fay and Richwhite had spent $65 million in trying to win the cup — $45 million on the 1986/87 and 1988 challenges, and $20 million at that time on the 1992 challenge. In the event the US retained the cup in

1992, but New Zealand's *Black Magic* won it convincingly off San Diego in 1995. It was Fay's confidence that made this David versus Goliath sporting victory possible.

Officially, Fay and Richwhite were not the owners of the 2000 defence of the cup in Auckland, but some members of the yachting fraternity suggested otherwise. The beneficial ownership, hidden behind a myriad of trusts and nominee shareholders, has never been disclosed, but when *Team New Zealand* lost the cup in 2003 to the Swiss challenge, *Alinghi*, the allegations of Fay and Richwhite's ownership re-emerged. They were promptly quashed by Team New Zealand's former directors.

The honeymoon Fay and Richwhite enjoyed with the public — and with the fourth Labour government — in the 1980s came to an abrupt end in the post-crash gloom of the early 1990s. The sources of the public's and the investment community's disenchantment were many:

▶ Fay Richwhite's receipt in 1988 of a substantial above-market premium for warehousing a strategic stake in L.D. Nathan & Co for Lion Corporation during the latter's takeover of L.D. Nathan;

▶ The 1990 reverse takeover of Capital Markets' parent company, Fay Richwhite, resulting in a $182.5 million goodwill payment to Fay and Richwhite;

▶ The National government's $620 million bailout of the Bank of New Zealand in 1990, to the benefit of the listed Fay Richwhite which held nearly 30 per cent of the former state bank;

▶ A $42 million BNZ loan to fund the building of Fay Richwhite's 'Big Pinky' tower in Queen St, Auckland, which was rolled over while Fay was a BNZ director;

▶ An undisclosed $28 million capital payback to Fay and Richwhite from Fay Richwhite's shareholding in New Zealand Rail following their buyout of the minority shareholders in the merchant bank in 1995; and

▶ Tax-dodge and finance-channelling activities through the Cook Islands-based European Pacific Banking Corporation, in which Fay Richwhite had held a minority stake until 1993.

The range of controversial deals involving Fay Richwhite during a period when shellshocked investors were looking for scapegoats was fertile ground for maverick National MP and later New Zealand First party

Self-made businessman Graeme Hart (born 1955) was named in 2002 as New Zealand's richest man and first individual billionaire, ending the long run at number one of cashed-up brewer Douglas Myers. Publicity shy and a loner in business, Hart suffered huge losses after his investment in Burns Philp & Co in 1997 turned sour. But he stayed firm and Burns Philp recovered, lifting his fortune accordingly. In 2003 Burns Philp took over the Goodman Fielder group, making Hart a dominant player in the trans-Tasman food business.

COURTESY *NBR*

founder-leader Winston Peters to exploit. He launched a highly personal attack on Fay Richwhite, and its principals' corporate behaviour. Fay Richwhite's law firm, Russell McVeagh McKenzie Bartleet & Co, also came in for a hammering (Peters had worked as a lawyer there from 1974–78). Peters' attacks turned into a nine-year campaign and while many of his claims were specious, made under the cloak of parliamentary privilege, he achieved some success in attacking Fay Richwhite's European Pacific connection — the so-called Wine-box Affair. This led to a three-year public inquiry which cost the taxpayer at least $12 million and corporate New Zealand upwards of $80 million.

As well as attacking several companies for engaging in offshore tax deals, Peters accused the Inland Revenue Department and the Serious Fraud Office of fraud and negligence by agreeing to, or not investigating properly, deals that in some cases had cut corporate tax bills by millions of dollars. The wine-box commissioner who investigated Peters' allegations, former chief justice Sir Ronald Davison, found no fraud, incompetence or

Merchant bank Fay Richwhite & Co got a public hammering during the three-year Wine-box Inquiry. David Richwhite (born 1948) fronted for the company in preference to his business partner and Fay Richwhite co-founder, Sir Michael Fay.
COURTESY *NBR*

wrongdoing on the part of public officials, and gave the tax transactions the big tick. Peters succeeded in having some of his findings overturned in court but the victory benefited one man only — Peters. The effect on the companies concerned, other than the cost of legal fees and the time involved in court and inquiry hearings, was negligible; the impact on public opinion about the behaviour of former sharemarket darlings like Fay and Richwhite was huge. In 1994 Fay, his wife, Sarah, Lady Fay, and their three children took a long sabbatical in Ireland, taking 1.6 tonnes of luggage with them. It was apparently not long enough. In 1997, fed up with years of sustained personal attack and negative press, the Fays and the Richwhites decided they had had enough. They packed their bags for Geneva, and have been there ever since, making occasional trips home. The Fay mansion in Godden Cr, St Heliers, Auckland, was sold to property developer Mark Wyborn — on the comeback trail after the 1987 sharemarket crash — for $5.1 million. The Richwhites' superior mansion a few kilometres away in Remuera Rd was sold for $8 million to property investor John Sanders (worth at least $50 million according to the 2003 *Rich List*).

The departure of Fay and Richwhite, the tallest of the corporate tall poppies to leave New Zealand, reflected the country's severe mood swing after the sharemarket crash. Fay and Richwhite retained extensive interests here, including Great Mercury Island off the Coromandel coast, which they bought in about 1979, but found it difficult to live in a country where the likes of Peters and talkback-radio hosts labelled them white-collar criminals.

In Geneva with other international corporate exiles, their business partnership remains as strong as it was in 1975 when Fay Richwhite was born. The essence of the merchant bank's outstanding success during its first fifteen years was the natural chemistry between the partners, although on the face of it their differences appear greater than their similarities. Fay, a Roman Catholic, is descended from poor Irish labourers who arrived in New Zealand in the late nineteenth century. His father, Jim, had been brought up by an uncle, Wellington barrister and later chief justice Sir Humphrey O'Leary, after his parents died in the influenza epidemic after World War I. Jim Fay was a prisoner-of-war during World War II, after which he rejoined his old employer, a foreign-owned insurance company, years later becoming its New Zealand manager. Michael Fay's education, with the exception of university all at Catholic schools, was split between Auckland and Wellington. Richwhite, on the other hand, is the epitome of what Americans would describe as a Wasp (White Anglo-Saxon Protestant). His family is solidly old money and he had the good fortune to be treated to a first-class private-school education. His father, Dr Lloyd Richwhite (born 1916), was a leading general practitioner in Remuera, Auckland, and his grandfather, Southland-born Cleave White (1890–1981), a businessman of note who had amassed considerable wealth through coalmining, especially open-cast operations in the Waikato in the 1950s with (Sir) William Stevenson. White, a man of style, changed his surname to Richwhite in 1909 to distinguish himself from other Whites working in the Napier insurance office where he was briefly employed. He entered the coal industry in 1910, acquiring his own coal and cement businesses more than 40 years later. His many outside directorships included New Zealand commissioner to the British Phosphate Commission and to the Christmas Island Phosphate Commission.

The partnership that made Sir Michael Fay and David Richwhite New Zealand's second-wealthiest individuals in 2003 ($600 million apiece)

National Business Review publisher *Barry Colman (born 1947)* with a Ralph Hotere painting which now hangs in his 'southern office' — his historic pub at Careys Bay, Port Chalmers. His wealth exceeded $100 million in 2003.
Courtesy *NBR*

would form the basis of a classic business case study. From his first days in business, Fay demonstrated the gift of the blarney and a devil-may-care passion for getting things done. Richwhite, the richer and possibly the smarter of the two, reflected a stolid, analytical approach to business in keeping with a family that took many years to build its fortune. The differences between the pair are borne out in how they celebrate anniversaries: Fay had the hide to print lookalike banknotes with his face on them to mark his fortieth and fiftieth birthdays; Richwhite, the King's College old boy whose sister, Rosslyn (born 1945), is married to a pillar of the Auckland establishment, Simon Caughey, would never have done anything so showy.

Showiness was very much a 1980s trait and for the early part of the 1990s, when New Zealand was wallowing in deep recession, wealth was something to hide, not flaunt. By the mid-1990s the beautiful people of Parnell and Queenstown had started to reappear at the right restaurants and venues. Journalists were again invited to slap-up corporate lunches and junkets. If you were rich it became de rigueur to build a big and extremely expensive house. But wealth in the 1990s is not the same as

Jeweller Michael Hill (born 1938) turned his back on the post-1987 recession and expanded his retail operation when others were shutting their doors. His success has been an inspiration to other retailers.
Courtesy *NBR*

The Rich List
July 2003

Top ten individuals, main sources of wealth and individual amounts

1. **Hart, Graeme Richard** (b. 1955) — $1.2b
   Food, investment

=2. **Fay, Sir (Humphrey) Michael Gerard** (b. 1949) — $600m
   Merchant banking, investment

=2. **Myers, (Arthur) Douglas** (b. 1938) — $600m
   Cashed up

=2. **Richwhite, David McKellar** (b. 1948) — $600m
   Merchant banking, investment

5. **Cooper, Peter Charles** (b. 1951) — $500m
   Property development

6. **Tindall, Stephen Robert** (b. 1951) — $420m
   Retailing

7. **Duke, Rodney Adrian** (b. 1950) — $320m
   Retailing

=8. **Erceg, Michael Anthony** — $300m
   Liquor

=8. **Gibbs, Alan Timothy** (b. 1939) — $300m
   Investment

10. **Watson, Eric John** (b. 1959) — $275m
   Investment

before the sharemarket crash. The old-money set, so despised by the brash investment bankers and smart-alec property developers of the mid-1980s, live on in the knowledge that history has proved them right.

Those without inherited wealth who prospered through the crash come

The Rich List
July 2003

Top ten families, main sources of wealth and individual amounts

1.	**Todd**	*Energy, investment*	**$2b**
2.	**Goodman**	*Investment, property*	**$550m**
	Formerly listed under Sir Patrick Goodman (b. 1929).		
3.	**Goodfellow**	*Fishing, chemicals*	**$375m**
	Formerly listed under (William) Douglas Goodfellow (b. 1917).		
=4.	**Stewart**	*Plastics*	**$170m**
=4.	**Paterson**	*Property development, investment, biotechnology*	**$170m**
	Formerly listed under Howard Paterson (1952–2003).		
6.	**Horton**	*Media*	**$165m**
7.	**Heatley**	*Investment*	**$150m**
	Formerly listed under Craig Heatley (b. 1956).		
=8.	**Barfoot & Thompson**	*Real estate agency*	**$125m**
=8.	**Norman**	*Jewellery*	**$125m**
10.	**Levene**	*Retail, property*	**$120m**

in many guises. *NBR* publisher Barry Colman (born 1947), whose personal fortune exceeds $100 million, developed a public profile through strategic sponsorship of the arts but in business is very much a loner. A former journalist from Rotorua, he demonstrates little of the cynicism associated with the printed word. A sign on his desk reads: 'We are not participating in the recession.' He has held true to that belief for more than twenty years. Colman enjoys the good life — his assets include artworks, several houses, a boat, a plane and an historic pub at Careys Bay, Port Chalmers

The Rich List
pre- and post-crash*

Year	No. individuals	No. families	Min. net worth ($b)
1986	56	12	5.296
1987	76	25	8.088
1988	36	22	4.474
1989	57	—†	3.101
1990	43	—†	2.777
1991	48	12	3.732
1992	44	10	3.711
1993	53	6	3.352
1994	76	14	4.657
1995	98	23	6.088
1996	107	23	6.285
1997	117	27	7.449
1998	131	32	8.603
1999	135	36	9.805
2000	139	36	11.205
2001	154	32	12.738
2002	156	33	15.096
2003	157	37	18.358

* Based on the number of individuals and families in the indices to the *National Business Review Rich List*. In some cases business partnerships and/or husband-and-wife teams have been included in the *Rich List* under a single entry, sometimes with a collective wealth estimate. The criteria for entry to the *Rich List* has varied over the years.

† Family entries excluded but some individual entries include other family members.

— but his feet are placed firmly on terra firma. His message is simple: if you want to do well in business, don't waste time planning, just make it happen.

Auckland-based children's book publisher Wendy Pye (born 1943), once dismissed as the 'brash West Australian' by NZ News' BIL-controlled management, shares the same philosophy. Some 85 million Pye-published

Cartoonist Bob Brockie has his say about the hype surrounding the National Business Review's 1995 Rich List.
Courtesy Bob Brockie

books distributed around the world make her hot property in publishing terms. She is valued at $35 million in the 2003 *Rich List*. Based on the number of horses she keeps on her farm southeast of Auckland and her many racing successes, she could be worth much more. Today Pye is in demand as a speaker, business awards judge and mentor. But she has not let it go to her head. She abhors cant and speaks her mind with impunity; political correctness is not one of her traits.

Another achiever, far more private than Pye, and far richer and more successful than he would ever admit, is Southland concrete and transport king Bill Richardson (born 1940). His companies include Allied Concrete, Southern Transport Co, Allied Petroleum and Greenhills Quarry. In 2003 his minimum net worth was $85 million.

Thoroughbred horsebreeder Sir Patrick Hogan (born 1939), owner of the legendary stallion Sir Tristram (which died in 1997), is living proof that quality begets quality in an industry notorious for price fluctuations, market swings and Flash Harrys. His personal wealth, centred on Cambridge stud, exceeded $65 million in 2003 and unlike so many on the *Rich List*, he is happy to talk to reporters about his business activities. Horsebreeding is in his blood: his father Tom, an Irish immigrant who settled in Taranaki, bred Clydesdales.

The rise of Kerry Hoggard (born 1941), chairman of Australian-listed chemicals company Nufarm (formerly Fernz Corporation), is a similar success story, although it carries a sting in the tail. The modest Hoggard joined Fernz's predecessor, the New Zealand Farmers' Fertilizer Co, as a seventeen year old, working his way up to become managing director and a major shareholder. His copybook was blotted in 1999 when he resigned as chairman of Fletcher Challenge after it was revealed he had bought Fletcher shares the day before a major restructuring was announced. The Securities Commission found in 2000 that he had been guilty of insider trading and in 2003 he paid $500,000 to settle a civil suit on the same matter brought against him by New Zealand Business Roundtable executive director Roger Kerr and Catharine Franks, wife of Act New Zealand MP Stephen Franks. The plaintiffs agreed to donate the money to a trust available to plaintiffs in further insider-trading cases. The maximum the court could have awarded against Hoggard was $535,000 — a minor dent in his fortune, estimated in 2003 to be at least $100 million.

Michael Hill (born 1938), of Michael Hill Jeweller fame, has succeeded despite swimming against the prevailing business tide. He expanded his Australasian retail empire during the most turbulent economic times imaginable and lived to tell the tale. Awarded the Air New Zealand Entrepreneur of the Year title in 1987, Hill's continued success has been a tribute to his dedication and an inspiration to other retailers. His personal wealth in 2003 was at least $100 million. These days he has less to do with the day-to-day activities of Michael Hill International than he used to and has taken a pay cut to reflect this. Whangarei-born Hill joined Queenstown's rich set in 1994 when his terracotta mansion — dubbed 'pink' by the conservative locals — was completed. He made the headlines more recently when he installed a five-metre-high stone sculpture, *Schist Strata*, by sculptor Chris Booth, at the head of his driveway. His property includes a nine-hole golf course, Hillbrook, a name that parodies that of the nearby international course, Millbrook. Despite the attractions of the Southern Lakes, Hill and his wife, Christine (née Roe), spend much of their time at a beachfront home on Australia's Gold Coast.

A retail success worth considerably more than Hill's is Stephen Tindall's nationwide discount retailer, the Warehouse Group. Tindall (born 1951), a great-great-grandson of pioneer Auckland retailer George Court, opened his first discount store by necessity after quitting the family emporium when Brierley Investments bought into George Court & Sons in 1982. Tindall's wealth in 2003, after allowing for his funding of a charitable foundation, was estimated to be at least $420 million, making him the sixth-richest Kiwi. He is a rarity in New Zealand terms — a business leader who is rich and popular with the public. A devout Roman Catholic, Tindall espouses good corporate citizenship as a regular part of his company's activities. He is an astute retailer, one of the first to profit when the government opened the doors to full-scale parallel importing in 1999, but lives modestly, insisting on dressing in Warehouse attire when he is doing business. He is a former ocean marathon swimmer.

Another who bucked the natural order of business is Christchurch-based Sir Gil Simpson (born 1948). He was a computer entrepreneur long before it was fashionable and is credited with creating a slice of Silicon Valley in New Zealand through Aoraki Corporation (now Jade Software Corporation) and its software system Jade. His personal wealth in 2003 was at least $60 million. Simpson is not the first Cantabrian to prosper from high-technology business. That honour probably goes to Sir Angus Tait (born 1919), whose company, Tait Electronics, has long been a world-class manufacturer of radio communications equipment. He has had his ups and downs in business but has always denied being in it for the money. 'This is an opportunity not given to many people, to help create something of substance,' he said in a newspaper interview in 1999. 'You can't put a money value on that.' PDL Holdings, the Christchurch plastics, electrical and consumer appliances group founded in 1947 by (Sir) Robertson Stewart (born 1913), is another example of a home-grown battler. Like Tait Electronics, it fought its way through recessions and bad governments, survived the sharemarket crash, and made the best of the removal of industry protection. Like Tait Electronics, it has had its problems but over the years has made a significant contribution to Christchurch and the wider community. In 2001, the Stewart family sold its 60 per cent holding in PDL to a French company, Schneider Electric, for $97 million, lifting the estimate of the family's collective fortune the following year to at least $170 million.

Dennis Chapman (born 1954) is another to thrive in Christchurch's technological 'hothouse'. His former business, Switchtec Power Systems — sold to a British company in 1998 — produces power-supply equipment for telecommunications. He started it after leaving an engineering position with Tait Electronics. Chapman is a long-time campaigner for high-quality education. He is also known for his trademark dress of walk shorts and jandals. (At the 1999 Ernst & Young Entrepreneur of the Year Award he surprised everyone by turning up in a dinner suit, complete with white shirt, black tie — and jandals.)

The fortunes of Christchurch's 'Silicon Valley' pale into insignificance when compared with those of the Kiwi dotcoms that started to emerge in the late 1990s. An outstanding example is Steve Outtrim (born 1973), whose Sausage Software (www.sausage.com), an electronic commerce solutions company, listed on the Australian Stock Exchange in 1996. Sausage only became known to the wider New Zealand public in 2000 when the *Sunday Star-Times* estimated Outtrim to be worth nearly $900 million after Sausage's planned merger with Solution 6, Australia's biggest supplier of accountancy software. In the event, the newspaper got its figures wrong and Outtrim was revalued at more than $A160 million (nearly $200 million), and that after the bubble burst in internet share prices in April 2000. His fortunes suffered after that — he was valued at a minimum $110 million in 2003 — but he had already established himself as a big spender, paying a reported $A2.5 million for the Stane Brae estate in metropolitan Melbourne — one of the city's larger home sites.

Outtrim was certainly luckier than another expatriate New Zealander, Chris Jones (born 1963), who was worth at least $125 million after the float in Australia of his telecommunications software company, Telemedia Networks International, but was removed from the *NBR Rich List* in 2002 after the dotcom tsunami took its toll. Jones, a dairy farmer's son, had founded the company in 1996 and floated it in 1999, lifting his wealth to the big league for New Zealanders anywhere — a good effort for someone who had dropped out of university before completing his bachelor of arts degree to 'chase the world of technology' and make money. Jones was philosophical about his fall and set about rebuilding his empire. By 2003 he was well on the way to becoming rich again, having created Argent Networks, which acquired the mobile phone billing-software assets of Telemedia. He made his comeback with the help of No 8 Ventures, which he praised as being part of a 'new breed of venture capitalists'.

The considerable hype over the dotcom wealth in New Zealand tends to obscure the fact that the so-called new economy has not overshadowed established wealth; the list of survivors from the 1987 sharemarket crash is in fact considerably larger than the list of casualties. Failed or battered entrepreneurs also have the ability to rise from the dead (several have) and family fortunes can be recreated (again, several have). That is certainly true of Graeme Hart (born 1955), who was the post-crash glamour boy for a time. After he cashed up in New Zealand, his principal investment — $A264 million paid for a 19.9 per cent stake in Burns Philp & Co in 1997 — shrank when the Australian food group announced catastrophic losses.

This dented his image as a value investor, undoing years of good dealmaking this side of the Tasman. Hart, to his credit, showed he had grown up. There were no fisticuffs with journalists, as happened in 1994 when he punched a photographer outside the Federal Court in Melbourne. Until then Hart had been Mr Nice Guy, but it seems that the pressure he was under through his takeover bid for West Australian food group Foodland Associated got to him. In the end Hart's bid was knocked back by the Australian regulators, leaving him on the prowl for another target. The venerable spice company, Burns Philp, was an easy catch. What has proved tough for Hart is not just the huge paper loss he suffered, but knowing what to do next. In 1998 he pumped in a further $A115 million to keep the company afloat in exchange for a generous options package that could lift his stake in the company to as high as 50 per cent. In 2000 the benefits started to shine through. Burns Philp reported a larger-than-expected interim profit, sending his shares rocketing. He was back in the *Rich List*'s top ten, with a minimum wealth estimated at $230 million, and by 2002 was by far the richest New Zealander with a fortune of at least $1.2 billion — the first individual Kiwi, officially at least, to reach billionaire status.

Burns Philp, the company that nearly destroyed him, became his saviour. In 2002 it paid $US110 million for Kraft Foods' Latin American yeast and ingredients business and in 2003 succeeded against the odds in its $A2.4 billion takeover of Australasian baking and flourmilling conglomerate Goodman Fielder.

In the first four weeks that Goodman Fielder was under Burns Philp control, Hart and Burns Philp chief executive Tom Degnan made cost savings of $A25 million. The casualties were mostly Goodman Fielder's head-office staff (legal, financial and executive), though five inefficient bakeries were also shut. In all, about 300 people lost their jobs. This was classic Hart — keeping things simple and tight (what he called 'fit').

Hart certainly never shed the trappings of wealth during the gloom of 1997 and 1998. Indeed, the problems with Burns Philp were temporarily overshadowed by publicity surrounding *Ulysses*, a 49-m superyacht he had built at an estimated cost of $US20 million. (*Ulysses* was damaged by fire at a New Orleans shipyard in 2002, robbing Hart of the chance to show off the vessel at the America's Cup regatta in Auckland in 2003.)

Rivalling Hart for a period as a sharemarket darling was Eric Watson. His aggressive Blue Star Group, initially funded by US Office Products in the United States, established his reputation as the country's most acquisitive and active investor. For a while it seemed he could hardly put a foot wrong, extending his personal interests well beyond stationery and office automation into areas such as healthcare, retirement homes, retailing, finance and e-commerce. The media gave the handsome businessman a dream run and for a time editors seemed more interested in Watson's young wife, blonde model Nicky (née Robinson), than what Watson was up to in business. Stories extended to the Watsons' various bloodstock purchases and to the state of their marriage and their eventual separation. Relatively little attention was paid to the controversial nature of some of Watson's deals, not least the insider-trading scandal at Blue Star Group where Watson was chief executive.

The Securities Commission found in 1997 that Watson had been involved in personal share trading in the lead-up to Blue Star's takeover of listed McCollam Printers. Watson sailed through the controversy, setting up a fund equivalent to the $680,705 profit made on his share dealings to compensate disadvantaged investors, with any unclaimed amount being paid to charity. He claimed the commission had cleared him of illegal share trading — something disputed by Auckland commercial law lecturer and commentator Mike Ross as insider trading was not illegal in New Zealand and had never been — but the issue died as quickly as it arose and Watson moved on to brighter things.

He won public favour in 2001 after he bought the troubled DB Bitter Auckland Warriors rugby league team, turned around the club's finances and lifted the players' performance. (The Warriors, rebranded the Vodafone Warriors, won the National Rugby League (NRL) minor premiership in 2002 before going down to South Sydney in the grand final.) In business, things were not quite so rosy. His IT interests turned out to be less than glorious and he took a bath on his retirement homes investment in 2002. The saving grace that year was a better performance from Pacific Retail Group, parent of lingerie maker Bendon.

Like Sir Ron Brierley, Sir Michael Fay, David Richwhite, Douglas Myers, Alan Gibbs, Charles Bidwill and others, Watson found New Zealand 'too small' and decided to live abroad, leaving his interests in the hands of apparently competent managers. But he was out of the country barely two months when, in November 2002, he was involved in a brawl at a London restaurant with another expatriate Kiwi, Oscar-winning actor Russell Crowe (born 1964). A fist-fight took place in the toilets of the swanky Zuma restaurant after the drunken Crowe allegedly made disparaging comments about the Warriors. According to the English tabloids Watson came out on top, but it was publicity the media-shy businessman could have done without and it did not do the soon-to-be-married Crowe much good either, being the latest in a number of fights he had been involved in.

Watson, who joined the *Rich List* only in 1995, was a coverboy on Auckland's *Metro* magazine in 1998. (His extranged wife, Nicky, is a former *Cleo* covergirl). *NBR* estimated his wealth in 2003 at a minimum $275 million. Others in the media have said he is worth up to $1 billion. One need only look back to 1987 to see how media fantasy can overtake logic.

Epilogue

In 1940 grammarian Sidney J. Baker, comparing New Zealand with Britain, wrote: 'We have no millionaires; our leisured class is negligible both intellectually and actually; our population is a working one and our standard of living is high; we are one of the greatest radio- and car-owning countries of the world; in much of our social development we are greatly envied by other nations.' While Baker was justifying the development of New Zealand English on the basis of social mores, his comments were merely a restatement of the old axiom, 'Jack is as good as his master'. In the eyes of many, the wealth explosion that occurred in the 1980s and 1990s shattered that belief. The most common catchcry after the sharemarket crash was 'the rich are getting richer'. Not that this was unique to that period: in the late 1880s and 1890s, following a prolonged and severe depression, New Zealand politicians, newspaper editors and social reformers were saying much the same thing. The fact is that wealth is more evenly spread now than at any time in the history of European settlement in New Zealand. It just attracts more publicity.

In 1940, when Sidney Baker was writing, the richest New Zealander was probably the brewer Sir Ernest Davis. He was also well connected in the Labour Party and highly popular with the public. No journalist then would have dared write about his wheeling and dealing, let alone his numerous extramarital affairs. It just was not done (unless, of course, a public figure's adultery reached the divorce courts). Wealth in 1940 was in far fewer hands than it is today, and the biggest holder was the government. It had the power to make or break business by the issue or removal of import licences and a host of other controls aimed ostensibly at creating a more efficient economy. When those controls disappeared in the 1980s the entrepreneurs went mad — and the share-buying taxi-drivers were just as bad as the new class of investment bankers. It was only when the financial markets turned sour that the hoary old argument about the rich getting richer resurfaced.

Even if such a belief were true, would it matter anyway? The zero-sum

Lucy Lawless (born 1968) is representative of a new generation of New Zealanders creating wealth through the performing arts. Thanks to her starring role in the TV show Xena: Warrior Princess, *as well as real estate investments with her husband, producer Rob Tapert, she has built up a fortune worth $15 million in 2003.*
Courtesy *NBR*

gain view that is still alive in the minds of many New Zealanders — Mr X is rich, therefore Mr Y is poor (or vice versa) — has been so discredited internationally that it is taken seriously only in North Korea and Cuba. (Even Russia and the People's Republic of China now have their own rich lists.) Fifty years of New Zealand governments redistributing wealth by way of punitive taxes and transfer payments have not made those living on the margins any richer. The New Right argues that it has robbed them of their self-esteem and will to work.

In actual fact, as Baker identified in 1940, the New Zealand leisured class is negligible compared with overseas. A University of Auckland study of the 1996 *Rich List* revealed that three-quarters of the country's wealthiest individuals earned their fortunes themselves 'in a variety of interests ranging from amusement parks and opera-singing to waste management and mushroom-growing'. The same study concluded that about two-thirds of New Zealand wealth came from competitive industries. In other words, if there were any idle rich, the numbers were small. In 2003 the whole New Zealand *Rich List* — the collective wealth of 157 individuals and 37 families — totalled nearly $18.4 billion — a fraction of the wealth attributed to the world's richest businessman, Microsoft supremo Bill Gates. We have only one home-grown billionaire, Graeme Hart, and only one family of billionaires, the Todds, and they have never been considered exciting enough for inclusion in *Forbes*' annual list of global billionaires. In fact, the United States has long since stopped counting millionaires (it has at least 3.5 million of them, in US-dollar millions at that) and bothers only with the super rich.

In New Zealand, despite our bad experiences after the 1987 crash, there are some encouraging signs in the pattern of wealth-creation. Kiwis were far quicker than their Australian cousins to take up shares in the 1990s life office demutualisations (National Mutual Holdings, Colonial and AMP). Sportspeople, long heroes in many New Zealanders' eyes but traditionally never especially rich, have started to become wealthy in their own right. Outside golf, their riches do not come within cooee of the wealth generated from public companies or family businesses, but it is a start. That All Black superstar Jonah Lomu had a net minimum worth of perhaps $10 million in 2003 is a message to every up-and-coming rugby player that professional sport can pay and pay well. The same might be said for the effect on the performing arts of the inclusion in the 2003 *Rich List* of *Lord of the Rings* filmmaker Peter Jackson ($70 million), actor-producer Sam Neill ($25 million), diva Dame Kiri Te Kanawa ($15 million) and actress Lucy Lawless ($15 million).

The emergence of a host of Maori entrepreneurs is a reminder that wealth is not an exclusive European domain. Gross tribal wealth, probably more than $2 billion, is made up mainly of Treaty of Waitangi settlements, raupatu settlements (in the case of Tainui) and about $500 million of Waitangi fisheries assets. It is a moot point whether tribal wealth should be included in the *Rich List* given the European/Maori divide over personal and collective ownership, but it can hardly be ignored.

Just as Maori wealth — mainly land and forests — made fortunes in the earliest days for European trader-speculators, so too has that repatriated wealth the potential to create individual Maori fortunes. But Maori wealth, like its European equivalent, has yet to trickle down in sufficient quantities to lift the lot of those on the bottom of the heap. It may never happen.

Business and media commentators have been obsessed with the wealth-creation potential of the 'knowledge economy'. Courtesy of Bill Gates, 'knowledge wealth' has been created on the back of hyped-up US internet and computer software stocks. But Gates' monopolistic tendencies have threatened to kill the golden goose. The shakeout in dotcom stocks worldwide in 2000 can be laid at least partly at his feet. Microsoft's market dominance, far from strengthening dotcom stocks worldwide, has actually weakened them. What the future holds is anyone's guess.

What is obvious to any intelligent observer is that the knowledge economy was not invented by Gates or, indeed, any other dotcom supremo and was not a creation of the 1990s. New Zealand knowledge economy in the broadest sense goes back to the earliest days of European settlement. Thomas McDonnell's ability to sniff out a bargain led him to acquire an ailing shipyard on the Hokianga in 1831 and make a base for himself in a new land. Sir Frederick Weld, the effete English aristocrat who tried his hand at sheepfarming by chance, became an expert pastoralist and wrote a bestseller for would-be farmers. William Davidson's foresight in the frozen-meat industry in the 1880s — the ultimate use of knowledge-based new technology — changed the nature of New Zealand farming life, as did Sir William Goodfellow's rationalisation of the dairy industry a generation later. Can these pioneers' achievements be said to be less significant than

Russell Coutts (born 1962), who led the Swiss challenge Alinghi to victory in the 2003 America's Cup. It was revealed he and colleague Brad Butterworth (born 1959) each received a contract fee from the Swiss of between $US5 million and $US7 million and a 'victory' bonus of perhaps $US2 million each in addition.
Courtesy *NBR*

those of the dotcom entrepreneurs? Only the arrogant or the ignorant would say so.

In our study of wealth-creation, we should not assume the rich have no feelings. Money notwithstanding, they are as sensitive to unfair criticism and ridicule as anyone else. Politician Winston Peters discovered this to his cost when he defamed the mild-mannered Hawke's Bay company director and *Rich List* entrant, (Sir) Selwyn Cushing, in 1992. Cushing brought a successful suit against the Tauranga MP, but not for the money. He was genuinely hurt by Peters' allegation — made partly under the cloak of parliamentary privilege — that Cushing had offered him money in return for Peters supporting free-market policies.

This was a lesson for Peters and others who casually link wealth with undue political influence or sleaze. The rich are not angels, as many personal accounts in this book show, but neither are many who throw mud at them. Far better we concentrate our efforts on the free lessons in wealth-creation history has to offer than condemning the rich as a race apart. Unless attitudes change toward wealth — and an Industry New Zealand study in 2003 revealed little public understanding of the relationship between wealth-creation and standard of living — rich New Zealanders will continue to leave our shores and take their money with them. The clean, green paradise New Zealand is billed as will not have the money to pay for the roads, schools, hospitals or electricity generation that a modern economy requires.

Wealth-creation and entrepreneurship are neither mutually exclusive nor the prerogative of the state. They are, quite simply, the products of a robust private sector that is not always perfect but is far better than anything governments have to offer.

Appendix A

National Business Review Rich List 2003

	Main source of wealth	$m (min)
Abel family	Investment	60
Adam, D.F.	Investment	20
Adams, P.H.	Property development	35
Alpe, C.C.	Tourism	35
Armstrong, L.S.D.	Hospitality, property	20
Aster, E.A.	Investment, hospitality	30
Avery, G.S	Wine	40
Bagnall, J.A.	Tourism	65
Baigent, H.K.	Retailing, investment	25
Baines, P.E.A.	Investment	17
Balcombe-Langridge, R.	Rental cars, property	37
Banks, J.A.	Property	16
Barfoot & Thompson families	Real estate agency	125
Bayley family	Real estate agency	110
Benton, J.G.E.	Investment	25
Bethell, G.J.	Rest homes	20
Bhatnagar, Sir R.S.	Investment, property	25
Bidwill, C.R.	Cashed up, share trading	130
Bowkett, G.D. & R.	Waste management, property	20
Brierley, Sir R.A.	Investment	180
Bryham, M.J.	Software, manufacturing	25
Bullivant, C. & D.V.	Vitamins, property	180
Burdon, P.R.	Mushroom growing, property	40
Burr, A.K.	Property development	120
Butterfield, W.J.	Hospitality, property	30

APPENDIX A – NBR RICH LIST 2003

	Main source of wealth	$m (min)
Carter, K.F.L. & Sir R.H.A.	Investment	40
Carter, P.M.	Property	75
Catley, D.H.	Nursing/inhome care	25
Caughey family	Retailing	45
Chapman, D.A.	Technology	35
Charles, Sir R.J.	Golf, property, consultancy	15
Clark family	Property, farming, wine	35
Cleary, E.J.	Agribusiness, bloodstock, property	200
Cleveland, L.H.	Transport, engineering	20
Collins, P.D.	Investment	15
Colman, B.N.	Publishing, investment	100
Coney, J.M.	Investment, wine	25
Congreve, Dr R.L.	Law, investment	60
Cook, C.J.	Retirement homes, property	100
Coon, C.L.	Investment	70
Cooper, P.C.	Property development	500
Copson, J.	Car insurance, property	110
Crichton, N.A.	Car dealing, yachts, auto engineering	100
Cushing, Sir S.J.	Investment	40
Davies, J.S.	Property, transport, tourism	30
Dick, M.S. & Presley, A.S.	Technology	60
Dickson, C.S.	Yachting, property	20
Douglas family	Pharmaceuticals	50
Drinkrow family	Civil engineering, property	85
Duke, R.A.	Retailing	320
Eagle, C.F.M.	Computer technology	30
Edgar, E.S.	Sharebroking, property	35
Erceg, M.A.	Liquor	300
Farmer, T.M.	Investment	120
Farrant, I.F.	Investment	25
Fay, Sir H.M.G.	Merchant banking, investment	600
Fistonich, G.V.	Wine	25
Fletcher family	Investment	50
Foreman family	Healthcare, manufacturing	115
Francis, P.E.	Investment	30
Friedlander, H.R. & M.	Property	75
Gallagher family	Electric fences	70
Gibbons family	Car and truck dealing	55
Gibbs, A.T.	Investment	300

	Main source of wealth	$m (min)
Gibbs, J.B.	Art, investment	35
Gilks, J.W.	Investment	20
Giltrap, C.J.	Car dealing	220
Glasson, T.C.	Clothes, property development	55
Gold, D.A.	Consultancy, radio, property	30
Goodfellow family	Fishing, chemicals	375
Goodman family	Investment, property	550
Gough family	Property, engineering, equipment	100
Green, H.	Property development, investment, livestock	170
Hagaman, E.R.	Hotels, investment	85
Hart, G.R.	Food, investment	1200
Harvey family	Property	35
Haszard, M.H.	Investment	45
Hay family	Housing, property	25
Heatley family	Investment	150
Hemi, H.A. & J.	Vehicle exporting	30
Hendriksen, J.	Internet advertising	15
Hendry, I.R.	Investment	25
Hickman, K.J.	Retirement homes	40
Hill, R.M.	Jewellery	100
Hogan, Sir P.	Horsebreeding	65
Hoggard, K.M.	Chemicals	100
Holyoake, N.V.	Heating, car dealing, forestry, property	55
Hopper family	Property development	55
Horton family	Media	165
Hoskins, P.A.	Software, property	15
Hotchin, M.S.	Finance, property	150
Hubbard, A.J.	Investment, finance	180
Huljich family	Property, investment	90
Hunter, R.K.	Fashion modelling, endorsements	20
Hunter, S.L. & Powell, T.G.	Investment	20
Hynds family	Drainage, concrete products	60
Inger, J.A. & P.G.	Investment, property	30
Izard, R.W.V.	Farming, property, aviation	50
Jackson, P.R.	Filmmaking	70
Jarvis, T.W.	Investment, horsebreeding	60
Johnson, B.E.	Investment	60
Jones, Sir R.E.	Property	100

	Main source of wealth	$m (min)
Jordan, N.	Information technology	65
Kirkpatrick, J.S.	Property	65
Krukziener, A.M.	Property development	20
La Grouw family	Housing	35
Lane, G.R.	Cashed up	170
Lawless, L.F.	Acting, singing	15
Levene family	Retail, property	120
Lowe, G.E.S.	Meat byproducts, property	65
Luney, C.S.	Construction, property	20
McCahill, B.J.	Cashed up, property	40
McCollam family	Investment, horsebreeding	35
McGurk, M.A.	Spa pools, property	25
McLaren, D.G.	Animal remedies	30
Mace, C.R.	Property, investment	80
Manson, E.C.	Property development	140
Marsh, G.J.	Manufacturing, property, car dealing	40
Martin, J. Mcc.	Property development, tourism	30
Masfen, P.H.	Cashed up, shares	230
Matthew, R.H.	Investment	40
Menzies, P.F.	Cashed up	25
Morgenstern, A.S.	Property development	20
Morrison, H.R.L.	Investment	70
Muller, D.F.	Property development	50
Myers, A.D.	Cashed up	600
Neill, N.J.D.	Acting, wine	25
Nightingale, A.J.	Paint, wine	45
Norman family	Jewellery	125
Outtrim, S.B.	Software	110
Paterson family	Property development, investment, biotechnology	170
Paykel family	Whiteware, healthcare	40
Perry family	Property, engineering, landfills, sand & aggregate	55
Petherick, S.G.	Property	30
Plested, B.G.	Transport	40
Plowman, N.H.	Investment	100
Pye family	Agribusiness	40
Pye, W.E.	Publishing	35
Ramsey, F.J.	Meat processing, farming	30

	Main source of wealth	$m (min)
Reynolds, C.W.	Property development	30
Richardson, H.W.	Concrete, transport	85
Richwhite, D. McK.	Merchant banking, investment	600
Ricketts, G.T.	Law, investment	45
Roberts, K.J.	Advertising	30
Rolleston, H.J.D.	Investment	35
Roy, J.	Investment	20
Ryder, J.W.D.	Retirement homes	40
Sanders, J.R.	Property	50
Savage, E.R.	Cashed up, retail	60
Schick, N.E. & S.D.	Horsebreeding	30
Schofield, R.T.	Property, hotels	40
Seaton, J.H.	Farming, property	35
Simpson, Sir G.	Software	60
Skeggs, Sir C.G.	Wine, hotels, fishing, shipping	35
Smith, J.C.S. & N.G.S.	Publishing, property, investment	50
Somers-Edgar, D.L.	Financial planning, investment	40
Spencer, J.B.	Investment, property	250
Spencer, P.A.	Farming, meat, clothing, internet	100
Staples, H.C.	Property development, investment	25
Stewart family	Plastics	170
Talley family	Fisheries	†25
Taylor family	Investment, horsebreeding	40
Te Kanawa, Dame K.J.C.	Opera singing	15
Thexton, D.J.	Beverages	20
Thom, M.N.	Music, promotions	25
Thomas, B.C.	Tourism	20
Timpson, A.C.	Carpets	55
Tindall, S.R.	Retailing	420
Todd family	Energy, investment	2000
Tololi, M.	Horsebreeding, property	25
Tonks, E.J.	Meat byproducts	35
Ullrich, G.W.	Aluminium	55
Vela family	Fisheries, horsebreeding	80
Walden, J.W.	Farming	18
Wale, D.H.	Investment	20
Wallace, J.H.	Meat, art	50

† Considerable wealth in trusts excluded from calculation.

	Main source of wealth	$m (min)
Wallis, Sir T.W.	Tourism, investment, deer farming	50
Watson, E.J.	Investment	275
Watt, M.H.	Sports promotion, entertainment	190
Williams family	Farming, property	35
Williams, T.	E-commerce	30
Wood family	Internet services	30
Wyborn, M.J.	Property development	50

Appendix B

National Business Review Business Hall of Fame 1994–2003

Inaugurated in 1994 by the Enterprise New Zealand Trust to recognise people who have made an outstanding contribution to business and to the nation, the *National Business Review* Business Hall of Fame includes many of New Zealand's richest achievers, although wealth is not a requirement for induction. Under the rules, living laureates must no longer be involved actively in their main business.

1994

Sir Woolf Fisher (1913–75): whiteware manufacturer, co-founder of Auckland-based Fisher & Paykel Industries.

Sir William Goodfellow (1880–1974): father of the modern dairy industry, leading light in the company that became New Zealand Dairy Group.

Sir Bryan James Todd (1902–87): founder of the New Zealand oil industry, head of the family-owned Todd Corporation.

Sir James Fletcher snr (1886–1974): New Zealand's first major industrialist, founder of the company that became Fletcher Challenge.

Sir James Wattie CBE (1902–74): pioneer food processor and manufacturer, founder of the company that became Wattie Industries.

Sir Jack Newman CBE (1902–96): pioneer transport operator who expanded the Nelson-based TNL Group (later Newmans) to become a national company.

1995

Sir Kenneth Ben Myers MBE (1907–98): liquor merchant, developed the family business, the Campbell & Ehrenfried Co, later part of Lion Nathan.

Edward Max Friedlander OBE (born 1922): clothing retailer, former chairman and managing director of Hallenstein Glasson Holdings.

Sir Clifford Ulric Plimmer KBE (1905–88): professional company director, leader of Wright Stephenson & Co.

Sir William Alfred Stevenson KBE CStJ (1901–83): civil engineering contractor, developed family company W. Stevenson & Sons.

Sir Robert James Kerridge CStJ Chevalier of the Order of Merit (Italy) (1901– 79): movie-theatre entrepreneur, founder of Kerridge Odeon Corporation.

Sir Robertson Huntly Stewart KBE (born 1913): plastics, electrical and consumer appliances industrialist, founder of Christchurch-based PDL Holdings.

1996

Sir Jack Richard Butland KBE (1896–1982): pioneer food manufacturer (Chesdale cheese) and philanthropist.

Chew Chong (1827/44?–1920): Taranaki dairy pioneer, entrepreneur and philanthropist.

Sir Angus McMillan Tait KNZM OBE (born 1919): world-class Christchurch-based telecommunications manufacturer (Tait Electronics).

Sir John Robert McKenzie KBE (1876–1955): discount retailer, founded McKenzies department store.

Richard William Vincent Izard OBE (born 1934): established world-class circular-sawblade company.

Sir Robert Arthur Owens KNZM CBE Order of Merit (Chile) (1921–99): transport industry driving force and respected public figure.

1997

John Anderson (1820–97): father of New Zealand engineering.

Sir John Logan Campbell (1817–1912): commercial leader, philanthropist and 'father of Auckland'.

Thomas Russell jnr (1830–1904): pre-eminent commercial lawyer and investor, driving force behind the formation of New Zealand Insurance Co and the Bank of New Zealand.

Assid Abraham Corban (1864–1941): Lebanese-born winemaker who commercialised New Zealand's wine industry.

Sir Alfred Hamish Reed CBE (1875–1975): book publisher and writer.

James Robert Maddren CBE Chevalier d'Ordre de la Couronne (Belgium) (1920–98): pioneer exporter and processor of venison and game.

Sir James Muir Cameron Fletcher ONZ (born 1914): built New Zealand's largest and most enduring industrial group, Fletcher Challenge.

Sir Francis Henry Renouf Order of Merit (Germany) (1918–98): pioneer merchant banker, sharebroker and benefactor.

Sir Thomas Edwin Clark jnr (born 1916): expanded family ceramics business into an export-led public company.

Robert Hannah (1846–1930): pioneer footwear manufacturer whose company, R. Hannah & Co, survives today.

1998

Te Kirihaehae Te Puea Herangi [Princess Te Puea] CBE (1883–1952): Waikato Maori leader, orator and promoter of tribal 'self-help'.

Sir Henry Joseph Kelliher KStJ (1896–1991): Auckland-based brewer (Dominion Breweries), monetary reformer and philanthropist.

Graeme James Marsh CBE (born 1933): Otago manufacturer, business leader and company director, former managing director of Donaghys Industries.

Raymond Watson Hurley (1923–78): entrepreneur, co-founder (with brother Desmond) of world-class lingerie manufacturer Bendon.

Maurice Paykel CBE (1914–2002): whiteware manufacturer, co-founder of Fisher & Paykel Industries.

Sir (Thomas) Harcourt Clarke Caughey KBE CStJ (1911–93): Auckland department-store head and public figure.

1999

John Jones (1808/09?–1869): entrepreneur whaler-farmer who helped launch Dunedin as a business centre.

Sir Ronald Ramsay Trotter (born 1927): talented company director who led Fletcher Challenge through its greatest period of growth.

Sir Laurence Houghton Stevens CBE (born 1920): retired managing director of Auckland Knitting Mills and a former president of the New Zealand Manufacturers' Federation.

Sir Apirana Turupa Ngata (1874–1950): outstanding Maori leader and scholar who devoted his time to Maori enterprise.

Rodolph Lysaght Wigley (1881–1946): entrepreneur who created New Zealand's largest tourist organisation.

Nathaniel William Levin (1818–1903): pioneer Wellington merchant, founder of Levin & Co.

Robert Graham (1820–85): pioneer tourism entrepreneur and farmer.

Donald George McLaren ONZM (born 1933): self-made owner of a major animal remedies company, Auckland-based Bomac Laboratories.

2000

Francis John Carter (1869–1949): sawmiller-contractor who established a business in 1895 that was to become Carter Consolidated.

Alexander Harvey (1841–1919): farmer and later manufacturer who established Alex Harvey & Sons (later Alex Harvey Industries), the country's largest manufacturer.

Robert Holt (1832/33?–1909): Hawke's Bay timber merchant who established Robert Holt & Sons.

Edward Elworthy (1836–99): prominent South Canterbury runholder-grain grower, director of South Canterbury Refrigerating Co.

Sir James Lawrence Hay OBE (1888–1971): Christchurch businessman, local body politician and philanthropist who established the Hay's (later Haywrights) department store.

Amy Maria Hellaby (1864–1955): saved and expanded the family meat business, R. & W. Hellaby, after the untimely deaths of her husband, brother-in-law and sister-in-law.

Robert Alexander Crookston Laidlaw (1885–1971): founder of Laidlaw Leeds, which became the country's largest department-store business, the Farmers' Trading Co.

Sir Clifford George Skeggs OStJ (born 1931): founder of family fishing business and inshore fishing fleet, former mayor of Dunedin and prominent philanthropist.

2001

Sir Geoffrey Newland Roberts CBE AFC LM(US) (1906–95): father of commercial aviation who helped create Air New Zealand.

John Brownlow Horrocks CBE MC ED (born 1920): lawyer, accountant and company director who specialised in the transport industry.

(John) Heaton Barker (1867–1947): pioneer food retailer who established Foodstuffs as the country's largest grocery group.

Brian Hall Picot CMG (born 1921): businessman who helped establish New Zealand supermarketing; leading education reformer.

Henry Alexander Horrocks (1893–1942): visionary lawyer who formed the company that became Whakatane Board Mills.

(George) Peter Shirtcliffe CMG (born 1931): company director who excelled in management; promoter of enterprise education.

2002

Thomas Henry Ah Chee (1920–2000): founder of New Zealand's first supermarket in 1958 and of the business that became Progressive Enterprises.

Romeo Alessandro Bragato (1858–1913): pioneer viticulturist who identified the country's best winegrowing regions and worked to eliminate phylloxera.

Dr Donald Thomas Brash (born 1940): economist who as Reserve Bank governor restored price stability to the national economy.

Sir Richard Henry Alwyn Carter (born 1935): third-generation sawmiller-forester who engineered the giant merger that created Carter Holt Harvey.

Peter Hanbury Masfen (born 1941): accountant who led Montana Wines to become New Zealand's largest and most successful winemaker.

Sir Timothy William Wallis (born 1938): aviator who pioneered deer recovery industry; tourism entrepreneur and founder of Warbirds Over Wanaka international air show.

2003

(Arthur) Douglas Myers CBE (born 1938): businessman who created Lion Nathan through a major merger and made it the largest trans-Tasman brewer.

Francis Holmes Chevalier of the Crown of Savoy (Italy) (1874–1947): father of the oil industry in Kuwait, Bahrain and Saudi Arabia.

Sir Wilson James Whineray KNZM OBE (born 1935): All Black captain and company director, including chairman of Carter Holt Harvey.

John Packard Goulter (born 1941): highly successful chief executive and later managing director of Auckland International Airport.

Peter Barr (1861–1951): father of New Zealand accountancy and founder of firm that became Barr Burgess & Stewart.

Robert Forsyth Barr QSM [known as Peter Barr, son of the above] (1907–67): founder in 1936 of Dunedin-based sharebroking house Forsyth Barr.

Appendix C

National Business Review Sporting Rich 2003

Professional sport showed its ugly face in New Zealand in 2002 and 2003 with a cricket pay dispute, bitterness over the America's Cup failure and fallout from the Rugby Union's loss of subhosting rights for the Rugby World Cup.

The America's Cup debacle highlighted New Zealand's inexperience in competing in the professional sporting arena. The public outcry that followed *Team New Zealand*'s 5–nil drubbing by Swiss challenge *Alinghi* was justified, but the inquiry into what went wrong brought few answers. As the Sydney-based Bulldogs rugby league team found out in 2002, sport demands accountability in much the same way as business does — especially so when the national interest is at stake.

But there were also some memorable successes, most notably the Vodafone Warriors making the National Rugby League grand final in Sydney and the Tall Blacks' astonishing performance at the basketball world championships in Indianapolis.

As the All Blacks prepare for the fifth Rugby World Cup, the interest in what Kiwi sportspeople earn is higher than ever. The opportunities for professional sportspeople in business are fewer than in the past because many have not developed skills outside their sport. Nevertheless, for people with sports skills but lacking academic qualifications or professional abilities, professional sport can provide a quick step to a comfortable lifestyle.

What follows is a snapshot of sporting wealth in this country with figures expressed as net worth, not earnings.

Top ten in sports wealth
July 2003

	Minimum wealth (not earnings)
1. Dickson, Christopher Stuart [Chris] (b. 1961) Food, investment	$20
2. Charles, Sir Robert James [Bob] (b. 1936) Golf, property, consultancy	$15
=3. Butterworth, Bradley William [Brad] (b. 1959) Yachting	†$14
=3. Coutts, Russell (b. 1962) Yachting	†$14
5. Tua, David (b. 1971) Boxing	$13
6. Lomu, Jonah Tali (b. 1975) Rugby union, endorsements	$10
7. Campbell, Michael Shane (b. 1969) Golf	$9
8. Nobilo, Frank Ivan Joseph (b. 1960) Golf	$8
=9. Dye, (Raymond) Shane (b. 1966) Jockey	$7
=9. O'Sullivan, Lance Anthony (b. 1963) Jockey	$7

† Conservative valuation because of uncertainty over level of earnings.

Bibliography

Use of the oblique (e.g. 1988/89) means a single volume, while use of the dash (e.g. 1987–89) indicates successive volumes. Reference material is arranged chronologically in some cases.

Books/publications

Acland, L.G.D., *The Early Canterbury Runs*, Whitcoulls, Christchurch, 1975 (4th edn).

Alexander, J.H., *Historic Auckland*, Whitcombe & Tombs, Christchurch, c.1961.

Allan, B., *The Geddes Family in Colonial Auckland*, Allan, Auckland, 1990.

Allan, B., *The Morrin Family of Early Auckland*, Allan, Auckland, 1990.

Anderson, J.C. & Petersen, G.C., *The Mair Family*, A.H. & A.W. Reed, Wellington, 1956.

Bade, J.J.D. Northcote (ed.), *West Auckland Remembers*, vols 1 & 2, West Auckland Historical Society, Henderson, 1991–92.

Bagnall, A.G., *Wairarapa: An Historical Excursion*, Hedley's Bookshop for the Masterton Lands Trust, Masterton, 1976.

Baker, J.V.T., *War Economy: The New Zealand People at War*, Department of Internal Affairs, Wellington, 1965.

Baker, S.J., *New Zealand Slang: A Dictionary of Colloquialisms*, Whitcombe & Tombs, Christchurch, 1940.

Barton, R.A. (ed.), *A Century of Achievement: A Commemoration of the First 100 Years of the New Zealand Meat Industry*, Dunmore Press, 1984.

Bassett, M.E.R., *Sir Joseph Ward: A Political Bioghraphy*, Auckland University Press, Auckland, 1993.

Bassett, M.E.R., *The State in New Zealand: Socialism Without Doctrines*, Auckland University Press, Auckland, 1998.

Bawden, P.M., *The Years Before Waitangi: A Story of Early Maori/European Contact in New Zealand*, Benton Ross, Auckland, 1987.

Belich, J.C., *Making Peoples: A History of New Zealanders from Polynesian Settlement to the End of the Nineteenth Century*, Penguin Books (NZ), Auckland, 1996.

Bentley, T., *Pakeha Maori: The Extraordinary Life of Europeans who Lived as Maori in Early New Zealand*, Penguin Books, Auckland, 1999.

Bidwill, J.C., *Rambles in New Zealand 1839*, Pegasus Press, Christchurch, 1952.

Bidwill, W.E. & Woodhouse, A.E., *Bidwill of Pihautea: The Life of Charles Robert Bidwill*, Coulls Somerville Wilkie, Christchurch, 1927.

Binney, J.M.C., Bassett, J.O. & Olssen, E.N., *The People and the Land: An Illustrated History of New Zealand 1820–1920*, Allen & Unwin, Wellington, 1990.

Birchfield, R.J., *The Rise and Fall of JBL*, NBR Books, Fourth Estate Publishing Co, Wellington, 1972.

Bohan, E., *To Be a Hero: A Biography of Sir George Grey*, HarperCollins, Auckland, 1998.

Bollinger, C.V.I., *Grog's Own Country: The Story of Liquor Licensing in New Zealand*, Minerva, Auckland, 1967 (2nd ed.).

Bolton, J.S., *Four Square: The Industry Behind the Shop Counter*, Foodstuffs (Wellington) Co-op Society, Wellington, 1997.

Boyd, J., *Pumice & Pines: The Story of Kaingaroa Forest*, GP Publications, Wellington, 1993.

Burdon, R.M., *The New Dominion*, A.H. & A.W. Reed, Wellington, 1965.

Burns, P. (Richardson, H. [ed.]), *Fatal Success: A History of the New Zealand Company*, Heinemann Reed, Auckland, 1989.

Bush, G.W.A., *Decently and In Order: The Government of the City of Auckland 1840–1971*, Collins, Auckland, 1971.

Bush, G.W.A., *Advance In Order: The Auckland City Council from Centenary to Reorganisation 1971–1989*, Auckland City Council, Auckland, 1991.

Butterworth, S.M., *Quality Bakers New Zealand: The First 25 Years*, Quality Bakers, Auckland, 1997.

Calder, M. & Tyson, J., *Meat Acts: The New Zealand Meat Industry 1972–97*, Meat New Zealand, Wellington, 1999.

Campbell, J.L., *Poenamo: Sketches of the Early Life in New Zealand: Romance and Reality of Antipodean Life in the Infancy of a New Colony*, Whitcombe & Tombs, Christchurch, 1952.

Carew, E., *Westpac: The Bank that Broke the Bank*, Doubleday, Sydney, 1997.

Caughey, A.M.R., *An Auckland Network*, Shoal Bay Press, Auckland, 1988.

Caughey, A.M.R., *The Interpreter: The Biography of Richard 'Dicky' Barrett*, David Bateman, Auckland, 1998.

Chappell, N.M., *New Zealand Banker's Hundred: A History of the Bank of New Zealand 1861–1961*, Bank of New Zealand, Wellington, 1961.

Christchurch City Council Town Planning Division, *The Architectural Heritage of Christchurch: 3. McLeans Mansion*, Christchurch City Council, Christchurch, 1983.

Coley, J., *Charles Luney: The Building of a Lifetime*, Hazard Press, Christchurch, 2000.
Colgan, W., *The Governor's Gift: The Auckland Public Library 1880–1980*, Richards Publishing & Auckland City Council, Auckland, 1980.
Cowan, J., *The New Zealand Wars: A History of Maori Campaigns and the Pioneering Period*, vols 1 & 2, Government Printer, Wellington, 1956.
Craig, E., *Breakwater Against the Tide: A History of Papakura City and Districts*, Ray Richards for the Papakura and Districts Historical Society, Auckland, 1981.
Cresswell, D., *Early New Zealand Families*, Pegasus Press, Christchurch, 1949.
Cresswell, D., *Early New Zealand Families: Second Series*, Whitcombe & Tombs, Christchurch, 1956.
Crocombe, G.T., Enright, M.J. & Porter, M.E., *Upgrading New Zealand's Competitive Advantage*, Oxford University Press and New Zealand Trade Development Board, Auckland, 1991.
Crosby, R.D., *The Musket Wars: A History of Inter-Iwi Conflict 1806–45*, Reed Publishing (NZ), Auckland, 1999.
Cumberland, K.B., *Landmarks*, Reader's Digest, Sydney, 1981.
Davis, E.R., *A Link with the Past*, Oswald-Sealy (New Zealand), Auckland, 1948.
Dienstag, E.F., *In Good Company: 125 Years at the Heinz Table*, Warner Books, New York, 1994.
Dyne, D.G., *Famous New Zealand Murders*, Collins, Auckland, 1969.
Eldred-Grigg, S.T., *A Southern Gentry: New Zealanders Who Inherited the Earth*, Heinemann Reed, Auckland, 1980.
Eldred-Grigg, S.T., *The Rich: A New Zealand History*, Penguin Books (NZ), Auckland, 1996.
Flude, A.G., *Henderson & Macfarlane's Circular Saw Line*, Flude, Auckland, 1993.
Foodstuffs (Auckland), *Four Square New Zealand Golden Jubilee*, Foodstuffs (Auckland), Auckland, 1982.
Gardner, W.J., *A Pastoral Kingdom Divided: Cheviot 1889–94*, Bridget Williams Books, Wellington, 1992.
Gilkison, W.S. (ed.), *Barr Burgess & Stewart 1871–1971*, Barr Burgess & Stewart, Dunedin, 1971.
Goldsmith, P., *John Banks: A Biography*, Penguin Books (NZ), Auckland, 2002 (2nd edn).
Goldsmith, P., *Gibbs: New Zealand Roots*, A.T. Gibbs, Auckland, 2002.
Goldsmith, P., *T.N. Gibbs*, A.T. Gibbs, Auckland, 2002.
Gore, R., *Levins 1841–1941: The History of the First Hundred Years of Levin and Company Limited*, Whitcombe & Tombs for Levin & Co, Wellington, 1956.
Graham, J., *Frederick Weld*, Auckland University Press & Oxford University Press, Auckland, 1983.

Grainger, J., *The Auckland Story: New Zealand's Queen City and its Citizens Through the Years*, A.H. & A.W. Reed, Wellington, 1953.

Grant, D., *Bulls, Bears and Elephants: A History of the New Zealand Stock Exchange*, Victoria University Press, Wellington, 1997.

Greenway, R.L.N., *Unsung Heroines: Biographies of Christchurch Women*, Canterbury Public Library, Christchurch, 1994.

Hall, D., *The Golden Echo: A Social History of New Zealand*, Collins, Auckland, 1971.

Hamer, D.A., *The New Zealand Liberals: The Years of Power 1891–1912*, Auckland University Press, Auckland, 1988.

Handley, C., *Receiving Orders: Caught in the Corporate Crossfire*, Random House, Auckland, 1999.

Hanham, H.J, 'New Zealand Promoters and British Investors', in *Studies of a Small Democracy: Essays in Honour of Willis Airey*, Paul's Book Arcade for the University of Auckland, Auckland, 1963.

Hawkins, A.R. & McLauchlan, G.W., *The Hawk: Allan Hawkins Tells the Equiticorp Story to Gordon McLauchlan*, Four Star Books, Auckland, 1989.

Healy, B., *A Hundred Million Trees*, Hodder & Stoughton, Auckland, 1982.

Holm, J., *Nothing But Grass and Wind: The Rutherfords of Canterbury*, Hazard Press, Christchurch, 1992.

Hunt, G.J., *Why MMP Must Go: The Case for Ditching the Electoral Disaster of the Century*, Waddington Press, Auckland, 1998.

Hunt, G.J., *Hustlers, Rogues & Bubble Boys: White-collar Mischief in New Zealand*, Reed Publishing (NZ) & Waddington Press, Auckland, 2001.

Hunter, I., *Man for Our Times: Robert A. Laidlaw*, Castle Publishing, Auckland, 1999.

Inkson, K., Henshall, B., Marsh, N. & Ellis, G., *Theory K: The Key to Excellence in New Zealand Management*, David Bateman, Auckland, 1986.

Irving, D.A. & Inkson, K., *It Must be Wattie's!: From Kiwi Icon to Global Player*, David Bateman, Auckland, 1998.

Jesson, B.E., *Behind the Mirror Glass: The Growth of Wealth and Power in New Zealand in the Eighties*, Penguin Books (NZ), Auckland, 1987.

Johnson, D.W., *Timaru and South Canterbury: A Pictorial History*, Canterbury University Press with Dan Cosgrove Ltd & D.C. Turnbull & Co, Christchurch, 1996.

Keene, F., *Legacies in Kauri: Old Homes & Churches of the North*, Keene, Whangarei, 1978.

Keith, H.H.C., *New Zealand Yesterdays*, Reader's Digest, Sydney, 1984.

Kirkland, A. & Berg, P., *A Century of State-Honed Enterprise: 100 Years of State Plantation Forestry in New Zealand*, Profile Books, Auckland, 1997.

Lambourn, A., *Kuwait's Liquid Gold: The NZ Connection*, Robert Allan Associates, Tauranga, c1991.
Lee, J., *Hokianga*, Hodder & Stoughton, Auckland, 1987.
Lee, J., *The Bay of Islands*, Reed Publishing (NZ), Auckland, 1996.
Lee, J.A., *For Mine is the Kingdom*, Alister Taylor Publishing, Martinborough, 1975.
Lion Breweries, *Lion Breweries: A Heritage of Brewing*, H.B. Publications, Napier, 1993.
Lloyd Prichard, M.F., *An Economic History of New Zealand to 1939*, Collins, Auckland, 1970.
Lockyer, R.H., *Jade River: A History of the Mahurangi*, Friends of Mahurangi Incorporated, Warkworth, 2001 (2nd edn).
Loftus, H.J., *The Tetley Affair: Colonial Dreams and Nightmares*, Heritage Press, Waikanae, 1997.
McAloon, J.P., *No Idle Rich: The Wealthy of Canterbury and Otago*, University of Otago Press, Dunedin, 2002.
McIntyre, R., *The Canoes of Kupe: A History of Martinborough District*, Victoria University Press, Wellington, 2002.
McKenzie, R.A., *Footprints: Harnessing an Inheritance into a Legacy*, Te Aro Press, Wellington, 1998.
McLauchlan, G.W., *The ASB: A Bank and its Community*, Four Star Books, Auckland, 1991.
McLintock, A.H., *Crown Colony Government in New Zealand*, Government Printer, Wellington, 1958.
McManamy, J., *Crash! Corporate Australia and New Zealand Fight for Their Lives*, Pan Books, Sydney, 1988.
Maddock, S., *A Pictorial History of New Zealand*, Heinemann Reed with David Bateman, Auckland, 1988.
Marton, J.E. (ed.), *People, Politics & Power Stations: Electric Power Generation in New Zealand 1880–1990*, Bridget Williams Books & Electricity Corporation of New Zealand, Wellington, 1991.
Moon, E.P., *Hobson: Governor of New Zealand 1840–1842*, David Ling Publishing, Auckland, 1998.
Morrison, I., Haden, F. & Cubis, G., *Michael Fay on a Reach for the Ultimate: The Unauthorised Biography*, Freelance Biographies, Wellington, 1990.
Morrison, J.P., *The Evolution of a City: The Story of the Growth of the City and Suburbs of Christchurch, the Capital of Canterbury*, Christchurch City Council, Christchurch, 1948.
Nathan, L.D., *As Old as Auckland*, L.D. Nathan Group of Companies, Auckland, 1984.
Newland, O.M., *Lost Property: The Crash of '87 and the Aftershock*, HarperCollins, Auckland, 1994.

Northern Club, *The Northern Club Auckland*, Northern Club, Auckland, 1954.

Ogilvie, G., *Pioneers of the Plains: the Deans of Canterbury*, Shoal Bay Press, Christchurch, 1996.

Oliver, W.H., *The Story of New Zealand*, Faber & Faber, London, 1963 (2nd edn).

Parker, S., *Made in New Zealand: The Story of Jim Fletcher*, Hodder & Stoughton, Auckland, 1994.

Parker, S., *Cutting Edge: 100 Years of Innovation, Leadership and Sheer Grit: The Carter Holt Harvey Story*, Penguin Books (NZ), Auckland, 2000.

Parry, G., *Thinking About Tomorrow: The Forsyth Barr Story*, Forsyth Barr, Dunedin, 2001.

Peters, T.J. & Waterman, R.H. jnr, *In Search of Excellence: Lessons from America's Best-Run Companies*, Harper & Row, New York, 1984 (Australasian paperback edn).

Phillipps, D., *Mission in a Secular City: Methodist Mission Northern 1851–2001*, Methodist Mission Northern, Auckland, 2001.

Phillips, J., *Douglas Myers: What I've Learned in Business*, Nahanni Publishing, Auckland, 1999.

Platts, U., *The Lively Capital: Auckland 1840–1865*, Avon Fine Prints, Christchurch, 1971.

Porter, F. (ed.), *The Turanga Journals: Letters and Journals of William and Jane Williams, New Zealand 1840–1850*, Price Milburn for Victoria University of Wellington, Wellington, 1974.

Pugsley, C.J., *On the Fringe of Hell: New Zealanders and Military Discipline in the First World War*, Hodder & Stoughton, Auckland, 1991.

Reed, A.H., *Historic Bay of Islands*, A.H. & A.W. Reed, Wellington, 1960.

Reed, A.H., *A.H. Reed: An Autobiography*, A.H. & A.W. Reed, Wellington, 1967.

Reed, A.W., *Auckland, the City of the Seas: An Illustrated Account of the Founding and Development of the City of Auckland and its Suburbs*, A.H. & A.W. Reed, Wellington, 1954.

Renouf, F.H., *Sir Francis Renouf: An Autobiography*, Steele Roberts & Associates, Wellington, 1997.

Rice, G.W., *Heaton Rhodes of Otahuna: The Illustrated Biography*, Canterbury University Press, Christchurch, 2001.

Robinson, N., *James Fletcher: Builder*, Hodder & Stoughton, Auckland, 1970.

Russell, S.T. (chairman), *Sharemarket Inquiry: Report of the Ministerial Committee of Inquiry into the Sharemarket*, Ministerial Committee, Auckland, 1989.

Scott, R.G., *A Stake in the Country: Assid Abraham Cordan and His Family*, Southern Cross Books, Auckland, 1973.

Scott, R.G., *Stock in Trade: Hellaby's First 100 Years 1873–1973*, Southern Cross Books, Auckland, 1977.

Scott, R.G., *Fire on the Clay: The Pakeha Comes to West Auckland*, Southern Cross Books, Auckland, 1979.

Scotter, W.H., *A History of Canterbury, Vol III: 1876–1950*, Whitcombe & Tombs, Christchurch, 1965.

Snedden, F.G., *King of the Castle: A Biography of William Larnach*, David Bateman, Auckland, 1997.

Stacpoole, J., *The Houses of the Merchant Princes*, University of Auckland, Auckland, 1989.

Stead, K., *One Hundred I'm Bid: A Centennial History of Turners & Growers*, Kestrel Publishing, Auckland, 1997.

Stewart, W.D., *Brief History of the Dunedin Club (Otherwise Known as Fernhill Club)*, Dunedin Club, Dunedin, 1948.

Stone, R.C.J., *Makers of Fortune: A Colonial Business Community and Its Fall*, Oxford University Press & Auckland University Press, Auckland, 1973.

Stone, R.C.J., *The Making of Russell McVeagh: The First 125 Years of the Practice of Russell McVeagh McKenzie Bartleet & Co 1863–1988*, Auckland University Press, Auckland, 1991.

Sturt, C.E., *Dirty Collars*, Reed Publishing (NZ), Auckland, 1998.

Sutch, W.B., *Poverty and Progress in New Zealand: A Re-assessment*, A.H. & A.W. Reed, Wellington, 1969.

Swainson, W., *Auckland, the Capital of New Zealand and the Country Adjacent: Including Some Account of Gold Discovery in New Zealand*, 1853 (facsimile edn) Wilson & Horton, Auckland, 1971.

Turnovsky, F., *Turnovsky: Fifty Years in New Zealand*, Allen & Unwin, Wellington, 1990.

Tyrrell, A.R., *The Fulton Hogan Story: 1933–1993*, Fulton Hogan Holdings, Dunedin, 1992.

van Dongen, Y., *Brierley: The Man Behind the Corporate Legend*, Viking, Penguin Books (NZ), Auckland, 1990.

Verry, L., *Seven Days a Week: The Story of Independent Newspapers Limited*, INL Print, Wellington, 1985.

Ville, S., *The Rural Entrepreneurs: A History of the Stock and Station Agent Industry in Australia and New Zealand*, Cambridge University Press, Cambridge, 2000.

Wallace, B., *Battle of the Titans: Sir Ron Trotter, Hugh Fletcher and the Rise and Fall of Fletcher Challenge*, Penguin Books (NZ), Auckland, 2001.

Ward, A.H., *A Command of Cooperatives*, New Zealand Dairy Board, Wellington, 1975.

Wild, L.J., *The Life and Times of Sir James Wilson of Bulls*, Whitcombe & Tombs, Christchurch, 1953.

Williams, T., *The Rise, Fall and Flight of Brierley Investments*, David Bateman, Auckland, 1999.

Wilson, J., *Cheviot: Kingdom to County*, Cheviot Historic Records Society, Cheviot, 1993.

Wilson, G.H.O., *Kororareka and Other Essays*, John McIndoe, Dunedin, 1990.

Wright Stephenson & Co Ltd, *A Century's Challenge*, Wright Stephenson, Wellington, 1961.

Biographical dictionaries

Oliver, W.H. (general ed.), *The Dictionary of New Zealand Biography: Volume One 1769–1869*, Allen & Unwin New Zealand & Department of Internal Affairs, Wellington, 1990.

Orange, C.J. (general ed.), *The Dictionary of New Zealand Biography: Volume Two 1870–1900*, Bridget Williams Books & Department of Internal Affairs, Wellington, 1993.

Orange, C.J. (general ed.), *The Dictionary of New Zealand Biography: Volume Three 1901–1920*, Auckland University Press & Department of Internal Affairs, Wellington, 1996.

Orange, C.J. (general ed.), *The Dictionary of New Zealand Biography: Volume Four 1921–1940*, Auckland University Press & Department of Internal Affairs, Wellington, 1998.

Scholefield, G.H. (ed.), *A Dictionary of New Zealand Biography*, vols I & II, Department of Internal Affairs, Wellington, 1940.

The Cyclopedia Co, *The Cyclopedia of New Zealand*, vols 1–6, 1897–1908, Cyclopedia Co, Christchurch, 1897–1908.

Thomson, J.A. (ed.), *Southern People: A Dictionary of Otago-Southland Biography*, Longacre Press & Dunedin City Council, Dunedin, 1998.

Who's who

Pine, L.H. (ed.), *Burke's Peerage, Baronetage & Knightage*, Burke's Peerage & Shaw Publishing Co, London, 1959 (102nd edn).

Scholefield, G.H. & Schwabe, E. (eds), *Who's Who in New Zealand and the Western Pacific*, Gordon & Gotch, Wellington, 1908 (1st edn)

Scholefield, G.H. (ed.), *Who's Who in New Zealand and the Western Pacific*, Scholefield, Masterton, 1925 (2nd edn).

Scholefield, G.H. (ed.), *Who's Who in New Zealand and the Western Pacific*, Rangatira Press, Wellington, 1931 (3rd edn).

Scholefield, G.H. (ed.), *Who's Who in New Zealand*, Scholefield, Wellington, 1941 (4th edn).

Scholefield, G.H. (ed.), *Who's Who in New Zealand*, A.H. & A.W. Reed, Wellington, 1951 (5th edn).
Simpson, F.A. (ed.), *Who's Who in New Zealand*, A.H. & A.W. Reed, Wellington, 1956 (6th edn).
Petersen, G.C. (ed.), *Who's Who in New Zealand*, A.H. & A.W. Reed, Wellington, 1961, 1964, 1968, 1971 (7th–10th edns).
Traue, J.E. (ed.), *Who's Who in New Zealand*, A.H. & A.W. Reed, Wellington, 1978 (11th edn).
Lambert, M. (ed.), *Who's Who in New Zealand*, Reed, Auckland, 1991 (12th edn).
Paul Hamlyn Ltd, *Famous New Zealanders of the 19th Century*, Paul Hamlyn, Wellington, 1973.
Paul Hamlyn Ltd, *Notable New Zealanders: First Edition*, Paul Hamlyn, Auckland, 1979.
Taylor, R.A.H., *New Zealand Who's Who Aotearoa: Volume 1, 1992, 1994 Edition, 1995 Edition*, New Zealand Who's Who Aotearoa, Auckland, 1992, 1994, 1995.
Taylor, R.A.H., *New Zealand Who's Who Aotearoa: 1998 Edition*, New Zealand Who's Who Publications, Auckland, 1998.
Taylor, R.A.H., *New Zealand Who's Who Aotearoa: Special New Millennium 2001 Edition*, Alister Taylor Publishers & New Zealand Who's Who Publications, Auckland, 2001.

Parliamentary records

Government Statistician (ed.), *The New Zealand Parliamentary Record*, Minister of Internal Affairs, Wellington, 1913.
Wood, G.A. (ed.), *Ministers and Members in the New Zealand Parliament*, University of Otago Press, Dunedin, 1996 (2nd edn).

Business who's who directories

Moffat, C. (ed.), *New Zealand Business Who's Who, 1958–59*, The Business Book Co of New Zealand, Wellington, 1958.
L.T. Watkins Ltd, *New Zealand Business Who's Who, 1960*, L.T. Watkins Wellington, 1960.
Moffat, C. (ed.), *New Zealand Business Who's Who, 1962*, L.T. Watkins, Wellington, 1962.
Solloway, G.F. (ed.), *New Zealand Business Who's Who, 1964, 1965/66, 1967/68, 1969/70, 1970/71*, L.T. Watkins Ltd, Wellington, 1964, 1965, 1967, 1969, 1970.
FEP Productions, *New Zealand Business Who's Who, 1970–86*, FEP Productions, Wellington, 1970–86.
Fourth Estate Holdings, *New Zealand Business Who's Who, 1987–88*, Fourth Estate Holdings, Wellington, 1987–88.

Fourth Estate Periodicals, *New Zealand Business Who's Who*, 1989, Fourth Estate Periodicals, Auckland, 1989.

New Zealand Financial Press, *New Zealand Business Who's Who*, 1989–2003, New Zealand Financial Press, Auckland, 1989–2003.

Peter Isaacson Publications (NZ)/Cranwell Publishing Group, *New Zealand's Top 50 Companies: First Edition 1988*, Peter Isaacson & Cranwell, Auckland, 1988.

Company shareholdings

Investment Research Unit, *Directory of Shareholders New Zealand Public Companies* 1980, Transvision Holdings, Auckland, 1980.

Investment Research (Services & Publications), *Directory of Shareholders New Zealand Public Companies* 1981–84, CBA Finance Holdings, Auckland, 1981–84.

Datex Services, *Directory of Shareholders New Zealand Public Companies* 1985–89, Westpac Merchant Finance, Auckland, 1985–89.

Datex Services, *The Bancorp Book: 1990 Directory of Shareholders New Zealand Public Companies*, Datex, Lower Hutt, 1990.

Datex Services, *Directory of Shareholders New Zealand Public Companies* 1991–99, Datex, Lower Hutt, 1991–99.

Mercantile Gazette Marketing, *The New Zealand Company Register Vol. 25 1986–87 and Mid-Year Supplement*, Mercantile Gazette, Christchurch, 1987.

Investment yearbooks

Fourth Estate Publishing Co, *Guide to the Top 100 NZ Companies*, 1973, 1975, Fourth Estate Publishing, Wellington, 1973, 1975.

FEP Productions, *Guide to the Comparative Performances of NZ Public Companies*, 1976, 1978, FEP Productions, Wellington, 1976, 1978.

Buttle Wilson & Co, *1985 Investment Year Book*, Buttle Wilson & Co, Auckland, 1985.

Datex Services, *The 1987 Broadbank Investment Yearbook*, Datex, Lower Hutt, 1987.

New Zealand Stock Exchange, *New Zealand Stock Exchange Annual Report 1988*, Stock Exchange, Wellington, 1989.

Buttle Wilson, *Investment Yearbook 1987, 1989, 1991, 1992*, Buttle Wilson, Auckland, 1987, 1989, 1991, 1992.

Datex Services, *New Zealand Investment Year Book 1992, 1995, 1998*, Datex, Lower Hutt, 1992, 1995, 1998.

Official yearbooks

Department of Statistics/Statistics New Zealand, *New Zealand Official Yearbook*, 1972–99, Statistics, Wellington, 1972–2002.

Atlases/gazetteers

McKenzie, D.W. (general ed.), *Heinemann New Zealand Atlas*, Heinemann Publishers with the DOSLI, Auckland, 1987.

Pope, D. & J., *Mobil New Zealand Travel Guide: South Island and Stewart Island*, A.H. & A.W. Reed, Wellington, 1974 (3rd edn).

Wilson, J . (ed.), *AA Book of New Zealand Historic Places*, Lansdowne-Rigby, Auckland, 1984.

Wilson, J. (ed.), *The Past Today: Historic Places in New Zealand*, Pacific Publishers, Auckland, 1987.

Wises Publications, *Wises New Zealand Guide: A Gazetteer of New Zealand*, Wises, Auckland, 1987 (8th edn).

General

Bassett, J., *The Concise Oxford Dictionary of Australian History*, Oxford University Press, Melbourne, 1994 (2nd edn).

Bromby, R., *An Eyewitness History of New Zealand*, Currey O'Neill, Melbourne, 1985.

Fraser, B. (ed.), *The New Zealand Book of Events*, Reed Methuen, Auckland, 1986.

McIntyre W.D. & Gardner, W.J. (eds.), *Speeches and Documents on New Zealand History*, Oxford University Press, London, 1971.

McLauchlan, G.W. (ed.-in-chief), *The Illustrated Encyclopedia of New Zealand*, David Bateman, Auckland, 1986.

McLintock, A.H. (ed.), *An Encyclopaedia of New Zealand*, vols 1–3, Government Printer, Wellington, 1966.

Thornton, G.G., *New Zealand's Industrial Heritage*, A.H. & A.W. Reed, Wellington, 1968.

Unpublished manuscripts

Hunt, G.J., *Forging New Zealand's Future: Carter Holt Holdings' Takeover of Alex Harvey Industries*, (unpublished) Hill & Knowlton (NZ), Auckland, 1985.

Hunter, I., *David Levene: A Man and His Business*, (unpublished) Castle Publishing, Auckland, 1999.

Newspapers/periodicals/articles

General

Berry, E.B. (ed.), *The Northlander*, No. 5, The News, Kaikohe, with Northland Newspapers, Kaitaia, 1965.

Eldred-Grigg, S.T., 'Whatever Happened to the Gentry: The Large Landowners of

Ashburton County, 1890–1896', in *The New Zealand Journal of History*, vol. 11, no. 1, 1977.

Hazledine, T. & Siegfried, J., 'How Did the Wealthiest New Zealanders Get So Rich', in *New Zealand Economic Papers*, 31(1), New Zealand Economic Association, Auckland, 1997.

Heritage New Zealand, New Zealand Historic Places Trust, Wellington, 2002–03.

Hunt, G.J., 'A Financial History of The Farmers' Trading Co Ltd', in *The Farmers' Trading Co Ltd Annual Report 1984*, Farmers, Auckland, 1984.

McAloon J.P., 'The Colonial Wealthy in Canterbury and Otago: No Idle Rich', in *The New Zealand Journal of History*, vol. 30, no. 1, 1996.

National Business Review, Fourth Estate Holdings, Auckland, 1970–2003.

NBR The Weekly Magazine, Fourth Estate Holdings, Auckland, 1990–91.

New Zealand Historic Places, New Zealand Historic Places Trust, Wellington, 1983–2002.

Personal Investment New Zealand, Personal Investment Magazines (NZ), Auckland, 1986–87.

Personal Investor, Personal Investor Joint Venture, Auckland, 1988–89.

Stone, R.C.J., 'John Logan Campbell, Frank Connelly and "Trespiano": Literary Evidence in Biography', in *The New Zealand Journal of History*, vol. 9, no. 1, 1976.

Rich lists

Greenwood, R., Myers, V.R., Parker, S., Cooke, M., Radojkovich, L. (compilers), *The Richest People in New Zealand*, special edn, *Personal Investment New Zealand*, December 1986.

Myers, V.R. (ed.), *The Rich 100*, special edn, *Personal Investment New Zealand*, August 1987.

Akers, B.J. (ed.), *Rich List 1988*, special edn, *Personal Investor*, August 1988.

Akers, B.J. (ed.), *Rich List*, special edn, *Personal Investor*, September 1989.

Byrnes, A.P.C. (ed.), *Rich List*, special edn, *NBR The Weekly Magazine*, 25 May 1990.

Byrnes, A.P.C. (ed.), *Rich List*, special edn, *NBR The Weekly Magazine*, 17 May 1991.

Byrnes, A.P.C. (ed.), *The Rich List*, special edn, *National Business Review*, 21 August 1992.

Gibson, A.P.C. (née Byrnes) (ed.), *The Rich List*, special edn, *National Business Review*, 20 August 1993.

Hunt, G.J. (ed.), *The Rich List 1994*, special edn, *National Business Review*, 12 August, 1994.

Hunt, G.J. (ed.), *The Rich List 1995*, special edn, *National Business Review*, 21

July 1995.

Hunt, G.J. (ed.), *The Rich List 1996*, special edn, *National Business Review*, 19 July 1996.

Hunt, G.J. (ed.), *The Rich List 1997*, special edn, *National Business Review*, 18 July 1997.

Hunt, G.J. (ed.), *The Rich List 1998*, special edn, *National Business Review*, 17 July 1998.

Hunt, G.J. (ed.), *The Millennium Rich List 1999*, special edn, *National Business Review*, 16 July 1999.

Hunt, G.J. (ed.), *The Rich List 2000*, special edn, *National Business Review*, 19 May 2000.

Hunt, G.J. (ed.), *The Rich List 2001*, special edn, *National Business Review*, 20 July 2001.

Hunt, G.J. (ed.), *The Rich List 2002*, special edn, *National Business Review*, 19 July 2002.

Hunt, G.J. (ed.), *The Rich List 2003*, special edn, *National Business Review*, 18 July 2003.

Business Hall of Fame (with laureate induction dates)

Hunt, G.J., in the *National Business Review*, 8 June 1994.

Hunt, G.J., special edn, *National Business Review*, 4 April 1995.

Hunt, G.J., special edn, *National Business Review*, 5 June 1996.

Hunt, G.J., special edn, *National Business Review*, 31 July 1997.

Hunt, G.J., special edn, *National Business Review*, 24 September 1998.

Hunt, G.J., special edn, *National Business Review*, 7 October 1999.

Hunt, G.J., special edn, *National Business Review*, 21 September 2000.

Hunt, G.J., special edn, *National Business Review*, 20 September 2001.

Hunt, G.J., special edn, *National Business Review*, 18 September 2002.

Hunt, G.J., special edn, *National Business Review*, 24 September 2003.

Index A

Individuals and families

Honorifics and titles have been omitted in most cases but titles and years of birth and death and other identifiers have been included where necessary to avoid confusion. Nicknames or petnames have been included in square brackets; maiden names and names not commonly used are enclosed in parentheses. Appendix A has not been indexed but Appendix B (the *National Business Review* Business Hall of Fame) and Appendix C (the *National Business Review* Sporting Rich) have been. Page numbers for illustrations are listed in bold type; references to photo inserts are denoted by *ff*.

Abel family 221, 243
Acland, Hugh John Dyke [Jack] (1904–81) 69, 72
Acland, Hugh Thomas Dyke (1874–1956) 69
Acland, John Barton Arundel (1823–1904) 57, 68–69, **98ff**
Acland, John Ormond (born 1936) 69
Acland, Leopold George Dyke [L.G.D.] 58, 69–70
Acton-Adams, William Acton Blakeway (born William Acton Blakeway Adams) 168
Adams, Ernest Alfred (1892–1976) 193, 195
Adams, (Ernest) Neil (1917–85) 195
Adams family 195
Adams, Hugh Alfred 195
Adams, Jessica 195
Adams, Ralph Howard 195
Adams, Sarah 195
Ah Chee, Thomas Henry [Tom] 165, 167, 170, 292
Aitken, William 85
Alpe, Christopher Carbrooke [Chris] 253
Anderson, John 114, **115**, 289
Anderson, Robert Albert 104
Anderton, James Patrick [Jim] 185
Andrew, John Watson [John W.] 148
Atkinson, Harry Albert 65
Aulsebrook, John 120
Austen, Jane 47
Baigent family (timber) 221
Baines, Paul Edward Alex 250
Baker, Sidney J. 277–78
Balfour, Thomas Waitt 53
Ballance, John 60, 124
Bankart, Alfred Seymour 158–59, 162
Banks, John Archibald 212, 217
Barfoot family 267
Barker, (John) Heaton 164, 291

Barker, Neil James 164
Barker, Philip Alwyn [Phil] 164
Barker, Reginald Malcolm [Reg] 164
Barr, Peter (1861–1951) 292
Barr, Robert Forsyth [Peter] (1907–67) 292
Barrett, Richard [Dicky] 41–42, 50ff
Barton, Richard John 53
Bassett, Michael Edward Rainton 124
Bayldon family 228, 231
Bayldon, (Harold) John 231, 254–55
Beauchamp, Harold 117–18
Beauchamp, Kathleen Mansfield [Katherine Mansfield] 118, **118**
Beatles 198
Beaumont, Richard 40
Beetham, Anne Palmer 24, 54–55
Beetham family 24, 54–55
Beetham, George 40, 54–55
Beetham, Hugh Horsley 53–54
Beetham, (Marie Zelie) Hermance (née Frere) 55
Beetham, Richmond 54
Beetham, William (1809–88) 54
Beetham, William Henry (1837–1925) 54–55
Bell, Caroline (née Robinson) 61
Bell, Francis Dillon (1822-98) 40, 79
Bell, Francis Henry Dillon [Harry] (1851–1936) 40, 45, 61
Bell, George Meredith 103
Bell, John 43
Bell, Margaret Joachim (née Hort) 40
Bellairs, Edmund Hooke Wilson 6
Benton, John Geoffrey Eric 250
Beyer, Trevor Jorgen Nielson 219
Bidwill, Catherine (née Orbell) (1825/26?–1894) 52, **52**
Bidwill, Catherine Carne (1852–1909) (later Mrs Barton, Mrs Hutton) 53

Bidwill, Charles Robert I (1820–84) 48–49, **49**, 52–54
Bidwill, Charles Robert II (1863–1902) 52
Bidwill, Charles Robert IV (born 1939) 53, 254–56, 274
Bidwill, Charlotte (later Mrs Balfour) 53
Bidwill, Eliza [Laila] (1862–1902) (later Mrs J.B. Rhodes) 53
Bidwill, Elizabeth (1862–1926) (later Mrs Warren) 53
Bidwill family **50ff**
Bidwill, Jessy (later Mrs R.H. Rhodes) 53
Bidwill, John Carne (1815–53) 53
Bidwill, John Orbell (1854–1923) 52
Bidwill, Ruth (later Mrs Beetham) 53
Bidwill, William Edward [Will] 52–53, **52**
Birchfield, Reginald James [Reg] 203
Black, William 148
Blundell, Ernest Albert 115
Blundell, Henry (1813?–78) 115, **116**
Blundell, (Henry) Neil (1909–2002) 116
Blundell, (Henry) Percy Fabian (1872–1961) 115
Blundell, Henry Thomas [Henry jnr] (1843/44?–1894) 115
Blundell, John 115
Blundell, Leonard Coker [Mr Len] 115
Blundell, Louis Proctor 115
Boag, William snr 63
Bolger, James Brendan [Jim] 98, 232, 256
Bolton, Murray John 211–12
Booth, Christopher Edwin (Chris) 270
Borthwick, James 137
Bowater, Stuart Waring 149
Bragato, Romeo Alessandro 292
Brash, Donald Thomas 206, 292
Brett, Henry 113
Bridges, John 103
Brierley, John Relf 219
Brierley, May Enez Evelyn (née Reader) 219
Brierley, Ronald Alfred [Ron] **178ff**, 194, 219–20, **220**, 222–23, 237, 242, 244, 274
Brierley, Thomas 219
Brockie, Robert Ellison [Bob] 269
Brown, Jessie (née Smith) 29
Brown, John Chinery 165
Brown, William 20, 29–32, 36, 78, 87
Browne, Gordon Davies 9
Browning, Samuel 80, 84
Bruce, Hugh 193, 195
Bryham, Maurice John 258ff
Buckland, Alfred 81
Buckland, William Thorne 80, 84
Buckley, George 66–67, 94, 121
Buckley, St John McLean 68, 168
Bunbury, Thomas 3
Burdon, Randal Matthews [R.M.] 123
Burr, Adrian Kenneth 230, 240
Burt, Alexander 114
Burt, Thomas 114
Burton, Ormond 136
Busby, James 10–15, 21–22
Butcher, W.G. 108
Butland family 221
Butland, Henry 195

Butland, Jack Malfroy (born 1919) 196–97
Butland, Jack Richard (1896–1982) **178ff**, 194–96, 289
Butland, Jack Richard (born 1946) 196–97
Butler, Samuel 246
Butt, J.M. 99
Butterworth, Bradley William [Brad] 280, 294
Calhoun, Phyllis Elizabeth (née Roland, later Mrs Kerridge) 199
Cameron, Duncan 69
Campbell, John Logan [sometimes J. Logan, Logan] 20, 29–32, 34, 36, 40, 77–78, 81, 84, 87–89, 94–95, **98ff**, 289
Campbell, Robert 75–76, 120
Campbell, Michael Shane 294
Campion, Edith (née Hannah) 107
Campion, Jane 107
Cargill, Edward Bowes 105, **106**
Cargill, John 105
Cargill, William 105–106
Carpenter, Avon Leavett 185
Carr, Harold 191
Carter, Francis John 181, 291
Carter, (Kenneth Clifford) Alwyn [K.C.A.] (1909–85) 181, 183–84, 194
Carter, Kenneth Francis Leslie [Ken] (born 1935) **182**, 183–85
Carter, Richard Henry Alwyn **182**, 183–85, 292
Cassidy, Hugh 63
Caughey, Andrew Clarke 142
Caughey, Angela Mary Ruxton (née Wilson) 143–44
Caughey family 142, 147, 178ff
Caughey, (George) Simon Marsden 142, 265
Caughey, (Patricia) Mary (née Finlay) 142
Caughey, Rosslyn (née Richwhite) 265
Caughey, (Thomas) Harcourt Clarke [Pat] 142, 290
Caverhill, John Scott 61, **98ff**
Caverhill, Thomas 50
Cawthron, Thomas 119
Cedeno, Simon 62
Chapman, Dennis Alan 271
Charles, Robert James [Bob] 294
Cheshire, Philip Max [Pip] 258ff
Chong, Chew [Chau Tseung] 107, 130–31, **130**, 289
Chong, Trevor Howard 131
Chrystall, Lillian Jessie (née Laidlaw) 139
Churchill, Winston Leonard Spencer- 69
Clark, David 9
Clark, Edwin [Eddie] 153
Clark, Errol Desmond 195
Clark, (James) McCosh [sometimes J. McCosh] 81, 94, 119
Clark, Malcolm Morison 155–56
Clark, Mary (née Cater) 154
Clark, Patricia Mary (née France) 156
Clark, (Rice) Owen (1816–96) 153
Clark, Rice Owen II [R.O.] (1855–1905) 153–54
Clark, (Rice) Owen III (1881–1969) 154
Clark, Thomas Edwin [T.E.] (1887–1964) 154–55
Clark, Thomas Edwin jnr [Tom] (born 1916) 155–56, **155**, 290

INDEX A - INDIVIDUALS AND FAMILIES — 311

Clarke, George 22
Clarke, Joseph 102
Clarke, William John Turner [W.J.T., Big Clarke, Monied Clarke] (1801–74) 102
Clendon, James Reddy 13–15, 19, 26–28, 32, 35, **50ff**
Clendon, John Chitty 13
Clifford, Charles 48–51, **51**, 57, 78, 121
Clifford family 121
Clifford, George Hugh 50, 121
Clifford, Roger Joseph Gerard [eighth baronet of Flaxbourne] 50
Clifford, William Hugh (later tenth Baron Clifford of Chudleigh) 51
Coe, Henry V. [Harry] 196
Cole, Noel 194, 254
Collins, Paul David 237, 244
Colman, Barry Neville 258ff, **264**
Conder, Gail Roberta (née Kerridge) 80–81
Congreve, Erika Margaret 258ff
Congreve, Robin Lance 258ff
Connell, William 80–81
Conner, Dennis 225
Cook, James 1–2
Cooke, George 3, 6
Coolahan, Hugh 81
Coon, Christopher Lawrence 257
Cooper, Peter Charles 235, 266
Corban, Alexander Annis [Alex, A.A. jnr] 209
Corban, Alwyn Alexander Annis 210
Corban, Assid Abraham [A.A.] (1864–1941) 208–209, **208**, 289
Corban, Assid Khaleel (born 1925) 209
Corban, Brian Phillip Najib 209–210
Corban, Corban Assid [C.A.] 210
Corban, David Wadier 210
Corban family 208–209
Corban, Joseph Annis [Joe, J.A.] 210
Corban, Wadier Assid [W.A.] 209
Cory-Wright, Silston 214
Costley, Edward 98
Court, George 270
Coutts family 163
Coutts, Morton William (see also Kuhtze) 163
Coutts, Russell **280**, 294
Cornwall and of York, George and Mary, Duke and Duchess of 89, 152
Cox, Alfred 85
Craig, James Joseph [J.J.] 201
Creech, Ellanora Sophia (née Beetham) 57
Creech, Wyatt Beetham 57
Crichton, Neville Alexander 149
Crowe, Russell Ira 274–75
Crum, Albert 154–55, 163
Crummer, Thomas 92
Cushing, Selwyn John 281
Dacre, Charles 8–9
Dacre family 9
Dacre, Henry 8–9
Dacre, Life Septimus 8–9
Dacre, Ranulph 8–9, 26–28
Daldy, William Crush 81, 84
Darby, John Gerard 253
Davidson, William Soltau 126, 280
Davies, John Llewellyn 218

Davis, Angelina Jean 200
Davis, Eliot Rypinski 161–62
Davis, Ernest Hyam (registered as Hyam Davis) 161–62, 173, **178ff**, 186, 191, 277
Davis, Morrison Ritchie [Morrie] 200
Davis, Moss 122, 161, 168
Davis, Trevor Moss 162
Davison, Ronald Keith 262–63
Daysh, (Harry Edgar) Duff 248
Deans, (Alister) Austen 47
Deans family 47–48, 50ff
Deans, (Ian) Bruce 47
Deans, John I (1820–54) 46–47, 50ff
Deans, John II (1853–1902) 46–47, **50ff**, 121
Deans, Nicola Anne (later Mrs Hobbs) 47
Deans, Robert George [Bob] (1884–1908) 47
Deans, Robert Maxwell [Robbie] (born 1959) 47
Deans, William 46–47, 50ff
Degnan, Thomas J. [Tom] 273
de Thierry, Charles Philippe Hippolyte 10–13, **11**
Dickson, Christopher Stuart [Chris] 294
Dilworth, James 96, **97**
Disraeli, Benjamin 79
Doig, James Nimmo Crawford [Jim] 185, **187**, 194, 207
Domett, Alfred 74
Douglas, Roger Owen 184, 213, 256
Drinkrow family
Driver, Henry 102–104, 112
Dryden, Gordon William John 185
Duke, Rodney Adrian 266
Duppa, Bryan Edward 74
Duppa, George 73–74, 120
Dwyer, Richard 203
Dye, (Raymond) Shane 294
Edgar, Eion Sinclair 252
Edinburgh, Philip Duke of 161
Edison, Thomas Alva 132
Ehrenfried, Bernard 159
Ehrenfried, Louis 159, 168
Elias, Sian Seerpoohi 175, 177
Eldred-Grigg, Stevan Treleaven 135
Elizabeth II, Queen 162
Elliott, John D. 193
Elworthy, Edward 70, 291
Elworthy family 70
Elworthy, Jonathan Herbert 71
Elworthy, Peter Herbert 71
Elworthy, Richard Frank 71
Elworthy, Samuel Charles (later Baron Elworthy of Timaru, New Zealand, and Elworthy, County Somerset) [Sam] 70
England, Robert West jnr 67
Ereeg, Michael Anthony 266
Evans, George Samuel [G.S.] 56
Falk, Hans Homman Jensen [see Phillip Tapsell] 17, **18**
Farmer, James 85
Farmer, Trevor Michael 254–56
Farrant, Ian Ferguson 253
Farry, Gabriel 109
Fay, (Humphrey) Michael Gerard 222, 235, 242, **257**, 257–60, 262–66, 274
Fay, James O'Leary [Jim] 263
Fay, Sarah Ann (née Williams) 263

Fenwick, George 112
Fenwick, Robert George Mappin [Rob] 112
Fergusson, James 85–86
Fernyhough, (Colin) John 255
Firth, Edward Buckland [Ted] (1905–78) 89
Firth, Edward Thompson Clifton [Ned] (1867–1951) 89
Firth, Guy Mortimer [Tony] 89
Firth, Josiah Clifton (originally Josiah Firth) 65, 81, 84–85, 89, 90, 123
Fisher, Benjamin James 189, 258ff
Fisher family 188–89, 221
Fisher, Gurshon [Gus] 189
Fisher, Joyce (née Paykel) 188
Fisher, Louis Jacob [Lou] (registered as Jacob Louis Fisher) 188, 258ff
Fisher, Stephen Barry 188–89, 258ff
Fisher, Virginia Jane (née Fenton) 189, 258ff
Fisher, Woolf 110, **178ff**, 186–89, 288
FitzGerald, Amy (later Mrs Levin) 40
FitzGerald, James Edward 40
FitzRoy, Robert 22, 35, 38, 95
Fleming, Thomas 192
Fletcher, Andrew 174–75
Fletcher, Angus Gregor 175
Fletcher, Christine Elizabeth [Chris] (née Lees) 175
Fletcher family 175, 177, 194, 243
Fletcher, Hugh Alasdair 175–77, **176**
Fletcher, James (1886–1974) 151, 171–72, 174–77, **174**, 186, 288
Fletcher, James Muir Cameron [Jim or J.C.] (born 1914) 174–77, **178ff**, 289
Fletcher, James Roderic [Jim] (1944–93) 175
Fletcher, John Shearer (1888–1934) 174
Fletcher, John Shearer (1913–84) 175
Fletcher, William John 172, 174–75
Forbes, George William 61
Foreman family 243
Francis, Peter Edward (born 1947) (Chase Corporation, Force Corporation) 230, 240
Francis, Peter James (New Zealand Equities) 185
Franks, Catharine Mary (née Mackenzie) 270
Franks, Stephen Leslie 270
Fraser, Peter 172
Freyberg, Bernard Cyril [Baron Freyberg of Wellington, New Zealand, and Munstead, Surrey] 162
Friedlander, Edward Max [Ted] 288
Friedlander, Harriet Rossi (née Nathan) 208
Friedlander, Hugo 154
Friedlander, Michael 208
Friedlander, Walter 208
Fulton, Julius Herbert [Jules] 218
Gates, William Henry III [Bill] 279–80
Gaynor, Brian Arthur 252
Gear, James 129–30, **129**
George, Ernest 113
Gibbons family 148, 173, 221, 223
Gibbons, Hopeful [Hope] 148–49, **178ff**
Gibbs, Alan Timothy 54, 228, 242, 251, 254–58, **255**, 266, 274
Gibbs, Ian Ogilvie 258
Gibbs, Jennifer Barbara [Jenny] (née Gore) 257–58

Gibbs, Theodore Nisbet [Theo, T.N.] 194, 256, 258
Gibson, Nevil James 232–33, 245
Gibson, William 30
Giltrap, Colin John [Lord Hubcap] 149, 222, 242, **258ff**
Gipps, George 5, 7, 14, 50ff
Glendining, Robert 111
Glew, Joseph Raymond [Seph] 230
Godley, John Robert 42–43, 50–51
Goodfellow, Eric Hector 135
Goodfellow family 135, 242
Goodfellow, (James) Gordon 135
Goodfellow, Richard Maclaurin 135
Goodfellow, William (1806–90) 132
Goodfellow, William (1880–1974) 130–35, **132**, 173, 194, 280, 288
Goodfellow, (William) Douglas [W.D.] (born 1917) 134–35
Goodman, Craig McCarthy 193
Goodman family 192–93, 202, 221, 267
Goodman, Gregory Leith 193
Goodman, Harold 204
Goodman, Hilary Gay (née Duncan) 193
Goodman, Patrick Ledger [Pat] (born 1929) **178ff**, 192–93, 195, 221
Goodman, Patrick Ledger (born 1961) 193
Goodman, Peter Harold 178ff, 192
Gough family
Gould, George 69
Goulter, John Packard 292
Graham, David 80, 84, 96–97
Graham, Douglas Arthur Montrose 98
Graham, John 97
Graham, Robert 96–98, **98ff**, 290
Graham, Walter Knott 81
Graham, William Franklin [Billy] 216
Grant, David 235
Griaznoff, Michèle Mainwaring (later Lady Renouf) 247
Green, Hugh [Hughie] 219
Greenwood brothers 48
Greenwood, Edward 48
Greenwood, George 48
Greenwood, James Dent 48
Greenwood, Joseph Hugh 48
Gregg, William 111
Grey, George (some early accounts call him George Edward Grey) 12, 22, 33, 36, 43, 61, 73, 95, 103, 105
Grigg, John 63–65, **64**, 69, 82, 89, 121, 124–25
Grose, David John 239–40
Gunn, (Owen) Robert [Bob] 193
Guthrie, Walter 101, 103
Halberg, Murray Gordon 218
Hall, John 65, **98ff**
Hallenstein, Bendix 110
Hancox, Bruce Alan 211, 244
Hannah, Robert **98ff**, 106, 168, 290
Hansard (Albert) William 81
Harris, Ambrose Reeves [A.R.] 132
Harris, John Williams 17, 19, 26–27
Hart, Graeme Richard 117, 193 242, 258ff, **261**, 266, 272–73, 279
Harvey, Alexander 183, **183**, 291

INDEX A – INDIVIDUALS AND FAMILIES

Hauraki 12
Hawkins, Allan Robert 222, 227–31, **227**, **229**, 237, 254
Hawkins family 228, 231
Hay, David John 216–17
Hay, Grant William 216–17
Hay, Ian Wilson 216–17
Hay, James Lawrence 291
Hay, Keith Wilson 216–17
Hay, William Catley [Scotty] 216
Hazard, Douglas Lenard [Doug] 203–205
Heatley, Craig Leonard **165**, 166–67, 237–38, **258ff**
Heatley family 238, 267
Heke Pokai, Hone Wiremu [Hone Heke] 21, 96
Hellaby, Amy Maria (née Briscoe) 126, **178ff**, 200–201, 291
Hellaby, Frederick Allan [Fred] (1892–1963) 136
Hellaby, (Frederick Reed) Alan (1926–2001) 127
Hellaby, John [Jack] 136
Hellaby, (Joseph) Arthur Burdett 136
Hellaby, Richard (1849–1902) 126–27, 136, 200–201
Hellaby, (Richard) Sydney [Syd] (1887–1971) 136
Hellaby, Rosina (née Burdett) 126
Hellaby, William (1845–1900) 126–27, 136
Hellaby, William (1890?–1940) 136
Henderson, George 94
Henderson, Henry William 94–95
Henderson, Thomas (1810–86) (some accounts call him Thomas Maxwell Henderson) 31–32, 78, 80, 84, 94–96, **98ff**
Henderson, Thomas jnr 94
Hendry, Ian Robert 256–57
Henry, David 179–80
Henry, Gerald Craig 235
Herangi, Te Kirihaehae Te Puea [Princess Te Puea] 282
Herbert, Colin Francis 222, 228
Hill, (Ann) Christine (née Roe) 270
Hill, (Richard) Michael **265**, 270
Hobbs, Michael James Bowie [Jock] 47
Hobson, William 8, 12, 14, 35
Hocken, Thomas Morland 119
Hogan, Patrick 269
Hogan, Robert [Bob] 218
Hogan, Thomas [Tom] 269
Hoggard, Kerrance Mervyn [Kerry] 242, 269–70
Holland, Sidney George [Sid] 175
Holmes, Francis [Frank] (parents' surname Holme) 292
Holt, Robert 182, 291
Holyoake, Keith Jacka 258
Hongi Hika 10
Horrocks, Henry Alexander 291
Horrocks, John Brownlow 291
Hort, Abraham snr (1799?–1869) 38
Hort, Abraham jnr (1819–62) 38, 78
Horton, Alfred George 99–100, **99**
Horton, (Elizabeth) Gael (later Mrs Levin) 144
Horton family 100, 243
Horton, Henry (1870–1943) 100
Horton, (Henry) Michael (born 1938) 100

Horton, Matthew William 100
Horton, Robert Duncan [Robbie] 100
Horton, Rosemary Anne [Rosie] (formerly Mrs Smith, née Moon) 100
Hotere, Ralph 264
Howell, John 3
Hudson, Richard 112
Hudson, Richard (1841–1903) 111–12
Huie, Edward Chalmers 164
Huljich family 243
Huljich, Paul Richard **258ff**
Hunt, William Duffus 125, 135
Hunter, Sharon Lee **258ff**
Hurley, Desmond Watson [Des] 290
Hurley, Raymond Watson [Ray] 290
Hutton, George T.F. 53
Hutton, John H.C. 54
Irving, David Andrew 191
Izard, Richard William Vincent 289
Jackson, Peter Robert **258ff**, 279
Jarden, Ronald Alexander [Ron] 248–49, **249**, 258
Jarvis, Terrence Wayne [Terry] 237–38
Jeffs brothers 194, 203
Jeffs, James Edward [Jim] 194, 203–204, **203**
Jeffs, Kevin Seamark 194, 203–204
Jeffs, Vaughan Joseph 194, 203–204
Jesson, Bruce Edward 224
Johnson, Bryan Ewart 248–49
Johnston, Walter Woods 38–39, 94, 168
Jolly, Wilson David 230
Jones, Christopher Gordon [Chris] 272
Jones, John [Johnny] 3–7, **4**, 8, 13, 26–27, 36, 48. 50ff, 78, 105, 290
Jones, Meryl Moye (later Mrs Kerridge) 199
Jones, Robert Edward [Bob] **178ff**, 205–207, 237
Joseph, Israel 32
Joy, Raymond 235
Judge, Bruce Raymond 127, 144, 147, 222, 228, **232**, 233, 237, 245–48, **258ff**
Julian, Harry Lancelot Hugh 258
Katchen, Julius 198
Kawiti, Te Ruki 21
Keesing, Henry (formerly Hartog Tobias Keesing, also Hartog ben Tobias) 36
Kelliher, Henry Joseph 162, 173, 194, 290
Kemp, Keith Lloyd 165
Kempthorne, Thomas Whitelock 116
Kendall, Thomas 10, 12, 17
Kennedy, Alexander 84
Kent, Norman [Norm] 165
Kermode, Anne [Annie] (later Mrs Moore) 60
Kermode, Robert Quayle 60
Kerr, Roger Lawrence 270
Kerridge family 199–200
Kerridge, Gail Roberta (later Mrs Conder) 199
Kerridge, John Robert 199
Kerridge, Robert James (1901–79) 25, 189–90, 197–200, **197**, 289
Kerridge, Robert James [Bob] (born 1938) 199
Kerridge, Roland Michael [Rolly] 199
Kerridge, Vanessa Ellen (later Mrs Tengblat) 199
Kirk, Norman Eric 190

Kirkpatrick, James Stewart [Jimmy] 207–208
Kiwiwharekete, Maraea (later Mrs Ormond) 71
Krukziener, Abraham 243
Krukziener, Andrew Mark 243, **258ff**
Krukziener, Veronica [Vera] 243
Kuhtze, Joseph Friedrich [Frederick Joseph] [see also Coutts] 163
Kuhtze, (William) Joseph [see also Coutts] 163
La Grouw, Cornelis [Corgi] 215–16
La Grouw family 215–16
La Grouw, Johannes snr [Jo] (born 1913) 215–16
La Grouw, Johannes jnr [Joe] (born 1940) 215
La Grouw, Tjeerd 215
Laidlaw, Arthur Frederick (1889–1918) 136–37
Laidlaw, (Arthur) Lincoln (born 1921) 139, 230
Laidlaw, John Ritchie Caldwell [Jack] 136
Laidlaw, Robert Alexander Crookston [Robert A.] 136–39, **137**, 291
Lamb, John 89
Lambert family 153
Lane, Gary Rodney 166, **166**
Larkworthy, Falconer 84–85
Larmour, R.J. 148
Larnach, Constance [Conny] (née de Bathe Brandon) 101
Larnach, Donald Guise 104
Larnach, Douglas John 101
Larnach family 100
Larnach, William James Mudie 84, 98ff, 100–104, **102**, 112
Lawless, Lucille Frances [Lucy] (née Ryan) **278**, 279
Le Cren, Frederic 63
Le Cren, Henry John 63
Lee, John Alfred Alexander [John A.] 162, 178ff
Lee, J.W. 181
Leigh, Vivien 162
Levene, David 211–12
Levene family 211, 243, 267
Levene, Lewis 211
Levene, Max [Mark] 211
Levin, Anne (later Mrs Beetham) 40
Levin family 144
Levin, Jessie (née Hort) 40
Levin, Nathaniel William 38–40, **39**, 50ff, 78, 144, 290
Levin, Peter Charles 40, 144
Levin, William Hort [Willie] 38–40, **50ff**, 120
Levy, Vera Anita (later Mrs/Lady Myers) 159
Leys, Thomson William [T.W.] 113, 120
Leys, William (1852–99) 120
Leys, (William) Cecil (1877–1950) 164
Lillie, James 60
Ling, Benjamin 129
Louisson, Cecil 157
Louisson, Charles 157
Lomu, Jonah Tali **258ff**, 279, 294
Love, John Agar [Jacky] 41
Low, William Anderson 75
Lowe, A.E. 46
Lowndes, Hilton Frank Noel 188–89
Lowndes, Noble 189
McAloon, James Patrick [Jim] 62

McArthur, John William Shaw [J.W.S.] 202, 254
McCahill, Bernard Joseph [Barney] (born 1928) 219
McCahill, Bernard Joseph [Bernie] (born 1964) 219
McCahill, Sean Anthony 219
McCahill, Theresa-Anne [Terry-Anne] 219
McCahon, Colin John 258
Macarthy, Mary Ellen (née Fitzsimons, later Mrs Reid) 169
Macarthy, Thomas George [T.G.] 169
McConnell, (Arnot) Malcolm [Buck] 222, 228
McCrystal, John 207
McDonnell, Edward 10
McDonnell, George 10
McDonnell, Thomas (1788–1864) 1, 9–10, 12, 26–28, 50ff, 280
McDonnell, Thomas (1831/33?–99) 10
McDonnell, William 10
McDougall, Robert Euning 120–21
McFadden, Monique Angela 236
Macfarlane, Henry 31, 94
Macfarlane, John (1816–50) 31, 94
Macfarlane, John Sangster (1818–80) 95
Macfarlane, Thomas 94–95
McGlashan, John 114
McGrath, John Joseph 200
McGuire, Felix 201
McGuire, Sarah-Jane (née Craig) 201
Mackelvie, James Tannock 119
Mackenzie, James 44
Mackenzie, Jessy Adela (née Bell) 79
McKenzie, John Robert 139–41, **140**, 289
Mackenzie, (Mackay John) Scobie 79
McKenzie, Roy Allan 141
McKenzie, Thomas [Jock] 61
Macky, James 8–9
Macky, Thomas 9
McLaren, Donald George [Don] 290
Maclaurin, Richard Cockburn 135
Maclean, Algernon Donald Douglas 73, 136
McLean, Allan 66–68, **67**, 98ff, 121, 168
McLean, Donald 71–73, 98, 136
McLean family (Canterbury) 121
McLean, John [Big Jock] 66–68, 94, 121, 168
McLean, Mary 68
Maclean, Robert 85
McLean, Robertson 66
Maclean, (Robert Donald) Douglas 73, 135
Maclean, (Thomas) Every 85
McSkimming family 153
Mace, Christopher Robert 235
Maddren, James Robert 289
Mair, Gilbert (1799?–1857) 13, 15, 22, 26–28, 50ff
Mair, Gilbert (1843–1923) 16
Mair, Henry Abbott 16
Mair, Kenneth Robert [Kenehi, Ken] 17
Mair, Robert 16
Mair, William (drowned 1836) 15
Mair, William Gilbert 16
Malpart, Emslie Marie (later Mrs Kerridge) 199
Maning, Frederick Edward 12–13, 26–27, 78
Mansfield, Katherine [Kathleen Mansfield Beauchamp] 118, **118**

INDEX A – INDIVIDUALS AND FAMILIES

Mappin, Frank Crossley 112–13
Mappin, (Eliza) Ruby (née Thomson) 112
Margrethe II, Queen of Denmark 211
Marryat, Frederick 8
Marsden, Samuel 17
Marsh, Graeme James 290
Marshall, John Ross [Jack] 203
Martelli, Peter Leeson 245
Martin, John Mccrae 253
Martini, Cushla Anne 258ff
Masfen, Peter Hanbury 292
Massey, William Ferguson 64
Mathew, Felton 15
Matthew, Robert Harry [Bob] 212, 244
Mayhew, William 16
Menzies, Peter Francis 214–15
Menzies, Robert Gordon 178–79
Middlemas, John 17
Mitchum, Robert 230
Mocatta, Solomon 38
Moller family 221
Montefiore, John Israel 17, 19–20, **20**, 26–27, 32
Montefiore, Joseph Barrow 19–21, 27, 32
Moodabe family 230
Moore, George Henry [Scabby] 58–61, 98ff, 120, 124, 168
Moore, William 60–62
Morrin brothers 90
Morrin, John Carsley 91
Morrin, Samuel 85, 90, 123
Morrin, Thomas 70, 85, 89–90, **91**, 123
Morrin, William 91
Morrison, J.P. 62
Morrison, (Hugh Richmond) Lloyd **250**, 250–51
Muldoon, Robert David [Rob] 190, 206–207, 213, 224, 259
Muller, David Francis 240–41
Mundella, Anthony John 86
Murdoch, David Limond 85, 87
Myers, (Arthur) Douglas (born 1938) 158, 160–61, **178ff**, 194, 222, 224, 235, 242, 261, 266, 274, 292
Myers, Arthur Mielziner (1867–1926) 158–59, 162, 168, 173
Myers, Catherine (née Ehrenfried) 159
Myers family 158–61, 194
Myers, Kenneth Ben **158**, 159–60, 173, 190–91, 194, 288
Myers, Louis 158–59
Myers, Margaret Blair (née Pirie) 159–60
Nathan, David 32–33, **33**, 78, 94, 144
Nathan family (Auckland) 33, 78, 144
Nathan, Joseph Edward 130–31
Nathan, Laurence David 32–33, 78
Nathan, (Nathan) Alfred 32–34, 78
Nathan, Peter Arthur Neville 208
Neill, Nigel John Demot [Sam] **258ff**, 279
Newland, Oliver Michael [Olly] 239, **258ff**
Newman, Henry [Harry] 149, **178ff**
Newman, Jack 149, **150**, 152, 288
Newman, Thomas [Tom] 149
Ngata, Apirana Turupa 290
Nobilio, Frank Ivan Joseph 294
Norman family 267
Norwood, Charles John Boyd 148

O'Connor, Kevin James 248
O'Donnell, Bernard Joseph [Bernie] 253
O'Leary, Humphrey Francis 263
Oliver, John S. 81
O'Neill, James 84
O'Sullivan, Lance Anthony 294
Orbell, John 52
O'Reilly, Anthony Francis J. [Tony] 100, 191
Ormond, Ada Mary (later Mrs Wilson) 71
Ormond, George Canning 71
Ormond family 111
Ormond, Hannah (née Richardson) 71
Ormond, John Davies (1831–1917) 71–72, 168
Ormond, John Davies (1871–1943) 71
Ormond, John Davies (born 1945) 72
Ormond, John Davies Wilder (1905–95) 72
Ormond, Katherine Wilde [Kit] (later Lady Acland) 72
Outhwaite, Thomas 82
Outtrim, Steven Bryce 272
Owen, George Burgoyne 81, 84
Owens, Robert Arthur [Bob] **178ff**, 207, 289
Paine, Warren Arthur 255
Palmer, Edwin 3
Palmer, Geoffrey Winston Russell 244
Parker, Selwyn 192
Paterson, Alexander Stronach [Alex] (born 1927) 193
Paterson, Alexander Stronach (founder, A.S. Paterson & Co) 193
Paterson family 267
Paterson, Howard James **251**, 252–53
Paykel, Dorothy Mary (née Bone) 189
Paykel family 188–89, 194
Paykel, Gary Albert 188–89
Paykel, George 187
Paykel, Maurice **178ff**, 187–89, 290
Paynter, (John) Richmond 24
Peters, Winston Raymond 260, 262–63, 274, 281
Petre, Francis William [Frank] 105
Petre, Henry William 48–50, 105
Petre, Margaret (née Cargill) 105
Petre, William Henry Francis [eleventh Baron Petre] 50
Petricevic, Rodney Michael [Rod] 233, 246–47, 258–59
Pharazyn, Charles Johnson 38–39
Phillips, David William 199–202, **200**, 234
Phillips, Steven Bruce 234
Philpott, Bryan Chesney 214
Philpott, Robert Halson 213–14
Picot, Brian Hall 165, **167**, 169–70, 291
Picot, David Willams 165
Picot family 165, 169
Picot, Francis Raymond [Frank] 165
Picot, Peter Horton 165
Picot, Suzanne Winton (née Brown) 169
Pinochet, Augusto 207
Platts, Una 31
Plimmer, Clifford Ulric 41, **50ff**, 289
Plimmer, Isaac 41
Plimmer, John 40–41, 50ff
Plimmer, William Harcus 41
Polack, Joel Samuel [sometimes J. Samuel] 17, 19, 26–27

Pomare II 13
Pompallier, Jean Baptiste François 12, 17
Porter family 189
Potter, William 143
Powditch, William 15
Preston family 251
Preston, Raymond 142
Prince, Walter 121–22
Prosser, Evan 116
Proudfoot, David 112
Proudfoot, George 112
Pye, Wendy Edith **258ff**, 268–69
Pym, Montague 103
Queen Mother, Queen Elizabeth the 162
Rabuka, Sitiveni Ligamamada [Steve] 202
Rainger, Owen Watson 207
Rank, (Joseph) Arthur [J. Arthur] 198
Rayner, Frederick John [F.J.] 254
Read, (Thomas) Gabriel 84
Read, George Edward 19
Reddy, Patricia Lee [Patsy] 244
Reed, Alfred Hamish [A.H.] 289
Reid, Donald 122
Reid, John 79, 121, 169
Renouf, Ann Marie (née Harkin) 247
Renouf, Francis Henry [Frank] 175, 233, **234**, 247–48, 290
Renouf, Susan (formerly Mrs Sangster, Mrs Peacock, née Rossiter) 247
Reynolds, Colin William 222, 227–28, 230, 237, 240–41, **258ff**
Reynolds, Henry 85
Rhodes, Arthur Edgar Gravenor [A.E.G.] 45
Rhodes brothers 42–44, 48, 50, 57, 62, 78
Rhodes, George 42, 44–45, 53, 78
Rhodes, Jessie (née Clark) 46
Rhodes, Joseph (1826–1905) 42, 53, 78
Rhodes, Joseph Barnard 53
Rhodes, Mildred Edith (later Mrs Bidwell) 53
Rhodes, Robert Heaton (1815–84) 42, 45, 78, 120, 168
Rhodes, (Robert) Heaton (1861–1956) 45–46, **50ff**, 53, 168
Rhodes, Robert Heaton [Bob, Bobby] (1857–1918, from Blue Cliffs) 53
Rhodes, William Barnard 42–43, **43**, 45, 78, 120
Rich, Francis 79, 85
Richardson, George Ernest G. 71
Richardson, (Harold) William [Bill] 269
Richardson, Ruth Margaret 256
Richwhite, Cleave McKellar [formerly Cleave McKellar Richmond White] 259
Richwhite, (David) Lloyd (born 1916) 264
Richwhite, David McKellar (born 1948) 222, 235, 242, 255, 257–60, **262**, 262–66, 274
Riddiford, Daniel (1814–75) 56–57
Riddiford, Daniel Henry Strothers (1883–1971) 56
Riddiford, Daniel Johnston (1914–74) 56
Riddiford, Edward Joshua [King] 56–57, 168
Riddiford family 55–56, 58
Riddiford, (Harold) Earle 56
Riddiford, Hugh Anthony Joshua 57
Riddiford, Richard Daniel 57, **58**
Riddiford, Rosemary Hope 56

Rillstone, Dougal 253
Ritchie, John Macfarlane 62–63, 103
Ritchie, James McLaren 63
Roberts, Geoffrey Newland 291
Robertson, James William 110
Robertson, Robert Miller 125
Robinson, Diana Elizabeth (née Seabrook) 202
Robinson, Noel Stuart 189
Robinson, Samuel 61
Robinson, William [Ready Money] 60–62, **98ff**, 120, 124
Rogers, Ginger 110
Ross, John 111
Ross, Michael James [Mike] 274
Rowling, Joanne Kathleen [J.K.] 258ff
Roy, John (formerly Jan Wojciechowski) 214–15, 254
Roy, Valerie Isobel (née Young) 215
Russell, George Frederick (Kohukohu trader) 10
Russell, George 86
Russell, James 82
Russell, John Benjamin [J.B.] 82
Russell, Spencer Thomas 244–45
Russell, Thomas 63–64, 80–87, **81**, 90–94, 96, 98–99, 101, 104, 121, 143–44, 254, 289
Russell, William 82
Rutherford, Andrew William 74
Rutherford, Duncan 74–75
Rutherford, Edmund Scott 75
Rutherford, George (1815–85) 74
Rutherford, George (1850–1918) 74–75
Rutherford, John Scott 74
Rutherford, Robert 74
Rutherford, Walter 74
Rutherford, William Oliver 74
Salmon, Cedric Whitby 214
Sanders, John Robert 263
Sandys, Diana (née Spencer-Churchill) 69
Sandys, (Edwin) Duncan (later Baron Duncan–Sandys) 69
Sangster, Robert 247
Sangster, Susan (later Renouf) 246
Sargood, Cedric Rolfe 135
Sargood, Lucy Constance (née Ormond) 111, 135
Sargood, Percy Rolfe 110–11, 135, 168
Savage, Michael Joseph [Mickey] 162, 186
Sax, (David) John 202
Saxe-Coburg and Gotha, House of 163
Schultze, George 7
Scott, Richard George [Dick] 155
Seabrook, Lalla Olga Spencer [Lal] (registered as Lela Spencer Olga Wilson but she later gave her maiden name as Munro Wilson) 201–202
Seabrook, Philip 173. 201
Seddon, Richard John [Dick, King Dick] 103–104, 118, 123–24, 171
Selwyn, George Augustus 22
Sew Hoy, Choie [Charles] 107–108
Sew Hoy, Hugh [also known as Choie Buck Pang] 108
Sew Hoy, Kum Poy 108
Shacklock, Francis Oakley 110

INDEX A – INDIVIDUALS AND FAMILIES   317

Shacklock, Henry Ely (1839–1902) **98ff**, 109–110
Shacklock, Henry Ely jnr 110
Shacklock, John Bradley 110
Shacklock, John Thomas [Jack] (1913–99) **109**, 110
Shacklock, Percival William 110
Shaw, Fred 119
Shaw, Henry 119
Shipley, Jennifer Mary [Jenny] 57, 98
Shirtcliffe, George (1862–1941) 192
Shirtcliffe, (George) Peter (born 1931) 192, 291
Shortland, Willoughby 35
Simpson, Gilbert [Gil] 271
Skeggs, Clifford George [Cliff] 256, 291
Skellerup, Peter Jensen Reid 211
Skellerup, Valdemar Reid 211
Skjellerup, George Waldemar (1881–1955) 210–11
Skjellerup, George Waldemar (born 1942) 211
Smallbone, David John 253
Smith, Henry Landon [Landon] 178–80
Smith, Henry Green [H.G.] 16
Smith, Ian Douglas 153
Smith, Mary Anne [Marianne] (née Caughey) **141**, 142
Smith, R.W. (flaxmiller) 181
Smith, Raymond William [Ray] 235–37, **258ff**
Smith, Reginald Caughey Seymour 142
Smith, William Henry 142
Snedden, Fleur Gwendoline (née Hjorring) 100–101
Snell, Peter George 218
Speight, Charles 156
Speight, Hugh Thomas **157**, 157
Speight, James 156–57, **178ff**
Spencer, Albert 246
Spencer, Berridge 246
Spencer, John Berridge 184, 222, 228, 233, 235, 242, 246–47, **258ff**
Spencer, Peter Albert 246–47
Spencer, (Mersti) Tytti Kaarina (née Laurola) 246
Spickman, William (parents' surname Spackman) 258
Spiers, Rodney James 230
Stafford, Edward William 57, 60, 81, 86
Steele, William 85
Stephenson, John 125
Stephenson, Samuel 13
Stevens, Laurence Houghton [Laurie] 290
Stevenson family 221
Stevenson, James Ross 217
Stevenson, John Kennedy 217
Stevenson, William 217
Stevenson, William Alfred jnr 217
Stevenson, William Alfred snr [Bill] (1901–83) **178ff**, 194, 217–18, 264, 289
Stewart, Charles 79
Stewart family 243, 267, 271
Stewart, Robertson Huntly [Bob] 271, 289
Stewart, William (1776?–1851) (sealer) 2–3, 6, 26
Stewart, William (hydrographer) 3

Stiassny, Michael Peter [the Terminator, Rambo] 185
Stone, Captain James 81, 84
Stone, Russell Cyril James 81, 85, 91, 159
Sturt, Charles Earl [Chas] 231
Studholme family 70, 121
Studholme, John snr (1829–1903) 69–70, 90, 121
Studholme, John jnr (1863–1934) 70
Studholme, Michael 69–70, 121
Studholme, Paul 69–70, 121
Suckling, John 107
Suckling, Nathaniel Joseph 107
Sutch, William Ball [W.B., Bill] 171
Sutton, W.A. 192
Swainson, William (1789–1855) (naturalist) 48–50
Swainson, William (1809–84) (attorney-general) 31
Tait, Angus McMillan 271, 289
Talley family 243
Tapert, Robert [Rob] 278
Tapsell family 17, 19
Tapsell, Kataraina **18**
Tapsell, Peter Wilfred 18
Tapsell, Phillip [formerly and sometimes Hans Homman Jensen Falk] 17, **18**
Taylor, Charles John 84
Taylor, Keith Ian Andrew 251
Te Hemara Tauhia 258
Te Kaha 258
Te Kanawa, Kiri Jeanette Claire 279
Te Kooti Arikirangi Te Turuki 16, 79
Te Puea, Princess [Te Kirihaehae Te Puea Herangi] 290
Tengblat, Vanessa Ellen (née Kerridge) 199
Tetley, Joseph Dresser 40
Theomin, David Edward [formerly David Ezekiel Benjamin] 98ff, 113
Theomin, Dorothy Michaelis 113
Thompson family 267
Thomson, Lorraine Vanessa Louise (née Hunt) 252
Thomson, Raymond John 251–52
Thornley, Samuel 151
Tindall, Stephen Robert 242, 266, 270–71
Titokowaru, Riwha 10, 79
Todd, Andrew 145
Todd, Bryan James 145–47, **145**, 148, 163, 288
Todd, Charles jnr (1868–1942) 144, 148
Todd, Charles Patrick (1896–1965) 145, 147–48
Todd, Charles snr 144, 148
Todd, Desmond Henry 145, 147–48
Todd family (auctioneering/prospecting) 152
Todd family (bricks and tiles) 152–53
Todd family (motor industry/oil) 144–48, 152, 173, 186, 194, 221, 243, 267, 279
Todd, James 144
Todd, Jeffrey Garfield [Jeff] 153
Todd, John Desmond 147
Todd, Louisa 153
Todd, (Reginald Stephen) Garfield 153
Todd, Thomas 152–53
Todd, William 152

Tole, John 137
Tombs, George 117
Tombs, Harry Hugo 117
Townend, Anne Quayle [Annie] (née Moore) 59–60, **98ff**, 168
Tripp, Charles George 68–69, **68**, 98ff
Trott, Steven T. 235
Trotter, Ronald Ramsay 175–77, 225, 290
Tua, David (born Mafaufau Sanarevi Talimatasi) 294
Turnbull, A.H. [meatworks owner] 127
Turnbull, Alexander Horsburgh 119
Turner family 221–23
Turnovsky, Frederick [Fred] 212–214, **213**
Turnovsky, Liselotte Felicitas [Lotte] (née Wodak) 212
Underwood, Frances (née Renouf) 248
Vaile, (Edward) Earle 108
Vaile, George 108
Vaile, Hubert Ernest 108
Vaile, Samuel 108
Valentine, Murray Graham 253
van Dongen, Yvonne 219
van Loghem, Johannes Jacobus [John] 215
Vavasour, Edward Joseph Everard [Ned] 51
Vavasour family 52
Vavasour, Henry Dunstan 51
Vavasour, William Joseph 48–51
Vela family 243
Vestey family 127
Victoria, Queen 131
Vogel, Julius 103, 121
von der Heyde, Gustav Ludwig Theodor 94
von Tempsky, Gustavus Ferdinand 10
Waikato 11
Wakefield, Edward Gibbon 36–38, **37**, 42–43, 56, 62, 74
Wale, David Houghton 252
Walker, Edwin Barnes 85
Wallis, Timothy William [Tim] **253**, 253–54, 292
Walsh, Fintan Patrick [Black Prince] (formerly Patrick Tuohy) 162
Ward family 173
Ward, Joseph George 104, 127–28, **128**, 173
Warren, Holmes 53
Watson, Eric John 238, 242, **258ff**, 266, 273–75
Watson, Nicky (née Robinson) 274–75
Wattie, Gladys Madeline (née Henderson) 191
Wattie, Gordon James 192
Wattie, James [Jim] 189–92, **190**, 197, 288
Wattie, Raymond Kingsford [Ray] 192
Webster, William 9
Weddel, William 127
Weld, Filumena Mary Anne Lisle [Mena] (née Phillipps) **50ff**
Weld, Frederick Aloysius 49–51, **50ff**, 57, 78, 280
Weller brothers 6–7, 26–27, 36
Weller, Edward 6–7, **7**, 27
Weller, George 6, **7**, 27
Weller, Joseph Brooks 6

Wentworth, William Charles 5
Wheeler, George Ronald 234
Whineray, Wilson James 292
Whitaker, Frederick (1812–91) 81–86, **83**, 92–93, 121
Whitaker, Frederick Alexander (1847–87) 92
Whitcombe, Bertie Ernest Hawkes 117
Whitcombe, George Hawkes 117
Whitmore, George Stoddart 79
White, Cleave McKellar Richmond [later Cleave McKellar Richwhite] 264
Whyte, John Blair 85
Whyte, Robert 246
Wigley, Alexander Grant [Sandy] 151
Wigley, Henry Rodolph [Harry] 151
Wigley, Jessie Christie (née Grant) 151
Wigley, Rodolph Lysaght [Wigs] 150–52, **178ff**, 290
Wigram, Agnes Vernon (née Sullivan) 173
Wigram, Henry Francis 151–52
Wigram, William Arthur 152
Wilks, William 8
Williams, Arnold Beetham [A.B.] 25
Williams, Desmond 25
Williams family 22–27, 50ff, 199–200, 221
Williams, Hamish 25
Williams, Heathcote Beetham [Bill] (born 1922) 25
Williams, Heathcote Beetham [H.B.] (1868–1961) 25, **50ff**, 198
Williams, Henry 15, 22, **23**, 24–27, 50ff, 54
Williams, Jane 19
Williams, Kenneth Stuart 25
Williams, Marcus 25
Williams, Samuel 22–23, **50ff**, 168
Williams, Thomas Coldham [T.C.] 24, 54
Williams, William (1800–78) 19, 22, 25, 198
Williams, (William) Leonard (1829–1916) 24–25
Williamson, James 81, 84–85, 91–93, **92**
Wilson, Emma (later Mrs Campbell) 77
Wilson family 98–99, 143
Wilson, (George) Hamish 71
Wilson, (John) Cracroft [Nabob] 76–77, **77**
Wilson, James Glenny 71
Wilson, (Joseph) Liston 98
Wilson, (George Hamish) Ormond (1907–88) 71–72
Wilson, William Chisholm (1810–76) 81, 84, 98
Wilson, (William) Scott (1835–1902) 84, 98–99
Windsor, House of 163
Winstone, family 144, 194
Winstone, George 143
Winstone, William 143
Wood family 241
Wright, Arthur 181
Wright, John Thomas 125
Wyborn, Mark John (registered as John Mark Wyborn) 240–41, 263
Wylie, Douglas Stuart 178–79
Yeates, A.B. 113
Young, Frederick George 162

Index B

Businesses and organisations

This index includes sole traders, business partnerships and limited-liability companies. 'Ltd', 'NL' (no liability, used by some mining companies) and 'Inc' have been omitted in most cases. The ampersand (&) rather than 'and' has been used throughout for the sake of form and to remove confusion where business partners and their partnerships or companies share the same names. Appendix A has not been indexed but Appendix B (the *National Business Review* Business Hall of Fame) and Appendix C (the *National Business Review* Sporting Rich) have been. This index also includes government agencies, newspapers, magazines, non-profit organisations and those of a recreational, charitable, educational or professional nature. Page numbers for illustrations are listed in bold type.

A. & G. Price (later part of Cable Price Downer) 122
A. & T. Burt 114
A2 Corporation 252
A.A. Corban & Sons 210
A.H. & A.W. Reed 117
A.S. Paterson & Co (later Goodman Group) 121, 178ff, 193
AB Consolidated Holdings (comprising Aulsebrook and Bycroft Macintosh) 121
Abraham & Williams 125
ACI International (formerly Australian Consolidated Industries) 183, 231
Act New Zealand (formerly Association of Consumers & Taxpayers) 72, 238, 256, 270
Active Equities 244
Adams Bruce 195
Admiral's Cup 249
Affco Holdings (formerly Auckland Farmers' Freezing Co-operative) 247
Afforestation 178
Air New Zealand (formerly Tasman Empire Airways) 150–51, 270, 291
Alexander Turnbull Library 119
Alex Harvey & Sons (later Alex Harvey Industries) 183, 187, 188, 291
Alex Harvey Industries (AHI, incorporating Alex Harvey & Sons) 181–84, 291
All Blacks 47, 249, 279, 292, 293
Alliance Textiles (NZ) 247
Allied Concrete 269
Allied Freightways (later Freightways) 256
Allied Mills 193
Allied Petroleum 269

Alpine Helicopters (later part of Helicopter Line) 254
Amalgamated Brick & Pipe Co 154–56, 163
Amalgamated Dairies 134
Amalgamated Marketing (a subsidiary of Amalgamated Dairies) 134
Amalgamated Theatres 199, 230, 241
America's Cup 225, 240, 259–60, 273, 280, 293
AMP (formerly AMP Society, Australian Mutual Provident Society) 279
Ansett Airlines of Australia 150
Ansett New Zealand (later Tasman Pacific Airlines of New Zealand) 150, 256–57
Aoraki Corporation (later Jade Software Corporation) 271
Apache Corporation 176
Archibald Clark & Sons 94
Argent Networks 272
Ariadne Australia (formerly South Pine Quarries) 127
Arthur Barnett 141
Arthur Yates & Co (later part of Yates New Zealand) 143
ASB Bank (formerly Auckland Savings Bank) 139
Associated Motorists' Petrol Co (later Europa Oil [NZ]) 146
Association of Consumers & Taxpayers (later Act New Zealand) 238
Astral Pacific 166
Atlas Corporation (later part of Ceramco Corporation) 54, 254–55
Atlas Majestic Industries (later Atlas Corporation) 214, 254

Auckland Agricultural & Pastoral Association 82
Auckland Agricultural Co 86, 92
Auckland Bridge Climb 212
Auckland Chamber of Commerce (later Auckland Regional Chamber of Commerce & Industry) 20
Auckland City Art Gallery 119
Auckland City Council 88–89, 93, 216, 241
Auckland Club 38, 92, 245
Auckland Coin & Bullion Exchange (later part of Goldcorp Holdings) 235–36
Auckland Farmers' Freezing Co-op (later Affco Holdings) 127
Auckland Freezing Co 126–27
Auckland Gas Co 219
Auckland Hospital Board 142
Auckland International Airport 292
Auckland Knitting Mills 290
Auckland Manufacturers' Association 139
Auckland Master Grocers' Buying Group (later Foodstuffs [Auckland]) 164
Auckland Master Grocers' Association 164
Auckland Polo Club 188
Auckland Provincial Council 84, 97
Auckland Public Library 119
Auckland Racing Club 90, 97
Auckland Regional Authority (later Auckland Regional Council) 209, 216
Auckland Savings Bank (later ASB Bank) 20, 88, 108
Auckland Star (formerly *Evening Star*, closed 1991) 113–14, 164, 221
Auckland Sun (closed 1988) 164, 221
Auckland University College (later University of Auckland) 53
Auckland War Memorial Museum 134
Aulsebrook & Co (later part of AB Consolidated Holdings) 120–21
Australasian Electric Light, Power & Storage Co 121–22
Australia & New Zealand Bank (later ANZ Banking Group [New Zealand]) 202–205
Australian Consolidated Industries (ACI) 183
Australian Grand Prix 156
Australian Mutual Provident Society (AMP) 69, 117–18
Australian Producers' Co-operative Federation 134
Australian Stock Exchange (ASX) 272
Bank of New South Wales (later absorbed by Westpac Banking Corporation) 84–85, 102, 196, 231
Bank of New Zealand (BNZ) 39, 53, 80, 84–87, 89, 91, 93–94, 98–101, 98ff, 118, 124, 127, 235, 258ff, 259–60, 289
Bank of New Zealand Estates Co 100
Bank of Otago 103
Barr Burgess & Stewart (later Coopers & Lybrand, later PricewaterhouseCoopers) 292
Baycorp Holdings (later Baycorp Advantage) 54
BBC World Service 256
Bell Gully (formerly Bell Gully Buddle Weir) 82
Belmont Presbyterian Church 216
Bendon Group (formerly Ceramco Corporation) 54, 156, 274, 290

Bendon Industries (formerly Hurley Bendon, later part of Ceramco Corporation) 54
Berlei (NZ) 118, 156
Bidwill Wakeman Paine & Co 53
BIL International (formerly Brierley Investments) 223
Bing Harris & Co (later part of Bing Harris Sargood) 111
Bing Harris Sargood 111
Blind Institute (later Royal New Zealand Foundation for the Blind) 141
Blis Technologies 252
Blue Star Group 117, 273–74
Bluebird Toys 223
Blundell Bros (later part of INL) 115
Board of Trade (United Kingdom) 86
Bolshoi Ballet 198
Bomac Laboratories 290
Botry-Zen 252
Boys' Gordon Hall Trust 65
Brett Printing & Publishing Co 113
Bridgecorp Holdings 246
Brierley Investments (BIL, later BIL International) 107, 110–11, 114, 116–17, 121, 144, 148, 150, 165–67, 178ff, 184, 199, 202, 211, 220–21, 223, 225, 230, 233, 237, 244, 258ff, 268
British Broadcasting Corporation (BBC) 72
British Everest Expedition 56
British Petroleum (BP) 147
British Phosphate Commission 264
Broadbank Corporation 231
Broadcasting Corporation of New Zealand 209
Broadcasting Council of New Zealand 249
Broken Hill Pty (BHP) 231
Brown & Campbell (later Brown Campbell & Co) 20–21, 30–34, **35**, 85
Brown Campbell & Co (later part of Campbell & Ehrenfried Co) 31, 87–89, 119, 159–60, 173
Bulldogs rugby league team 293
Bunting & Co 144, 167
Bureau for Industry 185–186
Burns Philp & Co 193, 258ff, 261, 272–73
Business & Parliament Trust 193
Business Hall of Fame (see the *National Business Review* Business Hall of Fame)
Butland Industries 196
Butland Tobacco 196
Buxton 212
Bycroft Macintosh (later part of AB Consolidated Holdings) 121
Cable Price Downer 211
Cadbury Fry Hudson 112
Cadbury's 112
Caltex Oil Co 180
Campaign Against Rising Prices (Carp) 190
Campaign for Better Government 193
Campbell & Ehrenfried Co (C&E, incorporating Brown Campbell & Co and Ehrenfried Bros) 31, 159–60, 162, 288
Canterbury Association 41, 43–44, 46, 48, 63
Canterbury Foundry 114–15
Canterbury Frozen Meat Co 64
Canterbury Jockey Club 157

INDEX B – BUSINESSES AND ORGANISATIONS — 321

Canterbury (NZ) Aviation Co 151
Canterbury (NZ) Seed Co 152
Canterbury Provincial Council 77
Canterbury Timber Products 182
Capital Markets (formerly Horizon Oil Exploration) 259–60
Carter Consolidated 181, 291
Carter Holt Harvey (CHH) 117, 181, 183–84, 246–47, 292
Carter Holt Holdings (Carter Holt) 181–83
Caspex Corporation 247
Catholics and Prohibition 148
Cawthorn Institute 119
Caxton Group 184, 233
Caxton Printing Works 246
Caxton Pulp & Paper 246
CBA Finance Holdings (later Westpac Merchant Finance) 231
CellularVision NZ 247
Ceramco (later Ceramco Corporation) 54, 156, 255
Ceramco Corporation (later Bendon Group) 54, 156
Cerebos Gregg's 111
Cerebos Pacific 111
Challenge Corporation (incorporating Wrightson NMA) 63, 175, 178ff
Challenge Phosphate Co 134
Chase Corporation 138–39, 199, 225–27, 230, 239–41, 252
Chase Holdings 230
Chong Press Clipping Bureau 131
Christ Church, Kororareka (later Russell) 15
Christchurch Star 113, 164
Christchurch Times (formerly *Lyttelton Times*, closed 1935) 164
Christchurch Town Board (later Christchurch City Council) 114
Christmas Island Phosphate Commission 264
Christ's College, Christchurch 53, 72, **124**, 125, 150, 253
Church Missionary Society (CMS) 15, 22–23
Church of Christ 153
Circular Saw Line (formerly Pacific Island Traders fleet) 32, 95
Clark Franchising 212
Clark Rubber 212
Clavell Capital 256
Cleo 275
Cobb & Co 63
Coles Myer 167–68
Colonial (formerly Colonial Mutual) 279
Colonial Bank of New Zealand 79, 100, 104
Colonial Motor Co (formerly Rouse & Hurrell) 148–49, 178ff, 223
Commercial Bank of Australia (CBA, later part of Westpac Banking Corporation) 231
Commission of Inquiry into Certain Matters Relating to Taxation (Wine-box Inquiry) 262–63
Community Pharmacy (CPL) 226
Compañia de Petroleos de Chile (Copec) 183
Congregational Church 110
Consolidated Brick & Pipe Investments 156
Continental (tyres) 210

Corban Revell 209
Corbans Holdings 209
Corbans Wines 208–10
Cornish Lamphouse Group 202
Corporate Cabs 211
Cory-Wright & Salmon (CWS) 213–14
Coulls Somerville Wilkie (later part of Whitcoulls) 117
Countdown 168
Court of Appeal 185, 204
Credit Suisse First Boston NZ Holdings (incorporating Jarden Morgan) 249–50
Cropper-NRM 192
Crown Lynn Potteries 156
Crum Brick & Tile Co 155
Crusaders (Canterbury) 47
CTV 264
D. Benjamin & Co 113
D.McL. Wallace (later Unity Group) 241
Daily News (formerly *Manukau Daily News*) 100
Dairy Produce Export Co 65
Dairy Products Marketing Commission (later part of New Zealand Dairy Board) 134
Dalgety & Co 94, 145
Dapoli Corporation (formerly Kia Ora Stud) 214
Daysh Longuet & Frethey (later Daysh Renouf & Frethey) 248
Daysh Renouf & Co (formerly Daysh Renouf & Frethey) 248–49
Daysh Renouf & Frethey (later Daysh Renouf & Co) 248
DB Bitter Auckland Warriors (later Vodafone Warriors) 274
DB Breweries (incorporating DB Group, formerly Magnum Corporation) 163, 244
De Luxe Motor Service (formerly Wilkinson's Motor Co) 198
Deak Morgan (later incorporated in Jarden Morgan) 249
Department of Lands & Survey, forestry branch 177
Development Finance Corporation (later DFC New Zealand) 213
DIC (formerly Drapery & General Importing Co) 110
Dilworth Ulster Institute Trust 96
Direct Capital Partners 258ff
DML Resources 212
Dominion 41, 56, 115
Dominion Breweries (later part of Magnum Corporation) 163, 173, 175, 186, 290
Dominion Motors (later part of New Zealand Motor Corporation) 148
Dominion Museum (later National Museum) 119
Dominion Salt 211
Donaghys Industries 290
Donald Reid & Co (later Donald Reid Otago Farmers, later Reid Farmers) 122
Douglas Credit 163
Drapery & General Importing Co (later DIC) 110
Dunedin Art Gallery 110
Dunedin Club (often Fernhill Club, formerly

Otago Club) 6, **50ff**, 79, 103, 112
Dunlop Pneumatic Tyre Co 210
East India Company 1, 9
Edinburgh Trust (see 'Tartan Mafia')
Egmont Co-op Box Co 131
Ehrenfried Bros (later part of Campbell & Ehrenfried Co) 159
El-Jay (NZ) 189
Elders IXL 193
Elders Resources Group 181, 233
Elders Resources NZFP (incorporating NZ Forest Products) 181, 184
Empire Carriage Factory (later Empire Steam Carriage Works) 148
Empire Dairies 134
Empire Steam Carriage Works (later Rouse & Hurrell) 148
Energycorp Investments 235
Enterprise New Zealand Trust 250, 288
Epicorp Investments 235
Equitable Group 247
Equiticorp Australia 229
Equiticorp Holdings 226–32
Equiticorp Industries Group 229
Ernest Adams 193, 195
Ernst & Young 271
Eton College 75
Euro-National Corporation 233, 246
Euro-National Finance 246, 259
Europa Oil (NZ) (formerly Associated Motorists' Petrol Co) 146–47
European Pacific Banking Corporation (EP) 260, 262
Evening Post 115, 147
Evening Star (later *Auckland Star*) 113
F.H. Hammond 126
Farmers' Trading Co (incorporating Laidlaw Leeds and Farmers' Union Trading Co) 136–39, **138**, 230, 240–41, 291
Farmers' Union Trading Co (FUT) 138
Farrier-Waimak (later New Zealand Equities) 185
Fay Richwhite & Co 34, 57, 235, 246, 257–60, 262–63
Federal Court 273
Federated Farmers of New Zealand (formerly New Zealand Famers' Union) 71, 146
Federation of Labour (later New Zealand Council of Trade Unions) 162
Fernz Corporation (later Nufarm) 134, 262, 270
Fielder Gillespie Davis (later part of Goodman Fielder Wattie) 193
Firth Concrete Co (formerly Ironclad Products) 89, 186
Firth Industries (incorporating Firth Concrete Co) 89
Fisher & Paykel Appliances Holdings 188
Fisher & Paykel Healthcare Corporation 188
Fisher & Paykel Industries (F&P) 109–10, 178ff, 186–88, 288, 290
Fisher International 189
Fletcher Bros 174
Fletcher Building
Fletcher Challenge (FCL) 63, 175–76, 181, 215, 233, 270, 288–90

Fletcher Challenge Forests (successor to Fletcher Challenge) 176
Fletcher Challenge Paper 176
Fletcher Construction Co (Fletcher Construction) 96, 171–72, 174–75, 216
Fletcher Holdings 89, 172, 175–76, 178ff, 182, 202
Fonterra Co-operative Group (incorporating New Zealand Dairy Group and Kiwi Co-operative Dairies) 133
Foodland Associated 168, 273
Foodland (NZ) Holdings 168
Foodstuffs (later Foodstuffs [Auckland]) 164, 291
Foodstuffs group 164–65
Foodtown Supermarkets (part of Progressive Enterprises) 165–67
Forbes 279
Force Corporation 241
Ford Motor Co 148
Ford Motor Co (Canada) 148
Ford Motor Co of New Zealand 149
Forestry Department 177
Forsyth Barr 252, 292
Four Square 164
Four Square Discount 164
Free Presbyterian Church 114, 216
Freightways Holdings (formerly Allied Freightways) 256, 258
Fuller–Hayward theatres 198
Fullers Corporation 258
Fulton Hogan (formerly J.H. Fulton & Co) 218
Fulton Hogan Holdings 218
Gazette 85
Gear Meat Preserving & Freezing Co of New Zealand 117, 129
General Foods Corporation (NZ) (incorporating Tip Top Ice Cream Manufacturing Co) 192
George Court & Sons (later absorbed by DIC) 143, 270
George Weston 192
Georgie Pie Family Restaurants (part of Progressive Enterprises) 166
Gibson & Mitchell 30, **35**
Girl Guides' Association 77
Gisborne Herald 198
Gisborne Times 198
Glaxo (later GlaxoWellcome) 131
Glaxo SmithKline (after merging with SmithKline Beecham) 131
Goldcorp Holdings (incorporating Auckland Coin & Bullion Exchange) 236
Goldman Sachs & Co 211–12
Goodman Fielder 192–93, 195, 261, 273
Goodman Fielder Milling & Baking New Zealand 89
Goodman Fielder Wattie (incorporating Wattie Industries, Fielder Gillespie Davis and Allied Mills) 192–93
Goodman Group 180, 192–93
Goods & Services Tax Co-ordinating Office 153
Goodyear 196
Gourmet Direct Investments (later GDI) 195

INDEX B – BUSINESSES AND ORGANISATIONS   323

Green & McCahill 218–19
Greenhills Quarry 269
Grocers' Review 164
Guinness Peat Group (GPG) 148, 178ff, 223
Guthrie & Larnach's New Zealand Timber & Woodware Factories Co (formerly Guthrie & Larnach) 98ff, 101, 103
H.C. Sleigh 180
H.E. Shacklock 109–10, 188
H.J. Heinz Co 191–92
H.R.L. Morrison & Co Group 251
Habitat for Humanity 217
Hallenstein Bros (later part of Hallenstein Glasson Holdings) 110
Hallenstein Glasson Holdings 110, 288
Hancock & Co 161
Harbour Steam Navigation Co (forerunner to Union Steam Ship Co) 5
Harmony Securities 233
Harry H. Tombs (later Wingfield Press) 117
Harry Potter 258ff
Harvard Business School 161, 170
Havelock Mail 115
Hawke's Bay Farmers' Co-operative Association 73
Hawke's Bay Farmers' Meat Co 191
Hawke's Bay Fruit, Produce & Cool Storage Co 191
Hawke's Bay Fruitgrowers 191
Hay's (later part of Haywrights) 291
Haywrights 291
Headliner 236
Heinz Wattie's New Zealand (formerly Heinz-Wattie, incorporating Wattie Foods) 191, 193
Helicopter Line (later Tourism Holdings) 254
Hellaby Holdings 127
Henderson & Macfarlane 32, 94–95, 98ff
Henderson & Pollard 182
Henderson Primary School (formerly Henderson's Mill School) 95–96
Hendry Hay McIntosh (later part of Merrill Lynch) 236
Hero 217
High Court of New Zealand (formerly Supreme Court of New Zealand) 180, 228
Highways Construction Co 149
Hocken Library 119
Hokitika Mental Hospital 210
Hong Kong Stock Exchange 233
Hope Gibbons (formerly J. Clarkson & Co) 149
Hort Mocatta & Co 38
House of Commons 36
House of Representatives (Parliament) 31, 50–51, 79, 83, 102, 104, 110
HSBC (formerly HongkongBank, Hongkong & Shanghai Banking Corporation) 243
Human Rights Commission 217
ICI (NZ) 118
Iddison Group Vietnam 252
Ihug (see Internet Group)
Impala Pacific 233
In Search of Excellence 225
Independent Newspapers Ltd (INL) 114, 116, 238
Independent Oil Industries 180–81

Industrial Equity (IEL) 166, 193, 223
Industrial Equity (Pacific) (IEP) 223
Industry New Zealand (later part of Trade and Enterprise New Zealand) 281
Inland Revenue Department (IRD) 26, 202, 262
International Paper 184
International Wool Secretariat 69
Internet Group (Ihug) 241
Inter-Pacific Equity (briefly incorporating McConnell Dowell Corporation) 234
Invercargill Licensing Trust 186
Investment Executive Trust of New Zealand 202
Ironclad Products (later Firth Concrete Co) 89
J.A. Corban & Family Nurseries 210
J. Arthur Rank Organisation 198–99
J. Ballantyre & Co 141
J.C. Williamson group 198
J.C. Williamson Picture Corporation 198
J. Clarkson & Co (later Hope Gibbons) 149
J.G. Ward & Co 128
J.G. Ward Farmers' Association of New Zealand 104, 127
J. Mercer Industries (later Judge Corporation) 147
J.R. Butland & Sons 196
J.R. Butland Pty 196
J.R. McKenzie Trust 140
J.R. McKenzie Youth Education Fund 140
J. Wattie Canneries (later part of Wattie Industries) 191, 194
J. Wattie Foods 192
Jackson Russell (formerly Jackson Russell Dignan Armstrong) 82
Jade Software Corporation (formerly Aoraki Corporation) 271
James Smith 142
James Speight & Co (later Speight's Brewery) 156–57, 178ff
Jarden & Co (later Jarden Corporation) 248–49, 254
'Jarden Boys' 249–52
Jarden Corporation (later part of Jarden Morgan) 249–50, 252
Jarden Morgan NZ (later part of Credit Suisse First Boston NZ Holdings) 249, 251
JBL Consolidated 203
JBL group 202–205
JBL Laboratories/Mill Valley 205
JBL Minerals 205
JBL Seafoods 205
JBL-Sargent Construction 205
Jeffs Brothers (later JBL) 203
John Andrew Ford (formerly John W. Andrew & Sons) 148–49
John Burns & Co 143
John Fairfax Holdings (Fairfax) 116
John McGlashan College 114
John W. Andrew & Sons (later John Andrew Ford) 148–49
John W. Andrew (later John W. Andrew & Sons) 148–49
Johnston & Co 39
Joseph Nathan & Co 131
Judge Corporation (formerly J. Mercer Industries) 147, 232–33

Keith Hay Homes 216–17
'Kelly Gang' 254
Kempthorne Medical Supplies (KMS) 117
Kempthorne Prosser 116
Kerridge Commercial College of Poverty Bay 198
Kerridge Odeon Corporation (later part of Pacer Kerridge Corporation) 25, 50ff, 198–200, 234, 289
Kia Ora Stud (later Dapoli Corporation) 214
King's College, Auckland 155, 265
King's School, Auckland 97
Kirin 158
Kirkcaldie & Stains 141
Kororareka Association 15
Kraft Corporation 196
Kraft Foods 166, 273
Kraft General Foods New Zealand 196
Krondor Corporation 184
Krukziener Properties 243
Kupe Group 232–33
L.D. Nathan & Co (later part of Lion Nathan) 32, 34, 139, 144, 234–35, 260
L.J. Fisher & Co 188
La Grouw Corporation 215–16
La Grouw Holdings 215–16
Ladies' Home Journal 187
Laidlaw Leeds (later merged with Farmers' Union Trading Co) 136–37, 291
Landmark Corporation 239, 243
Landmark Properties (later Landmark Corporation) 239
Lanes Food Group 166
Lanes Industries 211
Laura Fergusson Trust for Disabled Persons 189, 218
Legislative Council 6, 14, 39–40, 45, 50ff, 61, 65, 71, 75, 83, 93, 95
Levene & Co 211–12
Levin & Co (later part of National Mortgage & Agency Co of New Zealand) 38–40, 120, 125, 290
Leyland Growth (later part of Mainzeal Group) 215
Leys Institute 119–20
Liberal Party (New Zealand) 124, 162
'Limited Circle' 81, 84–85, 87, 91, 96, 98, 104, 143–44, 254
Lincoln Industries 139
Lincoln University (formerly Lincoln College) 62
Lion Breweries (later Lion Corporation) 158
Lion Brewery Co (later merged with Hancock & Co) 161
Lion Corporation (later part of Lion Nathan) 34, 158, 160–61, 234–35, 260
Lion Nathan (incorporating L.D. Nathan & Co and Lion Corporation) 33, 158, 288, 292
Lloyd's of London 153
Lockwood Buildings 215–16
London House 36
Lost Property 239
Lowe Walker NZ (later Lowe Corporation) 251
Lyttelton Times (later *Christchurch Times*) 115
Lyttelton Times Co 113, 164

McCollam Printers 274
McConnell Dowell Corporation (later part of Inter-Pacific Equity) 234
McKenzie Education Foundation 141
McKenzies (NZ) 139–41, 289
Maclean & Co 86
McLean Institute 68
Macquarie Bank 251
Madison Company of New York 235
Magnum Corporation (later DB Group, later DB Breweries) 167, 237, 244
Maine Investments (formerly Skellerup Group) 211–12
Mainline Corporation (Australia) 215
Mainzeal Corporation (later Mainzeal Group) 214–15
Mainline Corporation (NZ) (later Mainzeal Corporation) 215
Mainzeal Group (formerly Mainzeal Corporation) 199
Mair Astley Holdings 215
Malayan Breweries (later Asia Pacific Breweries) 235
Marac Finance (formerly Pacific Factors) 231, 254
Marianne Caughey Smith-Preston Memorial Rest Homes Trust 142, 178ff
Matsushita Electric Co 188
Mason & Porter (Masport) 187–89
Masport (formerly Mason & Porter) 189, 210, 237
Meat New Zealand (formerly New Zealand Meat Producers Board) 69, 72
Medical Research Council of New Zealand 189
Mega First Industries 195
Mercury Bay Boating Club 259
Metro **258ff**, 275
Metro-Goldwyn-Mayer (MGM) 198
Michael Hill Jeweller 270
Michael Hill International 270
Michelin 210
Microsoft Corporation 279–80
Mill Valley 205
Ministerial Committee of Inquiry into the Sharemarket (Russell Inquiry) 244–45
Ministry of Forestry 177
Mitsui OSK Lines 207
Mobil Oil 231
Montana Group (NZ) 208
Montana Wines (part of Montana Group [NZ]) 292
Montgomery Ward 136
Morning Report 256
Morrison-PIM Holdings 211
Motor Holdings 247
Mount Cook Group 150–51
Mount Cook Motor Co 151
Mount Cook Motor Service 151
Mount Cook Tourist Co 151
Mr Chips Holdings 252
Mutual Life Association of Australasia 100
Mutual Rental Cars 151
Nathan & Co (briefly Nathan & Joseph, later L. D. Nathan & Co) 8, **35**
National Art Gallery 110

INDEX B – BUSINESSES AND ORGANISATIONS

National Association of Retail Grocers of New Zealand 164
National Bank of New Zealand 62, 103
National Business Review (title of Fourth Estate Holdings including 1990–2003 *Rich Lists*) 53, 100, 134, 146, 169–70, 175, 189, 196–97, 206–208, 211–12, 214, 228, 232, 238, 240–45, 250–53, 255–58, 258, 258ff, 263, 266–69, 272–73, 275, 278–87
National Business Review Business Hall of Fame 6, 41, 98, 107, 142, 151, 170, 177, 189, 207, 218, 234, 248, 250, 254, 288–92
National Mortgage & Agency Co of New Zealand (NMA) 40, 62–63, 125, 128
National Music Council of New Zealand 214
National Mutual Holdings (later Axa) 279
National Mutual Life (later part of Axa) 181
National Provident Fund 216
National Radio 256
National Rugby League (NRL) 274, 293
Nelson Bros 128
Nelson Cathedral 119
Nelson Forest Industries 150
Nelson Museum 119
Nelson Provincial Council 74
New Millennium Party (NMP) 202
New World 164
New York State Court of Appeals 259
New York Supreme Court 259
New Zealand & Australian Land Co 126
New Zealand Aero Transport Co 151
New Zealand Agricultural Co 103
New Zealand Agricultural Society 82
New Zealand Alliance 148
New Zealand Banking Co 14, 84
New Zealand Breweries (later Lion Breweries) 157, 160–63, 186
New Zealand Business Roundtable 176, 225, 270
New Zealand Candle Co 117
New Zealand China Clays (formerly part of Ceramco Corporation) 54
New Zealand Company 10, 37–38, 41–42, 46, 48, 50, 56
New Zealand Co-operative Dairy Co (later part of New Zealand Dairy Group, later part of Fonterra Co-operative Group) 131, 133–34
New Zealand Dairy Association (later merged with Waikato Co-operative Dairy Co to form New Zealand Co-operative Dairy Co) 133
New Zealand Dairy Board (formerly New Zealand Dairy Control Board) 134, 195–96
New Zealand Dairy Control Board (later New Zealand Dairy Board) 134
New Zealand Dairy Group (incorporating New Zealand Co-operative Dairy Co, later part of Fonterra Co-operative Group) 288
New Zealand Deer Farmers' Association 71
New Zealand Distillery Co 161
New Zealand Electric Light Co (later part of R.E. Fletcher & Co) 122
New Zealand Equities (formerly Farrier-Waimak) 185, 187
New Zealand Farmers' Fertilizer Co ('Farmers Fert', later part of Fernz Corporation) 116–17, 202, 270

New Zealand Farmers' Union (later Federated Farmers of New Zealand) 146
New Zealand Federation of Music Societies 212
New Zealand First party 260
New Zealand Forest Service (later New Zealand Forestry Corporation) 177
New Zealand Forestry Corporation (formerly New Zealand Forest Service) 177
New Zealand Freezing Co 73
New Zealand Frozen Meat & Storage Co (later Auckland Freezing Co) 127
New Zealand Herald (title of Wilson & Horton) 98–99, 113–14, 164, 252
New Zealand Historic Places Trust 65, 69, 99, 106
New Zealand Insurance Co (NZI) 80, 84, 87, 94, 98, 100, 289
New Zealand Inventions Development Authority 189
New Zealand Journal of Agriculture 108
New Zealand Labour Party 161–62, 206, 224–25, 232, 256, 259–60
New Zealand Land Association (formerly Waikato Land Association) 86–87, 93
New Zealand Land Mortgage Co (later New Zealand & River Plate Land Mortgage Co) 99
New Zealand Loan & Mercantile Agency Co (Loan Co or 'Loan & Merc') 85–87, 89–91, 94, 96, 127
New Zealand Manufacturers' Association 109
New Zealand Manufacturers' Federation 139, 213, 290
New Zealand Metropolitan Trotting Club 157
New Zealand Motor Corporation (incorporating Dominion Motors) 148, 201
New Zealand National Party 206, 224, 232, 256, 259–60
New Zealand Newspapers 113–14
New Zealand Opera Company (later part of Opera New Zealand) 214
New Zealand Paper Mills (later part of NZ Forest Products) 180
New Zealand Party 178ff, 206, 257
New Zealand Passenger Transport Federation 149
New Zealand Perpetual Forests 178–79
New Zealand Political Reform League (Reform Party) 162, 254
New Zealand Polo Association 56
New Zealand Press Agency 112
New Zealand Press Association 112
New Zealand Rail (later Tranz Rail Holdings) 260
New Zealand Refrigerating Co 126
New Zealand Rugby Football Union (Rugby Union) 293
New Zealand Seamen's Union (later New Zealand Seafarers' Union) 162
New Zealand Shipping Co 114
New Zealand Social Credit Political League 162
New Zealand Society of Viticulture & Oenology 209
New Zealand Sports Foundation 54
New Zealand Steel 188, 228–29
New Zealand Stocks and Shares 219–20

New Zealand Stock Exchange (and metropolitan exchanges before its formation in 1983, now New Zealand Exchange — NZX) 53, 144, 166–67, 180, 210, 215, 220, 225, 235, 245, 252, 254
New Zealand Thames Valley Land Co 86, 96
New Zealand Theatres 198
New Zealand Travel Association 149
New Zealand United Corporation (NZUC, later Barclays New Zealand) 248
New Zealand Wine Council 209
New Zealand Wines & Spirits 160
New Zealand Wool Board 69
Newman Bros 149–50, 178ff
Newmans Airways (later Ansett New Zealand) 149–50
Newmans Group 149–50, 226, 288
News 256
Ngatarawa Wines 210
Ngauranga Meat Processors (later part of Taylor Preston) 251
NMA Wright Stephenson Holdings (Wrightson NMA) 63
No 8 Ventures 272
Norske Skogindustrier (Norske Skog) 176
North British (tyres) 210
North British Freezing Co 73
Northern Club 33, 38, 92, 254
Northern Roller Milling Co 89
Nufarm (formerly Fernz Corporation) 270
NZ Brick, Tile & Pottery Co 154
NZ Cheese 196
NZ Forest Products (later Elders Resources NZFP) 179–82, 233–34
NZ News 114, 258ff, 268
NZI Corporation (formerly New Zealand South British Group) 234
Odeon Theatres (part of J. Arthur Rank Organisation) 198
Oji Paper Co 182
On the Spot 164
Opotiki Volunteer Forest Rangers 16
Oriental Bank Corporation 84
Otago Daily Times 112, 115
Otago Farmers' Co-operative Association of New Zealand 122, 220
Otahuhu Agricultural Association 82
Outward Bound Trust of New Zealand 188–89
Owens Group (formerly R.A. Owens) 178ff, 207
P. & O. 207
Pacer Kerridge Corporation (incorporating Pacer Pacific Corporation and Kerridge Odeon Corporation) 199
Pacer Pacific Corporation (later part of Pacer Kerridge Corporation) 25, 50ff, 199–200, 234
Pacific Area Travel Association (Pata) 149
Pacific Factors (later Marae Finance) 231
Pacific Island Traders fleet (later Circular Saw Line) 32
Pacific Metropolitan 239
Pacific Pine Industries 216
Pacific Retail Group 274
Pak 'N Save 164
Palliser Estate Wines of Martinborough 57

Palmers Gardenworld 211–12
Para Rubber Co 210–12
Paxus Corporation (part of NZI Corporation) 234
Paykel Bros 187
Paynter Corporation 245
PC Direct 258ff
PDL Holdings 271, 289
Penguin Books 117
Personal Investment New Zealand (including 1986 *Rich List*) **226**, 230, 235, 246, 252, 258ff, 268
Personal Investor (including 1987–89 *Rich Lists*) 221, 228–29, 237–38, 244, 246, 268
PharmaZen 252
Piako Land Association (later acquired by Waikato Land Association) 86
Pioneering the Pumice 108
Porirua City Council 130
Port of Nelson 119
Ports of Auckland (formerly Auckland Harbour Board) 184, 240
Post & Telegraph Department 191
Poverty Bay Petroleum & Kerosene Co 19
PPCS (see Primary Producers' Co-operative Society)
Presbyterian Social Services (later Presbyterian Support Services) 141
Press, Christchurch 164
Preston Russell 82
Price Tribunal 139
Price Waterhouse (later part of PricewaterouseCoopers) 153
Primary Producers' Co-operative Society (PPCS) 253
Printing & Publishing Corporation (Printpac) 117
Printpac 117
Printpac-UEB 117
Privy Council Judicial Committee 236
Progress Party 82
Progressive Enterprises (Progents) 165–69, 237, 292
Progressive Greens party 112
Public Service Investment Society (PSIS) 203
Purr-Pull Oil Industries (formerly Smith Wylie Australia) 180
Putaruru Pine & Pulp Co 179
Putaruru Pine Products 179
Pyne Gould Corporation 71, 75, 122
Pyne Gould Guinness (later briefly Pyne Gould Guinness Reid Farmers) 122
Quality Bakers of New Zealand 192
Queen Elizabeth II Arts Council (later Creative New Zealand) 214
Queenstown-Mount Cook Airways 151
R. & W. Hellaby 126–27, 136, 143, 178ff, 291
R.A. Brierley Investments (later Brierley Investments) 219–20
R.E. Fletcher & Co (incorporating New Zealand Electric Light Co) 122
R. Hannah & Co 106, 290
R.O. Clark 153–54
Rada Corporation 180, 233–34
Radio Broadcasting Co 132

INDEX B – BUSINESSES AND ORGANISATIONS — 327

Radio Corporation 212
Radio Hauraki (NZ) 54, 256
Rainbow Corporation 165–67, 226, 237
Raine & Ramsay (later Raine Ramsay & Browne) 9
Raine Ramsay & Browne (formerly Raine & Ramsay) 9
Rangatira 140
Rank Group 117
Ranks Hovis McDougall 111, 193
Ravensdown Fertiliser Co-operative 71, 116
Reform Party (see New Zealand Political Reform League)
Reid Farmers (later Pyne Gould Guinness Reid Farmers, then Pyne Gould Guinness) 122
Rendells 143
Renouf Corporation 232–33, 247–48
Reserve Bank of New Zealand 206, 244, 284, 292
Riccarton Trust Board 47
Riddiford Holdings 57
Robert Campbell & Sons 75–76
Robert Holt & Sons 182, 291
Robt Jones Investment Group 205
Robt Jones Investments (later Trans Tasman Properties) 178ff, 205–206, 236
Robinson Industries 189
Ross & Glendining 111
Rotary International 141
Rothmans 196
Rothmans Holdings of Australia 244
Rothmans Industries (later Magnum Corporation) 196, 244
Rothmans International 244
Rouse & Hurrell (formerly Empire Steam Carriage Works) 148
Roy McKenzie Foundation 141
Royal Air Force 70
Royal Commission on Forestry 177
Royal Commission on Licensing 186
Royal Flying Corps 145, 152
Royal Naval Air Service 136
Royal Navy 3, 8–9, 35, 145
Royal Navy, New Zealand Division 162
Royal New Zealand Air Force 154
Royal School of Dungannon 96
Rubicon 176
Rugby World Cup 293
Russell Inquiry (see Ministerial Commission of Inquiry into the Sharemarket)
Russell McVeagh (formerly Russell McVeagh McKenzie Bartleet & Co) 82, 262
Russell Ritchie & Co (later part of National Mortgage & Agency Co of New Zealand) 62
St Kentigern College 135
St Kentigern Trust 135
St Patrick's College, Silverstream 214–15
St Paul's Cathedral, London 46
St Paul's Church, Auckland 9
St Paul's Church, Taitapu 46
St Paul's Church, Waipara 59
St Thomas' Church, Auckland 218
Salvation Army 141
Samuel Vaile (later Samuel Vaile & Sons) 108
San Diego Yacht Club 259

Sandhurst Military College 53
Sanford 134
Sausage Software 271–72
Sanyo Pulp 182
Sargood Son & Ewen (later part of Bing Harris Sargood) 110
Schneider Electric 271
Scout movement 110
Seabrook Fowlds (later part of New Zealand Motor Corporation) 201
Sealord Products 182
Sears Roebuck 136
Securitibank 202–203, 258
Securities Commission 232, 234, 270, 274
Security Discounters (later part of Fay Richwhite & Co) 258
Self Help 164
Serious Fraud Office (SFO) 231, 262
Sew Hoy & Sons 108
Shalfoon Bros 117
Shell BP & Todd Oil Services 147
Shell New Zealand (formerly Shell Oil [NZ]) 176
Shell Oil (NZ) 147, 249
Shipping Corporation of New Zealand 72
Shirley Golf Club 121
Shotover Big Beach Gold Mining Co 108
Sisters of Mercy 93
Skeggs Group 256
Skellerup Group (later Maine Investments) 211
Skellerup Industries (later part of Skellerup Group) 211
Sky City Entertainment Group 241
Sky Network Television 165, 237–38, 241, 256
Smith & Caughey (formerly Wm H. Smith) 141–43, **178ff**
Smith Wylie & Co 178–79
Smith Wylie Australia (later Purr-Pull Oil Industries) 179–80
Smith Wylie Journal (later *Wealth*) 178
Smithfield market 65, 125
Smiths City Market Group 226
Society for the Prevention of Cruelty to Animals (SPCA) 199
Soldiers' & Airmen's Christian Association 139
Solution 6 272
South British Insurance Co (later part of New Zealand South British Group) 108, 160
South Canterbury Refrigerating Co 70, 291
South Eastern Utilities (formerly Amuri Corporation) 71, 75
Southern Cross (later part of *New Zealand Herald*) 31, 80, 99, 113
Southern Transport Co 269
Southland Times 80
Sovenz 134
Sovereign (formerly Sovereign Assurance) 253
Speight's Brewery (formerly James Speight & Co) 156–57, 161
Spirit of Adventure Trust 189
Standard Footwear Co 110
Standard Insurance Co 202
Standard Oil Co 180
Staples & Co (later part of New Zealand Breweries) 161

State Advances Corporation of New Zealand (later Housing Corporation of New Zealand) 230
State Forest Service (later New Zealand Forest Service) 177
Stevens KMS Corporation (later Zuellig New Zealand) 117
Stonyhurst College 48–49
Strathmore Group 251
Suckling Bros (later Suckling Industries) 107
Sun, Auckland (closed 1930) 164, 179
Sun, Christchurch (closed 1935) 164
Sun Insurance Co 219
Sunday Star-Times 272
Sunday Times (UK) 258ff
Supreme Court of New Zealand (later High Court of New Zealand) 22, 82
Switchtec Power Systems 271
Sydney Alliance Insurance Co 8
Symphony Group 240–41
T. & D. Asquith 2
T. Macky & Co 9
T.G. Macarthy Trust 169
Tainui 279
Tait Electronics 271, 289
Tall Blacks 293
Tappenden Holdings 254, 256
Tappenden Motors 254
'Tartan Mafia' (also known as Edinburgh Trust) 252–53
Taskforce on Private Provision for Retirement 153
Taskforce to Review Education Adminisration (Tomorrow's Schools) 170
Tasman Pulp & Paper Co 175, 178ff, 182, 246
Tatra Leather Goods (later Tatra Industries) 212
Tatra Industries 212–14
Taylor Preston 251
Te Aute College 23, 26
Team New Zealand 260
Telecom Corporation of New Zealand 256
Telemedia Networks International 272
Television New Zealand (TVNZ) 209–210
Temperance & General Group (T&G) 121
The Lord of the Rings 258ff, 279
Theory K 225–26
Thos Borthwick & Sons 53, 137
3 Guys group 166
Tip Top Ice Cream Manufacturing Co (later part of General Foods Corporation (NZ)] 192
TNL Group (later Newmans Group) 149, 288
Todd & Sons (bricks and tiles) 153
Todd Bros 144
Todd Charitable Trust 147
Todd Corporation 147, 288
Todd Foundation 147
Todd Motor Co 145
Todd Motor Corporation (later Todd Corporation) 146
Todd Motor Industries 145
Todd Motors 145
Tokanui Hospital 210
Tokomaru Harbour Board 25
Tongariro-Rangipo prison 236

Tourism Holdings (formerly Helicopter Line) 150, 254
Tower Corporation Holdings (formerly Government Life Office) 223
Tramco Investments (later Tramco Harbour Holdings) 240
Trans Tasman Properties (formerly Robt Jones Investments) 206
Transport (Nelson) 149
Transport (Nelson) Holdings (later TNL Group) 149
Transvision Holdings (later CBA Finance Holdings) 231
Treasury 232, 245
Triple M 199
Truth 137–38
Turners & Growers 223
Tyndall Australia 223
UEB Industries (formerly United Empire Box) 185, 187
Unigroup Pacific (formerly Unity Group) 199, 241
Union Bank of Australia 8, 60, 84
Union Steam Ship Co (Union Company, later Union Shipping Group) 5, 207
United Buyers [later Foodstuffs (Wellington)] 164
United Empire Box (later UEB Industries) 185, 187
United Nations Educational, Cultural & Social Organisation (Unesco) 214
United States District Court 235
United Temperance Reform Council 148
Unity Group (later Unigroup Pacific) 241
Universal Motor Co 149
University Club (formerly Brett home) 114
University of Auckland (formerly Auckland University College) 134, 215, 218, 278
University of Cambridge 10, 100, 158, 161
University of Otago 178, 251–52
University of Oxford 72, 248
US Office Products 117, 258ff, 273
Victoria University College (later Victoria University of Wellington) 205, 214, 219, 258
Vodafone Warriors (formerly DB Bitter Auckland Warriors) 274, 293
W.B. Rhodes & Co 42
W.H. Smith 117
W.M. Bannatyne & Co 117
W. Stevenson & Sons 178ff, 217–18, 289
Waiapu County Council 25
Waiapu Hospital & Charitable Aid Board 25
Waiapu Racing Club 25
Waiapu Returned Soldiers' Trust 25
Waihi Gold Mining Co 87, 90
Waikato Co-operative Cheese Co 133
Waikato Co-operative Dairy Co (later merged with New Zealand Dairy Association to form the New Zealand Co-operative Dairy Co) 133
Waikato Dairy Co (later part of Waikato Co-operative Dairy Co) 133
Waikato Land Association (later the New Zealand Land Association) 86–87, 93
Waipuna International 252
Wairarapa Energy 71

INDEX B – BUSINESSES AND ORGANISATIONS

Wairarapa Frozen Meat Co 125
Waitaki International (formerly Waitaki NZ Refrigerating) 192
Waitangi Tribunal 210
Waitemata brewery 163
Wall Street Journal 233
Warbirds Over Wanaka international air show 253–54, 292
Warehouse Group 270–71
Wattie Book Awards 192
Wattie Industries (Wattie's, incorporating J. Wattie Canneries) 180, 192, 233, 288
Wellington & Manawatu Railway Co 40, 50ff
Wellington Chamber Music Society 214
Wellington Club 38, 40
Wellington College 219
Wellington Gas Co 117, 148
Wellington Publishing Co 56
Wesleyan mission station, Mangungu 10
Westmed Group 240
Westpac Banking Corporation 231
Whakatane Board Mills (formerly Whakatane Paper Mills, later part of NZ Forest Products) 180, 291
Whakatane Cattle Co 95
Whinney Smith & Whinney 159
Whitaker & Russell 82–84, 94
Whitcombe & Tombs (later part of Whitcoulls) 117
Whitcoulls (incorporating Whitcombe & Tombs and Coulls Somerville Wilkie) 117

Wilkins & Davies Construction Co 226
Wilkinson's Motor Co (later De Luxe Motor Service) 198
Wm H. Smith (later Smith & Caughey) 142
Williams & Kettle 26
Wilson & Horton 57, 99–100, 114, 143–44
Wilson Neill 258ff
Wine Institute of New Zealand 209
Wine-box Inquiry (see Commission of Inquiry into Certain Matters Relating to Taxation)
Wingfield Press (formerly Harry H. Tombs) 117
Winstone group 143–44, 237
Winstone Pulp International (formerly Winstone Sumsung Industries) 144
Winstone Samsung Industries (later Winstone Pulp International) 144
Woolf Fisher Trust 188
Woolworths Australia 166, 237
Wrightson (formerly Wrightson NMA) 41, 125
Wrightson NMA (later Wrightson) 63
Wright Robertson & Co (later Wright Stephenson & Co) 125
Wright Stephenson & Co (later Wrightson NMA) 40–41, 50ff, 63, 125, 135, 289
Write Price 164
Xena: Warrior Princess **278**, 279
YMCA (formerly Young Men's Christian Association) 141
Zuellig Group 117
Zuellig New Zealand (formerly Stevens KMS Corporation) 117

Index C

Properties, ships, boats and horses

This list includes houses, farms, stations, works, mills, mines, breweries, hotels, horses and other property holdings, as well as all sailing and motor vessels (in italics). Where known, earlier names are included. Page numbers for illustrations are listed in bold type; references to photo inserts are denoted by *ff*.

Acacia Cottage 30, 89
Addington station 74
Adelaide 56
Adventure (renamed *Tahora*) 41
Akhbar 76
Akito station 73
Albert Plaza 208
Albion Club 19
Alinghi 260, 280, 293
Annedale block 55
Antrim House 106, **107**
Ashfield station 66
Asp 17
Auckland Magistrates' Court 244
Aurora 42
Australian 42
Balruddery estate 79
Barrett's Hotel 41, **50ff**
Bella Vista (later Newman Hall) 33
Benmore station (or Ben More station, Canterbury) 74–75
Benmore station (Otago) 75
Birch Hill station 73
Birchbank 207
Birchlands (Epsom, Auckland) 113
Birchlands (Sheffield, England) 113
Bird Grove 36
Black Magic 260
Blandford Lodge stud 196
Blue Cliffs station 53
Bolina 30
Bramcote (Epsom, Auckland, later Florence Court) 126, 136, 178ff, 200–201, **201**
Bramcote Hall, England 126
Brancepeth station 24, 53–55, **55**
Britomart scheme 241
Broadlands estate (Taupo) 108
Broadlands station (Canterbury) 76

Brookdale station 121
Buccaneer 156
Bunnythorpe dried-milk factory 131
Burnside freezing works 126
Burwood station 75
Callooa 246
Cambridge stud 269
Camp, the (later Larnach Castle) **98ff**, 100–101, 104
Campbell Park (Otekaieke) 75–76, **76**
Canterbury block 43–44, 48
Carbine 90
Careys Bay Historic Hotel 264, 267
Cargill's Castle (formerly the Cliffs) 105–106
Cashmere estate 76
Castlepoint station 39
Chateau Tongariro 151
Cherry Farm 4–5, **5**, 48
Cheviot Hills station 60–62, **98ff**
Cintra 159
City brewery (later Speight's brewery) 156
Civic Theatre 241
Cliffs, the (later Cargill's Castle) 105–106
Clive Grange estate 53
Cloudy Bay whaling station 38
Coburg Hotel 160
Coldstream station 70
Colman house **258ff**
Commercial Hotel 32
Congreve house **258ff**
Conical Hill station 102
Cornwall Park (formerly One Tree Hill estate) 89
Cottage, the (Sir Donald McLean, Sir Douglas Maclean) 73
Cottage, the (Thomas McDonnell) 10
Cracroft House 77
Cracroft station 76

INDEX C – PROPERTIES, SHIPS AND BOATS — 331

Crown brewery 157
Crown Lynn potteries 155–56
Culverton station 76
Dalethorpe station 74–75
Deans Bush (formerly Potoringamotu bush) 46
Deans Cottage 47, **50ff**
Deepdell station 79
Deptford sawmill/shipyard 9–10, **50ff**
Deveron 16
Dilworth farm 96, **98ff**
Domain brewery 87
Dunedin 126
Edinburgh Castle Hotel 160
Eight Hours mill (later part of Northern Roller Milling Co) 89, **90**
Elderslie 79
Elderslie estate 79
Ellerslie Hotel 160
Ellerslie House 97
Ellerslie racecourse 97
Endeavour 8
Erewhon station 247
Eyre Creek station 102
Farrant house (Wanaka) 253
Fay mansion 263
Fay Richwhite Building (Big Pinky, now IAG Building) 260
Fellworth House 119
Fern Hill 6, **50ff**
Finance Plaza 240
Fisher house **258ff**
Flaxbourne station 50–51, 121
Florence Court (formerly Bramcote) 126, 178ff, 200, **201**
Fortitude 13
Galloway station 75
Gear Homestead (formerly Okowai) 129–30
Gear meatworks 129
Gibbs house (Orakei) 257–58
Glenbrook steelmill 218
Glenmark station 58–61, **59**, **98ff**
Glynn Wye station 75
Godley Peaks station 75
Golden Crown goldmine 119
Government House (Auckland, destroyed 1848) 32–33
Government House (Auckland, 1856–1975) 32
Government House (formerly Birchlands; Auckland, from 1975) 113
Great Barrier Island copper mine 9
Great Mercury Island 263
Gymnotus 143
Hannibal 14
Harbour City 240
Harley House 119
Hart mansion **258ff**
Heatley house **258ff**
Heaton Park estate 42
Henderson's Mill estate (later Henderson) 95
Herald (Church Missionary Society) 15
Herald (HMS) 3
Heretaunga block 71
Heriot fellmongery 144

Heritage Auckland hotel 138–39, 240
Hermitage, the 151
Highden 39
Highland Park estate 42
Highpeak station 75–76
Hill River station 61
Hillbrook golf course 270
Hobson Park 96
Hobson St store, Farmers' Trading Co **138**
Hobsonville pottery 153–54
Holly Lea (later McLeans Mansion) 66–68, **98ff**
Holme station 70
Homebush station 46–47
Imax 241
Inconstant 41
Independence (renamed *Tokerau*) 15
Industry 10
Infidel 156
Jacobs River whaling station 3
Jade Stadium (formerly Lancaster Park) 62
Joseph Weller 6
Jubilee dairy factory 131
Kaingaroa State Forest 182
Karamu stud 71
Karewa estate 59
Karere 15
Kaukapakapa farm 257
Kawau Island 105
Kawerau pulp and paper mill 175
Kawerau mill (Spencer family) 246
Kawhia Harbour trading station 21
Kekerengu station 75
Kilbryde 88–89, **88**
King's Wharf freezing works 126–27
Kinleith pulp and paper mill 180
Kinloch development and marina
Koputaroa sawmill 181
Kulnine station 74
Kyeburn station 79
KZ-7 225
Lady Lilford 29
Lagmhor station 66
Lake Grassmere saltworks 210
Lamb Hill 97
Lansdown(e) station 60
Larnach Castle (formerly the Camp) **98ff**, 101
Leslie Hills station 74
Leslie station 74
Levels, the 44, **44**, **50**, 53
Lochinvar station 218
Lockerbie estate 70, 89–91, 123
Logan Bank 89
Longbeach station 63–65, 69, 82
Longridge station 102
Lord Rodney 3
Lucy Dunn 95
McLeans Mansion (formerly Holly Lea) 66–68, **98ff**
Mahurangi spa station 9
Maketu pa trading station 17
Makino dairy factory 131
Manawaora farm 13–14
Mangatoki dairy factory 131

Mangaweka sash and door factory 181
Mansion House (Sir George Grey) 105
Mansion House (William Robinson) 61, **98ff**
Maraekakaho station 73
Mararoa station 75
Maria 46
Marinoto 111
Matahiia station 25
Matamata estate 89–90, 123
Matheson Homestead 54
Mavora station 75
Meadowbank (suburb) 91
Meadowbank estate 91
Melanesian Mission 210
Melness 79
Mendip Hills station 74
Mercury Bay sawmill 9
Metropolis, the 244
Middle Dome station 102
Millbrook golf course 270
Milton Grange estate 53
Moa Flat station 103
Moanatuatua swamp 85
Moerewa **178ff**
Molesworth station 75
Mona Vale 59–60
Monte Cecilia (formerly the Pah) 93, **93**
Montrose station 74
Morven Hills station 66
Motuihe Island farm 97
Motutapu Island farm 97
Mt Lebanon vineyards 209
Mt Neesing station 75
Mt Peel station 68–69, **98ff**
Mt Possession station 69
Mt Somers station 69
New Brunswick flourmill 110
Nihotupu dam 218
Northern Wairoa timbermill 87
Ocean Beach freezing works 127–28
Ohinemutu Hotel 98
Okiato estate 13–15, 35, **50ff**
Okowai (later Gear Homestead) 129–30
Olveston **98ff**, 113
Om Santi vineyard 57
One Queen Street 243
One Tree Hill estate (later Cornwall Park) 85, 88–89
Onoke estate 12–13
Opawa station 74
Opou estate 19
Opuha Gorge station 150
Orari Gorge station 69
Orongorongo station 56–57
Oroua Downs station 75
Otago whaling station 6
Otahuna 45, **45**
Otekaieke (see Campbell Park) 75
Pah, the (later Monte Cecilia) 92–93, **93**
Pah Farm estate (later the Pah) 91
Pakaraka estate 22
Pakatoa Island 198
Palace picture theatre 198
Palmyra 29
Pan Pacific pulp mill 182

Paradis sur Mer (formerly Toison d'Or) 247
Paritai Dr, Auckland **258ff**
Parramatta 21
Pegasus 2
Petone slaughterhouses and boiling-down works 129
Piako swamp 82, 85
Pihautea station (formerly Kopungarara) 49–50, **50ff**
Pirinoa station 53
Planet Hollywood 241
Plimmer City Centre 240
Poenamo Hotel 160
Pt Piper mansion (Spencer) 246
Porangahau block 71
Port Pegasus settlement 3
Posthumous 48
Preservation Inlet whaling station 3
Prince of Denmark 3
Prospect Farm 4
Puketiti station 25
Purau farm 48
Pye farm 268
Queen St store, Smith & Caughey **178ff**
Ra Ora stud 188
Rainbow station 75
Rainbow's End 237
Rangataua sawmill 181
Redcastle station 66
Retreat, the 22
Riccarton farm 46
Riccarton House 47, **50ff**
Richmond meatworks and fellmongery 126
Richwhite mansion 263
Rissington station 79
Rocky Pt station 75
Roslyn mill 111
Roydon Lodge stud 141
Run 333 73
St Keven's 33
St Leonards station 73
Saracen 156
Schist Strata 270
Sequoia estate 25
Sherwood station 74
Shortland meatworks 127
Sir George Murray 9–10
Sir Tristram 269
Sirdar 196
South Malvern pipeworks 152
Southdown freezing works 127
Spartan 8
Spirit of Adventure 189
Springfield station 69
Stane Brae estate 272
Stars & Stripes 225
State housing **172**
Station Peak station 75
Stony Batter 247
Stonyhurst station 50, 121
Strand Arcade 160
Sunny Hills estate 188
Surrey Hills estate 92
Sydney Packet 3
Sylvia Park stud 53, 89–90

INDEX C – PROPERTIES, SHIPS AND BOATS

Tahora (formerly *Adventure*) 41
Tarndale station 75
Te Awaiti block 56
Te Kitiroa 113
Te Parae stud 24, 55
Te Rau Kahikatea **24**
Te Wahapu Inlet trading station 15–16, **50ff**
Te Waimate station (see Waimate station) 69–70
Team New Zealand 260, 293
Terrace Hotel 98
Terrace station 65, 98ff
Teviotdale station 48
Tintagel 71
Tiraumea station 53
Toison d'Or (later Paradis sur Mer) 247
Tokerau (formerly *Independence*) 15
Tory 41, 56
Totara Estate station 126
Towers, the 97
Trelawney stud 251
Turanganui River trading/whaling station 19
Turihaua station 25
Ugbrooke station 51–52
Ulysses 258ff, 273
Urewera Mural 258
Valley, the **66**, 67
Viaduct Basin 240
Victoria township (never built) 21–22
Viking 162
Waikakahi station 66–67
Waikiwi brickworks 153

Waikouaiti whaling station 3
Waimanu station 248
Waimate station (or Te Waimate station) 69–70
Waingawa boiling-down works 55
Waiotahi goldmine 119
Waitaki Plains station 66
Waitangi estate 21–22
Waiwera spa 97, 98ff
Wallingford station 71
Wanaka station 111
Weiti block 8
Weekly News building 57
Wellington 17
Wellington Park stud 89
Wentworth House **258ff**
Westfield freezing works 126–27
Whakatane farm 87–88
Whale Island whaling station 15, 17
Wharekaka station 48–50
White Island 17
Whitford town hall 258ff
Wickford 33, **34**
Wigram aerodrome (formerly Sockburn aerodrome) 151
Winchmore station 69
Windsor Castle 71
Woburn 56
Woolston brickworks 152
Woodlands brickworks 153
Zuma restaurant 274